DATE DUE

WITHDRAWN

HERBERT EUGENE BOLTON

Albert L.
Hurtado   ·   HERBERT EUGENE BOLTON

Historian of the American Borderlands

University of California Press

Berkeley   Los Angeles   London

University of California Press, one of the most distinguished
university presses in the United States, enriches lives around
the world by advancing scholarship in the humanities, social
sciences, and natural sciences. Its activities are supported by
the UC Press Foundation and by philanthropic contributions
from individuals and institutions. For more information, visit
www.ucpress.edu.

University of California Press
Berkeley and Los Angeles, California

University of California Press, Ltd.
London, England

Library of Congress Cataloging-in-Publication Data

Hurtado, Albert L., 1946–.
    Herbert Eugene Bolton : historian of the American
borderlands / Albert L. Hurtado.
        p.   cm.
    Includes bibliographical references and index.
    ISBN 978-0-520-27216-3 (cloth : alk. paper)
    1. Bolton, Herbert Eugene, 1870–1953.
2. Historians—United States—Biography.
3. Mexican-American Border Region—
Historiography.   4. United States—Territorial
expansion—Historiography.   I. Title.
    E175.5.B66H87   2012
    907.2092—dc23
    [B]   2011035056

Manufactured in the United States of America

20 19 18 17 16 15 14 13 12
10 9 8 7 6 5 4 3 2 1

In keeping with a commitment to support environmentally
responsible and sustainable printing practices, UC Press
has printed this book on Rolland Enviro100, a 100 percent
postconsumer fiber paper that is FSC certified, deinked,
processed chlorine-free, and manufactured with renewable
biogas energy. It is acid-free and EcoLogo certified.

To the memory of David J. Weber

CONTENTS

ILLUSTRATIONS

ACKNOWLEDGMENTS

This project began on the patio outside the snack bar at the Huntington Library in the summer of 1987. Wilbur Jacobs, my doctoral advisor, asked me if I would like to be part of an OAH roundtable on Frederick Jackson Turner that Robert E. Smith was organizing. I allowed that I did not know much about Turner but that I would like to do something on one of Turner's students, Herbert Bolton. I suggested a paper on Bolton's ethnocentric view of history, which I would contrast with Turner's ideas. Wilbur and Bob agreed. I thank them for setting me on this accidental journey.

I have worked on this project off and on ever since my first foray into the Bolton Papers at the Bancroft Library in 1987. Along the way I accumulated the usual personal and professional debts that I acknowledge here with gratitude. The National Endowment for the Humanities funded a summer seminar on the Spanish Borderlands that David J. Weber convened in 1986. Arizona State University provided a series of grants that funded research at the National Archives and the Bancroft and Huntington Libraries between 1987 and 1998. Since that time the endowment of the Paul H. and Doris Eaton Travis Chair, which I hold at the University of Oklahoma, has generously provided research and travel funds.

The bulk of the research was done at the Bancroft Library. The Bancroft staff has been unfailingly helpful and supportive of me and this project for the more than twenty years that I have been going to and fro. My old friend Walter Brem's knowledge about Bolton, Berkeley, and the Bancroft Library added immeasurably to the pleasure and joy of researching this book as well as to its substance. Theresa Salazar arranged for me to see Bolton's famous classroom maps and has helped in other ways. Bancroft director Charles Faulhaber gave me the opportunity to present a paper on Bolton at the celebration of the library's 150th anniversary.

I am grateful to several of Bolton's grandchildren for their assistance. Robert Brower offered help, but sadly, did not live to see the book completed. Steven Johnson gave me his sketch of Bolton and other materials. Thomas Johnson reminisced about Bolton when Johnson was a student at Berkeley and about other matters relating to the Bolton family. Gale Randall graciously invited me into her home and shared photographs and memories of her grandfather. She also provided copies of family letters and other helpful information.

A host of colleagues and friends have suffered through my telling of hundreds of gossipy tales about Bolton back in the day. Some of them were actually interested, or kindly pretended that they were. My friend and mentor Kenneth N. Owens heard my first seminar presentation on Bolton in 1974, when I was a master's student. Consider this book my final response to the criticism you offered then. Sorry it's late. At Arizona State University my friend Peter Iverson encouraged me to write this book. He also arranged for me to interview his mother, who was a student at Berkeley in Bolton's time. David A. Hollinger helped me with a few details about the history department after Bolton's time and sent me *History at Berkeley: A Dialog in Three Parts*, which he coauthored with George A. Bruckern and Henry F. May.

Several of Bolton's graduate students have shared their reminiscences with me. Donald Cutter, Woodrow Borah, Engel Sluiter, and Earl Pomeroy were especially helpful. Edward Von der Porten and Robert J. Chandler were kind enough to read the chapter on the Drake Plate. My University of Oklahoma colleague Donald J. Pisani, who happens to be the son-in-law of Bolton student Engel Sluiter, arranged for me to meet with him. Don is also a Cal alum with a lively interest in his alma mater. Consequently he has been a willing and informative conversationalist about all things Berkeley and Bolton.

My friend and student William Carter sent me the Alfred Barnaby Thomas–Bolton correspondence from the University of Texas Pan American Library. Fellow Bolton scholar Russell Magnaghi generously sent me Bolton materials gleaned from the Georgia State Archives. Martin Ridge and Steven Hackel invited me to present papers about Bolton at the Huntington Library that helped me to sharpen my arguments.

David Wrobel and two anonymous readers carefully read the first draft of this book and made helpful suggestions. Thanks to them, the book is more succinct and readable. My graduate assistants David Beyreis, Matt Pearce, John Rhea, and Ryan Sturdevant helped me to prepare the final version of the manuscript. Jean Barman, Rose Marie Beebe, Iris Engstrand, Richard Etulain, Pamela Herr, Paul Hutton, W. Turrentine Jackson, William P. MacKinnon, and Samuel Truett have helped along the way. Steven Baker's copyediting of the manuscript added precision and polish to the finished product.

And as always, my wife, Jean, has been a willing listener and a knowing critic. Without her, where would I be?

By 2007 I had finished almost all of the research for this book and was ready to write. Then came an unexpected gift. Robert C. "Roy" Ritchie, W. M. Keck Foundation Director of Research at the Huntington Library, offered me the one-year *Los Angeles Times* Distinguished Fellowship in American History. So I crated up eight file drawers of documents, notes, and my computer database and hauled them to San Marino. I conceived of the fellowship as an opportunity to write without distractions, and so it was. I had already reviewed the correspondence between Turner and Bolton held by the Huntington, but the collections there proved to be far more helpful after I looked more deeply into them. The Frederick Jackson Turner Collection, Max Farrand Papers, and the Institutional Archives provided important new information not available anywhere else. Because of the *Times* fellowship the book is significantly different than it would have been otherwise. At the Huntington, Peter Blodgett helped me in myriad ways with his incomparable knowledge of the collections. While I did not quite finish the manuscript at the Huntington, most of the first draft was written there. It is fitting that the book ended more or less where it began, under the spreading trees of that most wonderful place for scholars. Thank you, Roy.

This book is dedicated to David J. Weber. More than any other historian David deserves credit for revitalizing the Spanish Borderlands as a respected field of study. Over the years he helped me and many others to achieve our professional dreams while building his own superlative record of scholarly achievement. I had hoped that this book would be in print before he died, but it was not to be. In his last few months of life I sent him some bits and pieces that I thought he would enjoy, and I trust that he did. David personified the scholar's life well lived. I hope this book is a fitting tribute.

A NOTE ON LANGUAGE

In most cases I have used the words that Bolton and his peers used. Their language included sometimes objectionable racial slurs, although these words and phrases are rare in Bolton's voluminous correspondence. I have quoted them in order to reveal as much about him and his views as possible.

I have used the terms "Anglo" and "Anglo-American," although these categories are usually not accurate representations of actual ethnic identities. Anglophone would perhaps be a more accurate way to describe the mass of non-Hispanic white people. In Bolton's time "Anglo" was often used as an ethnic identifier. There was a Crocker Anglo National Bank (where my parents had an account), as well as a Hibernia Bank. The Bank of America, as all Californians know, got its start as the Bank of Italy. I use the term "Anglo" because in the American West it is commonly understood as a means to distinguish Hispanic from non-Hispanic people; it should not be understood to indicate a precise ethnic identity.

I sometimes use the terms "America" and "Americans" to refer to the United States and its citizens. Bolton must be spinning in his grave. He strenuously argued that everyone who lived in the Western Hemisphere was an American. Indeed they are, but it is awkward to use the phrase "United States citizens," so I have used the commonly accepted "American" instead.

For the sake of variety and to avoid the repeated use of cumbersome institutional names (Leland Stanford Junior University, for example), I often use shortened names of universities or their common nicknames. "Cal" and "Berkeley" are used interchangeably. When unpunctuated initials (UCLA and USC) are commonly understood, I have used them. Readers should understand from the context that "Texas" and "Austin," "Wisconsin" and "Madison" mean the universities rather than the places. If these literary decisions cause confusion or offense to any readers, I apologize in advance.

Introduction

The Border Lord

On one of his southwestern expeditions Herbert Bolton clambered atop an Anasazi ruin tucked into a canyon wall. From there he surveyed his domain like a conquistador viewing his latest conquest. The pose suited him. Bolton was the undisputed master of a scholarly domain that he had pioneered and conquered. It is a memorable image of Bolton at the height of his powers. Of course, the snapshot did not capture a true conqueror, but a historian doing field research for one of his books. Yet the pose reveals the aspect of Bolton's work that today's historians find most objectionable—his complete identification with Spaniards who *were* conquerors. This is the Bolton that is easy to dismiss as an artifact of colonialism's bygone days.

But there is another Bolton whose work suggested a tolerant and capacious view of American history, an outlook more congruent with today's values: the transnational Bolton of the borderlands who was equally at home in Mexico and the United States. This Bolton conceived of the borderlands—the southern tier of states that extended from Georgia to California—as a liminal space that transcended national boundaries. Within this space he found a Spanish past that illuminated and expanded United States history. According to Bolton, Spanish explorers, missionaries, and soldiers were heroes who paved the way for Anglo pioneers who came later. The story of the Spanish Borderlands was the indispensable preface to the national history of the United States. Thus Bolton's borderlands comprised a transnational region that told a national tale. His essential concept, that the borderlands were the meeting place of diverse cultures, is an important foundation for today's multicultural borderlands studies.[1]

Bolton conceptualized a second broad idea that has continuing significance: hemispheric history or the history of the Americas. His sojourns in Mexico and his study of the history of colonial New Spain and the Spanish borderlands of the United States convinced him that national histories could be better understood in a hemispheric setting. When seen in hemispheric context, the history of one nation sheds light on the history of the others, he argued. He also claimed, too grandly for many specialists, that there was an essential unity in the history of the Western Hemisphere. His Americas course aimed to provide a broad comparative foundation for Berkeley's undergraduate students. He hoped that his course would be generally accepted in American universities, and he met with some success. Although critics charged that Bolton too easily glossed national and cultural differences, Bolton's hemispheric perspective was influential for decades. In recent years some of Bolton's ideas have been resurrected in the guise of transnational history.[2] These coexistent, sometimes incompatible Boltons—the colonial apologist and the progressive transnational scholar—make his legacy a debatable matter that demands scrutiny before it can be fully appreciated.

Bolton was one of the most respected historians of his generation. His professional accomplishments were prodigious. He was a prolific publisher. Hundreds of graduate students studied with him. He helped to establish the academic reputation of the University of California in the eyes of the world. The presidency of the American Historical Association and many other professional honors marked him as one of the elite academics of his time. Yet his once towering reputation gradually faded and became the subject of scholarly debate.[3] There were several reasons for Bolton's decline. The rise of Native American history made Bolton's appreciative treatment of Spanish missionaries and explorers seem an apology for colonialism. Latin American historians regarded his studies of the far northern reaches of the Spanish American empire as marginal episodes of limited significance and explanatory power. The romantic tone of Bolton's triumphalist narrative no longer matched the critical sensibility of American historians.

Yet, when all is said and done, there he stands, like a colossal ruin on the intellectual landscape of the borderlands. Right or wrong, au courant or passé, Bolton is impossible to ignore. Historians and anthropologists continue to rely on his many volumes of carefully translated and edited documents and detailed maps. His ideas about the borderlands and the Americas are once again relevant to historical studies. Bolton's graduate students added hundreds of scholarly articles and books to the corpus of essential borderlands and Latin American studies. He personally contributed thousands of pages of original and transcribed Spanish documents to the Bancroft Library and, as its director, acquired tens of thousands more—an essential cache of primary documents for scholars to use now and in the foreseeable future.

Now, more than a century after Bolton began to investigate the Mexican archives, with a steady stream of revisionist borderlands and transnational studies issuing from academic presses, the time has come for a new assessment of Bolton and his work.[4] The appreciative biographical treatments of Bolton by his students emphasize his scholarly contributions but do not adequately contextualize his work.[5] I believe that Bolton's work is best understood when it is seen in a world that was not always prepared to accept his ideas. Today Bolton's critics emphasize his ethnocentrist, pro-missionary perspective, but in valorizing Catholic missionaries, Bolton (a Methodist) challenged the commonly held anti-Catholic prejudice of his day. Some Californians (Bolton called them "local patriots") objected to Bolton's Hispanophilia and wanted the University of California to emphasize the history of their Anglo ancestors (see the "Note on Language" herein). In the University of California Bolton also met resistance that was sometimes intellectual and sometimes personal. Long-forgotten political controversies sometimes influenced Bolton, and vice versa. Thus I have explored Bolton's larger world in order to fully comprehend his work.

I have paid particular attention to Bolton's relationship with his mentor, Frederick Jackson Turner. Bolton's ideas about the Spanish frontier offered a counterpoint to Turner's writings on American frontiers and sections, so it is natural to look into the influence that Bolton may have had on his mentor over their more-than-thirty-year association. Alas, there seemed to be none, but in comparing Bolton and Turner, the present study offers a new way to understand and interpret the work of both historians.

This volume gives some attention to Bolton's graduate students because they helped to disseminate his work. They formed an unusually large and diverse group. More women than men studied with Bolton. Most of the women were master's students who became public school teachers. The majority of his doctoral students found academic employment at the college level all over the United States. Still other graduate students worked as what we now call public historians for the State Department, National Park Service, National Archives, and other federal and state agencies. Through them Bolton created a professional empire that spread his ideas about borderlands and the Americas in schools at every level and in historic parks and monuments. Artifacts of the once extensive domain of Bolton and his students may still be seen at the national monuments today.

Bolton established a professional empire perhaps without parallel, but he was not primarily an academic politician. He was a scholar. The central purpose of this book is to explore the development of his historical ideas, their impact on scholarship and society in his day, and their relevance to historical studies today. It is my hope that this study of Bolton will deepen our understanding of the American historians' ongoing challenge: writing the history of a people who are racially, ethnically, and religiously diverse.

ONE · The Scholars' Hard Road

In late December 1922 Herbert Eugene Bolton boarded an eastbound train at the Berkeley station and settled into his seat. Even in repose Bolton was a striking figure. At fifty-two years old, he was six feet tall with neatly trimmed sandy hair that was still full. Smiles broke easily upon his open face. He wore glasses over large blue, attentive eyes, and chain-smoked Lucky Strike cigarettes, but still looked fit in middle age. Bolton was chairman of the history department at the University of California, director of the Bancroft Library, and one of the most important historians of his day. Everyone in the history profession knew it. He was on his way to New Haven for the annual meeting of the American Historical Association (AHA).

The wintry landscape that slid past the Pullman car window triggered memories about his own past, as well as the history he had written. At some points Bolton's personal story and his grand narrative of the North American frontier seemed to merge. As the train sped across Nebraska, Bolton recalled his family's covered-wagon trek when he was only three. Seeking new farmland in the West, the Boltons had left Wisconsin in 1873. Busted, the family returned to Wisconsin, but this sad memory of frontier failure did not divert Bolton for long. Now riding down the Platte River Valley, "where ran the trail of the fur traders, the Oregonians, and the Californians, and along which Parkman came," Bolton saw only prosaic haystacks instead of teeming herds of wild animals. "I would much prefer to see buffaloes, or Pawnee Indians, who belong here." One of his friends interrupted this reverie with pleasant conversation, but Bolton "could not help looking out from time to time, to see if perchance I might get a trace of [Pedro de] Villazur or of [Pierre] Mallet, or of the Pawnee."[1]

Through New York the rails paralleled the abandoned Erie Canal, which his New England ancestors had traveled. "I can see them now, peering over the edge of the railing of a can[al] boat drawn by a tow line. That brown-eyed girl is my mother."[2] Not content with conjuring his mother, Bolton "saw old Leatherstocking or some of his associates 'moving noiselessly' through the thickets over the hills." As the train rolled through the Hudson River Valley, Bolton imagined that he could see Rip Van Winkle and all the heroes of Sleepy Hollow.

Herbert Bolton was a romantic. For him the landscape was a grand stage upon which heroic figures, historical and imaginary, acted their parts. In his imagination, long-dead explorers and literary heroes joined him in the places where they had lived so memorably. He admired their exploits, and—in his own mind at least—shared their glory. One cannot understand Bolton or his work without recognizing his romantic attachment to the people and places about which he wrote. Where did this romantic historian come from?

Bolton was not born to be a romantic professor of history. Far from it. He came into the world on a small farm in Wisconsin on July 20, 1870. He was the fourth in a family of eleven children, three of whom did not live to maturity. The circumstances of his birth and early family life are the common stuff of nineteenth-century rural America. His father, Edwin Latham Bolton, was born in Leeds, England, and migrated with his family to Utica, New York. They worked at the weavers' trade, as they had done in England. According to family tradition, young Edwin took up surveying and led the Boltons out of the mills and across the country to western Wisconsin, although family mill earnings may have financed the move. In 1856 they settled on a farm in Wilton near Kickapoo Creek, about twenty-five miles from La Crosse. There the Boltons became independent farmers, working the raw land to build a new life for themselves.

Bolton's father was an immigrant, but his mother, Rosaline Cady, was not. She came from old New England stock. Ten generations back, one of her forbears, Richard Warren, had arrived in the New World aboard the *Mayflower*. She even had a distant connection to Ralph Waldo Emerson. Her family had been settled in Vermont for two centuries before her father and mother moved to Wisconsin in the 1840s or 1850s. The children of Edwin and Rosaline were culturally and genetically Anglo-American right down to the soles of their feet.

By the time Herbert entered the world, the eighty-acre homestead near Wilton was doing well. Edwin built a larger house to accommodate his growing family. His rheumatic condition, a legacy of his Union Army service during the Civil War, was the only cloud on the horizon. In the early 1870s his illness was still manageable, but it would steadily grow worse. In 1873 the prospect of new lands on the Nebraska frontier filled Edwin with optimism. He sold his farm and moved his family to a new homestead near Lincoln. It was a bad year to go west: grasshoppers and drought ruined the farm before it was fairly begun. The Boltons returned to Wisconsin, and Edwin bought another farm there, but it was not as productive as the old one. Located at LaGrange, the new farm had poorer soil, fewer resources, and a mortgage. The Boltons had to scratch harder than ever. Even so, the family was poorer at the end of 1873 than they had been at the beginning, when they had turned their hopeful faces west.

Large families like the Boltons' were the rule on American farms where children soon became useful. The Bolton boys were of inestimable value on the farm. By 1880 three of them were teenagers, old enough to work at men's jobs. Even Herbert could pick berries and do light farmwork. Everyone worked an "eight-hour" day, Herbert's older brother Frederick joked: "8 hours in the forenoon and 8 more in the afternoon!"[3] Hoeing, weeding, and harvesting occupied the farmer's sons in season. Caring for livestock, building fences, repairing barns, and countless other farm chores took whatever time remained.[4] There was work to do at the neighbors' places, too. Planting, haying, harvesting, cutting, and hauling wood all demanded labor that the Bolton boys could supply in return for produce, handmade clothes, or other goods; they sometimes got cash but rarely. As soon as Herbert was big enough, he became his older brother Fred's constant work partner. A life of hard labor seemed to stretch endlessly before them.

Constant hard work was not the only discipline that the Bolton boys knew. Their Methodist parents "were both quite religious and we received rather strict, but wholesome counsel," Fred recalled. "Had we told a lie, committed a theft, or damaged others' property, the punishments would have been severe." Swearing, smoking, and playing hooky from school were also infractions worthy of punishment. Fred thought that he and Herbert inherited their drive and perseverance from their father. "He was the personification of those traits." The elder Bolton augmented his income by teaching school in the winter, an occupation that probably first inspired Fred and Herbert to become teachers.[5] Fred and Herbert wanted to escape rural life and understood that education offered them a way to do it. Both parents encouraged their children to get an education, and the boys often saw their father studying when he took a break from farmwork. In January 1883 Edwin gave Herbert some advice in the autograph book that his mother had given him for Christmas: "Make the most of the advantages you may have. E. L. Bolton."[6] Herbert took his father's counsel to heart.

Herbert's introduction to history no doubt came from his father. Full of vivid tales about his Civil War experiences, Edwin also told admiring stories about the heroes of the American revolutions, such as the Marquis de Lafayette and Simón Bolívar. Poor as he was, Edwin subscribed to two periodicals that inspired Herbert and Fred, the *Chicago Inter-Ocean* and the *Youth's Companion*. The boys walked five miles to the post office to pick up the latest issues. The *Inter-Ocean* opened their eyes to world affairs and a life beyond rural Wisconsin. The *Youth's Companion* fired the boys' imaginations with adventure stories by Jack London, Barrett Willoughby, and Samuel Woodworth Cozzens. Cozzens's serialized "The Lost Trail," a story about two boys who went to California with a trading caravan, was a particular favorite of the Bolton boys. The southwestern setting for Cozzens's vivid tale with its deserts, mesas, and perpetually blue skies was dramatically different from western Wisconsin. The story was full of youthful heroism and narrow escapes from Comanche and Apache Indians, who were the villains of the piece. Cozzens even described the mission San Xavier del Bac, near Tucson, as "one of the most interesting relics of the old Spanish rule to be found in the country." Cozzens's exciting serial was doubtless Herbert's introduction to the Southwest as a place of romance and adventure.[7]

With incessant labor the Boltons made a go of their hardscrabble farm, but in the late 1870s Edwin's rheumatic condition grew debilitating. He began teaching in the summer as well as the winter in order to replace the income that he could no longer earn by manual labor, but even this occupation became too much for him.[8] He died in 1885 at age forty-nine, leaving Rosaline with eight children and the widow's share of his Civil War pension. Forty-one years old and pregnant, Rosaline was responsible for a poor farm and a large family. Every dollar counted. From Edwin's pension Rosaline received eight dollars a month plus two dollars for each child under the age of sixteen. Herbert and his five younger siblings thus added twelve dollars per month to the family treasury, but only briefly. He turned sixteen in 1886. One year later his thirteen-year-old brother, Johnnie, was thrown from the driver's seat when his team bolted; he was killed in the fall. Herbert's maturity and Johnnie's death reduced the family income by four dollars per month.[9]

All of the boys pitched in to keep the farm and the family together. Fred went to La Crosse to teach school and sent money home. Herbert started high school in

Tomah, where he worked for room and board at a local hotel. School was a common topic in the letters of the two education-minded brothers. "I get along very well with my studies," Herbert wrote, "all except English Language and that I detest." Teachers had already noticed that tall, blonde, good-looking Herbert was a likely prospect for their calling, because they sometimes allowed him to teach classes. He was in the same business that Fred was, "teachin skule," he once joked, because the teacher was sick.[10] Herbert liked school, although he described many of his fellow pupils as "country Jakes." Of course, he was a country Jake also, fresh from the farm. In high school he studied history, but at fifteen Herbert did not think of this subject as a professional option. He studied "very hard evenings as well as day time. Don't have much time for mischief."[11]

But Herbert did find a little time for devilment. He cut school once to look over the old Bolton farmstead at the Ridge, perhaps wishing that his father had not left his good farm for a dream in Nebraska. Sometimes he got a "good 'solemn lecture'" at school for failing to keep up with his homework, but these occasions were rare.[12] Another time, spring weather inspired Herbert and some friends to skip school and go fishing. They were caught in a cold rain, but Herbert persevered and returned home with a bit of doggerel that described his experience:

Thirty-six trout.
Fisherman's luck:
Wet ass
And a hungry gut.[13]

He was not above a practical joke. One night Herbert and some friends saw one of their schoolmates visiting his girl. They "tied the [barn?] doors when he was up there and he stayed till morning too." If this adventure became common knowledge, it would have set small-town tongues wagging. "He don't know who 'twas," Herbert told his brother, and "you needn't tell him ever either."[14]

Rural life was not Herbert's idea of an attractive future, but the countryside had its charms for an active boy. He loved to saddle a horse and ride around the country with his friends. In Tomah Herbert made a name for himself as an athlete. He played baseball with the local team, the unfortunately named Skunks. Herbert was the fastest sprinter in high school, and the best broad jumper.[15] He would always revel in the outdoors and in physical activity as long as they had nothing to do with farming.

Herbert was a likable youth who liked other people. Affability was one of his most endearing traits, though he committed himself to solitary habits of study. In some ways, the adult would become almost monkish in his pursuit of scholarship, but the teenaged Herbert was no monk. He liked his friends and enjoyed parties. "Had a good time," he reported to Fred after attending a social. "I guess it wouldn't be me if I didn't, would it?" he added with a touch of self-awareness that pegged him as a good-natured, social animal.[16] Yet Herbert's teen years were marked by unusual seriousness of purpose. He had his fun but worked to make a success of high school just as he worked hard on the farm. As he said, he would have to work hard if he ever intended "to be anybody, which I cert[ainly] do."[17] Herbert's ambition to be somebody marked his whole life.

Girls noticed the blonde boy with the sunny disposition. They smiled at him, and he smiled back, although he sometimes reported that he was giving up girls in favor of hard work so that he could get ahead. One girl in particular commanded Herbert's attention: Gertrude Janes of Tunnel City—"snapping-eyed, beautiful Gertie Janes," as Fred remembered her.[18] Herbert met her when carrying blueberries from the farm to sell at the Tunnel City trading post. Eventually she attended high school in Tomah, so Herbert saw a lot of her there. He kept her in sight on Sundays by going to church in Tunnel City. In his senior year Herbert liked Gertrude well enough to be jealous of a boy who competed for her affection. Consequently he planned to attend church a little oftener than usual, "till he has withdrawn from the field."[19]

In the summer of 1888 Herbert worked as printer's devil at the weekly *Tomah Journal*. It paid six dollars per week and was preferable to "granging it," as Herbert derisively called farmwork.[20] His stint with the weekly may have sharpened his interest in current events. "What are your politics?" he asked Fred. "I don't know what mine are, I'm either a Pro[hibitionist] or a Republican." Herbert's adult political sympathies seemed to hover around the progressive side of the Republican Party, but he made it a point not to discuss his party affiliation (at least not in writing).

Essentially apolitical in the partisan sense, Bolton had a keen sense of personal and institutional relations that would serve him well throughout his career. He probably acquired these skills in the Bolton family matrix. As historian Frank Sulloway argues, siblings must develop strategies for obtaining their shares of family resources such as food, shelter, wealth, affection, and encouragement. Thus each child develops a niche in the family and a way of maximizing his or her chances for survival.[21] The fourth son in a very large family, Herbert capitalized on his innate strengths and developed talents that set him apart from his older brothers. His good looks, athletic prowess, pleasing personality, affability, sense of humor, good health, capacity for hard work, attention to detail, and ability to get along with people made Herbert a good son, a successful student, and a valued employee. These personal qualities served him well throughout his life.

Fred, the second son, blazed the trail of higher education and escape for Herbert, but his older brother's struggle for advancement showed that the scholar's life was not a perfect meritocracy. A certain amount of shrewdness was needed in order to succeed, and Herbert, even as a teenager, seemed to have it. In 1887 Fred wanted a teacher's job at Tunnel City, so he wrote to Mrs. Janes (Gertrude's mother), who was a school board director.[22] After Fred's mother went to see Janes and the board clerk about the position, Herbert reported to Fred, "I guess they want *you*."[23] Herbert was certain that his brother was the best man for the place, but it helped to know someone. His brother got the job.

Such jobs were just stepping stones for the Bolton boys. The following year, Fred resigned so that he could attend the state normal school in Milwaukee. Education was a family affair, with most of the older siblings helping to pay for expenses whenever they could. Fred was only the third graduate of Tomah High School to attend college, so his matriculation in Milwaukee was a big thing, especially to Herbert. He asked his older brother about everything—girls, extracurricular activity, books, everything.[24] Herbert was already looking past Milwaukee and hoped to attend the state university in Madison. He knew that he would "have to work a while," but the dream was there. Fred was showing that with hard work and some help from home, the dream could be realized. "You encourage me," Herbert wrote.[25]

A senior now, Herbert was anxious to be out on his own. Graduation was fast approaching. The teachers had chosen him to speak at commencement, and this honor brought out his insecurity. "But I can do my best."[26] As always, doing his "best" meant working hard on the task at hand. Commencement evidently came and went without great trauma caused by a botched valedictory. At least Herbert never mentioned it in his letters to Fred.

Now the road was open to the future. Nearly nineteen, Herbert had accomplished as much as he could have in the little community bounded by the farm, Tomah, and Tunnel City. Optimistic, attractive, and outgoing, Herbert faced the future certain of only one thing: a lot of hard work. Even so, success was not assured. The track for advancement he had chosen, higher education, was virtually unknown to him. From Tomah he could see only a few paces ahead as his brother proceeded. Yet he was determined to make something of himself through ambition and hard work.

Herbert did not know it, but a place was already being prepared for him. In 1884 forty-one historians had gathered at a resort in Saratoga, New York, to found the AHA. Their purpose was straightforward: the promotion of historical studies "without limitations of time or space," as Harvard professor Justin Winsor explained.[27] "The future of this new work is in the young men of the historical instinct," he continued, "largely in the rising instructors of our colleges." Founded for the promotion of history, the AHA would become primarily an organization of, by, and for college professors of history. They would form a new professional class: college professors with a doctorate. The AHA founders took the German academy and its faculties as their model. The new American doctor-professors would transform their universities into Germanic research institutions whose mission was to investigate history rather than to merely reiterate well-worn moral tales about the past. The transformation involved the establishment of doctoral programs so that as time marched on new generations of American-trained PhDs would fill the ranks of the professorate in the United States. It followed that institutions with doctoral programs would attain the highest level of prestige among colleges and universities.[28] Thus research universities, graduate schools, and doctoral production formed a self-perpetuating and self-justifying regime. None of this was laid out in the AHA constitution, but it nevertheless came to pass.

The first AHA members' historical interests embraced the American West. In 1885 the AHA passed a resolution that called for the careful recording of the history of the western states and territories.[29] A second resolution called for cataloging historical documents concerning the United States held in European archives. A third resolution commended the German historian Leopold von Ranke, "the oldest and most distinguished exponent" of "historical science."[30] These resolutions were not unrelated. The AHA founders envisioned their historical enterprise as an excruciatingly detailed Rankean effort that would be global in extent. Before there could be a proper history of the United States, specialists must assemble the documents, whether they were in Leadville or London. The teen-aged Herbert had no way of knowing about these resolutions, but they defined his life's work.

In the summer of 1889 the arcane discussions of historians did not concern Herbert. He was looking for a job. Like his brother, he hoped to teach school, but it was not an easy matter for an inexperienced high school graduate to convince school boards that he was up to the task. He searched for a position with characteristic energy and thoroughness. In a flurry of writing he sent letters to fourteen schools. Whenever possible, Herbert spoke with board members and clerks.

Surely, he explained to Fred, after all of this activity he "must get something of a place."[31] Fred was especially interested in his brother's employment prospects because a portion of Herbert's meager salary would go to support Fred's education. Once Fred's schooling was complete, he would help finance Herbert's college years. The striving brothers would alternate years of school teaching with stints as college students. This was the scholars' hard road of upward mobility that would culminate in university professorships for the Boltons.

But first Herbert had to get a job, and school boards were remarkably unimpressed with the nineteen-year-old inexperienced (but earnest) applicant. In the summer Fred worked for a lumber company in Granite, Wisconsin, so Herbert followed him there. When Fred departed for Milwaukee in late summer, Herbert took his job as store manager. This brought him into contact with a rough, migratory laboring class of lumberjacks and shingle weavers. It must have been difficult for a boy so young to look such men in the eye and tell them what they owed the company store.

Fred and Herbert may have been college men, or at least college bound, but they were not pansies. They wrestled with the lumberjacks on their days off and gave a good account of themselves. Herbert made friends with some of the more colorful characters who worked in the woods. He recounted some of their misadventures— and their debts to the store—in his letters to Fred.[32] These encounters must have reminded the Boltons that they were not too far removed from the laborers' life that they were trying to escape for good.

In September Herbert finally heard that the small town of York had decided to take a chance on him. He settled business in Granite and departed for his new job with a sense of purpose and affection for "the renowned (new) York," the "home of my heart and the center of all rural attractions."[33] The school suited him. Most of his scholars were almost as old as he was. Some young men already had moustaches. The school was ungraded, which meant that he taught students of all ages in the same room. He was grateful that all but two of his charges were able to read and write.[34]

Teaching in York was good experience for Herbert, but he led a solitary life while preparing for Normal. As usual he asked Fred for advice about books to read. The uncertainty of regular pay at York troubled him too, because he had a hard time forwarding money to Fred. His affection for the small town quickly wore thin. "I should *like* to get into a town somewhere in civilization. It is so lonesome here. No one to talk with on a subject that interests me, or *any-one* wishing to pursue any line of book study."[35] The boy from a two-horse town looked down on the one-horse town that claimed his services. He quit at the end of the first semester.

Herbert's loneliness was real enough. He and Gertrude occasionally exchanged letters and saw each other when he went home, but he may have taken her for granted.[36] "I'll be terribly sweet when I go home . . . and make up for it all. Someday I'll get left, won't I?" he cavalierly added. He had also heard a false rumor that Gertrude and several other Tunnel City students would not graduate on time. The story might have lowered Gertrude a bit in the estimation of a young man who was betting everything on the power of education to improve his condition in the world. Gertrude's intelligence and excellent academic performance had been among the qualities that recommended her to Herbert. Now, perhaps, she was lowering her sights, looking ahead to a life as wife and mother with some local farm boy or merchant. Besides, Herbert had a long way to go before he was ready for marriage and capable of supporting a family. Gertrude, "old girl," as he sometimes called her, might turn out to be Herbert's *old* girl. In the fullness of his young manhood he no doubt assumed that the choice would be his, but life would be full of surprises for Herbert.

Once home, Herbert hoped to work and save enough to join Fred at Wisconsin Normal in the fall. He had managed to save a hundred dollars from his York earnings, but he put this in the family common fund and so was not able to use that money to go to Milwaukee or to help Fred. But he was not the only Bolton who was banking on higher education to lift the family out of penury. Mrs. Bolton had mortgaged the farm to help the boys through college. Then she sold a horse for $85 and sent some money to Fred. To Herbert's great surprise and satisfaction, the family urged him to go to normal school immediately and provided money to do it. On March 1 he informed Fred that he would arrive in Milwaukee the next Monday on the midnight train.[37]

The budding scholar who had looked down on little York was now in Milwaukee, which was probably the first sizable city he had ever seen. With its bustling Lake Michigan port, burgeoning industry, and growing immigrant population Milwaukee must have been exciting and overwhelming at first.[38] Wisconsin Normal was located near the heart of the city. Normal schools were meant to train professional teachers with a two-year college curriculum designed with pedagogy in mind.[39] Professionalization was one of the watchwords of the late nineteenth century. Self-taught physicians and lawyers gave way to university-trained men (and a few women) who increasingly dominated their professional worlds. The time would soon pass away when a likely high school graduate, perhaps one who was big enough to "handle" the larger pupils, could find a job at a country school as the Bolton boys had done. Indeed, Fred and Herbert would eventually help hasten the day when college training was a prerequisite for school teaching at all levels. The brothers saw no irony in this development.

Herbert and Fred roomed together in the spring. With his brother's help Herbert adapted and prospered, in the personal sense if not financially. Still, scholastic success in this new and strange atmosphere was not guaranteed, and Herbert did not immediately impress Wisconsin Normal students as a comer. One of his friends later recalled that he was not sure if the green boy from Tomah would make it through Normal.[40] He was well established at the school by the fall of 1890, when his brother, diploma in hand, departed for Fairchild to be principal of the high school there.[41] Fred's new job was convincing evidence of the value of higher education. At age twenty-four, with less than two years' teaching experience, Fred's normal school certificate made him a high school principal. Here was tangible proof that the Boltons' faith in higher education was well placed. Fairchild was only a way station for Fred. He was headed to the state university in Madison eventually but needed to make money to finance Herbert as well as gain experience in the field. Fred was turning to education as his academic specialty. As a teacher of teachers he might land a job at one of the new normal schools that were being established in Wisconsin and elsewhere.

Wisconsin Normal offered college-level courses, but was by no means a comprehensive university. As its graduates were expected to teach many subjects, the curriculum was general. The normal school diploma was not a bachelor's degree, but a certification of the holder's competence to teach school in specific disciplines. Mastery of a textbook in the field seemed to be the common standard for each course. Herbert studied mathematics, grammar, political economy, history, rhetoric, science, Latin, modern languages, pedagogy, and practice teaching all crammed into a year and a half of intense study.[42]

Social life in Milwaukee was far more interesting than anything Herbert had experienced before. After Fred's departure Herbert roomed with other Normal students. Despite his sometimes cloistered study habits Herbert easily made friends among the students, men and women alike. Gertrude apparently slipped off of his list of preferred female companions. There was no lack of attractive young ladies to escort to dances, sleigh rides, and other entertainments at Wisconsin Normal. Besides, Gertrude was younger and still in Tunnel City.

Gertrude, perhaps sensing that Herbert was losing interest, then stunned him by announcing that she intended to teach. "She always swore against it," he wrote his brother. "But so we do change. I think she will be a success with smaller children," he added, not quite willing to grant Gertrude full credit for a career move that was identical to his own.[43] Gertrude landed a job in suburban St. Paul, Minnesota.[44] This was a bold move, revealing an unexpected streak of independence and drive in the small-town girl Herbert thought he knew. And she did not have to go to York to teach bumpkins, he no doubt noticed. His correspondence with Gertrude had dwindled (at least he seldom mentioned it to Fred), and he no longer regarded their relationship as a courtship, if he ever had. But Gertrude, well, Gertrude had other plans.

All the while, Herbert portrayed himself as a carefree youth playing the field. "Now I'm not in love—with anybody, but my Dutch and my Norwegian girls used to bother me somewhat, for I did not know which to please. I settled it by trying to please them both. Hope I succeeded."[45] One school incident hints that he was not quite the sophisticated lover that his letters made him out to be. Miss Faddis, an instructor at Normal, held regular classes in manners. Herbert attended infrequently, but decided to put in an appearance one day. He was the only man among fifteen young women for whom Miss Faddis was demonstrating the correct method of shaking hands, a procedure evidently more complicated in 1891 than it is today. Perhaps she failed to notice the lone gentleman in the room, or maybe she just forgot herself in the midst of a teachable moment. Whatever the case, in order to make clear the particularities of correct posture, she raised her dress "nearly up to her ___," Herbert reported to Fred. This display of feminine pulchritude was too much for the blushing young brother, who left the room. He immediately reported the incident to Professor Mapel, but did not get the response that he expected. "'*Oh my dear boy!*' said he. 'you don't like it because you are not interested. If Mr Gillan should give you the work you would do your best.'" Herbert evidently did not quite follow the gist of Mapel's remark. "I soon made him understand that he had told the truth for Gillan is a teacher, and Miss F. is not."[46] The boy from Tomah was not yet up to the droll humor of the urban sophisticates in Milwaukee.

The end of the spring semester 1891 found Herbert preparing for graduation and looking for employment. Fred was going to the University of Wisconsin in the fall, so Herbert needed a good job in order to support his brother's further education. The brothers put an amazing amount of time and energy into their search for employment. They seemed to know of openings in every school throughout the state and shared information about each place, who they knew there, and who could help them with a recommendation. Herbert's best chance for employment came from his brother's recommendation to replace him at Fairchild. He considered a position in Montello, but Professor Gillan thought it would go to a Catholic, so he advised Herbert to concentrate on Fairchild.[47] Religious and ethnic prejudice worked both ways in the 1890s, as the Protestant Herbert learned.

With neither summer nor fall plans firmed up, Herbert looked forward to graduation. If not quite a lettered man, he at least would have a diploma that certified his professional standing among the ranks of Wisconsin teachers. He was relieved to pass this milestone in his diligent program of self-improvement and upward mobility.[48]

In July Fairchild finally decided to hire Herbert as principal at seventy dollars per month. At about the same time he learned about Fairchild, something else popped up. Gertrude, fresh from a year of teaching at St. Paul, wanted to study with him during the summer. He thought it would be a good idea, but the plan did not materialize as Gertrude had hoped.[49] Herbert took a job as a traveling salesman of memberships in an association that sold books to members at discount prices. "Now if a man has time and wants a trip to California he can get there all right if he will work."[50] He liked the money, but selling on the road was not the path to status that he had in mind. A traveler did "not belong to any society, and of course" was "a *fraud*."[51] Herbert would find another way to get to California.

A letter from Gertrude found Herbert while he was on the road. She had heard about a teaching position at Fairchild and asked Herbert to help her get it. He was willing, but it turned out that the position had already been filled. Too bad, but Gertrude, a young woman of remarkable resilience, persistence, and determination, was not finished with Herbert yet.[52]

At summer's end Herbert went to Fairchild to take up his post as high school principal. He was twenty-one and only two years out of high school, yet now he taught pupils who were nearly as old as himself, managed the school, and oversaw teachers who were far older and more experienced than he was.[53] Of course, he taught his own classes, so preparation was part of his day. As always, he worked at night for as long as the light and his energy held out. In addition to his myriad duties Herbert prepared himself to enter the University of Wisconsin, where Fred was now a student. Herbert would maintain this demanding schedule for two years, sending Fred whatever money he could spare.

It should come as no surprise that Herbert managed to do all of this work. By then discipline and labor were ingrained in him, but there was more to the principal's job than work. The management of older teachers who must have resented a mere youth as their new chief required sound judgment. Before long one of the teachers began to give him trouble, but he stood firm and eventually forced her to resign.[54] "The one who wears the *slipper* can kick hardest and hurt most," he observed.[55] Despite his youth Herbert was willing to take charge, give orders, and insist that they be carried out. He did not like subordinates who challenged him. In his world, even in little Fairchild, status and authority went hand in glove. For the most part Herbert wore authority lightly, but he wielded it without compunction.

Principals had to deal with superiors as well as subordinates. The state school superintendent, Oliver E. Wells, had to approve the work done at Wisconsin high schools. He also had something to say about who taught summer institutes and was an ex officio member of the University of Wisconsin Board of Regents. Wells's win was something of a surprise in the 1890 election that swept him and other Democrats into office.[56] Needless to say, getting along with Superintendent Wells was crucial for high school principals. Wells, however, was not well liked by the Bolton brothers. He hoped to revamp the University of Wisconsin to emphasize practical subjects that would better serve the people of Wisconsin, or so he believed. Fred wrote a critical newspaper article about Wells. "Good for you!" wrote brother Herbert. "I endorse your sentiment . . . exactly."[57]

Herbert disliked Wells, but he had to cultivate him while he was in office. When finally he met Wells, Herbert ingratiated himself with pleasantries and good humor. In November 1892 Herbert voted against Wells, but the superintendent won reelection.[58] Herbert had little choice but to go along cheerfully with a superintendent whom he happened to despise. This small incident foreshadowed a lifetime of pleasing the men who held authority over him. When in charge, Herbert expected to be obeyed; to his betters, he returned the favor with a smile on his face.

Success at Fairchild High School was important to Herbert, but it was a means to an end. He studied hard for the university and kept asking Fred for advice about his studies. The brothers were dreaming big dreams for farm boys with two-year teaching diplomas. They began to consider the doctorate as the consummation of their educational and social advancement. Herbert drew a figure at the bottom of a letter to Fred. At the left margin a fingerpost pointed to the right, followed by five arrows that ended at "Ph.D." on the opposite margin. "I will follow in your wake, or break a road for myself," he told his brother.[59]

The same letter contained another foreshadowing. Herbert asked Fred about bringing Wisconsin history professor Frederick Jackson Turner to Fairchild for a lecture. There is no reason to suppose that Herbert wanted to study with Turner, but the brothers probably knew enough about him to regard the young history professor as a role model. Turner was also a small-town Wisconsin boy, who was only five years older than Fred and nine years senior to Herbert. If Turner could do it, there was hope for the brothers.

Herbert was beginning to take more than a perfunctory interest in history. With a friend he read Prescott's *Conquest of Mexico*.[60] He selected an assortment of histories for his school and hoped to read them, but feared he had "more good works" than he could "get time to read."[61] The little library included books about Hannibal, Alfred the Great, Peter the Great, William the Conqueror, Rome, and Greece. He also had Parkman's *Pontiac*, Fiske's history of the American Revolution, and miscellaneous books about U.S. history. This was not a bad little library, considering the state of historical scholarship in 1892. Dipping into it would have given him a broad education in history.

While at Fairchild Herbert found time for romance with a local woman, but she threw him over for someone else. The experience left him wounded and a little discouraged about women. "I would not trust any of them with my heart if I wanted it to remain whole. They would *bust* it, sure!"[62] Fred was probably in no mood for Herbert's dreary philosophy about women and love, for he planned to marry his fiancée after he graduated from Wisconsin in June 1893.[63] But Herbert continued with his casually misogynistic ramblings. "It is well for me that there is no danger of female eyes gazing on some of my charges made against their sex," he wrote; "otherwise I should be doomed to lifelong celibacy."[64]

Permanent celibacy was not the sort of life sentence that Gertrude Janes had in mind for Herbert. He had come to respect her educational and professional goals, although in the fall of 1892 he regarded her merely as an old friend. Nevertheless, his respect for Gertrude was growing. When he told someone that Gertrude "ought to be at the U.W.," his friend replied, "Yes, nice thing—lots of money," referring to the Janes family's comfortable circumstances. "I suppose that's as far as he sees," Herbert thought.[65] But Herbert now saw Gertrude as someone with serious mental ability, a likely prospect for the state university, where he was headed himself. In the spring of 1893 his feelings for her would deepen.

During the Christmas holiday Herbert went home to his family and likely saw Gertrude. Whatever transpired then, their relationship took a turn in the new year. In early February Gertrude visited Fairchild, and it was not because she was looking for a job. Herbert, who usually wrote long, detailed letters to his brother, resorted to breathless stabs of information. "Janes is here to spend Sat & Sun[.] Dance last night." It must have been a big night. "Still in the ring, though slightly disfigured," he told Fred.[66] Gertrude had him now and Herbert was a willing captive.

In the fall Herbert went to Madison, while Fred and his new wife, Olive, moved to Kaukauna, Wisconsin, for a principalship at the high school. Once again the brothers traded places, now with Fred gaining practical experience and subsidizing Herbert's education. At last Herbert stood at the door of the institution that he had dreamed about since high school, an institution that he hoped would grant him the keys to the kingdom of professional recognition and social advancement. The professors he met there would change his life.

The University of Wisconsin was less than fifty years old when Herbert Bolton arrived in 1893. The student body of nearly three thousand was small by today's standards, but it had grown rapidly from only five hundred in 1887. Located on College Hill along the shores of Lake Mendota, the university's environs were nothing if not scenic, but its political geography was as important as its physical location. Madison is the state capital, and the state house is within walking distance. Politicos had only to cast their eyes westward to see the fruits of the state's investment in higher education. Most Wisconsinites judged the university approvingly; some thought otherwise.[1]

The University of Wisconsin was poised to become a great institution of higher learning. Funding from the sale of public lands under the federal Morrill Act had enabled the expansion of faculty, student body, and curriculum. By the 1890s Wisconsin was recognized as one of the emerging progressive centers of higher education.[2] Thousands of working-class urbanites, villagers, and farm boys like the Boltons were among the beneficiaries of this magnificent public donation.

Two young professors in the history department when Bolton arrived in 1893 would influence his development as a historian: Frederick Jackson Turner and Charles Homer Haskins. Turner, at age thirty-one, was a rising star. The Wisconsin native had received his undergraduate and early graduate training at the state university, where he was influenced by William F. Allen. Turner had studied for the doctorate under Herbert Baxter Adams at Johns Hopkins

University before returning to the University of Wisconsin faculty. In July 1893 he read his influential essay "The Significance of the Frontier in American History" at the AHA meeting in Chicago. Frontier conditions and the settlement of the West, he argued, had made the United States what it was. This was a distinctive departure from the prevailing historical idea which held that the beginnings of American institutions and character were to be found in European antecedents. "It seems exceedingly valuable and important," Haskins wrote of Turner's essay, "but I feel so 'westernized' that I cannot appreciate how it would appeal to an eastern man."[3] Turner's essay eventually established him as one of the leading American historians of his day, even among easterners. Needless to say, westerners (including Wisconsinites) were glad to learn that they were on the cutting edge of history rather than mere primitives who lived on the margins of American civilization.[4]

Haskins had also earned his doctorate at Johns Hopkins, where he became Turner's friend. He wrote his dissertation on the Yazoo land frauds but eventually became America's leading medieval historian, with interests in Norman institutions and the development of medieval science. Something of a child prodigy, he completed his undergraduate degree at Johns Hopkins at the age of sixteen, then studied in Paris and Berlin before returning to Hopkins for his doctorate. Professor Haskins was only twenty-three, the same age as the undergraduate Bolton. By the time Bolton met him, Haskins was known as a meticulous researcher who had mastered several languages. Haskins impressed Bolton because of his thoroughness and because he worked his students very hard, which appealed to Bolton's dogged work habits. One of Haskins's friends, F. M. Powicke, likened his approach to teaching and writing to that of a builder. First, he amassed sufficient research material with which to build his edifice; then, he deliberately laid its foundation, "each sentence . . . like a block of hewn stone, laid in its place by a skilful mason." Haskins's construction "was directed by a clear and powerful mind, but every stone . . . was left to make its own impression, without the aid of external graces." Anything "wild and extravagant" from Haskins "was unthinkable," Powicke recalled. Yet, when listening to Haskins lecture, Powicke found himself "hoping, and I knew I hoped in vain, for a touch of mischief or something just a trifle hazardous." The resulting intellectual structure, however, spoke "of purpose and achievement; its austere lines reveal unexpected lights and shadows."[5]

Turner's teaching methods also impressed Bolton. His undergraduate lecturing style must have seemed offhand, perhaps even ill-prepared to the casual undergraduate, but Herbert was anything but a casual student. In a time when most professors delivered carefully prepared lectures from detailed notes, or perhaps written essays that were read word for word, Turner would walk into the hall with a stack of note cards often based on primary source material. Turner spoke to the students from the cards, which he would sometimes fumble while he looked for some particular datum; so the effect was informal, almost casual, except for his voice, which had a melodic, almost hypnotic quality. Bolton's friend, historian Carl Becker, wrote that Turner's "voice was everything: a voice not deep but full, rich, vibrant, and musically cadenced; such a voice as you would never grow weary of, so warm and intimate and human it was."[6] Turner's lectures were analytical and full of ideas, rather than strictly narrative. He amply illustrated them with lantern slides and maps, just as Bolton would do when he became a professor. To an attentive student, such as Bolton, Turner seemed to be creating history from the raw materials before his very eyes. Many of the undergraduates called the good-looking, approachable, and brilliant professor Freddie or Fred, but never to his face. His graduate students called him "the Master."[7]

As historians Haskins and Turner could not have been more different. Haskins's history was founded on a massive archival base that seemed unassailable, if a bit prosaic. Turner was quick, incisive, intuitive, deeply immersed in primary sources, but willing to write in advance of supportive evidence for his brilliant ideas. There were similarities as well as differences between the two men. Both of them were inspiring teachers. Handsome and gregarious, they were ambitious for professional advancement and recognition. They were alive to the idea that they were helping to build a new university and a new profession. Turner and Haskins were active in the AHA, and each would serve as its president. Students, especially serious ones interested in history, found both of them to be accessible and helpful. Turner and Haskins had high hopes for the development of a graduate program in history at Wisconsin, and they needed earnest disciples like Bolton.

The rapid development of the University of Wisconsin and its impressive young faculty had not gone unnoticed in the hallowed halls of Harvard University, whose president, Charles W. Eliot, toured the university in 1891. Eliot pointedly asked Haskins and Turner why they had studied at Hopkins. "Didn't we know that Harvard was the place to study history," Haskins wrote to historian J. Franklin Jameson, "that they alone had the libraries and instructors?" According to Haskins, Eliot spent much of his time in Madison maligning his Baltimore competitor. Eliot's rudeness aggravated Haskins. "Even in the West one is expected to be a gentleman."[8] Eliot was known as a reserved and forbidding figure at Harvard—William James called him a "cold figure at the helm."[9] But Eliot's manner at Madison was not merely due to his personality: he feared that upstart institutions would somehow undercut Harvard's paramount standing among American universities. If he had misgivings about advanced study at Hopkins, one can only surmise what he thought about graduate education at Madison, especially under tyros like Turner and Haskins.

A few months after Eliot's visit Daniel Coit Gilman, president of Johns Hopkins University, showed up in Madison. Gilman was the man who had so speedily made Hopkins a force in higher education. Before going to Baltimore, Gilman had been president of the University of California and is credited with laying the foundations for that western university's rise to prominence.[10] Described by one of his Berkeley friends as a pleasant and tactful man, Gilman's personal qualities served him well during his visit to Wisconsin.[11] "The contrast with Harvard's agent was significant and helped the cause of Hopkins in the Northwest," Haskins told Jameson. "We shall have nine and possibly ten Hopkins men in the faculty next year."[12] It was no wonder that eastern university presidents visited institutions in the West. Wisconsin and other developing colleges and universities sent their students to eastern graduate schools and hired the finished products of those schools. Sometimes, as in the case of Turner, the departing student and the returning professor were one and the same.

The Wisconsin visits of Eliot and Gilman illuminated the quandary over doctoral training in American universities. Once doctoral training became the sine qua non for elite institutions, they faced the dual problems of attracting the best students and then placing them when they were finished. Moreover, enterprising faculty at budding western universities were eager to establish new doctoral programs of their own. Thus, developing institutions added to the pool of doctors qualified for professorships, but there was no guarantee that the number of faculty positions would grow enough to absorb them. Even when the supply of PhDs exceeded demand, the pressure was great to maintain doctoral programs, because they were indispensable status symbols in which institutions had heavy investments. Bolton's professional life would be greatly entangled with these intractable issues, which remain salient today.

In Bolton's era, graduate education was developing rapidly at Wisconsin. In 1892 the university had hired the renowned political economist Richard T. Ely from Johns Hopkins to head a new School of Economics, Political Science, and History that would offer graduate instruction. Turner and Haskins had studied with Ely at Hopkins; Turner thought that Ely's presence would give Wisconsin a leg up on its new regional rival, the University of Chicago. The younger men chafed under Ely's sometimes heavy-handed leadership, but respected him nonetheless.[13] In those days duty (and good judgment) required faculty to obey department heads, deans, and university presidents. Turner and Haskins kept to that form.

Faculty relations and the struggle for institutional recognition did not immediately concern Bolton. In his first semester he enrolled in Haskins's course on English constitutional history as well as German, algebra, economics, and elementary law classes. He briefly considered law as a profession, perhaps because it was a more direct route to the sort of social and financial success that he coveted, but history appealed to him.[14] Haskins demanded twice as much work as his other professors, "but the work is interesting," Bolton thought, "hence easily done."[15]

Herbert moved into a rooming house and settled into college life. The freshmen and sophomores recruited him for field day, "but rather than have one class haze me for helping the other I'll keep away from them both."[16] Football, however, attracted Herbert's attention. He played halfback in intramural games, scored a touchdown, and thought the game was great fun, although it was a bruising experience in those helmetless, padless, and dangerous early days of the sport. He gave it up after a few games. He enjoyed competitive rowing but abandoned that sport, too, as he devoted more attention to his studies.

Gertrude's presence in Madison sharpened Herbert's sense of purpose. Now he wished to achieve something not only for himself but also "for her sake, and [to] be somebody of whom she can be proud . . . her nearness to me keeps the motive more vividly before me."[17] Perhaps hoping to plant a seed in Herbert's mind, she passed along news of various friends who had recently married.[18] Formerly, Herbert regarded the marriage of old chums as if he had heard news of their execution. Not now. Perhaps Fred's marriage had reconciled him to the inevitability of his own matrimonial future. By the beginning of 1894 the couple had reached an "understanding," a locution that must have meant that they were privately if not formally engaged. Herbert had gone so far as to quit working on Sundays, which gave the couple more time together. Still Herbert insisted that he studied "all the more earnestly because . . . every time I see her I receive anew the strongest inspiration and incentive for work."[19]

The couple could not marry until Herbert finished his studies in the spring of 1895. Until then he needed better bachelor living arrangements. He decided to join a fraternity. "The fellows here who belong to no society and stay in their shells all the time are in danger of losing their earmarks of civilization and lapsing into savagery." It was as if Herbert believed that manners were a mere husk that covered the raw farm boys who had made it to Madison. Without constant reinforcement, the newly acquired veneer would slough off and reveal the rougher stuff that lay within. Herbert had worked too hard to make something of himself to allow that to happen. "I feel it to be almost a duty, and that not chiefly to myself," he explained, "to mingle to a certain extent with as good society as my limited qualifications will make me eligible to."[20] He intended to rise in the eyes of his community, whether it consisted of the small town of Tomah or the university student body. For him, fraternity membership was a means to that end.

Fred, a former frat member himself, loaned his brother the fifteen-dollar initiation fee for Theta Delta Chi. Two other Tomah boys had rushed the fraternity but were voted down. Herbert must have felt some pride in knowing that he had been admitted to an exclusive club.[21] Indeed, his fraternity proved to be more exclusive than he could have guessed in 1894. Like Bolton, two of his fraternity brothers, Carl Becker and Guy Stanton Ford, would become presidents of the American Historical Association. If professional connections and upward mobility were the objects of his membership, Bolton joined the very best fraternity for his purposes, although there was more than a bit of luck involved. The odds against three AHA presidents coming from the same fraternity chapter must have been enormous; that the three presidents-to-be studied with two other AHA presidents in the making is perhaps unique in the history of the profession.

Theta Delta Chi was exclusive in ways unappealing today. Like other college fraternities at the time, Theta Delta Chi excluded Jews.[22] This was not a matter that Herbert discussed openly, but it was probably tacitly understood that the "good society" with whom Herbert wished to associate did not include Jews. While public and most private institutions admitted qualified Jews, Jewish college students faced social discrimination of the sort that fraternities dished out.[23]

Bolton shared the common racial, ethnic, and religious prejudices of his time. As he put it many years later, his outlook in college was "typically 'American,' that is to say, provincial, nationalistic. My unquestioned historical beliefs included the following: Democrats were born to be damned; Catholics, Mormons, and Jews were to be looked upon askance."[24] It is impossible to fathom how deeply these bigotries ran in the young Bolton's psyche, but in 1894 he was a conformist who sought the approval of the dominant society.

Bolton, Becker, and Ford accepted the institutionalized prejudice of their fraternity, but later in life each of them would interrogate deeply held intellectual and cultural assumptions. Becker is well known for questioning the purposes and explanatory power of history. He was deeply intellectual, philosophical, and skeptical about the historian's ability to re-create an objective account of the past through an uncolored reading of historical documents as the so-called scientific historians claimed to do. For Becker, written history (as opposed to the past itself) was transitory, to be rewritten by each succeeding generation in ways that would best serve that generation.[25] Ford eventually settled on German history as his field. In the 1930s he became an outspoken critic of Nazi Germany with its "hideous intolerance."[26] By then, it would seem, Ford had left his anti-Semitic fraternity days far behind.

If by comparison with his fraternity brothers Bolton did not have quite the intellectual acuity and literary panache of a Becker, or the political courage of a Ford, he should not be condemned as intellectually lightweight or permanently prejudiced against Jews and other groups. Bolton had a good and sensitive mind.[27] Even though he was deeply marked by Turner's incisive brilliance and Haskins's rigorous scholarship, Bolton had an indelible strain of romanticism that would influence his historical writing throughout his life. As a mature historian he would cast the history of the Spanish Borderlands in that romantic light. And he would abandon his youthful prejudice against Catholics and Jews.

Hard work, not introspection about social problems, occupied Bolton's time in Madison as the year 1893–94 wore on. Medieval history under Haskins and American history with Turner were claiming more of his attention. He won a top grade from Turner. Law was becoming less attractive to Bolton.[28] History, or perhaps Haskins and Turner, had won him over.

By the end of the school year in June 1894, Bolton was again looking for summer work. Gertrude had decided to return to teaching in Minnesota in the fall of 1894 so that she could save money for their impending marriage. Bolton feared that she had exhausted herself to get good marks at the university.[29] Herbert spent part of his summer teaching school in Neillsville, Wisconsin, but hated it. "I hope I may be 'hanged by the neck until dead' if I ever agree to teach another arithmetic class," he wrote Fred.[30]

During the summer a crisis arose at the University of Wisconsin. While Herbert had no direct part in the affair, it demonstrated the vulnerability of faculty and the university to the manipulations of a striving politician. Oliver Wells, the superintendent of public instruction whom the Boltons despised, was ex officio member of the Board of Regents. He published a letter in *The Nation* accusing Professor Ely of advocating "utopian, impractical and pernicious doctrines," including the right to unionize, boycott, and strike against employers.[31] This was a very serious matter that threatened Ely's career and the university. The Board of Regents named a committee to investigate the charges. Some faculty feared that if substantiated, the accusations would lead to a witch hunt for other professors with politically unpopular views. Turner wrote a lengthy report that rebutted Wells's charges against Ely. In the end the regents exonerated Ely, and Wells was discredited. The regents also approved a declaration that the university "should ever encourage that continual and fearless sifting and winnowing by which alone the truth can be found."[32]

There is no mention of this episode in the Boltons' letters, but they no doubt knew about it. Certainly they knew all of the principals involved. While one might conclude that all was well that ended well, the incident offered other lessons for an aspiring professor of history. The conflict was resolved satisfactorily (from the standpoint of the faculty), but only because of the hard work of Turner and the wisdom of the Board of Regents. Moreover, Ely's defense was that he was innocent of the charges. What if he *had* advocated unions, strikes, and socialistic ideas in his classes? What might have happened under the hands of a more popular and skillful politician than Wells? The regents' resounding and inspiring defense of academic freedom was good only for as long as they continued to support it. New regents with new ideas could put aside the resolution of the old board. And, of course, the statement applied only to the University of Wisconsin.

While the Wells-Ely controversy percolated in Wisconsin, one of Ely's former students, Edward W. Bemis of the University of Chicago, made the mistake of criticizing the railroads during the Pullman Strike. William Rainey Harper, president of the University of Chicago, quickly informed Bemis that his speech had caused Harper a great deal of annoyance. "It is hardly safe for me to venture into any of the Chicago clubs," Harper complained. "During the remainder of your connection with the University . . . exercise very great care in public utterance about questions that are agitating the minds of the people."[33] At the end of the academic year Bemis was dropped from the faculty without further explanation. If Bolton learned anything from the Ely and Bemis controversies, it was to avoid them.

When Herbert returned to the university in the fall of 1894, his younger brother Roy accompanied him. Roy had just finished high school, and his immediate enrollment in the university seemed to vindicate Bolton family sacrifices for higher education. Fred had worked for five years before attending college, and graduated at age twenty-six. Herbert worked intermittently before earning his baccalaureate at twenty-four. Roy enrolled in the university when he was seventeen and graduated in four years. Eventually he became a physician. For Herbert and for Roy the path to higher education was shorter than it had been for his older brother. Nor were the Bolton women left out of this educational parade of upward mobility. Each of the sisters attended college and some became schoolteachers. That the

Boltons continued to attend college in the midst of the economic depression of the 1890s was a testament to their conviction that education would improve their lot.

Herbert's life in his final undergraduate year assumed the familiar routine of study, work, and planning for the future. His determination to study history was now fixed, largely because of the influence of Turner and Haskins, who were "ahead of all the others I have been under," he told Fred.[34] He was taking courses in U.S. constitutional history, social and economic history, and medieval history. By March Herbert was strategizing a campaign for employment after graduation. As usual, no stone was left unturned.[35] Fred, who had been subsidizing Herbert for two years, planned to enter graduate school in Madison in the fall while anticipating additional study in the future at one of the great German universities. In the meantime, Herbert arranged for Fred to teach two "easy classes" in Madison to help meet expenses.[36]

In June 1895 Herbert graduated from the university. Now he had letters behind his name and all the rights and privileges that they conferred. He went off to Neillsville for the summer to teach with Fred. He was slated to replace Fred as principal of Kaukauna High School, so he and Gertrude could set a date: August 20, at the Janeses' home in Tunnel City. The Bolton wedding was quite an affair. Herbert and Gertie took their vows before one hundred witnesses, including some of his fraternity brothers, who sang college songs. The festivities lasted until evening when "amid showers of congratulations and rice and attended by the Theta Delta Chi yell," the couple departed on a train. "We compassed our journey in due time," Herbert wrote, "and very pleasantly."[37]

Married life in Kaukauna was good, but the newlyweds knew that it was only a temporary home before returning to Madison for Herbert's graduate studies.[38] He was already making plans. To make sure that the Wisconsin faculty did not forget him, he invited Turner to give a public lecture in Kaukauna.[39] Not about to let his day job get in the way of his ultimate goal, Herbert did just enough to keep his employers satisfied and worked at night to prepare for graduate work. "*Duty* on the one hand holds me to my school work, and *desire* to rise lashes me on to burn the midnight oil for personal advancement."[40]

After one year of study in absentia Herbert decided to go back to Madison. He hoped for a fellowship but knew that he could work at teaching and odd jobs as he had done while an undergraduate. The year in Kaukauna had been profitable. For the first time in his life Herbert had money in the bank. "We have saved about $100 every month." Gertrude's household economy had no doubt helped that small nest egg grow. Teaching in a summer institute would add to the treasury.[41] In the meantime Herbert was reading as much U.S. history as he could get his hands on, including works by Reuben Gold Thwaites, Francis Parkman, George Bancroft, John Bach McMaster, James Ford Rhodes, Woodrow Wilson, John Fiske, and Justin Winsor. In the summer he studied for an exam on slavery from Turner.[42]

By the time Herbert reached Madison, Fred and his family were embarked on the long journey to Germany.[43] Herbert buckled down to study in earnest. His instinct was to specialize and to investigate primary sources rather than to cover comprehensively the whole field of American history for exams, the results of which would soon be forgotten (as long as one passed). Cramming, or "bucking," for exams "takes time and grubbing," he wrote to Fred, "but investigation takes brains and luck in striking *something good.*" By November Herbert believed that he had already found a good thesis subject, what he described as "the Abolition vote of 1844 [and] its effect on the different parties." Orin G. Libby, one of Turner's doctoral students, said it would "open up a *new field* of investigation."[44] Libby was well qualified to appraise Bolton's subject. His published master's thesis was a pathbreaking study of voting patterns that foreshadowed the cliometric studies of the 1970s.[45]

Once again Bolton fell under Turner's classroom spell. Turner conceived his seminar to be a collaborative effort in which everyone, including him, worked on topics. They met in the Wisconsin Historical Society and used the collections and library there. Bolton listened carefully and offered useful suggestions. Turner's criticisms were gentle but pointed up the shortcomings of ill-prepared work. Bolton assimilated Turner's collaborative seminar philosophy and his gentle but revealing interrogation technique. Like Turner, Bolton presented himself as a helpful and well-informed coworker, although he eventually became a bit more avuncular with his own students than "the Master" was.[46]

Turner had his eye on Bolton. He asked him to teach extension courses at six dollars per student. Bolton agreed to do it for the money, which was always needed, and "to get a more personal hold on Turner."[47] He even hoped he might land a job on the Wisconsin faculty if he did a good job in the classroom, although he knew it was a long shot.

There is no question that Herbert favorably impressed the faculty and students at Wisconsin. His fellow graduate students elected him as their delegate to the Federation of Graduate Clubs, which was to meet in Baltimore at the end of December.[48] The Wisconsin club paid his expenses, so Herbert jumped at the opportunity to go east. In Washington, D.C., he saw all of the sights that he could fit into forty-eight hours. He judged the capital to be "truly a magnificent city" with "an air of 'swell-dom'" seen only rarely in other cities. Like any good tourist, he took in the Capitol, Library of Congress, Navy Yard, National Museum, Smithsonian Institution, Ford's Theater, and the White House. Then he went down to Mount Vernon, saw "Lee's confiscated estate," Washington's Masonic Lodge, and Christ Church, where both Washington and Lee worshiped. "I sat in both pews," he added. Mount Vernon captured his imagination: "Truly a beautiful home in any age! And such a view up and down the grand old Potomac!" Then he "viewed *The Tomb* with such sacred memories for every American. Really such a visit is inspiring!"[49]

After these breast-swelling sights, the Federation of Graduate Clubs meeting in Baltimore was a bit of a letdown. Still, in a room full of strangers, Herbert soon became a center of attention. The delegates elected him secretary pro tem for the meeting and secretary for the coming year.[50] This was the beginning of Bolton's national reputation among his academic peers.

To complete the PhD in two years Bolton needed a fellowship in his second year. The need became imperative in January 1897, when Gertrude gave birth to their first child, Frances. Turner thought that the prospects for a fellowship were good for Herbert and Fred, who would be back from Germany in the fall.[51] "If one or two fellowships pan out right, then O.K.," he told Fred; "if not then O___."[52] Turner wanted to keep Bolton at Wisconsin but offered to nominate him for fellowships at other universities including Harvard.[53] Such a fellowship did not necessarily mean a complete transfer away from Wisconsin. In the 1890s it was not unusual for graduate students to take a fellowship for a year at another university and return to their home institution to complete the degree. This was a way to broaden graduate training, and (from the perspective of Turner and Haskins) advertise the bright young graduate students of the University of Wisconsin to the elite East Coast schools.[54]

Neither the Harvard nor the Wisconsin fellowship came through for the Boltons. The experience left the usually optimistic Herbert feeling a little abused. "Turner told me right up to [the vote] that my chances were strong." "The *policy* of the Univ. . . . was to turn down home men," he fumed. Turner and Haskins were now plumping Herbert for a fellowship at the University of Pennsylvania, but he had "no strong hopes."[55]

Herbert's judgment was a bit harsh. Turner probably told Bolton much the same thing about fellowships that he told Carl Becker. "It would give me pleasure to see you win a fellowship," Turner explained. Of course, "we have to settle them purely on the basis of competition, but I should be glad, other things being equal, to see one of the men trained entirely by us win the honor. Of course I cannot make any promises, and you, I understand, are not asking for any."[56] Herbert probably heard what he wanted to hear without registering Turner's careful qualifiers.

Nevertheless, Turner offered him a place as his assistant and some extension work. Herbert thought that things might turn out all right after all. "I felt pretty blue last night but there's a good deal of India rubber in me and I bound back into shape pretty easily."[57] Herbert's disappointment was somewhat assuaged with his election to an alumni fellowship, but it did not pay as much as the one he had lost. "Turner says that if I get something in the East I'd better resign . . . which I think I'll do." Three weeks later the University of Pennsylvania faculty elected him to a Harrison Fellowship.[58] Still, Herbert's failure to obtain major support at Wisconsin rankled. "It is the policy of the UW profs. to get outsiders and to widen their own reputations. I know Turner was very anxious to get me a place but he preferred it to be abroad. I hardly think that a fair policy."[59]

Herbert had drawn an astute assessment out of the disappointment that he felt over losing the Wisconsin fellowship. He had been a pawn in a larger game of professional and institutional politics. Haskins and Turner were brilliant young comers who assiduously cultivated their reputations with older men at more prestigious institutions. Promising graduate students like Bolton, Becker, and Ford could be moved around on the academic map to further the careers of their mentors. Improvements in the mentor's status sometimes created opportunities for students. Indeed, in April, the month before the fellowship election was held at Wisconsin, the prominent American historian John Bach McMaster had invited Turner to take a position at the University of Pennsylvania. Although he did not want the job, Turner visited Penn and returned to Wisconsin no doubt armed with knowledge about the Harrison Fellowship for which he recommended Bolton.[60] The move to Pennsylvania would benefit Bolton, but he resented being forced out of his alma mater in order to succeed in his chosen field. The graduate student who wanted to rise had gotten a lesson on just how that was done in the historical profession. He did not think it fair, but he would not forget the lesson.

Bolton left Wisconsin reluctantly, but he must have thrilled to the historical associations of Philadelphia and the University of Pennsylvania.[61] Founded in 1740, Penn was one of the older institutions of higher learning in the United States. The university had struggled to become a first-rate institution until the 1880s when private endowments and an aggressive new administration began to improve things.[62] In 1883 Penn hired John Bach McMaster to teach American history. Only thirty-one at the time, McMaster had an unusual background for a historian. He had graduated from City College of New York, where he had distinguished himself in the sciences. After college McMaster surveyed the Civil War battlefield at Winchester, Virginia, a task that supported General Philip H. Sheridan's *Memoirs*. McMaster's technical books on engineering qualified him for a faculty position at Princeton in 1877. He taught surveying and led Princeton's fossil-collecting expedition to the Wyoming Bad Lands. In these early days of bone collecting McMaster's experience as a surveyor no doubt outweighed his inexperience in paleontology. The experience gave McMaster a lasting interest in the American West.[63]

McMaster began writing the *History of the American People* as a diversion from teaching Princeton boys the art of surveying. He intended his multivolume work to be a story about ordinary people that was entirely unlike the accounts of political affairs that dominated historical writing at that time. When the first volume appeared in 1883, it became an instant best seller. Almost overnight McMaster had become one of the nation's leading historians. Two months after his book appeared, a representative from Penn offered McMaster a new chair in American history.[64]

McMaster's enthusiasm for Penn was matched with a deep hatred of Princeton. He detested teaching the surveying courses, and was certain that he would never be promoted or allowed to teach history at Presbyterian Princeton, because he was not a church member. Thus, when he headed for Pennsylvania, McMaster penned in his diary, "Left Princeton, Thank God forever."[65]

Bolton found that McMaster was a very different sort of teacher than Turner or Haskins. McMaster was a poor lecturer and inattentive mentor. Although he demanded much from his graduate students, his mentoring style is best described as benign neglect.[66] But McMaster had connections and used them to benefit his students. He arranged for Bolton to attend a dinner for Herbert M. Friedenwald, superintendent of manuscripts in the Library of Congress and formerly McMaster's doctoral student. "The party was very select, only the club and three history Fellows," but it was costly at $1.50 per plate.[67] Bolton bore the expense so that he could make the connection with Friedenwald. To Herbert, fresh from the western provinces, Penn must have seemed the center of a social and scholarly world he had only dreamed of in Wisconsin.

Brother Fred had also moved east, to Worcester, Massachusetts, where he won a fellowship at Clark University. The Clark faculty had already accepted the thesis he had written in Germany for a doctorate in psychology, although he had yet to pass his exams.[68] Fred was developing a specialty in educational psychology. He soon arranged to publish his thesis as a book and began submitting articles to professional journals. Once again, Fred proved to be Herbert's role model.

By the end of October Herbert had decided on a thesis subject, the "status of negro as a slave in 1860; changes effected in his status by emancipation, reconstruction, and the attempts of the south to make these laws inoperative." This was his general plan, "but think a doctors thesis may be written on the first chapter."[69] His interest in slavery seems to have developed over a period of a year or so. He began studying slavery intensively in 1896 before returning to Madison for graduate work with Turner.[70] Within weeks he could report that he had already written the first few pages of his thesis after going through "at least 100 vols of state statutes and digests," demonstrating the prodigious capacity for primary source investigation that would distinguish Bolton's career ever after.[71] By the end of the fall term he had written forty pages for McMaster's seminar and hoped to finish the dissertation in six months.[72]

Thesis writing did not go as smoothly as Herbert had hoped. In late December the meeting of the Federation of Graduate Clubs in Chicago took a week out of his crowded schedule.[73] Family life had its satisfactions, but "you know the difficulties of studying with small babes in small quarters," he groused to Fred. Gertrude was nearly worn out. She had been reduced "to a mere nurse and kitchen maid," he said. To make matters worse, Herbert caught a winter cold. On top of all those distractions he had to write "reports—reports—reports" for every graduate seminar, which were "fatal to thesis work."[74]

In February 1898 the explosion of the USS *Maine* in Havana harbor added the prospect of war with Spain to Herbert's list of distractions. The catastrophe was widely believed to be an act of Spanish sabotage, and war fever was at a high pitch. One week after the explosion President McKinley tried to cool public passions against Spain with a temperate speech to a huge crowd at the University of Pennsylvania. Herbert may have been at the event; he sent the program to his brother without comment.[75]

Herbert was "no jingo," he told Fred. Nevertheless, he concluded that the United States was "not to be wholly condemned for interfering in Cuban affairs," citing "disorder at our doors," "un-Christian barbarities," and the "Commercial interests of the United States." Herbert thought that the United States would ultimately prevail if war came and that Spain should lose its last colonial possessions as a result. Current events compelled him to take a historical view of Spanish America, perhaps for the first time in his career. "At the opening of the century [Spain] was in possession of the whole American continent from the headwaters of the Missouri to Terra [*sic*] del Fuego." But now "most of her possessions have been lost by revolution, all by incompetency."[76] No one could accuse Herbert of Hispanophilia in 1898.

Bolton's ruminations about the Spanish Empire show a distinct lack of interest in what would become his chief field of study. He emphasized his disinterest in things Spanish when he speculated about "learning a language (Not Spanish)" and preferred picking up Italian so that he could master Renaissance history.[77] The days when he would defend Spanish civilization still lay far in the future.

Herbert's opinions about the war and Spain were influenced by McMaster, who thought the sinking of the *Maine* reason enough to go to war. McMaster's newspaper and magazine articles and speeches were widely publicized. Territorial expansion had been a good thing for the United States in the past, he analogized, and it would be a good thing now. McMaster thought that war would stimulate patriotism and might quiet social discontent in the United States, a position that eventually helped to convince historian Charles Beard to conclude that the Spanish-American War was launched to quell domestic unrest. McMaster gave visual reinforcement to his bellicose ideas by decorating his office with Frederick Remington's "savage paintings," as McMaster's biographer styled them.[78]

McMaster's choice of art and his high-blooded rhetoric must have impressed Herbert. His prominence as a public intellectual was impossible to miss. Politicos who found academic support for their views deeply appreciated McMaster. As Henry Cabot Lodge said, McMaster's ideas about expansion and the war were significant because he spoke "with the authority of an historian."[79] At Penn Bolton found a new model for professional success: a professor of history who wrote for popular audiences about the historical origins of the important issues of the day.

By the end of the school year Bolton's dissertation was not finished but Penn had renewed his fellowship. Bolton's work pleased McMaster, so one more year of effort would bring the degree if all went well. Fred's success brought renewed encouragement. He passed his examinations and secured the doctorate. Then came the perfect culmination of events when Wisconsin Normal in Milwaukee hired Fred. This justified everything that the Boltons had invested in higher education. If anyone doubted their wisdom, they had only to consider the esteemed professor, Dr. Frederick Bolton, the published scholar who lectured in Milwaukee. "I shall be glad when I have accomplished as much," Herbert averred, and who could doubt his sincerity?[80]

With another summer behind him and Fred's gleaming success before him, Bolton plunged back into his work at Penn. Hoping to alleviate the distraction of having a toddler in the house, he rented a three-room, third-floor flat with a living room that was arranged as a study for Herbert. "Herbert is so nicely shut off from us that he is quite certain that he will be able to accomplish a good deal," Gertrude wrote.[81]

It was time to finish the degree, and Herbert intended "to make every day *count* toward the desired end." Scholarship was not all that Herbert had to think about. He had more privacy in the new home, but in some ways it was not as convenient as their former Philadelphia room, where a neighbor routinely took care of Frances so that Gertrude could get out during the day. Now Herbert babysat when Gertrude had errands or social engagements. Gertrude was not entirely shut in. During the evenings while Frances slept and Herbert studied, she enjoyed the cultural attractions of Philadelphia. She attended lectures and musicals at the Drexel Institute, only three blocks from their apartment.[82] Nor had she forgotten her scholarly interests. At home she studied English Medieval history, perhaps as Herbert's study mate.

Bolton plugged away "under the lash 'must'" in this crowded but companionable setting. "McMaster accepts all my ideas without much comment," Herbert wrote. "I don't know whether that augurs well or ill. He may tear me to pieces at the end." In December McMaster accepted Bolton's most recent "batch of 'negroes' with the comment that it was 'very good.'"[83] This was where matters stood at Christmas 1898.

In January disaster struck the Boltons when Frances developed a fever and then severe convulsions. The frightened Boltons, who were loving but inexperienced parents, doused Frances with cold water and called for a doctor who decided that Frances's intestines were inflamed. After two days and nights of nursing, Frances's condition did not improve, although the doctor visited twice daily and Herbert got a woman in to help Gertrude during the day. Then Frances developed hives and a severe cold.[84] The cash-strapped Boltons hired a nurse. The doctor prepared them for the worst when he said that Frances was "*desperately sick.*"[85] Complications set in. Frances's bowels had stopped and poison was building up. Her abdomen, face, and limbs were bloated "fearfully" and her pulse ran at 150 beats per minute. It was "now a question of which way the tide goes." "We only *hope*," Herbert told his brother. "My faith in the result is weak."[86]

With everything in the balance and the outlook bleak, on the last day of January the tide carried Frances back to the Boltons. The worst symptoms had abated and Herbert thought that she would survive, although the recovery period proved to be lengthy. It had been an expensive illness, but family members pitched in to defray expenses.[87]

Amidst the uncertainty and chaos of late winter, Herbert returned to his thesis. McMaster thought that it was better than the work he had seen from Harvard and that it should be published.[88] With the dissertation approved, Bolton still had to pass his examinations. "I do not see how they can pluck me," he mused, "but they *might*."[89] It was not likely that the Penn faculty would "pluck" Herbert at this stage of the game. They had arranged for him to lecture on his thesis before the Professors' History Club, a group of faculty from Penn and other Philadelphia colleges.[90]

If he won the degree, Herbert believed, his best opportunity for college teaching would be in a normal school. Sometimes he wished that he had taken pedagogy and psychology like his brother, because it would have given him "a pull" at the normal schools.[91] If he could not get a normal school job, Herbert was willing, even anxious, to teach high school if the pay was good. He was tired of being poor, tired of annual searches for summer jobs, tired of subjecting his wife and child to the inconvenience and risk of a life without money to spare. And while he was sure that he was a good teacher, uncertainty about his other abilities dogged him. "I have never thought I am a *whale* at originality," he explained to Fred, "but I always thought I could *teach some*."[92] Herbert's insecurity in the final stages of his graduate education was natural enough. Like many doctoral students, he had taken in a mass of data and detail and was uncertain about how to digest it. Nor did he know whether his work was worthwhile in the eyes of others. He thought it would take an additional year to turn it into a book, if that feat was even possible.

Examinations still loomed. He was prepared, but no matter what he had accomplished thus far, a few professors could take it all away from him. Yet the preliminary signs were all there. Bolton had received nothing but praise and recognition at Penn—two prestigious fellowships with an even better one promised, an invited lecture, generous support from a nationally recognized mentor, an office in a national organization. Turner was still thinking about him too. In April Turner informed Herbert that he had put his name in for a position, but he did not tell him where.[93] Herbert should have gone into his exams with a high degree of confidence, but like virtually all well-prepared graduate students, he worried nonetheless.

His anxiety was misplaced. Bolton passed written examinations in economics and European and American history in early May, days of "severe travail," as he called the process.[94] The oral examination was the only hurdle that remained. Finally, Herbert could see the dawn coming. At Penn the orals were "supplementary 'farces,'" he told Fred. "Unless I am inordinately asinine on Tuesday, I shall pull through."[95] A few days later he reported that he had passed the orals "with no great honor and no bad scars or scares." Now that the ordeal was over, he was glad that he was "no longer a school boy. That gives me more satisfaction than the *degree*, (which has depreciated much within 24 hours)."[96]

But would it pay? Bolton still did not have a professional position, although McMaster had promised him a postdoctoral fellowship at Penn if a job did not materialize. Bolton was understandably concerned about his professional prospects, but he was in a very strong position to compete for jobs. At Wisconsin and Penn he had studied with some of the country's most important historians, who showed confidence in him at every turn. In the early summer, however, Bolton returned to Wisconsin without a job.

Bolton's fondest hope was that he would land a professorship with his brother at Wisconsin Normal. He expected Fred to help him get it, but there were no guarantees. He sent letters to high schools while teaching a summer institute for teachers in Appleton.[97] Then a job opened at Albion College, a Methodist school in Michigan. Herbert applied, hoping that his acquaintance with a prominent Methodist minister would help his cause.[98] Turner wrote for him too. Bolton's reliance on a church friend to vouch for him bordered on hypocrisy. He no longer belonged to the church. The word "church" appears only rarely in Herbert's correspondence with his brother; "prayer," "God," and "Bible," were never used. If he prayed for a good job, he never told his brother about it. Any appeals to God during his child's desperate illness likewise went unreported. Nevertheless, Albion called Herbert to Michigan for an interview. Methodist or not, Herbert was "elected OK," he wrote Fred. "You fix up the newspaper accts," he added. "They are going to give me a column here, & [in] Detroit."[99] Evidently Fred did more than fix up newspaper announcements, for soon Wisconsin Normal offered Herbert a position teaching economics and civics at $1,000 per year, $100 more than Albion, but $300 less than Herbert had hoped for. So much for Methodism at Albion; back to Wisconsin.[100]

And so it came to pass that the Bolton brothers engineered the perfect ending to their years of struggle. Herbert's salary was small but it was secure, and he hoped for raises. Living near his brother in Milwaukee gave him great personal satisfaction. The feeling was mutual. As Fred wrote many years later, "No two young couples ever experienced greater mutual enjoyment than we did that year."[101] Surely this happy ending foreshadowed many years of contentment for the brother professors in their alma mater. Some happy endings are not destined to last.

THREE · Gone to Texas

Life in Milwaukee was good, but despite Herbert's happiness in being with Fred, the reality of normal school teaching soon set in. Herbert's teaching load was heavy: four classes in three subjects, while more favored faculty taught only three classes in two subjects.[1] This was a matter of preferential treatment rather than merit, Herbert believed. He had little control over what he taught. "He had to teach what was handed to him at the opening of each term," Fred explained; "mathematics, economics, ancient history, etc." Herbert was rarely permitted to teach U.S. history in Milwaukee. He taught in a college, but his colleagues and administrators did not value his hard-earned PhD. What had the sacrifice been for? Institutional life at Normal was riven with pettiness, politics, and the narrowest sort of pedagogical cant, at least as far as Bolton's letters told the story.[2] Then there was the matter of salary. The Boltons had a second child, Helen. Despite Gertrude's careful management, $1,000 did not go far with Herbert's growing family. He even considered taking a sales job with a publishing house.[3] Surely he had not invested so heavily in the doctorate merely to become a traveling salesman.

Herbert became increasingly unhappy at Milwaukee and was anxious to get out. In a surprising move in the spring of 1900 he applied for the presidency of Oahu College, a small preparatory school in Honolulu originally founded to educate the children of Congregationalist missionaries. A more remote, insignificant posting for the ambitious Herbert can scarcely be imagined. The title of president may have appealed to him as much as anything else. At least he would have been in charge of a school. Perhaps the idea of being in a balmy land far away from the ordinary pressures of academic advancement and petty politics charmed him, but it was only a dream. He did not get the job.[4]

Herbert was not the only Bolton who was dissatisfied in Milwaukee. In September 1900 Fred left for the University of Iowa, where he would head an education program. This turn of events, while unwelcome from a personal standpoint, lit the forward path for Herbert: be patient, get more experience, publish, establish yourself in your field, then move to a better place where you will be in charge. Fred's move to Iowa was an important step upward, but Herbert's happiness for him was tinged with sadness. The brothers would never again live in the same town or even in the same state.

Herbert toiled on alone. He condensed his dissertation for a magazine.[5] That essay was not accepted, but he published his first short article for a teachers' magazine, "Our Nation's First Boundaries," which in a general way foreshadowed his interest in the borderlands. He was also working on a textbook manuscript on U.S. territorial development. A sketch of his ideas about the U.S. acquisition of Florida included a section called "Race Antipathy and Spanish Weakness," which declared that "Race dislike between Spaniards and Americans was . . . a constant spur inciting the stronger to encroach upon the other." Spaniards, Bolton thought, "lived in constant dread of the irresistible westerner."[6] At the turn of the century, Bolton's thinking about Spain in America had not penetrated beyond the common prejudices of the day.

Herbert applied for jobs in late 1900, but to no avail.[7] He had to get out of Milwaukee, but "I do not know where I'll land, I'm sure," he wrote. "I hope I'll be a teacher of *something, somewhere, sometime*. Now I'm a teacher of every thing."[8] He fit in as best he could while waiting for something to break.

While Herbert chafed at Normal, events one thousand miles away conspired to take him away from Wisconsin. George Pierce Garrison, chair of the history department in the University of Texas, needed a replacement for his assistant professor, Lester Gladstone Bugbee, who was mortally ill with tuberculosis. Bugbee taught medieval history, but he and Garrison had been developing the archival basis for the history of Texas and the Southwest. Bugbee had been instrumental in the university's acquisition of the important Bexar Archives, which documented the history of Coahuila y Texas from 1717 to 1836.[9] Garrison, who dreamed of making the University of Texas a great center for historical research and graduate training, needed someone to replace Bugbee in the archives as well as the classroom.

Garrison would have an important influence on Bolton's career. He was "an impressive man with a commanding presence and a cultivated, urbane manner," according to historian Llerena Friend. He was born in Georgia in 1853, and after attending college and teaching school, he moved to Texas in 1874.[10] Five years later he studied at the University of Edinburgh in Scotland, where he received certificates in mathematics, natural philosophy, logic, metaphysics, rhetoric, and English. The suave southerner even won the David Masson prize for poetry while he was there. Returning to Texas in 1881, Garrison was immediately stricken with tuberculosis, but by 1884 he was well enough to join the faculty of the one-year-old University of Texas as part of a two-man department of English language, history, and literature. Four years later Garrison was teaching all of the history courses at Texas, a fact that determined him to enroll for the doctorate in history at the University of Chicago, which he completed in 1896. He put his personal stamp on all things historical at the University of Texas and insisted on teaching all of the courses in U.S. history.

Garrison and Texas were attracting favorable attention in the historical profession. In 1898 J. Franklin Jameson, editor of the *American Historical Review*, invited Garrison to submit an article. There was a wealth of hitherto unknown and unworked material on Texas and the Southwest, Garrison explained. He, Bugbee, and his students were all at work on it and would have something ready for publication soon. "At least some of it shall be offered to the Review," as indeed it was.[11] He sent Jameson some articles by his students about Spanish missions in Texas and the wanderings of Cabeza de Vaca.

National notice of Texas made the replacement of Bugbee all the more pressing. Garrison had obtained some help from Eugene C. Barker, who held a fresh new Texas MA, but with Bugbee gone Garrison needed a new wheelhorse. Barker was not yet the proper animal; he needed to complete doctoral work before he would be credible in the estimation of the historical profession. In search of the right man Garrison initiated a "furious correspondence," as Barker put it.[12]

One of Garrison's letters fell on the desk of Jameson, who knew almost everyone in the history profession. "It is important that the man selected should not only be of high scholarship," Garrison explained. "I am anxious especially that the man chosen should be of high character and an inspiring and effective teacher, ready to devote himself . . . to the general interests of the School of History and the University at large."[13] Where could Garrison find such a man? In all likelihood, though letters have not surfaced, Garrison (and perhaps Jameson) sent queries to Turner and Haskins, perhaps only the latter since Garrison wanted someone to teach European courses. In any case, Haskins recommended Bolton for the Texas job.[14]

Meanwhile Bolton had almost given up looking for jobs when a graduate school friend recommended him for a place at Dartmouth College. He got the offer, but it was not a permanent position as had been promised. There was a chance the position could be made permanent, but he could not justify moving his family on that uncertain basis.[15] Bolton turned it down. Neither Turner nor Haskins encouraged him to go. Turner said that he would "be *more* ready to help me into a university if I stay than if I go out of his territory." Turner admitted that he was selfish in recommending that Herbert stay so that he could "help build up in Wis a history centre."[16] Turner's advice was no doubt sound, but there was an edge to it. *Do my bidding here for a while,* Turner seemed to say, *and I will help you. If you leave, I may not.* In 1901 the world of American history was Turner's world. Turner knew it and so did Herbert.

Within a month Herbert regretted his decision to stay in Wisconsin. His raise at Normal was fifty dollars less than he had expected, and he was unlikely to be promoted over other faculty with more seniority. Nevertheless, as the fall semester approached, he seemed determined to make the best of his situation. Perhaps in an effort to make his teaching more congruent with the objects of the normal school mission, Herbert developed a proposal to team-teach an innovative history course on "the child in history—an historical child study course," with Vande Walker, one of the women on the faculty. Herbert thought it should be "evolutionary in character," examining the childhood experience over time and across cultures.[17] He would use anthropology and psychology as well as historical sources. This unrealized idea—it never got off the drawing board—surely was a pathbreaking approach to historical study. In an age when the lives of great men and important political movements were considered to be the proper stuff of history, Herbert was thinking about the history of children, a topic that would not come into its own until the rise of social history in the 1970s. In some ways it was not surprising that Herbert would consider such a subject, for it combined his own interests with those of his brother in child psychology. Turner's interest in social-scientific approaches to history also may have influenced Bolton. The history of childhood proved to be a road not taken, but it revealed an innovative streak in a developing young historian who was struggling to find himself.

Herbert's ruminations about new courses were interrupted when baby Helen suddenly fell ill with intestinal complaints all too similar to those that had almost killed her older sister in Philadelphia. Herbert hired a nurse and gave Helen all of his attention. (Gertrude was eight months pregnant at the time.) "She is a very dear child—Beautiful in temperament and feature. We can't spare her."[18]

Herbert was so consumed with the welfare of his child that Garrison's letter scarcely registered. The Texas professor offered Bolton a position, which would become permanent "providing Prof Bugbee does not recover from consumption—an improbability." The starting salary would be $1,500 with the rank of instructor the first year and the possibility of promotion through the ranks to "head of the school." "The work will be European history. What do you think of the prospects?" he asked Fred.[19] Herbert worried about the impermanent nature of the appointment, but Garrison assured him that Bugbee was unlikely to live and that prospects at Texas were bright. Garrison's words seemed unambiguous, but after his experience with Dartmouth Herbert was looking for fine print and disappearing ink. He wanted his brother's advice but could not wait for a reply. "I wired that I would accept." Once the decision was made, Herbert found his courage. "I am going in to win and hope to succeed."[20]

Herbert knew that Haskins had recommended him for the Texas job, but there is no reason to believe that he knew Jameson and Turner may have been involved. If Haskins knew about the Texas position, surely his best friend, Turner, knew. Bolton's name may have come to Garrison from University of Texas president W. L. Prather, who had a doctorate from Penn and who was also searching for a likely candidate.[21] The ambitious (and sometimes jealous) Herbert complained about "pull" when it benefited others, but he had plenty of pull, even though it operated out of his sight. Bolton's offers from Wisconsin Normal and Texas show how murky the hiring process was at the turn of the twentieth century. Searches were not advertised. The selection process was opaque and connections mattered; inside candidates often got the nod. A few prominent historians and university presidents controlled the professional destinies of aspiring academics, who often did not know that they were being considered for a professorship. Although Doctor Bolton was still a pawn in other men's games, this time he was the happy beneficiary of the secretive dealings of presidents and professors.

Herbert's decision to go to Texas settled his professional future, but important personal matters hung in the balance. Helen's health slowly improved, but Herbert was reluctant to leave until Gertrude gave birth. He lingered in Milwaukee until their third daughter, Laura, was born on October 7. "Easy labor, fine child, mother doing nicely," he scrawled in a hasty note to Fred.[22] The following day Herbert was on the train south, leaving Gertrude and the children, who would follow in December. It was the most decisive journey of his life.

As Bugbee convalesced in El Paso, a letter arrived from his admiring friend and former student, Eugene C. Barker. Texas had hired the new man from Wisconsin, Barker wrote. "He is rather good looking, a blond, about six feet tall; and I believe he will prove a pretty good teacher." Barker, peeved with Garrison for having given Bugbee's summer courses to Bolton instead of him, "exploded."[23] Explosions in front of Garrison were not wise. He expected professional behavior at all times, and the men who worked under him soon understood that there was an iron hand in Garrison's velvet glove.

Garrison and the university made a fine first impression on Bolton. "Prof. Garrison is a royal good man, well-trained, 48 years old." Garrison's age (seventeen years older than Bolton), meant that Bolton might eventually head the history department (or "school" as it was then called), even if Garrison remained in harness into his sixties. "Barker is a young fellow, perhaps 26, rather 'green' looking, but pleasant," Bolton wrote. Bolton's teaching load was relatively light: two European history courses in three sections that each met thrice weekly. His university accommodations included a "beautiful recitation room, with good maps and a private office," in Old Main, which in Bolton's time was still comparatively new.

Garrison had some "odds and ends" for Bolton in addition to teaching. Founding editor of the *Texas State Historical Association Quarterly*, Garrison gave Bolton editorial assignments. The new instructor did not complain. Garrison was "building up a centre for southwestern history for which Texas has unsurpassed opportunities," Bolton thought. He quickly intuited that Garrison would encourage him to work in this new field, southwestern history. "I shall get up Spanish at once, which they say is easy." All in all, Bolton thought he had "fallen into good quarters" where he thought he could rise to the top.[24] For the first time Bolton believed that he was well positioned to succeed in his chosen profession.

Bolton liked Austin. The October weather was "perfect." The city was "a big village in type and appearance, the good and bad all mixed." The capitol impressed him. He lodged in "a 'swell' residence" where Garrison had put him "to avoid making a social error *before* I get started." He noticed that almost everyone rode single footers (horses with an unusually quick and comfortable gait almost as fast as a trot). They were "common as niggers," he wrote, an unfortunate choice of terms that signaled Bolton's quick assimilation of white southern sensibilities and values.[25] "I like the southern people extremely well," he told his brother. He found them to be "kind, courteous, hospitable," and the students "much more courteous than in the north."[26] He did not mention that the university was racially segregated.

Moving to Texas to teach European history for a fifty-dollar raise had been a gamble. Once he surveyed the situation in Austin, Bolton knew that he had won his bet. Now he could specialize in history instead of teaching everything under the sun. Noticing that he was a more demanding teacher than either Garrison or Barker, he decided to modify his own teaching so that he would have more time for research. Even the administration stars seemed to be aligned in Bolton's favor. President Prather's association with Penn probably helped Bolton, who judged Prather to be an "honest, warmhearted, provincial man" who would "give one free scope." The Board of Regents had treated Bolton "liberally," paying him from September 1, rather than docking his pay for the days he had missed while waiting for his daughter's birth.[27] Texas was going to be a good thing for Bolton, and Bolton intended to be a good thing for Texas.

But the University of Texas was not quite as calm as it seemed in Bolton's first appraisal. The university had been embroiled in political controversies concerning funding, its relationship with Texas Agricultural and Mechanical College, and whether the university should serve the immediate, practical needs of the state's farmers or less concrete but loftier scholarly goals. Funding of the university by munificent land grants and oil revenues would eventually secure its future, but this inchoate treasury was also a source of political conflict.[28]

The university was vulnerable to powerful political figures in Austin. In 1897 a state representative asserted that some university professors "not in sympathy with the traditions of the South" were teaching "political heresies in place of the system of political economy" cherished by Texans. A house committee investigated the charges. They questioned professor of political science David F. Houston, and Garrison. Both men assured the legislators that nothing was being taught that reflected poorly "on Southern institutions or that would be unacceptable to Southern people." The committee closely questioned Houston (a South Carolinian) about his Harvard University Press book on nullification in South Carolina, which the committee believed to be "unacceptable from a Southern standpoint," and "contrary to Southern teachings."[29] Houston explained that he had written the book before coming to Texas and that he did not assign it or refer to it in his classes. The committee learned that the regents hired faculty on the basis of fitness rather than which region they haled from. Nevertheless, "other things being equal," the regents hired "Texas men first and Southern men next." The committee was satisfied that nothing was taught at the university that was "objectionable to Southern people," but called for an annual investigation of the university by the state legislature to make certain that this happy circumstance was not disturbed. The regents appended a statement to the report that no political or religious tests were used in the selection of faculty, who were expected to be "in sympathy with the people whom they teach," and that while the university "was in no sense partisan, sectarian, or sectional," it was "in sympathy with the life, character, and civilization of the Southern people."[30]

At about the time Bolton arrived in Austin, controversies had arisen concerning certain professors' interpretations of historical events and other educational matters. Representatives from church-supported colleges complained that some University of Texas professors held unorthodox religious views that "inculcated infidel ideas in the minds of the students," as one observer put it.[31] Other critics had complained that a professor of political science had said uncomplimentary things about the free coinage of silver, a key plank in the 1896 platform of the Democratic and Populist Parties, one that had strong support in Texas and the West. To eliminate the possibility of professors expressing such unpopular opinions, some newspapers advocated the elimination of the university's political science chair. Happily, the regents decided against that drastic measure. However, a member of the Board of Regents grilled the errant professor, and he agreed not to mention the topic of silver again.

Another Texas professor, speaking at a teachers' meeting in Denver, made the flabbergasting mistake of saying that it was a good thing that the South had lost the Civil War. "The great question in the South is the lifting up of the colored man to citizenship," the professor argued. "And it is being done," he added. He spoke in defense of southern states (including Texas) restricting the political rights of African Americans, but this did not mollify Texans with diehard Confederate sympathies. Race relations were a touchy subject in turn-of-the-century Texas, a former slave state where racially motivated lynching was common.[32] The Board of Regents excused the incident by claiming that it had been an impromptu address on the subject of "southern patriotism" given on short notice. If the gentleman had had more time to reflect before speaking, the regents implied, he would not have uttered such inflammatory statements. All of these incidents led J. J. Lane, a University of Texas professor, to write in his 1903 *History of Education in Texas* that he disapproved of student and (in some cases) faculty participation in politics. Such activities could only harm the university.[33]

As in many other public institutions at the turn of the previous century, the University of Texas faculty were judged by bedrock cultural assumptions, shifting political currents, and the whims of crafty politicians. According to Garrison, political controversy involving President Prather's predecessor George T. Winston had caused "such a storm" that "two years of [Prather's] wise and sympathetic administration have hardly enabled us to orient ourselves."[34] Garrison had been personally involved in those controversies and in helping to right the ship after Prather's arrival in 1899. He must have worried about how the Yankee Bolton would fit in. Surely he would never allow Bolton to teach anything about his doctoral specialty, free blacks in the South. The astute Bolton must have soon realized that his dissertation was a dead letter in Austin. If he objected to abandoning the field he had pioneered, he never mentioned it.

In the fall of 1901 Bolton simply put his head down and went to work in the classroom and on the *Quarterly*.[35] Meanwhile Garrison wrote a report on the status of historical studies on the southwestern United States for the annual meeting of the American Historical Association. He sketched the regional situation in broad terms but concentrated on research activities in Texas, especially the acquisition of the important Bexar Archives. Garrison thought there was still more to be discovered in Mexico, which he had scouted in the summer of 1900.[36] "No man living," he averred, "could estimate it accurately or indicate, except in a general way, the nature of the documents."[37] The repositories in Mexico City were virtually unexplored. Mexico's provincial archives doubtless held additional treasures for the curious researcher. The archival investigations that Garrison outlined would become Bolton's lifework. Garrison had no doubt hoped when he hired him that Bolton would work the Mexican archives, but in late 1901 he could not have guessed how completely Bolton would embrace that project.

Garrison's report heralded his own ambitions for the University of Texas while paving the way for Bolton. At that time there were no other significant university libraries with historical research collections west of Missouri, so the University of Texas was well positioned to become a center of graduate training.[38] This situation would change in a few years, but for the moment there was no better place in the West for an aspiring historian. Bolton scrambled to get on board Garrison's southwestern express. "Garrison was *the* man in this year's national association," Herbert told his brother. "Texas has the key to Spanish American history." Bolton was "grubbing Spanish" so that he could "help turn the lock."[39] Garrison enhanced his scholarly reputation in 1903 with the publication of *Texas, A Contest of Civilizations* in the respected American Commonwealths series.[40]

Early in 1902 Garrison revealed to Bolton his long-range thinking about the younger scholar's future. In the fall of 1902 Bolton would begin teaching a course on "European Expansion, commercial and colonial activities" in colonial America. "I think I shall in time be able to block out a field of *my own* here," he wrote Fred.[41]

This new course would at least have Herbert teaching American history, even though it was not in the area of his special training. Perhaps it was just as well that Garrison redirected Bolton's intellectual interests. By December Bolton had taken to describing his work on freedmen simply as "Niggers," which suggests neither sympathy with nor a deep interest in the subject.[42]

The rest of the Bolton family arrived in Austin as expected. Once settled, the Boltons fit into the social round of the young faculty and their families. "This is a great place for callers," Herbert told his brother. People visited in the "forenoon, afternoon, and evening." One couple in particular visited frequently. "They come in with a pack of cards to spend the evening," or might invite the Boltons for singing. He liked his colleague, but he wasn't "a very hard worker, I think. Likes too well to go to church and calling." Organized religion was not going to get in the way of Bolton's ambition. "Do you people attend church?" he asked Fred. "We do not," though most of the Texas people did. "I haven't the time."[43]

Moving expenses had staggered the Boltons' finances, a situation that usually caused Herbert to think about greener pastures. Garrison had virtually promised Bolton a raise, but the regents did not promote him. In the past, personal pride and pecuniary needs had made Bolton rail against politics and outrageous fortune, but not this time. "I shall not worry for another year," he wrote. "Promotions are slow here, in spite of what they told me before I came."[44] Rather than excoriating Garrison for misleading him about early promotion, Bolton worked hard to please him. Bolton was more philosophical at Texas because for the first time he was reasonably certain things were going his way. With his $1,500 salary he no doubt knew that he was getting top pay in his grade.[45] And now he saw the beginnings of something that would prove more important to him than money: the possibility of developing a field of historical investigation entirely his own.

Bolton rapidly developed his knowledge of Spanish and southwestern history so that he could begin archival research. "I have a new bee in my bonnet," he told Fred in July. He had decided to go to Mexico City. "I want to lay my lines here deep enough, and my plans broad enough, so that if, in the future, chance should leave an open field, I will be master of the situation." Bolton was tired of being at the mercy of others. To control his destiny, he planned to dominate the field of southwestern history that Garrison had pioneered. "To do it one must know the Spanish archives and the Spanish language."[46] The department head must have been pleased that his hardworking instructor was willing to go to Mexico at his own expense. He did not yet understand the extent of Bolton's aggressive plans.

Once summer school was out, Bolton boarded a train for the four-day ride to Mexico City. After quickly orienting himself in the Mexican capital—"beats Milwaukee in many respects," he observed—Bolton turned to the Archivo Nacional. "It's a bold venture, but I have the nerve."[47] He burrowed into the Archivo with characteristic energy but struggled with the strange orthography and lack of finding aids. On Sundays he found time to sightsee. As might be expected, Bolton was a historically minded tourist. What he saw appealed to his romantic imagination. He traced the route of Cortés's entry into the city and saw the tree under which Cortés wept on *la noche triste* because he had lost so many of his men during his retreat from the Aztec capital in 1520. Bolton visited the Zocolo, the main plaza, and ventured out to Coyoacán, where Cortés had lived. Sites of American feats of arms during the Mexican War also seized his attention. He ambled along the remains of old causeways that harked back to the Aztec empire. There were sixteenth-century churches cheek by jowl with modern structures. "Everything here is a mixture of the very ancient and the very new." Mexico City's modernity was perhaps most surprising to Herbert. "They tell me there are 400 miles of street railway in this city of the Aztecs—mostly electric." Not everything in Mexico was commendable: once he left the modern city center, there were "myriads of peons—Indians of the laboring class—barefooted, blanketed &c. Someone said a yard of cotton will cover 4 Mexicans."[48]

After spending about one month in Mexico, Bolton returned to Austin with "enough powder for shooting off historical fireworks most of the year." Within weeks, Bolton's first article about his findings appeared in the *Quarterly:* "Some Materials for Southwestern History in the Archivo General de Mexico." This piece described in a general way about three dozen bound volumes of original and copied documents comprising many hundreds of pages. He pointed out some of the most important and interesting things he had discovered—eighteenth-century Texas settlements, missions, explorations, and personalities. This, Bolton revealed, was just a small portion of the archival riches in Mexico. What the remaining 273 volumes of bound documents contained could "be learned only by patient investigation." Some arrangement should be made, he argued, to "systematically seek out, sift, copy, edit, and publish the more important sources."[49] And Texas was only a portion of Spain's northern frontier. There was much else on New Mexico, Sonora, and the Californias. By way of example, he published in the January 1903 issue of the *Quarterly* his translation of an inspection of eighteenth-century Laredo.[50] Beginning in 1903, Bolton contributed translated documents to a fifty-five-volume collection concerning the history of the Philippine Islands.[51] It was a fair start for the founder of Spanish Borderlands history.

Bolton's first publications from the Mexican archives show him to be a meticulous researcher with a comprehensive, though as yet undeveloped, view of the subject as he understood it—the history of those parts of the U.S. Southwest (especially Texas) that had been a part of the Spanish Empire. This definition, furnished by Garrison, was created as much by the need to appeal to Texans as it was by strictly scholarly considerations. In Mexico he again exhibited his capacity for hard work. Reading in a language still new to him, Bolton was able to review intensively about one volume of one hundred or more pages of handwritten documents per day. He also took time to copy out some of the most important items. He recognized that the Archivo General was only the tip of the iceberg. Local and provincial Mexican archives held much more, including the originals of many of the copies he encountered in 1902. He believed that it was necessary to track down those originals and to plumb the more remote repositories where even more documentary riches remained to be discovered. This was the true beginning of Bolton's lifetime of scholarly labor and achievement.

His hard work paid off. The regents gave him a modest raise of $100 and a two-year appointment. In the summer of 1903 Garrison arranged university funding for Bolton to return to Mexico to copy documents for the university. While there Bolton copied additional Philippines documents, which added a few dollars to his state-supported budget. Things were looking up. He and Barker were now close friends and cowriting *With the Makers of Texas*, which he thought would "have a good market" because the state's history was required to be taught in every school. The University of Washington asked him to apply for an assistant professorship there, but he decided to stay in Texas, probably with Garrison's encouragement. The university was growing. The student body had increased from 353 to 1,348 in the past ten years.[52] In the long run Texas was the best place for Bolton, or so it seemed in 1903.

From Garrison's point of view Bolton's work in Mexico advanced his plan for Texas and Southwest history. He thought of Bolton as his assistant in a program of research that Garrison managed. In 1903 he sought funding from the Carnegie Institution for Bolton's work in the Mexican archives. Garrison would send a party from Texas "composed of an instructor . . . and two assistants, all of them well trained and competent."[53] The proposal was not approved on account of uncertainty about whether the Mexican documents were merely copies of original records in Spanish archives. Until that question was answered, the Carnegie Institution was unwilling to fund translation work in Mexico.[54]

Nevertheless, Bolton and three University of Texas student assistants (all young women) went to Mexico City that summer. The Texas women had "worked in Spanish four or five years each," he explained to Fred. Herbert could speak more fluently, but the women read more accurately because they worked full-time with the Spanish manuscripts in the Bexar Archives. With the help of these assistants Bolton greatly improved his ability to decipher colonial writing.[55] The researchers set a grueling pace. They entered the Archivo General at eight in the morning and worked until it closed at two. Then they ate before going to the library of the National Museum, working there from about three until it closed. After supper they translated Philippines documents.[56] Adhering to this taxing schedule, Bolton and his assistants collected more than a thousand folios of material on Texas history. He thought that in two or three years he would be an authority on the manuscript sources of southwestern history—"a thing worth accomplishing."[57]

The Texas women helped him immensely in Mexico. He especially appreciated their work on the Philippine translations. Bolton told his brother, "They have helped me to the last and it will be published as a joint product."[58] Bolton was as good as his word. When the document was published, he shared credit with the two young women.[59] This small act of scholarly generosity told much about Bolton as a man and about his conception of the scholarly enterprise. While he demanded all the credit he thought he deserved, Bolton also believed that scholarship was essentially a cooperative enterprise. A hard worker himself, he recognized and rewarded hardworking men and women. Though not a feminist, throughout his career Bolton helped women scholars, took women graduate students, and worked to get them fellowships and jobs.

Bolton actively sought competent Spanish-language students to help him with his work. One semester he prefaced a medieval history lecture with a question: was there anyone who knew "Spanish and would like to work in the history of the old Spanish Southwest? If so, please see me after class." Freshman William E. Dunn came forward. Bolton put him to work in the state capitol, indexing and copying Spanish and Mexican government manuscripts at twenty cents per hour. The work fascinated Dunn, who thereafter accompanied Bolton on his summer excursions to Mexico and became his graduate student.[60]

In the spring of 1904 two prominent Americans visited Austin—President Theodore Roosevelt and David Starr Jordan, then president of Stanford University. They arrived on the same train. Teddy gave his stump speech and moved on. Jordan remained to deliver a formal lecture. Bolton took the opportunity to drive Jordan through the Texas hill country in a buggy.[61] Jordan remembered that the Texas faculty had a spirited debate about whether to serve wine for dinner at their club, where Jordan would be guest of honor after his lecture. The Stanford president was, after all, a man of the world. What would he think of a place that did not serve wine with dinner? The epicures lost by one vote. Worried that the lack of spirits would give Jordan a negative impression of Texas, several heroic professors missed Jordan's lecture and repaired instead to the club, where they furiously smoked in order to fill the rooms with a convivial blue haze that would make Jordan feel at home. But instead of appreciating the club's cosmopolitan atmosphere, Jordan requested that the windows be opened to evacuate the smoke.[62] Whether Bolton—a chain smoker—had a hand (or lung) in the smoke-out is unknown, but he had made an important acquaintance in Jordan. They would become better acquainted in the future.

Bolton did not go to Mexico in the summer of 1904, perhaps because Gertrude was in the final stage of pregnancy with their fourth daughter, Eugenie, who was born in September. He was also working on an article on the Spanish abandonment and reoccupation of Texas and finishing his textbook with Barker.[63] Garrison, who no doubt regarded the book as the latest good advertisement for the University of Texas school of history, wrote a graceful introduction.[64]

Book royalties may have improved Bolton's financial situation somewhat, but he was betting on future prospects associated with his Mexican research. Money problems pestered him, yet in the same letter in which he complained of grim prospects for promotion at Texas—"They are terribly stingy"—he reported that he had rejected the presidency of Vincennes University.[65] There is little doubt that, had Bolton remained in Milwaukee, he would have jumped at a university presidency. But Texas had changed the trajectory of his ambitions. Now he was a dedicated scholar who was convinced of the importance of his work and the eventual rewards that it would bring. Bolton's reputation was spreading. Texas would have to recognize his achievements or he would go. In June 1905 the regents promoted Bolton and raised his salary to $1,800.[66] He was finally a regular member of the faculty with an improved salary (plus a stipend for managing the *Quarterly* and other university publications). There would be bigger payoffs in the future.

As Bolton continued to develop his expertise in the Mexican material, his relationship with Garrison became fraught with jealousy and mistrust. In early 1905 both men were evidently involved in Garrison's new application for Carnegie money to support Bolton's work in the Mexican archives.[67] Andrew McLaughlin, the Carnegie Institution's director of research, had apparently given Garrison strong assurances that the project would be funded, because the *Quarterly* carried an announcement about it. But McLaughlin's successor, J. Franklin Jameson, was mainly interested in underwriting the publication of guides to U.S. materials in foreign archives.[68] In February Jameson informed Bolton (and probably Garrison) that the Carnegie Institution's executive committee had turned down the Mexican project.[69] Jameson reasoned that without sound guides to foreign archives, historians could not make reliable decisions about what should be copied. Jameson's desire for a guide to the Mexican archives eventually would raise Bolton's professional stature and wound Garrison's pride.

Before leaving for Mexico in the summer of 1905, Bolton scattered a little professional seed corn. He wrote Turner about documents in the Archivo General that might be of interest to him. Heading the list was correspondence concerning the 1819 Transcontinental Treaty. There were also eighteenth-century documents about England and Texas. "Do you suppose that the *American Historical Review* would care to publish good material of this sort?" he asked.[70] Turner immediately (and without telling Bolton) forwarded Bolton's letter to Jameson, who was editor of the *Review*. "Bolton is a good man—trained here and at University of Penna," he explained. "The stuff sounds interesting and . . . copies ought to be gotten, I imagine."[71]

Turner's note prompted Jameson to contact Bolton, who sent a detailed report to Jameson. He revealed that he had found new Spanish material on the Lewis and Clark expedition and mentioned the possibility of renewing Garrison's application for funds to pursue work in Mexico. "If there are any questions that you would like to ask me personally," Bolton offered, "I shall do my best [to] answer them." He had done a great deal of research at his own expense, he explained, but he needed more funds to work more extensively. "The field is rich here, and it ought to be harvested."[72]

Garrison knew that Bolton and Jameson were in contact, but he may not have known the details of Bolton's correspondence or the sort of papers that Bolton had used to bait the hook for Jameson.[73] The documents bearing on Lewis and Clark and the Transcontinental Treaty were in the class of material that Garrison expected to monopolize himself, documents reflecting the Anglo advance in the West. Bolton was now on Garrison's turf. Furthermore, Bolton invited a direct correspondence with Jameson that undercut Garrison's role as the nominal director of research in Mexico while simultaneously establishing Bolton's reputation with Jameson as the true expert in the field.

Professional courtesy dictated that Jameson ask Garrison about Bolton's fitness to compile a guide to the Mexican archives.[74] Garrison's response was lukewarm. "I will only answer yes in a general way to the questions you ask me about him.

You would, I believe, find his work reliable and satisfactory." He added that he hoped to see Jameson personally at the AHA meeting and thought it best to put off further consideration of the work in Mexico until then. Garrison explained that he had intended to do the Mexican archival work himself, and he diplomatically suggested that he would go if Jameson could provide funding. In his honeyed but pointed conclusion Garrison remarked that he was pleased to learn of Jameson's interest in Mexico. "I shall take pleasure in doing anything I can to further your plans relative thereto, whether Mr. Bolton or I should have a personal share in them or not."[75]

There was no mistaking Garrison's preference as to whom the Carnegie Institution should fund to work in Mexico. Garrison had welcomed and applauded Bolton's work in Mexico as long as it had been seen as part of his larger operation, but he well understood that if Bolton authored a guide to historical materials in Mexican archives, he would become the leading authority, not Garrison. And Bolton understood this too. The opportunity to work in the Mexican archives under Jameson's direction was "just the kind of work I have been preparing to do and am intending to do independently and unaided if I cannot have the advantages of cooperation and financial help," Bolton explained. He had a bibliographical essay "relative to the Mexican archives about ready" for the *Quarterly*, "but I shall withhold it at present."[76] This was bait that Jameson was interested in. He rejected the publication of the Transcontinental Treaty documents, but placed Bolton's essay on the Mexican archives in the *Review*.[77] This publication alone made Bolton the leading candidate for the Mexican guide project.

In early January 1906, presumably after seeing Garrison at the AHA meeting in Baltimore, Jameson invited Bolton to compile "a comprehensive guide to the materials for the history of the United States in the Mexican archives."[78] He offered to pay Bolton's salary and expenses for one year. Jameson advised Bolton to consult with Garrison to determine when he might begin the work. Garrison put a smiling face on these developments in a newspaper article announcing the project. He claimed that Bolton had taken up the work because Garrison's other duties prevented him from doing so.[79] Bolton noted that Garrison figured "with characteristic prominence" in the article. "He claims everything in sight," he added, "but this does not greatly trouble me."[80] Bolton was coming into his own, and he felt secure enough to risk alienating Garrison. With Jameson on his side (not to mention Turner, Haskins, and McMaster), he could afford to be bold.

Bolton's serenity was well founded. He had shrewdly played an inside game that enabled him to get around Garrison. He outmaneuvered his department head in

Austin by winning the support of the new university president, David F. Houston, who had replaced Prather. Bolton asked Houston if he had made a mistake in studying southwestern history, because Professor Garrison was "(let me whisper it) very sensitive to competition." Houston told Bolton to "create the field and the chair will be made in due time. This is what he [Houston] wants me to do." Bolton did not intend to be Garrison's errand boy at Texas.[81]

But Garrison was not yet finished with Bolton and Jameson. The question of the timing of Bolton's leave of absence depended on arrangements for someone to take Bolton's duties at the University of Texas and the *Quarterly*. Barker was in Pennsylvania finishing his doctoral work with McMaster, and Bolton could not leave until Barker returned. Bolton proposed to do part of the work in the summer of 1906 and return to Texas for the academic year 1906–1907. He would complete the Mexican work in the succeeding academic year.[82] Just when everything seemed set, Jameson reported that the Carnegie Institution executive board had deferred funding for the guide projects.[83] He hoped that funding would be forthcoming, but in the summer of 1906 Bolton proceeded to Mexico without Carnegie assistance.

Bolton had found new work that subsidized his Mexican research trip. William A. Holmes of the Bureau of American Ethnology had asked Bolton to revise some articles and to write additional ones for a handbook on American Indians.[84] More than one hundred articles in the published book came from Bolton's pen, and much of it was written from documents he found while he was in Mexico in 1906. He was paid $1,000 for the first half of this work, a considerable infusion of outside income.[85]

Bolton reported his new findings to Jameson, who finally secured the appropriation for the Mexican guide at $150 per month plus expenses. The two planned to meet in Washington to firm up plans before proceeding to the AHA meeting in late December.[86] "Please express my thanks to Professor Garrison for his kindness in making the arrangement possible," Jameson concluded, but he expressed his gratitude too soon.[87] The very next day Garrison asked Jameson for financial assistance to examine in the Mexican archives "materials belonging to the period of the Anglo-American movement southwestward." Bolton, he clarified, was working in the "earlier period of Spanish-American history," and his archival research had dealt exclusively with that area. "My own judgment is that his work for the Carnegie Institution had best be prosecuted under the same restrictions." Garrison believed that he had earned the right to exploit the Mexican archives in his own field, because he had pioneered research in Mexico. "I do not like to press my claims," Garrison wrote, but "I trust that you yourself see the situation clearly, and that argument is unnecessary."[88]

Jameson's response was unequivocal. He had engaged Bolton for the preparation of "*one* comprehensive guide to the materials for United State history" in the Mexican archives. Turning to Garrison's long-standing hope that the Carnegie Institution would help him get documents from the Mexican archives, Jameson planned to aid in "the more elaborate exploitation" of foreign archives "that would do the greatest good for the greatest number," but these projects lay "so much in the future that I have not considered them carefully."[89] Jameson hoped that Texas and other state governments would be moved to fund projects of the sort that Garrison proposed. Garrison was out in the cold.

Everything seemed to be set. Barker would finish his degree, return to Texas in June, and Bolton would leave for Mexico. Then came Garrison's letter to Jameson. "I regret greatly the little hitch that seems likely in the matter of Dr. Bolton's leave of absence." Barker was going to Harvard on a one-year fellowship. Garrison proposed to put off Bolton's leave for a year. Garrison insisted that he had no desire to interfere with Jameson's plans. "This is said in the frankest and most cordial spirit."[90] There was a limit to Jameson's patience and it had been reached. Delaying Bolton's leave would cause much "difficulty and regret," he informed Garrison.[91] Just when was Barker expected to finish his degree, and when would Bolton's leave finally be decided? the irritated Jameson asked. Bolton solved the problem by going directly to the university president, who approved the leave.[92] Houston also promised Bolton a promotion to associate professor with a good salary raise when he returned.[93]

President Houston realized that Bolton's work had practical applications as well as scholarly merit. In May Houston referred several "Dallas capitalists" to Bolton for information about the long-lost Los Almagres silver mine.[94] Discovered in the eighteenth century, the mine was located somewhere north of San Antonio, Texas. Comanches had driven out the miners, and the mine's exact location had been forgotten. Anglo Texans learned of the place, assumed that the mine was fabulously rich, and fruitlessly searched for it. In 1904 Bolton had found an official account of the mine together with precise information about its location. After hearing from Houston's acquaintances, he sent to Mexico for the records and met with the Dallas men, who made him one of nine partners in the venture. Then he and one of his partners found the mine "exactly where the papers directed us . . . with startling precision." Iron deposits as well as silver might make money for the partnership. "But, thunder," he exclaimed, "I never expect anything except in return for a day's work, and in the form of wages."[95] The mine proved not to be a moneymaker but was still useful to Bolton because it connected him with Texans who appreciated his knowledge of Spanish land records.[96] And from Houston's perspective Bolton's work demonstrated the utilitarian value of historical research in the university.

Six years in Texas had made a big change in Bolton's professional fortunes. He had carved out a field of his own and established the beginning of a national reputation. Hungry for professional recognition and advancement, Bolton now felt sure enough of his future to turn down tempting offers when they came. He was also secure enough to risk the wrath of Garrison by taking over the Mexican project that his department chair had pioneered and wished to dominate. Bolton established a legitimate claim to the field by virtue of hard work and significant publications. But he made his claim stick by adroitly outmaneuvering Garrison at every turn. President Houston supported Bolton because he recognized the value of his work to the university. Garrison *wanted* to do the work, but Bolton was actually doing it.

Bolton had established a substantial scholarly reputation in Texas, but he had had a lot of help. Jameson, Turner, Haskins, and perhaps others behind the scenes promoted his career. Nor should Garrison be forgotten. Without a Garrison, there could not have been a Bolton. By founding the state historical association and its journal, he created an organizational structure that promoted and published southwestern research. He was the first historian to foresee that the systematic exploitation of the Mexican archives by Texas faculty and students could elevate the scholarly reputation of the University of Texas. And he knew that the historian who opened those archives would become a very big man in the historical profession. By the time Bolton left for his year in Mexico, Garrison no doubt understood that he would not realize his dream of being that big man. But in a very real sense Garrison had founded his Texas school of southwestern history through Bolton, and there was no other way he could have done it. Garrison would die of a heart attack in 1910, just about the time he promised Jameson that he would be free to get back to Mexico.

When Bolton stepped onto the train to Mexico in the summer of 1907, he knew that his career had entered a new phase. He was looking at a big future. Texas would not be able to hold Bolton.

FOUR · Many Roads to California

While Bolton negotiated the terms of his work in Mexico, Frederick Jackson Turner was engaged in high-level professional discussions of his own. From 1904 until 1909 Stanford University and the University of California avidly competed for Turner's services. Bolton would be the ultimate beneficiary of Turner's long courtships on the Pacific Coast.

In 1902 Turner had called Max Farrand to Madison to teach a summer seminar in American constitutional history, "to the delight" of the students, Turner noted. "I am finding him a most companionable friend," he explained to Professor Henry Morse Stephens. Farrand was head of the history department at Stanford, and Stephens had just moved from Cornell to the University of California. "I am very confident that your removal to the coast is full of significance to the development of historical study in the country," he added.[1] This was the beginning of a delicate, three-sided courtship between Turner, Stanford, and Berkeley.

Turner's friendship with Farrand lasted all of their lives. A few years younger than Turner, Farrand had earned his PhD at Princeton University, where he had studied with Woodrow Wilson, Turner's friend and teacher from his Hopkins days.[2] Turner and Farrand had much in common intellectually, and they were both avid anglers who spent summer weeks fly-fishing.[3] Farrand, of course, saw much more than a fishing buddy in Turner. Adding Turner to the Stanford faculty would immeasurably enhance that young institution's intellectual reputation. He discussed the matter with university president David Starr Jordan, who enthusiastically agreed to recruit Turner.[4]

Selling Stanford to Turner would be tough. The institution had opened in 1891 as a memorial to Leland Stanford Jr., the son of railroad baron and California U.S. senator Leland Stanford. After their son died at age fifteen, Stanford and his wife, Jane, invested millions in the creation of the university, which they conceived as a gift to the people of California as well as a lasting memorial to their son. When her husband suddenly died in 1893, Jane Stanford carried on the work of building the university, but it still lacked a significant library, a shortcoming that hindered faculty research as well as graduate training.[5]

Farrand and Jordan recognized that Stanford needed a better library in order to attract Turner. It so happened that two major private libraries were available in California, the Bancroft and the Sutro. The former was named for Hubert Howe Bancroft, a wealthy San Francisco stationer and bookseller who wrote a multivolume history of California and the West.[6] He scoured the world for manuscripts and books pertaining to his subject, acquiring copies when the originals could not be had. The Bancroft Library's special strengths were in the Spanish and Mexican periods of California and the Southwest. Bancroft erected a special building for his library in San Francisco and hired a staff of librarians and writers. In 1883 the first of thirty-nine volumes of *The Works of Hubert Howe Bancroft* issued from the press. Once *The Works* were completed, Bancroft was faced with the question of what to do with his vast private library and archive. The city of Sacramento, the University of Chicago, and the Library of Congress all were rumored to have been offered the library for prices ranging from $50,000 to ten times than figure.[7]

Adolph Sutro was a Prussian-born mining engineer who became wealthy through his mining investments and the development of the famous Sutro Tunnel, which drained the silver mines near Virginia City, Nevada. Sutro had refined tastes that he satisfied by amassing a huge private library. He and his agents searched Europe, Mexico, and the United States to add to his collection. Sutro would buy the entire stock of a bookstore, or an entire library, to obtain one treasured item. He prevailed on poor monks to sell centuries-old monastery libraries with their rare incunabula (books printed before 1501). Sutro's library may have amounted to 200,000 books, pamphlets, and newspapers. It was one of the largest privately held libraries in the world, and in some ways one of the richest. Sutro owned more than 4,000 incunabula, perhaps more than any other library anywhere. His interests were different from Bancroft's, as reflected in Sutro's holdings in science, natural history, and European subjects. But there was some overlap, as in the cases of Mexican history and American newspapers. Cornell University historian and librarian George Lincoln Burr judged Sutro's holdings in some categories as being unrivaled in America and perhaps even in Europe.[8]

Unlike Bancroft, who wished to sell his collection, Sutro offered his library to the public. In 1895 he promised to give the library, a building to house it, and twenty-six acres in San Francisco to the University of California, which turned him down because accepting would have required the abandonment of the new Berkeley campus. Sutro's heirs continued the search for a suitable public recipient, but no one would have it. So it was that two of the worlds' great private libraries were spurned by the people of California, who would neither purchase nor receive a great library as a precious gift.

Like a good fisherman, Farrand lured Turner with libraries. He asked Turner for his estimation of the value of the Bancroft and Sutro collections. Like a wary trout, Turner circled the bait. Turner was not familiar with the Sutro holdings but supposed it was a good modern European library. As for the Bancroft, "if the $200,000 or so" that was supposed to be its price was "to be expended chiefly on early Indian and Spanish records," Turner felt "less confident . . . if the documentary material for the American period of the history of the Rocky Mountains and the Pacific Coast" could be obtained elsewhere. Remarkably, Turner believed that too large a proportion of Spanish records actually devalued the Bancroft collections as a resource for a university library—or at least for *his* university library. He thought the record of the American period of about a half century outweighed three and one-half centuries of Spanish and Mexican history. The very sort of materials that Bolton was laboriously collecting in Mexico were of no concern to Turner.[9] Nevertheless, if Bancroft's library had the Anglo-American materials that Turner valued so highly, or if they could be obtained and added to the collection, Turner supported the purchase.

Turner made it clear that if the Bancroft (or the Sutro) did not have the materials that he needed, Stanford should find or build a library that did. Jordan and Farrand agreed. On Christmas Eve 1904 Farrand wrote Turner that "one by one the obstacles are being removed in the most satisfactory way," though there were still details to be worked out that Farrand would not reveal.[10]

What was Farrand unwilling to tell Turner? The new library building at Stanford was about to open, and Jordan was undoubtedly pressing Jane Stanford on the need for books to fill it, a need that coincided with Turner's recruitment. Stanford decided to fund the proposed acquisitions, but before she could act, she had a frightening experience. In January 1905 she sipped some water at her bedside table, but the foul taste made her spit it out. There were no lasting ill effects, but analysis revealed that the water had been tainted with strychnine. Investigators thought the poisoning had been an accident, but Stanford believed that someone had tried to murder her. She decided to go to Honolulu, where she hoped she might be safe. Before sailing on February 15, she took care of the library business.[11] "We need books at present more than anything else," she wrote. The new library had room for one million volumes and she intended to acquire them. Therefore, she requested that the trustees establish an endowment from the sale of her "diamonds, rubies, and other precious stones," to be known appropriately "as the Jewel Fund."[12]

The story of the Jewel Fund does not have a happy ending. A few weeks after announcing her plans for the library, Stanford died in Honolulu, the victim of a second strychnine poisoning. Her murderer was never found. Indeed, the police did not investigate the crime. President Jordan, who evidently hoped to spare the Stanford family as well as the university from a scandal, insisted that she had died of heart failure even though an inquest in Hawaii indicated otherwise. Jordan's unfounded version of events was widely believed until recently when researchers examined the autopsy report and other testimony from Hawaii.[13] Nevertheless, as Jane Stanford had wished, the Jewel Fund was established and became the essential endowment for Stanford's library.[14]

In January 1905 Jordan made an offer to Turner of $5,000 per year, a $1,000 raise over his Wisconsin salary. Turner did not jump at the offer, but he did not turn it down. He decided to wait for a year to see what Stanford would do about a library.[15] The California rumor mill turned. A San Jose newspaper erroneously reported that Turner was going to Stanford.[16] In Berkeley Professor Stephens, who was by then the history department head, heard the false report and implored Turner not to go to Stanford until he visited Berkeley. He promised to match any offer that Stanford made. Turner assured Stephens that Jordan had made no offer, but of course the Stanford offer was on the way.[17]

Turner's delaying tactics with Stanford gave Stephens time to address Berkeley's library problem. Like Stanford, Berkeley lacked a library that could support serious research in history. Stephens was a European historian, but he recognized the immense value of the Bancroft for the study of history on the Pacific Coast. He convinced President Benjamin Ide Wheeler that acquisition of the Bancroft was crucial to the future of the university. Wheeler then won over the regents, but money stood in the way, for Bancroft wanted a quarter of a million dollars for his library. Bancroft himself helped to overcome financial obstacles by agreeing to "donate" $100,000 toward the purchase while agreeing that the balance could be paid him in three $50,000 installments. On September 15 Stephens and Bancroft reached an agreement that Stephens sealed, in his decorous way, by kissing Mrs. Bancroft's hand.[18]

The regents feared a public outcry because Bancroft was portrayed in the press as a self-promoter who was prying money from the public treasury for a worthless lot of old books and papers, mere "rubbish" as some people thought.[19] To mute criticism, the regents called for an expert appraisal. The choice of appraisers was especially shrewd considering Stephens's cherished desire to recruit Turner. The call went out to Reuben Gold Thwaites, Turner's colleague and friend and the superintendent of historical collections for the State Historical Society of Wisconsin. His praise was unstinting. Bancroft's library was "astonishingly large and complete, easily first in its own field, and taking high rank among the famous general collections of Americana, such as exist at Harvard University, the Boston Public Library, the Library of Congress, the New York State Library, and the Wisconsin Historical Library." The library would "at once attract to the University a body of graduate students in American and Spanish-American history and allied studies, who are to find here a practically unique collection of material of the highest order of excellence."[20]

Thwaites recommended creating at Berkeley a repository of material for all of Spanish America. Nor was Anglo-American history to be forgotten. Bancroft had amassed a huge collection of newspapers, books, documents, reminiscences, business records, and other materials bearing on the Anglo-American phase of California and the West. The opportunities for research were "quite unexampled elsewhere in America." As to its monetary value, the Bancroft Library was "a bargain" worth far more than the price that Bancroft had put on it.[21] Thwaites made one additional suggestion: that Frederick J. Teggart, librarian of the fine Mechanics' Institute Library in San Francisco, be put in charge of moving the library to Berkeley. Teggart had been working in the library for some time and was already a University of California extension lecturer.[22] Accordingly he organized the move and eventually became curator of the Bancroft in Berkeley.

Bancroft's splendid rubbish now belonged to the university, but it remained in San Francisco until the university completed the Doe Library, which was still on the drawing board. In the meantime the newest building on campus, California Hall, was made ready to house the collections until Doe Library was on its footings. President Wheeler quickly used the library to good effect by inviting Turner to teach in the summer of 1906. "The presence of the Bancroft Library . . . might add to the attraction." Turner accepted.[23]

President Jordan continued to work on Turner. In March he obtained an agreement from the Stanford trustees to give Turner an annual two months' leave of absence to enable his research in other libraries "until such time as our library becomes adequate."[24] In early April Jordan went to Madison and made Stanford's best offer to Turner: $5,000 per year, plus two months' annual leave for research until a library suitable for Turner's purposes had been gathered at Stanford. On April 17 the Wisconsin regents countered Stanford's offer. They did not advance Turner's salary, but freed him from teaching for one semester per year to carry on his research and writing.[25]

Had the world continued to turn on its axis as usual, Turner might have waited to hear something from Cal before giving an answer to Wisconsin or Stanford, but the earth quaked. Early in the morning of April 18 the San Andreas Fault gave way, causing catastrophic damage in San Francisco and the surrounding area. Jordan was in bed at his Stanford home. "We were all awakened by tremendous jolts, after which the house was shaken with great violence as a rat might be shaken by a dog, and objects began to fly through the air."[26] Devastation from the quake was terrific. Ceilings collapsed, buildings toppled, roads buckled, and the earth yawned. Fire soon added to the destruction in San Francisco, which burned for three days. Perhaps three thousand people died during the cataclysm.[27]

Stanford University, whose impressive stone buildings had only recently been completed, was in ruins. On the day of the quake President Jordan found a typewriter and someone who could work it. He sent a heartbreaking letter to Turner. "All of the beautiful buildings are gone, the loss being about $2,800,000." Who could even imagine such stupendous losses, much less their replacement? He asked Turner to "let our matter rest in abeyance for the present until we can know just where we are."[28] Jordan's letter to Farrand in Ithaca was more specific: the losses included the new library.[29] Still, two days later Jordan wrote encouragingly to Turner, "Better come to us in 1907 as you have [previously] suggested."[30] It was too late. As soon as Stanford toppled and San Francisco burned, the game was over. In April it was impossible to know the long-term impact of the earthquake on the California economy. Jordan had told Turner that the damage to San Francisco alone was more than a billion dollars. It was reasonable to assume that the disaster would adversely affect the University of California's future as well as Stanford's. Turner folded his hand, accepted Wisconsin's counteroffer, and informed his Stanford friends. He claimed that he had made up his mind the day before the earthquake, but this was probably a white lie intended to make Farrand and Jordan feel better.[31]

Quite by chance, when the San Andreas Fault gave way, President Wheeler was in Austin for the inauguration of University of Texas president Houston. Bolton had heard about Cal's acquisition of the Bancroft and asked Wheeler about it, probably before news of the earthquake reached Austin. "We mean to exploit it ourselves," Wheeler said, a response that seemed to indicate that it might be closed to outsiders.[32] Whatever restrictions Wheeler might place on the use of the library, Bolton had his eye on it and the man who would control its fate.

But there might not be a library to exploit. While Bolton and Wheeler spoke, the fire raced through the streets of San Francisco. Two great libraries stood in the path of catastrophe, California's Bancroft and the Sutro. In Berkeley Stephens anxiously wondered if California's newly acquired library would be lost. After three days of fire the Bancroft was unscathed, though the building "was a little racked by the earthquake," as Stephens said.[33] Although legend has it that Stephens sent students to man bucket brigades to save the Bancroft, Cal was just lucky. Bancroft's building was outside the fire zone. Sutro's library was not so fortunate. More than half of it was lost in the flames, including nearly all of the priceless incunabula.[34]

Stephens was practically giddy with relief when he informed Turner that the library was safe. He hoped to move it to California Hall on the Berkeley campus as soon as possible.[35] Summer school would go ahead as planned, Stephens explained. By the end of May the books were in California Hall, ready for Turner's inspection in the summer. Teggart oversaw the transfer of the collection and also managed to effect his own transfer to Berkeley as curator of the Bancroft and history instructor.[36]

Despite the earthquake and attendant damage, Stephens and Jordan still hoped to appoint Turner. In early August Turner joined President Jordan in a visit to the renowned botanist Luther Burbank in Santa Rosa, which was near the earthquake's epicenter.[37] From Santa Rosa the Turners went to the Bohemian Grove campground, the famous resort of the Bohemian Club, an important gathering of influential Californians.[38] Jordan, Wheeler, and Stephens belonged to the club and were probably there. After seeing the *Jinx*, an annual play put on by the members, the Turners returned briefly to Berkeley and then went to Lake Tahoe for a month.[39] The California competition for Turner was not over.

It is impossible to read about Turner's leisurely summer gambols without recalling Bolton, who meanwhile labored without surcease. Turner knew that he was on top of the world and could afford to take long vacations without fear of losing reputation. However, one must conclude that he did not advance his research and writing in the summer of 1906. Turner was a brilliant man who perhaps believed that there was time enough for him to do his work, and that it would be best if he did it under the most pleasant of circumstances. Bolton was driven to work from daylight to dark and into the night if he could find a candle.

Bolton regarded his year in Mexico funded by Carnegie as a unique, career-making opportunity. He worked accordingly. "I was hunting materials, not pleasure," he told Fred, "and found both." In Mexico City Bolton rented a furnished two-story house for about $60 a month, which was more than he had ever paid anywhere. It was in the American quarter and had all the modern conveniences— electric lights and indoor plumbing. He hired a Mexican woman who cooked and cleaned. The large house and servant were necessary: the Boltons now had a fifth daughter, Gertrude. The family especially liked the cool summer weather in Mexico City. "So far," he reported, "all are delighted."[40]

The presence of Gertrude and the children must have been a great consolation for Bolton, who was in the libraries and archives six days a week. "I am over my ears in work," he remarked. He arrived at the Archivo General at 7:30 each morning and worked there until 1:30, when it closed. Every other afternoon he went to the Museo Nacional, which was open until 6:00, or to the Biblioteca Nacional, which closed at 8:00. On the other afternoons he stayed home to arrange his notes. Nights and weekends he worked on the articles for the American Indian handbook and his own book on Texas Indians.[41] "Besides, I have to keep preparing the way for future work in the archives."[42] He seemed able to keep up this pace indefinitely.

Hard work was nothing new to Bolton, but he had to learn how to apply his energy in a way consonant with Mexican social and political conditions. The short hours and unhelpful officials in the Archivo General aggravated him. The records custodians thought Bolton was a rude Yankee—worse, a Texan—who made demands on them. It was up to Bolton to adapt to local conditions. At first he did this grudgingly; it would take him many years to develop sincere appreciation for Mexican culture and gratitude for the assistance that many Mexicans had given to him and his students. Decades later Bolton reminisced that "there were numerous occasions on which the Mexicans concluded that the American [Bolton] didn't know good manners."[43] That sort of self-awareness did not exist in the Bolton of the first decade of the twentieth century.

Bolton was ethnocentric, but he was able to succeed in Mexico because he would not take no for an answer and because he did business with a smile on his face, his complaining letters notwithstanding. He also understood that letters of introduction from high U.S., Mexican, and church officials were needed to unlock doors. Accordingly, before going to Mexico, he asked Jameson to provide him with letters from a Roman Catholic cardinal, Secretary of State Elihu Root, and other important people.

He also contacted Father Zephyrin Engelhardt, a German-born Franciscan priest who was writing the history of California missions. Engelhardt gave Bolton detailed information about the Church's archival holdings in Mexico and wrote a letter of introduction to the father president of the Franciscan Colegio de Guadalupe in Zacatecas.[44] A grateful Bolton sent Engelhardt a cache of copied documents from Mexican archives.[45] This was the beginning of a lifelong friendship with Engelhardt and other Franciscan historians.

Secretary of State Root's visit to Mexico in October precipitated a telegram and letter to Bolton from Jameson. Root sat on the Carnegie Institution executive committee. "I thought it would be advantageous if Secretary Root could be given a more vivid idea of what sort of work the 'foreign missionaries' [such as Bolton] are doing when they have a rich field of virtually virgin soil to work in." However, Jameson warned, Root was "not a person easily kindled about such objects."[46] Bolton did not need to be prompted to meet the secretary of state. By the time Jameson's telegram reached Bolton, he had already finagled an interview with Root, who appeared to be interested in his work. Root "ventured particularly, a hope that I might run across some of the missing [Zebulon Montgomery] Pike papers."[47]

Root was no doubt thinking about Pike because it was the centennial year of the American lieutenant's arrest in Mexico. Pike had been released, but his papers had been confiscated. Within a month Bolton found the papers except for a few that had been lost. When opportunity knocked, Bolton answered the door, and then pulled it wide open. Perhaps Jameson might consider publishing the recovered documents along with Bolton's introduction in the *American Historical Review?* The irresistible conjunction of personal ambition, professional accomplishment, public relations, and scholarship was not lost on Jameson, who published the documents with Bolton's introduction and gave Bolton a place on the upcoming AHA conference program.[48] The news of Bolton's discovery was no doubt met with general acclaim in Austin, except perhaps for one man. Bolton's Pike triumph was carved from the heart of the field that George Pierce Garrison had wished to reserve for himself.

We can only imagine Bolton's exhilaration when he unearthed the Pike papers. This feat was the beginning of a long career marked by impressive discoveries of important documents and historical sites that had been unknown or given up for lost. Such finds came to define the sort of history Bolton did. He was as much an explorer-detective as a historian. For Bolton these discoveries were the big emotional payoff for his unstinting labor in airless rooms. Here was a primary difference between Bolton and Turner as scholars. For Turner, satisfaction came with intellectual inquiry and explanation—his history lived in the mind. But Bolton found his rewards in the discovery of the physical thing itself, whether it be artifact, document, or place. Both men were alive to the physical and metaphysical aspects of history, but the difference in emphasis placed them at different spots on the philosophical spectrum. Turner was quick, intuitive, intellectual, willing to write hypothetically, theoretically. He was very much a modern historian and as such was ahead of his time. Bolton, despite his studies with Turner, was at heart a Rankean historian who labored to construct the documentary edifice of history. His work—find the documents, publish the documents, write the history from the documents—was the very definition of scientific history, as that term was commonly understood in the late nineteenth century. There seemed little room for individual interpretation in this scheme. This was a point of view that likely came from his early work with Haskins. Yet Bolton was a romantic who thrilled to the tangible remains of the past that fired his imagination. His approach to history and enthusiasm for discovery would bring him great rewards; in time it would lead him into error.

In December 1907 the AHA met in Madison. The anticipation of returning to his alma mater with the announcement of his great discovery of the Pike papers must have been sweet indeed.[49] Bolton was a comer in the historical profession. Haskins, who was now on the Harvard faculty, approvingly told his colleagues about Bolton's paper.[50] Bolton's accomplishments were undeniable, but it is equally true that he had useful connections with the men who operated the levers of power in the historical profession. Bolton returned to Mexico sure of that.

Back in Mexico Bolton continued to survey the archives at a sprintlike pace. Even so, he was willing to take on additional work for a Dallas law firm.[51] This small job was the start of a lifetime of litigation support for attorneys in the Southwest.[52] The legal research took longer than expected because of the lack of finding aids and uncooperative archivists. Bolton often faced such difficulties. Hoping to see the archives in a Catholic cathedral, he presented a letter of introduction from the archbishop of Mexico to the local vicar, who asked Bolton to return the following day at noon. When he returned, a subordinate official met him and asked him to return the next day. And so it went for twelve days. "Finally they capitulated and then I was given the courtesy of the place," Bolton recalled. "Of course they thought I was ill mannered." He told many similar stories in later years. In time he "learned to play [his] fish," as he put it.[53]

In San Luis Potosí Bolton sought records about the Mexican-American War, or Guerra de Tejas, as his Mexican hosts called it. The old clerk said that Benito Juárez had taken them when he was president of Mexico in the 1860s. Bolton doubted the story, so he stayed in the clerk's office for three hours making small talk. When the clerk complained of a bad cough, Bolton told him about the fine climate for consumptive patients in New Mexico. This information interested the clerk. "I told him all I knew about how to cure consumption." Pretty soon he took Bolton through a door with the date 1565 carved above and into the archives, "the best I saw in Mexico." As they perused the shelves, Bolton stopped. "Señor," Bolton said, "here is a whole bundle labeled *La Guerra de Tejas.*" The clerk replied, "Of course."

One by one Bolton overcame the resistance of suspicious and cynical officials. In Monterey he looked for the missionary archives of Zacatecas, which were thought to be lost. The local bishop told him about a great fire that had destroyed the records. "You must have had a very fine archive here," Bolton mused. "*Sí, magnífico,*" the bishop replied. "It must have occupied a large place." "*Sí, señor, mucho.*" "Just out of curiosity I would like to see the room where the documents used to be kept." The bishop obliged, and there were the "lost" Zacatecas records.

Sometimes Bolton dealt with cooperative people who did not know what they had in their libraries. At Querétaro Bolton searched the archive of the College of the Holy Cross for missionary records concerning Sonora and Pimería Alta. The friars were helpful, but the library contained only books that Bolton had seen before. Sensing that there might be more than met his eye, Bolton remained at the college admiring the library and browsing its contents. After two days he noticed a trap door in the ceiling. In the attic he found "a *great* trunk . . . packed nearly full with missing records," plus a complete list of the documents that existed in 1772. Two-thirds of the records were there. Bolton spent two weeks putting them back in their original order.

Perseverance usually won the day for Bolton, but he sometimes had raw political power behind him, as in the case of his survey of the Secretaría de Gobernación, which was under the control of the vice president of Mexico, Ramon Corral, an unpopular man with a reputation for ruthlessness.[54] Bolton described him as "one of those hard fisted soldier like men from Sonora." "Everybody feared him," he continued, "and because of that they hated him." Bolton wanted to look at the Gobernación papers, so he asked to meet Vice President Corral in order to smooth the way. When Bolton made the request to see Corral, one official "pretty nearly turned pale at the mention of the 'hombre terrible.'" Corral frowned at Bolton but gave him "all the privileges in the world" and a pleasant office off the main patio.[55] The vice president held no terrors for Bolton, but as the Díaz regime began to collapse, the unpopular Corral would become one of the main targets of critics, reformers, and revolutionaries. The Mexican Revolution was only a few months in the future when Bolton got his room at the Gobernación.

Bolton's personal acquaintance with Mexican politicians, priests, librarians, clerks, archivists, diplomats, and scholars broadened and deepened his knowledge of Mexican culture and people. And they began to accept, like, and even to admire Bolton and his single-minded pursuit of the materials of Mexican history. Friars, who had at first been reluctant to cooperate, gave him bed and board in their monasteries. Those times "were very pleasant indeed," he reminisced, but they would be interrupted by Mexican political events as well as Bolton's professional peregrinations.[56]

While in Mexico Bolton asked Turner for advice about getting a job at the University of California so that he could have access to the Bancroft Library. Now that Bolton had mastered the materials relating to Spanish colonial Texas, "the best of all points of attack, is California," he reasoned. "Somebody is sure to fall heir to a professorship in California that will put him in control of the great mass of material that Bancroft collected." He did not know if anyone else had "preempted" a position at California, but he wanted a shot at it. "I know that whenever such a position opens up in California you will be quite certain to know about it and to be consulted."[57] Turner promptly wrote to Stephens and suggested that Bolton contact the Berkeley department head. "I have not yet screwed up the nerve to write to Professor Stephens," Bolton confessed, "but I may come to it soon."[58]

Evidently Bolton was reluctant to write Stephens because his first meeting with him at the 1903 AHA meeting in New Orleans had not been encouraging. As they sat side by side on a round settee in a hotel lobby, Bolton said that he was using Stephens's *Revolutionary Europe* as a text.[59] "'Tisn't worth a damn!" Stephens snorted, and that was the end of the conversation. Bolton felt that this was how the "great man" told a young professor that he did not know how to select a proper textbook.[60] So Bolton hesitated to contact Stephens even after Turner had smoothed the way.

Then a reconfiguration of the California planets changed the orbits of Bolton and Turner. "You have probably heard that Farrand is going to Yale," Eugene Barker gossiped from his desk in Cambridge. "Stanford would be right in your field, wouldn't it?"[61] Perhaps it would, but Stanford now had another gardener in mind. Everything but the church had been restored to its pre-earthquake appearance, President Jordan told Turner. Could Turner suggest anyone to replace Farrand? The Jewel Fund had been established and was "devoted exclusively to buying books" at the rate of about $25,000 per year. A fine library was within reach. Perhaps Turner was too. "And are there any terms on which we could 'do business' with you?" Jordan asked?[62]

As usual, Turner left the question of his availability open while he considered his options, but he made some recommendations.[63] Evidently Bolton was on Turner's list of candidates, because Stanford sent an offer of a temporary appointment that reached him in San Luis Potosí, probably in July. Bolton rejected a temporary job out of hand, but was willing to entertain a permanent position. Even so, Bolton was not certain about leaving Texas, where he expected "to hold the whip" himself soon, he told Fred. In August, Ephraim Adams, the new department chair, informed Bolton that there were two permanent positions to be filled, one in political and constitutional history (Farrand's courses) and the other covering "aspects of western history." Adams invited Bolton to explain "the type and character of work in which you are interested."[64]

In the minds of Jordan and Adams, the alluring Turner was still the leading candidate for the western position. Turner's semester on–semester off for research arrangement did not look good to some Wisconsin regents, and he feared they might raise the issue again.[65] This was more than enough to convince Adams and Jordan that Turner could be had and that the time might be right. And if Stanford hired Turner, they surely would not hire Bolton. So, as Bolton composed his letter to Adams, he had no way of knowing that his chief competition was Frederick Jackson Turner.

One week after encouraging Bolton to apply for the western position, Adams made a strong appeal to Turner. After consulting with President Van Hise at Wisconsin, Turner once again turned down Stanford in the middle of October.[66] Adams did not waste time mourning. "I want to get your opinion of Professor Bolton of Texas," he asked Turner. Adams was already favorably impressed with him.[67] "He seems to have cut out a rather new and important field in Spanish-Mexican-American history," Adams thought. Evidently Turner thought so too.[68]

Adams immediately offered Bolton an associate professorship at $3,000. Perhaps as important as salary to Bolton was Adams's assurance that "each man in the Department above the rank of Instructor, is absolutely equal in all Departmental matters, and is absolutely independent." The majority ruled in department meetings, but as far as each professor's work was concerned, he was "totally independent." After years of working under the imperious Garrison, Bolton could imagine the shackles falling from his ankles. At Stanford Bolton could teach and publish whatever he wanted. In addition to scholarly freedom, Adams promised financial support for Bolton's Mexican research. The Stanford library was "rather unusually equipped in the general field of Western History in the line originated by Professor Turner," Adams explained, although not in Spanish-American history.[69] Over time the proceeds from the Jewel Fund would ameliorate the deficiency. But Bolton was interested in a nearby library. Would "the Bancroft collection . . . be opened with good will to a Stanford man specializing in the Southwest and West?" he asked Adams.[70] Adams assured him that it would be.[71]

Bolton was a rising star that Texas did not want to lose. President Sidney E. Mezes offered Bolton a full professorship at $3,000, freedom from teaching medieval and elementary history courses, and funds for his Mexican archives work.[72] It was not enough. After further negotiation Bolton accepted a full professorship at Stanford with a salary of $3,500 and the understanding that the university would support his Mexican research. He would teach undergraduate courses on westward expansion and Spain in America. His graduate seminars would cover the Anglo-American West and Southwest.[73]

In June Bolton bid a fond farewell to President Mezes and the University of Texas. He was grateful for the opportunity to work in Texas, but the Stanford offer and the chance to research in the Bancroft was too good to pass up. "I believe that the University of Texas has a bright future," he concluded, "which I shall watch with a warm personal interest and sympathy."[74]

Turner congratulated Bolton on his Stanford appointment. "I think you are right in going to the coast," Turner wrote. "You probably have a better opportunity, particularly if the Bancroft Library is accessible, to continue your studies of Spanish American relations, and Stanford is an exceedingly attractive place."[75] Turner's enthusiasm for the Bancroft was genuine. He surveyed the collections when he taught in the 1908 summer school. He promised to return to Cal and write a new book based on what he had learned.[76]

So, it would seem, the die was cast. Bolton would go to Stanford with the expectation that he could use the Bancroft Library across the bay. His desire to join the Berkeley faculty had to be put away because the two university presidents had an understanding that they would not recruit faculty from each other.[77] Such were Bolton's expectations when he and his family arrived in Palo Alto in the fall of 1909, but unexpected shifts in the professional firmament would influence his placement once again.

As Bolton prepared to move to Stanford, Turner once again became the pivot around which Bolton's professional life rotated. "Here I am out in the redwoods," Morse Stephens wrote Turner from his camp in Bohemian Grove, "and thinking of you."[78] Stephens had a serious heart problem and was planning a leave in the spring of 1910 in order to relieve the strain of university work while gathering documents for the Bancroft in Spain. Would Turner pinch-hit for Stephens in the spring? Stephens had thoughtfully delegated the administrative work to Frederick J. Teggart, so Turner would be relatively free to research in the Bancroft. The offer of a temporary appointment was only the leading edge of a much broader proposal. President Wheeler wanted to hire Turner permanently at $5,000 per year, $1,000 more than he was getting in Madison. "And the Bancroft Library!" Stephens exclaimed as he warmed to his task. "Here we give you a field to work on and materials to burn." Stephens painted a dreamy scene for Turner: "Here in my tent among the redwoods, I think of you; I think of California, which needs you; I think of the U. of C. with its certainty of being a great historical school owing to its Dr. Turner and the Bancroft Library." It was a hard sales pitch and Stephens left nothing out. "You and I could always work together, for we love each other." Stephens's love was of the courtly variety, and he was ardently courting Turner. "Now I cannot argue well on rotten paper in a tent," Stephens complained, but urged Turner to come to California in the spring to resolve all doubts.[79]

California had propositioned Turner at the right moment. Some Wisconsin regents had become unsympathetic to Turner's special teaching arrangement.[80] So Turner, the reluctant (but experienced) maiden, responded with serious flirtation. The Bancroft was the chief dower that Stephens offered Turner. "The purchase of the Bancroft Library shows the trend of the University towards historical productions, and the Academy of Pacific Coast History will be our own publishing mechanism."[81] The regents had founded the academy in 1907 to fund acquisitions and publications.[82] Its publishing function was important because the University of California did not yet have a scholarly press as such, but maintained a small printing plant for syllabi and other campus publications. The academy council included President Wheeler, Phoebe Apperson Hearst, James K. Moffitt, and other representatives of San Francisco fortunes. These well-heeled donors, Stephens hoped, would support the work of the Bancroft Library as well as scholarly publication.[83] With a great library and a mechanism for publishing in place, Turner might as well face the facts and accept his fate. "Now, my dear boy," Stephens proposed, "I wish you could see President Wheeler," who would be in Chicago the following month.[84]

When Wheeler made his offer in writing, he insisted that Turner begin his permanent appointment in January 1910. "I think you know us pretty well already, and can estimate reasonably the factors to be considered in making a decision" without having to look over the university during the spring. "I should rather you would decide the matter at once," Wheeler insisted.[85] Turner agreed to meet Wheeler in Chicago on September 16.

News that Turner might be available spread quickly. Adams made another pitch from Palo Alto, which Turner quickly rejected.[86] Bolton must have known about Stanford's approach to Turner and probably had heard of California's offer.

So Wheeler went to Chicago, and the world waited on Turner's decision. No one waited with more anticipation than Morse Stephens, who stewed in Berkeley on the day Turner and Wheeler met. "The result of that interview means so much to the Pacific Coast, to California, to the U. of C., and—oh! selfish that I am— to me. I think my cup of happiness would run over, if you were to be my colleague here." Everything was in readiness for Turner if only he would come. If only. Perhaps Stephens's nervousness sprang from his intuitive understanding of Turner. Turner intended to leave Wisconsin, but this did not mean that the great prize was in California's hands; it meant that the great prize was truly up for grabs.

When Turner and Wheeler met in Chicago, Turner was almost certain that he would cast his lot with Berkeley, but he wanted to give his alma mater the courtesy of one more opportunity to hold him in Wisconsin. Wheeler gave Turner some time to think it over.[87] Turner had a second reason for stalling Wheeler in Chicago. Haskins had learned of the meeting with Wheeler and sent a telegram directly to the meeting place. "Can't you delay decision?" it read. "If you leave should like to see what can be done elsewhere."[88] Elsewhere, of course, meant Harvard. Turner was an expert delayer, so he easily acceded to Haskins's wish. Luckily for Haskins's cause, Turner was slated to receive an honorary doctorate from Harvard on October 5 as part of the inauguration of President A. Lawrence Lowell. It was a grand occasion with many university presidents and prominent academics in attendance, including Wheeler and Stephens. In Cambridge Turner finally made up his mind. Seeing the sickly Stephens convinced Turner that he might soon die or retire. Then the responsibility for building the history department would fall entirely on Turner's shoulders, a prospect decidedly repugnant to him. Turner would go to Harvard.

When the announcement of Turner's move to Harvard finally came, congratulations flooded in to him. In acknowledging Bolton's letter, Turner responded: "Needless to say, I shall watch your conquest of the Pacific coast and southwestern history with keen interest. Let me know what you are doing."[89] Turner's decision to go to Harvard had left Morse Stephens in the lurch. "Poor Morse," Turner wrote his wife, was "badly cut up. And it hurts me too."[90] Stephens's wounds stemmed from a practical problem as well as emotional distress. He had a great library and no one of great stature to work in it. The development of graduate studies in history was one of the reasons for the acquisition of the library, but there was no nationally recognized specialist in American history at Berkeley. He wanted a big name, but if not Turner, who? Bolton was a rising star. His experience in the Mexican archives, his spectacular discovery of the Pike papers, his publications, and his research interests made him the most obvious candidate for the Berkeley position, but now the gentlemen's agreement between Jordan and Wheeler prevented Stephens from directly approaching Bolton. With Turner finally out of reach and no plausible alternative in sight, Stephens departed for Europe.

When Stephens went to Spain in 1910, he made Teggart acting department head even though he did not have a regular appointment and only held a bachelor's degree. This proved to be a revealing mistake. Teggart took it upon himself to openly accuse his department brethren "of wholesale bad teaching." At his urging, the department met weekly rather than monthly, a schedule that would carry into the summer too, if the interim chair had anything to say about it. Teggart was concerned that the doctoral program was not up to snuff. Consequently, the department named a committee of three to consider changes in the graduate program. When the committee presented its report, Teggart offered an alternative that the department adopted instead of the committee's. In short, Teggart's new rules required that students be examined in fields determined by the faculty before being advanced to doctoral candidacy, which seemed reasonable enough. However, Teggart decided to apply the new regulations by requiring a student who was *already* advanced to candidacy to stand for a snap examination. The poor chap failed, as Teggart suspected he would. Teggart claimed that the man was studying for reexamination, "was entirely satisfied with the treatment accorded," and regretted only that he had "not been held up last year," a comment that must have been read as a rebuke of the student's unnamed advisor. The upshot of all of this meddling, Teggart claimed, was a "remarkable bond of unity." The faculty were resolved to maintain "the new spirit that has been developed this year," a remark that implicitly criticized Stephens's leadership of the department.[91]

Stephens must have gone slack-jawed when he read Teggart's letter. It was as if Teggart had set out to destroy departmental harmony while undermining Stephens's authority. His sheer effrontery was mind-boggling. A lecturer by annual appointment with comparatively little classroom experience had taken it upon himself to condemn the teaching of the entire department. Without a PhD himself, Teggart believed he should determine standards and procedures for the degree instead of professors who had earned the doctorate. Having never been a doctoral student, Teggart decided to terrorize graduate students in the name of standards he had never had to meet himself. The department went along with him, but that only speaks to the power that a department chair in those days had over his colleagues, if only temporarily in Teggart's case. They could wait for Stephens to return and put things right, but their docility may also speak to the considerable power of Teggart's personality and intellect. If Stephens had not recognized that Teggart was a loose cannon, he certainly knew it after reading the interim chair's letter.

When Stephens returned to Berkeley, he faced the problem of appointing a respected scholar to the Berkeley history department, a need that Teggart reinforced with his high-handed behavior. But Wheeler and Stephens could do nothing to actively recruit Bolton away from Stanford without risking a controversy between the two universities. And then came the gift. On July 3, 1910, George Pierce Garrison suddenly died.[92] Bolton still had strong personal ties to the University of Texas, so on July 30 he sent a telegram to President Mezes indicating his interest in Garrison's old job. "From the very first I have been very desirous of returning to Texas," Bolton explained. He was interested in the entire Southwest, but "Texas is the center," and because of the "sympathetic atmosphere," Bolton's work could "be done better there than elsewhere." He liked Stanford, but Bolton felt that "local patriotism" would force him "into the study of Pacific Coast problems" instead of Texas and the Southwest, which he preferred.[93]

Bolton looked forward to building a "really distinctive and distinguished School of History" in Texas. For the next twenty-five years, Bolton believed, Spanish-American and western history would be the most promising fields in American history. Three universities would lead the way. Wisconsin covered the Old Northwest and Mississippi Valley, the University of Texas naturally commanded southwestern history, and the University of California dominated the study of "the Far West and the Pacific Coast" because of the Bancroft collection. With a "proper organization . . . nothing" could stop Texas's ascendance in the field of history. To all of these reasons Bolton added his "real fondness" for Texas.[94] "A larger institution" had asked him to consider a place, "but my preference is for Texas." Bolton did not reveal the identity of the university that had made the offer, but it must have been Berkeley, though Stephens claimed that Bolton was on his way to Texas before he recruited him.[95]

Mezes offered Bolton the position but not a raise in salary.[96] Within days of Bolton's receipt of Mezes's offer Stephens invited him to Berkeley, where he met Stephens and Wheeler. The three men reached an understanding. Bolton would be Stephens's "second-in-command with entire charge of . . . everything pertaining to American history." If Berkeley could not have Turner, "let us have Turner's most promising pupil." The Berkeley chairman was punctilious about having Bolton's assurances that he had intended to leave Stanford for Texas before Stephens contacted him.[97]

Stephens recommended Bolton for a full professorship at $4,000. "It is clearly understood," Stephens added, "that you will have resigned from Stanford to accept the call from the University of Texas, before any call can come from the University of California."[98] Bolton had not "resigned from Stanford" to go to Texas, as Stephens directed Bolton to acknowledge. He could not bring himself to tell such a bald-faced lie and would only say that he was "on the point of resigning" when the California position was offered.[99] This sophistry was meant to justify Wheeler, Stephens, and Bolton in the eyes of Stanford critics while accomplishing the objective of pulling Bolton over to Berkeley.

Would Bolton have gone to Texas if Cal had not hired him? Possibly, but Barker's letters to Bolton reveal that an inside game was being played in Texas as well as in California. "Just once more: you can't come for 1910–1911." As Barker had artfully put it, "They won't take another man so long as you dicker with them—couldn't get one before next winter, if then; uncertainty may help me to get out of the rank of Adj. [assistant] Prof. into Asso. class; so if my logic seems good to you hang on without giving a definite answer." He added a note asking Bolton to delay his decision until the September meeting of the Texas regents. Otherwise, Barker wrote, "I would be merely what I am—*nothing*." Bolton hung on through most of September, and Barker was made acting chair of the history department.[100]

"I have decided to cast my lot with you," he informed the worried Stephens on September 21. "Now that the decision has been made," he wrote, "I am all for California, and I shall not look back."[101]

Bolton's decision hinged in part on Stephens's assurance that the university would purchase some of his Mexican transcripts for $1,000.[102] Wheeler agreed to this arrangement and Stephens asked Phoebe Apperson Hearst to provide the money. Hiring Bolton was California's victory, but Texas gained too. The Texas regents soon made Barker's chairmanship permanent. He held the position for decades, constructively guiding the development of the history program, the library, and the university.[103]

Bolton got a nice raise by going to Berkeley, and he needed it. The Bolton family now included six daughters. The Bolton's new baby, Jane, was born in 1910. "I of all the 'boys,'" Herbert wrote his bother, "most resemble our father in exemplifying the proverb, 'a rich man for luck and a poor man for babies.'"[104] Money had more than practical significance for a family man who was strapped for cash. At Berkeley Bolton was going to pull down the same salary that Turner had commanded at Wisconsin.[105] Bolton's new salary declared that he was on his way to the top of the history profession.

Negotiations with Stanford, Texas, and California had not prevented Bolton from finishing his guide to the Mexican archives, but the manuscript still sat on his desk. "I hate to 'turn it loose,' to use a Texanism," he explained to Fred.[106] Three days after telling Stephens that he was "all for California," Bolton sent the manuscript to Jameson. "I submit it to your tender mercy, with no comment as to what I think of it." Bolton had worked on it for so long that he "could scarcely work on it any more—I was paralyzed in sight of it," he confessed.[107]

Once the manuscript was off of his desk, Bolton began to anticipate his move to Berkeley and the peerless resources of the Bancroft. "I shall be very glad indeed to have my work and office across the hall from the great Bancroft Collection," he wrote Jameson.[108] Much to his satisfaction, Bolton's new teaching responsibilities would consist mostly of graduate work. "You probably know that I am going to the University of California next year," he reported to Turner. "The Bancroft Collection is a magnificent one and I could not have collected it better myself from the standpoint of my own purposes." Bolton hoped to build a strong department in western and Spanish-American history at Berkeley. "My own interests lie on the border between the two and I expect plenty of help on the two flanks."[109]

Indeed, it is impossible to imagine a better situation for Bolton. He would be assistant department head with entire responsibility for building the program in American history. Through hiring professors and training graduate students, Bolton could shape the Berkeley history program, the field of Spanish-American history, and the profession. He could continue his own march to scholarly prominence with the finest library in his field literally at his fingertips. Hard work would make it so, but Bolton's success in California would not come without opposition or conflict. Frederick J. Teggart would see to that. In the summer of 1911 the regents made Teggart associate professor of Pacific Coast history in recognition of "the invaluable services . . . rendered without charge" in moving the Bancroft to Berkeley.[110] Now slated to teach American history, Teggart would fall under Bolton's purview.[111] Stephens appointed Bolton assistant curator of the Bancroft under Teggart, creating dual arrangements that would inevitably cause friction.

In the summer before moving from Palo Alto to Berkeley, Bolton finally heard from Jameson about the long-delayed guide. Jameson was "the dean of the history faculty and can make or unmake one's future," he explained to Fred. Jameson's opinion was all that Bolton could have hoped for. After carefully reviewing the manuscript, the editor praised its "remarkable merits in respect to both planning and general composition on the one hand, and to execution on the other." The *Guide* would contain "an enormous amount of useful material" for future researchers, who would be "very grateful to you, and so am I." Bolton quoted Jameson's praise to his brother. "These are boyish things for me to write, but they are very pleasing to me," Bolton confessed.[112] Forty-one years old, a full professor with a good salary at an improving university with the very best library in his field, Bolton for a moment revealed the uncertain Wisconsin farm boy who wanted to impress important people so that he could rise in the world.

FIVE · In Stephens's Grove

Like other institutions of higher learning in Bolton's time, the University of California existed as a complex web of interlocking political, social, cultural, and economic relationships. We may imagine those connections as a series of intersecting rings, much like the circles used to illustrate set theory in mathematics. A large circle represents the university. A cluster of smaller circles signifies a collection of departments assembled to form a college within the university circle. A large circle that intersects with the university circle represents the Board of Regents, which consisted of influential men and women of wealth. Likewise the governor and the state legislature have circles that overlap with the university and each other. Students, alumni groups, fraternal organizations, historical societies, important donors, and other interest groups are represented by circles that indicate their relative force and relationships to the other circles.

If completely and accurately elaborated, the set theory model eventually would become too cluttered to convey useful information. Nevertheless, the weblike interlocking network illustrates the complicated structures of power and influence within the university as well as its connections with public and private entities. A simplified diagram for Bolton's situation in 1911 would have shown the large university circle, containing a much smaller history department circle, which enclosed an even smaller American history circle. The Bancroft Library intersected with both history circles and with a general university library administration circle. Because the circles represent human institutions and relationships, the diagram is perhaps too mechanistic. One must imagine the personalities who were in charge of each circle to fully grasp how the university functioned. Morse Stephens, Herbert Bolton, and Frederick Teggart presided over their respective circles, with President Wheeler reigning over them all. Overlapping areas of responsibility required cooperation, but convergence could sometimes cause conflict among strong personalities. While making every effort to cooperate with his colleagues, Bolton also sought to enlarge his circle of influence. Eventually some of the circles would merge into a single system of coincident parts with Bolton at the center.

Lines of authority could be complicated, but there was no doubt about who was in charge of the university. Benjamin Ide Wheeler was known to Cal students as a kindly, distinguished-looking man with a white moustache who patrolled the campus on horseback. Born in Massachusetts, Wheeler had been educated in New England preparatory academies and had graduated from Brown University as a member of Phi Beta Kappa. After earning a master's degree at Brown, he continued his graduate studies at Heidelberg University, where he received the PhD summa cum laude. With special fields of interest in comparative philology and Greek, he taught briefly at Harvard before settling into a distinguished career at Cornell University. In 1899 the University of California offered him the presidency, which he held until his retirement in 1919. Wheeler is generally regarded as one of Cal's great presidents. The honorary degrees conferred on him by Princeton, Harvard, Yale, Brown, Johns Hopkins, Dartmouth, Columbia, and other universities were emblematic of the respect that President Wheeler enjoyed in academic circles.[1]

Wheeler's inaugural address at Berkeley explained his ideas about the relationship between the university and society. The university president was "a representative to its public constituency," Wheeler explained, "whether that constituency take the form of state or sect or community of graduates and friends." The university president mediated "between the divergent ideals of the supporting constituency and those of the university life." Ideally, Wheeler thought, presidential mediation meant "harmonizing the university to the demands of its constituency." With these ideas in mind Benjamin Ide Wheeler embarked on his presidency of the University of California.[2]

After nearly ten years of service in California, Wheeler had adopted a westerner's point of view, at least for public consumption. In 1908 he told his audience how he felt about the American West. "I have always noticed when the train passes North Platte coming west," he said, "that men stop wiping their necks at the edge of the collar . . . they begin to ask each other for a match, without reference to present condition of bank account or previous condition of servitude." These social changes seemed to accelerate as the train continued westward. "By the time we have passed Buffalo Bill's ranch, agriculture begins to yield to grazing, men sit on top of the horse instead of behind him, and the hat brims grow stiffer." "Who has ever shifted his life from one side of this frontier to the other without feeling he is in another world?" he asked rhetorically. Out West "the air is thinner, but the skin is thicker," he continued. "It has to be—a little. The sticks are thicker. And almost everybody carries one." The western atmosphere even invigorated men's cardiovascular function. "Hearts beat several times a minute more here than over yonder, but then there is more here for hearts to do than there." As Wheeler warmed to his subject, he touched on Turner's well-known tropes of frontier history—free men living on free land where they created a new society unencumbered by the restrictive customs of Europe. Despite the presence of hundreds of thousands of American Indians, Latinos, and Asians in the western United States, Wheeler insisted that "only the people of the prairie schooners and their successors . . . really set their faces toward the West."[3] The West as a place and an idea about freedom, Wheeler implied, was the invention of Anglo-Americans, and it was their inheritance alone. To judge Wheeler by this speech, it would seem that he had completely absorbed the meaning and prejudices of Turner's hypothesized frontier. One of Bolton's important tasks would be to educate Wheeler and other Californians about the Spanish-American frontier's importance in California history.

H. Morse Stephens was a warmhearted, jowly, full-bearded fellow with a British accent and courtly manners. To Cal's students he was avuncular and friendly, among the most popular teachers on campus. Stephens's decorous ways and extravagantly expressive speech—one need only recall his florid Turner courtship letters to get the full flavor of his language—disguised a shrewd man who managed well the political currents in which the university sailed. His membership in the Bohemian Club was not an accident, one supposes, but a calculated way to meet some of the most powerful and wealthy people in California. Not all of the faculty admired him. Arthur W. Ryder, a classicist, remarked upon seeing Stephens surrounded by his colleagues at the Faculty Club, "There goes a fake giant surrounded by real pygmies."[4] Professional jealousy may have sparked Ryder's bon mot, for Stephens was a man of real accomplishment and certain power on the University of California campus and in the historical profession.

For all his personal foibles, Stephens deserves great credit for establishing the University of California as an important center of historical research and graduate study. He, like Turner and Garrison, understood that a school of history in the West could grow from local resources, local history, and local support. That is what Stephens meant in reminding Turner that he had "at once grasped" what Turner was doing at the University of Wisconsin when he visited the summer school in 1895.[5] Accordingly, Stephens and Wheeler put together the money and political support to acquire the Bancroft and build a California school of history. Adding Bolton to the faculty set off the hoped-for chain reaction of scholarship and graduate study that created the California school of history, a school that Bolton stamped as his own.

In the early twentieth century Stephens was a respected historian and a major force in the historical profession.[6] Born and educated in England, Stephens had received his graduate training at Oxford's Balliol College before teaching the history of India at Cambridge University. In 1894 he was called to Cornell, where he became a close friend of Wheeler. Stephens, ambitious to promote the reputations of Cornell and himself, proposed a national historical journal and convinced the board of trustees to underwrite the new review that Stephens would edit. Harvard and Penn had similar ideas, but each wished to house the journal at its campus. Stephens shuttled among the eastern campuses to promote a diplomatic solution and agreed to give up any claim to the editor's chair while assuring that the Cornell trustees' generous financial support would remain intact. The group chose J. Franklin Jameson, then on the Brown University faculty, to edit the new magazine, with Stephens and others serving on an editorial board. Thus the *American Historical Review* was born. And thus, a recent immigrant, with "his genial social traits," as Jameson recalled, "his talent for friendship, and his gift of entertaining speech," shot to the top of the American historical profession. As for his scholarship, the claim that Stephens's history of the French Revolution "bade fair to replace at last the classical narrative of Carlyle," as his *AHR* eulogist wrote, was intended as a high compliment.[7] President Wheeler called his friend to Cal in 1902 to run the extension program. Soon he also became the Sather Professor of History and head of the history department. Stephens was not a fake anything. He was one of the founders of the American historical profession and the creator of a respected University of California department.

Stephens was one of those underappreciated academics who worked selflessly for the profession, his university, his department, and the colleagues who resided in it. Bolton became his right-hand man. As such Bolton came into regular contact with President Wheeler, university regents, and the important alumnae and supporters of the university. Stephens taught Bolton the political ropes in California, just as the smooth Garrison had done in Texas. Bolton was an avid learner.

Stephens probably introduced him to Phoebe Apperson Hearst, arguably the university's most important donor. The Bolton family was soon making weekend trips to Hearst's Pleasanton estate, visits that no doubt were meant to solidify her enthusiasm for university benefactions.[8]

Stephens had granted Bolton control over the American part of Berkeley's historical domain.[9] The other Americanists included Assistant Professor Eugene I. McCormac, a Yale PhD who had already published his dissertation on Maryland's indentured white servants. In years to come, his publication and teaching would range over the colonial and early-republic periods.[10] Donald E. Smith, also an assistant professor with a new PhD, had evidently come with Stephens from Cornell in 1902. He was listed as the history department secretary and also as an assistant professor of geography. Before Bolton arrived, Smith completed his doctorate in history at Berkeley with work on the viceroyalty of New Spain.[11] The third Americanist was Frederick J. Teggart, who taught Pacific Coast history as well as historical bibliography and historical theory. With the assistance of Smith Teggart published Spanish California documents from the Bancroft collections.[12]

Outside the history department there was a collection of prominent faculty with interests in Bolton's field. Although he was listed as a professor in Berkeley's political science department, Bernard Moses was a noted historian of Spanish America.[13] After earning the PhD at Heidelberg University, Moses joined the University of California faculty in 1876. At one time Moses had been head of the history department, but when he took a leave from 1900 to 1902 to serve on the U.S. Philippine Commission, Wheeler took the opportunity to bring in his friend Stephens to fill Moses's place as head. When Moses returned to Berkeley, he moved into the political science department. Bolton recalled him as a "rather cold and austere" man whose teaching was more "intellectual than inspirational." Still, Bolton credited Moses with calling attention to "the importance of Spain's great work for the spread of European civilization in the western hemisphere," and for teaching the first formal college course in Latin American history in the United States.[14]

Political science professor David Prescott Barrows, though not a Latin Americanist by training, had interests in common with Bolton. A graduate of Pomona College, Barrows was awarded the PhD by the University of Chicago in 1897. From 1900 to 1907 he served as superintendent of schools in Manila and director of education for the Philippine Islands. Wheeler called him first to the school of education and later appointed him professor in the political science department. His experience with postcolonial Hispanic society in the Philippines and extensive travels in revolutionary Mexico gave Barrows and Bolton much to talk about.[15]

Because of Bolton's contributions to the *Handbook of North American Indians*, Alfred L. Kroeber, who headed the department of anthropology, recognized Bolton as a kindred spirit. A student of Franz Boaz, Kroeber received the first PhD in anthropology granted by Columbia University. At first he directed the university's small museum in San Francisco (a job he detested), but by the time Bolton arrived, he had moved to the Berkeley campus. Working with native tribes of California, Kroeber would become one of the towering figures in the anthropology profession. Kroeber was soon inviting Bolton to participate in anthropological conferences, and they served together on numerous university committees as senior members of their respective departments.[16] By chance, the famous Yahi Indian Ishi became a resident of the university museum during Bolton's first semester at Berkeley. While not a part of the faculty or student body, Ishi became Kroeber's friend and informant. The trip across the bay to the campus was one of Ishi's favorite excursions. There is no evidence that he and Bolton ever met, but Ishi was a familiar figure on campus.[17] He was one of the few people of color whom Bolton would have seen while strolling the Berkeley grounds.

Bolton arrived in the midst of a great campus building boom. Construction of the Doe Library with its magnificent reading room and facilities to house the Bancroft Library was under way. Made possible by the bequest of Charles Franklin Doe, the new library would be Bolton's professional home for nearly forty years. The university had many generous donors, but none were greater than Phoebe Apperson Hearst, heir to the mining fortune of her husband, Senator George Hearst. In 1896 she had provided funds for an international competition to draw an architectural plan for the university. "I have only one wish in this matter," she wrote, "that the plans adopted should be worthy of the great University whose material home they are to provide for; that they should harmonize with . . . the beauty of the site . . . ; and that they should redound to the glory of the State whose culture and civilization are to be nursed and developed at its University."[18] She would spend nearly $200,000 on the plan. Hearst funded women's scholarships and built Hearst Hall, a women's gymnasium and social center. She underwrote the construction of the Hearst Memorial Mining Building (completed in 1907), supported the university museum and worldwide archaeological research, and had continuous influence on the university through her gifts and as a regent.

The winner of the architectural competition was the French architect Emile Henri Bénard, who conceived a monumental plan that would have been impossibly expensive to construct. Architect John Galen Howard revised and built Bénard's concept in a more economical form. The erection of landmark structures such as Doe Library, Wheeler Hall, and Sather Tower during Bolton's first years at Berkeley marked the advancement of the Bénard-Howard plan.[19]

When the university opened the Berkeley campus in 1873, the site appeared to be an open, gently rolling field with few large trees. Over the years redwoods, oaks, eucalyptus, and other trees were planted, giving the campus a heavily wooded appearance. The faculty built their clubhouse in Faculty Glade. Organized in 1901, the next year the Faculty Club opened the Great Hall, an impressive room that resembled a hunting lodge. The masculine character of the place was in keeping with the club's membership, which was exclusively male even though there were a few women faculty at the university.

Fourteen faculty, including Stephens, lived at the Faculty Club.[20] At night, after the library closed, he sometimes recited his favorite lines from Rudyard Kipling from the window of his third-floor apartment:

Lord God of Hosts, be with us yet
Lest we forget, lest we forget![21]

He no doubt intended the performance to edify undergraduates who might be tempted to unwholesome activities.

Student life was lively. A continuous round of formal, informal, and spontaneous doings for men and women students animated the Berkeley campus. Hazing of various sorts was ubiquitous among the men from the different classes. As one historian of the university put it, class hazing resulted in "a spirit of individualism and lawlessness" so severe that it became "continuous class hostility and warfare which partook of primitive and savage periods of life." Some unrestrained students became "flagrant violators of statutory law" involved in "the destruction of property and the endangerment of life."[22] When students destroyed street car property in 1902, the public outcry finally roused President Wheeler to action. From that date Wheeler gave more responsibility to the student government, which gradually brought hazing and other abuses under better control.

Sports were important, especially football. In 1898 San Francisco banker and mayor James D. Phelan offered sculptor Douglas Tilden's life-sized bronze depiction of two football players to the team that won two out of three annual games between California and Stanford. Cal won the first two games and claimed the statue, placing it on a shady path near Strawberry Creek.[23] Numerous sorority and fraternity houses surrounded the campus. Theta Delta Chi, Bolton's old frat house, had a chapter at Berkeley and listed him as a faculty member of the fraternity.[24]

The fraternities and sororities observed the usual ethnic, racial, and religious prejudices against people of color, Jews, and Catholics.

University enrollment was open to men and women without racial restrictions, but class pictures indicate that the general student body was decidedly white.[25] Trying to identify race on the basis of nearly century-old black-and-white yearbook photographs and names is prone to error, yet a few observations are in order. Of 372 student pictures the class of 1911 included only one indisputable person of color, Nai Lamoon, probably a Thai man. There might have been one Hispanic, Joseph Dias. There were no discernible African Americans, although the quality of the photographs does not reveal subtle skin tones. Nor can one pick out faces that are unambiguously of mixed racial descent. Names reveal four men and one woman who were perhaps Italian. There was a scattering of names that could be Jewish but might be German or Polish. On the basis of names and photographs the class of 1911 was overwhelmingly of northern European extraction. This demographic estimate, while lamentably incomplete, should not astonish anyone. Female enrollment is the only category in which the Cal student body showed a progressive tendency. More than 42 percent of the people shown in the class photographs were women.

This was the relatively homogeneous group of undergraduates that Bolton found in 1911. He never said anything about the makeup of the undergraduate student body, but he paid much closer attention to the graduate students. He understood very well that it was his job to attract graduate students to the University of California. A large number of graduates already were built into the Cal system because all high school teachers were required to have a fifth year of college training beyond the bachelor's degree. Bolton applauded this requirement but thought that these graduate students "would not amount to much for higher work," although they would improve the quality of the state's teaching force.[26] At the end of his first year four women completed the master's degree under his direction, the first of hundreds of his graduate students who would fill the teaching ranks in California's primary and secondary schools. Training school teachers was a good thing, but Bolton (not to mention Wheeler and Stephens) aimed to train doctors. Accordingly, Bolton brought in doctoral students from Texas and Stanford. In 1909 he recruited Charles W. Hackett, a talented University of Texas undergraduate, for the Stanford graduate school.[27] When Bolton moved to Cal, Hackett followed him, although he finished the master's program at Stanford before moving across the bay.[28] Thomas Maitland Marshall, a University of Michigan product, got his master's degree with Bolton at Stanford and moved to Berkeley, where he became Bolton's first PhD in 1914.

Bolton picked up one student who was already enrolled in the doctoral program: Charles Edward Chapman, a native of New Hampshire with a bachelor's degree from Tufts and a law degree from Harvard. Chapman was also an exceptional athlete who had played professional baseball and moonlighted as a scout for the St. Louis Cardinals and Cincinnati Reds. When Bolton moved to Berkeley, Chapman was working with Frederick Teggart.[29] Although Chapman did not mention Teggart by name, he was the only plausible professor (other than Bolton) to direct a doctoral student in Spanish-American history. Evidently Chapman had been promised a position on the faculty if he completed his degree. For some reason Teggart had decided that Chapman should not get the doctorate. "At length one of my enemies . . . proposed to Professor Bolton that I should be failed in my examination, in order to keep me from getting an appointment in the Department." Bolton carried this news to Chapman, who dumped Teggart for Bolton, duly completed his doctorate in 1915, and received a regular appointment as assistant professor of Hispanic-American and California history. He eventually published a guide to the archives of Spain similar to Bolton's on Mexico.[30] Needless to say, Chapman was an ardent admirer of Bolton.[31] One may reasonably suppose that Teggart did not appreciate Bolton's role in saving Chapman's career.

Among Bolton's first group of doctoral students, none was more important to him than Herbert Ingram Priestley. A native of Michigan but raised in Southern California, Priestley had graduated from the University of Southern California in 1900. He had taught school in the Philippines from 1901 to 1907 before returning to his alma mater for the master's degree.[32] After a few years as supervising principal of the Corona city schools, east of Los Angeles, Priestley corresponded with Bolton about studying with him at Berkeley.[33] In 1912 the university hired him as an assistant curator of the Bancroft, a post he continued to hold after completing his degree under Bolton in 1917. Students remembered him as the heart and soul of the Bancroft Library.[34] As soon as he had the doctorate, Priestley was appointed assistant professor of Mexican history. With Chapman and Priestley Bolton shaped the American section of the history department in his own image.

In his first ten years at Berkeley, fourteen graduate students earned the PhD under Bolton. It was just the beginning of a long parade of doctoral students whom Bolton hooded at commencement. He was close to these men, whom he called his "boys." Sometimes he took them into his home as temporary boarders. The experiences of J. Fred Rippy, a Tennessean who arrived in Berkeley in 1917, suggest how involved Bolton was with his graduate students in that period. After finding an apartment that would accommodate himself, his wife, and mother-in-law,

Rippy went to the Bancroft Library, where he met Bolton for the first time. "Have you found a place to live?" Bolton asked. When Rippy replied in the affirmative, Bolton was disappointed that he had not asked for Bolton's help, but by chance, the Rippys had rented an apartment across the street from the Bolton family home on Scenic Avenue. Bolton told Rippy to call on Mrs. Bolton and his daughters. "They will be glad to help any way they can," Bolton said. He was sincere. A few days later Bolton arrived on Rippy's front porch at 7:30 A.M., asking if he was ready to go to campus. Rippy was ready, and Bolton was favorably impressed. Thereafter they briskly walked six blocks to campus each morning. Rippy had a hard time keeping up with Bolton on the street and in the library. When the student complained that he did not have enough time to do research, Bolton gave him a library key. "I often work in my office until eleven or twelve." "Be careful," he added, "or this might get us both into trouble."[35] Over the years Bolton provided many of his students with library keys.[36] Of course, they loved him for it. They became coworkers in Bolton's historical enterprise, working day and night in the Bancroft's vast holdings. They also became coconspirators against petty bureaucratic rules imposed by the university, including those that Teggart made and enforced.

Bolton's nocturnal habits included chain-smoking cigarettes as a stimulant for late-night study. There is no record of when Bolton started smoking, but one of his children thought he took it up late in life. "He had a peculiar way of puffing that gave him away as a rank amature [sic]," his son recalled. "I doubt if he ever inhaled; his hands, though, were always tobacco stained." Bolton may have started the habit in college, as many college students have done before and after Bolton's time. Perhaps his "boys" introduced him to smoking as a relaxing social ritual. Whatever the case, Bolton was a confirmed smoker with a habit that many observers noticed. Lucky Strike was his brand. His customary welcome to office visitors was "Come in! Sit down! Have a Lucky?"[37] That Bolton's smoking was remarked on at all in an age when cigarettes were almost universally accepted suggests that his habit was pronounced. On the other hand, no one thought Bolton's drinking habits out of the way. He was probably a social drinker, but evidently nothing more than that. Smoking supported decades of demanding study sessions that extended far into the night; heavy drinking likely would have made him less effective in the graveyard shift.

Obsessive, nicotine-fueled late-night sessions were needed to complete the heavy publication schedule that Bolton had in mind. He prepared a report for President Wheeler, "Need for the Publication of a Comprehensive Body of Documents Relating to the History of Spanish Activities within the Present

Limits of the United States."[38] John Francis Bannon, Bolton's student and biographer, believed this to be Bolton's earliest comprehensive statement describing the Spanish Borderlands project.[39] Bolton proposed publishing twenty-five volumes, if the money could be found.

During his first five years at Berkeley Bolton cleared his desk of old business from his Texas days. The first item was the long-delayed guide. "I have never had such luck with any manuscript," Jameson apologized.[40] Bolton adopted an ironic attitude. He told his brother that the *Guide* had "not yet appeared to damage my reputation. Blessed are the printers."[41] The Mexican Revolution added to the delays. In January 1913, just as the final preparations for printing the *Guide* were under way, Bolton learned that fighting in Mexico City may have damaged the government repositories. He feared the revolution might destroy the archives or force them to be relocated for safekeeping. Bolton had spent years making sense out of Mexico's scattered documentary record for the *Guide*. The revolution might shuffle the deck again and make his painstakingly assembled *Guide* worthless for future research, a mere artifact of things as they had been before 1913. The building that housed the Secretaría de Gobernación, where Vice President Corral (now deposed) had given Bolton an office for three years, seemed to have suffered the most, but Bolton had little reliable information.[42]

Jameson reckoned that "ordinary damage incident to street fighting" was not worth reporting on. He expected the conflict to continue for several years. "We could not keep up with events of that sort." He suggested that Bolton ascertain damage to the archives through correspondence in order to prepare a short supplement if needed.[43] In the end, there was no supplement, only a brief disclaimer about the inability to determine the extent of damage caused by "recent disturbances in Mexico."[44]

Bolton was also concerned about acknowledging the government officials in the defunct Díaz regime, but Jameson convinced him to thank the people who had assisted him, "as we usually do."[45] Thus Bolton acknowledged the "official courtesies" of Díaz, Corral, and many other officials and dignitaries of the ancien régime.[46] Scholars on both sides of the border were grateful to Bolton for providing the most comprehensive handbook to Mexican archives in existence. The utility of the *Guide* has diminished with the passage of time, but even today it retains some usefulness.

In 1914 and 1915 Bolton published two books about Texas that illustrated his strengths and weaknesses as a historian, as well as a path not taken. The first, *Athanase de Mézières and the Louisiana-Texas Frontier, 1768–1780*, is a heavily annotated two-volume collection of translated documents with a large detailed map by Bolton.[47] Bolton had developed this information while writing his essays for the *Handbook of North American Indians*. The book was in many ways a model for the many documentary editions he would publish in the coming years. It included his long introduction and notes, which were often as informative as the text itself. *Athanase de Mézières* displayed Bolton's command of the archives and the deep knowledge of his subject that had taken him years to establish. He also began to emphasize Spain's missionary effort, which he called "the principal weapon" in the contest for the frontier.[48]

Focused on New Spain's northeastern frontier at the time of the French cession of Louisiana, the book emphasized relations with American Indian peoples. The text and the map described the location, movements, and relationships of the many tribes that lived in the area. The oversized "Map of Texas in the Eighteenth Century" deserves special attention because it prefigured both Bolton's subsequent cartographic contributions and a multicultural, multinational historical perspective. The map shows general tribal regions, such as the "Caddo Tribes," "Hasinai Tribes," and "Attacapan Tribes" on the Texas-Louisiana border. Bolton also located specific tribes within the general regions. Trails, each grandly called "Camino Real," crisscrossed Texas linking Spanish missions, presidios, and Indian villages. One trail leads eastward across the Sabine River to the French outpost of Natchitoches. Another track extends southwest across the Rio Grande to Monclova in present-day Coahuila, Mexico. These tendrils were the beginnings of a transnational network of Spanish trails that Bolton would traverse and map. The *De Mézières* map connected the Spanish empire with the elaborate American Indian cultural geography of Texas and French Louisiana. By inference it connected the histories of the United States and Mexico.

The map is a cartographic representation of a transnational world and the meetings of disparate empires, nations, and cultures. It illustrates a remote chunk of the Spanish Empire whose borders were jealously (if ineffectively) guarded, but the map infers the insubstantiality of borders, the mutability of imperial claims, and the significance of Native peoples in the contest for North America. Of course, words like "transnational" and "multicultural" would have been foreign to Bolton, but he mapped a world now understandable in these terms even though he lacked the interpretive framework to thoroughly explicate its meaning.

Although Bolton was poised to pioneer in the field of American Indian history, he could not quite figure out how to interpret their past. He wrote a short book about the Hasinai Indians but could not bring himself to publish it. Russell

Magnaghi, the editor of the posthumously published Hasinai book, suggests that Bolton was too busy with the move to California and his many other projects to bring the book to completion.[49] This is no doubt true, but not the entire explanation. Bolton lacked useful models for Native American history. Parkman was the most obvious precedent, but the Texas Indians did not seem to offer Parkman-like narrative possibilities, at least not to Bolton. His book reads more like descriptive anthropology than history. Bolton presents useful cultural and geographic information, but he did not figure out how to convert his ethnology into ethnohistory. In short, he did not know how to make Indians the subject of American history. Bolton was already shifting his interest toward Spanish missionaries whom he could portray in a heroic light. If missionaries were the subject of his work, Indians were the objects of the friars, so after 1914 Bolton described American Indians from the missionary perspective—as prospective converts or resistant miscreants.

Bolton's next book, *Texas in the Middle of the Eighteenth Century,* published in 1915, helps to explain his aspirations as a historian and how they might have taken him away from a career as a historian of American Indians. Like everything else that Bolton published, this book was based on meticulous archival investigation. Although some of it was published previously as journal articles, Bolton added additional information and interpretive sections. The result was not a seamless narrative, but as Bolton frankly admitted, a collection of special studies.[50] The book has useful information, but its prose may be characterized as workmanlike at best.

The preface, however, hints that Bolton had something larger in mind than reprinting his old essays. "My quest has been as romantic as the search for the Golden Fleece," he wrote. He had dug into the forgotten archives of Mexico City and a dozen Mexican state capitals, not to mention those in Texas and Louisiana. Ambassadors, secretaries of state, governors, cardinals, archbishops, and other luminaries had helped him in his work. Humble padres had given him food and shelter. Bolton's research had taken him not only to distant archives but over "hundreds of miles of old trails in . . . the Southwest, in search of topographical and archaeological data," he explained.[51] Whether by horse team, horseback, rail, or automobile Bolton had followed in the footsteps of his Spanish frontiersmen. He had found the sites of long-forgotten missions, a lost mine, and the location of La Salle's old fort on the Texas coast.[52] Bolton was not merely a historian who haunted dusty archives and wrote turgid monographs, but an explorer who searched the world for lost empires and then wrote romantic historical narrative history about his discoveries. Indoors and out, he practiced history as high adventure. His research had transformed him from a striving young professional historian into a romantic adventurer, at least in his own mind.

The chapters that followed did not measure up to Bolton's high-blooded preface. He aspired to be the Francis Parkman of the Southwest, but his literary style did not yet match Parkman's, as Bolton's most astute critic explained. Bolton often sent Turner offprints of his work and his students' as well. Turner acknowledged these publications with grace, but once responded with what seemed like critical advice. "The definiteness of information presented regarding facts of settlement[,] dates of advance, etc." astounded Turner.[53] Bolton, who could be sensitive, understood Turner's criticism: Bolton and his students were mere chroniclers who recapitulated the facts of Spanish-American history without providing critical analysis. It was dull reading, and what did it all mean? Bolton's response was defensive. He knew that his work was loaded with detail, but he thought that such densely written publications were needed to provide a "clear understanding of the Spaniards in the American west." That goal explained "the dreariness of most of what I have written," Bolton concluded.[54]

Turner waited several months to reply to Bolton, pleading the press of work at the end of the semester. When summer came, Turner explained, he had found "so fascinating a trout country in the Bitter Root Mountains that letters seemed sacrilegious!" Once he had caught enough trout to clear his mind, he informed Bolton that "there wasn't a vestige of subconscious or implied criticism in my compliments of the seminary work exhibited by your pupils and yourself." Such details were "essential," and Turner had "no doubt" of Bolton's "ability to see the forest" as well as the trees.[55]

But Turner was not through advising Bolton on matters of style and substance. After perusing *Texas in the Middle Eighteenth Century*, Turner complimented Bolton, but the book was not easy reading. "You must water your rum, and offer it in a small glass to the man who is brought up on the Parkman light wines," Turner advised. "Sometime you are going to complete your Parkman-like work," he continued, "by putting your material in a format of interpretation and generalization suited to the general reader, not for the *sake* of the general reader only, but because by doing this you will make clear to eastern and northern scholars also what a rich field you are working and what its bearings are in general American history, in the larger sense."[56] Bolton replied that he understood Turner's remark about watering the rum, but first he needed a good supply of rum. Besides, "when I have to plant the seed and grow the cane before even beginning to distil, its a slow process."

Bolton asked Turner to be patient. "I mean to live a long time yet."[57] He would remember Turner's remark about Parkman.

Bolton's growing list of publications, burgeoning reputation, and attractive personality were not enough to assure a steady stream of graduate students. They needed funding. The university provided some financial support by appointing several graduate assistants. Research in foreign archives for dissertations and for augmenting the Bancroft's collections required outside funds. Professor Stephens had foreseen the need and was already working on the problem when he was recruiting Turner in 1909.[58] Stephens convinced the Native Sons of the Golden West, a fraternal organization founded in 1875 and interested in Pacific Coast history, to establish fellowships. Sons membership had at first been limited to those born in California under the American flag, on or after July 7, 1846.[59] This restriction, which precluded membership by *californios* (Mexicans born in California before 1846), was eventually lifted, but many of the Native Sons were interested primarily in celebrating the state's Anglo-American past, the gold rush in particular.

Judge John F. Davis was a Native Son who had a much broader outlook on history. Born on Angel Island in San Francisco Bay in 1859, Judge Davis was a Roman Catholic and a Republican, a graduate of Harvard and the University of California Law School, and an active participant in state politics. He became a lawyer, then an Amador County judge, before serving in the state senate. By the time Stephens and Bolton knew him, Davis was in private practice in San Francisco. He had a deep interest in California history and was an influential member of the Native Sons and the Bohemian Club.[60] As a Catholic lawyer, judge, and politician in a state dominated by Anglo Protestants, Davis was sensitive to California's cultural currents. An admirer of author Charles F. Lummis, Davis had a particular interest in California's Spanish and Catholic heritage.[61] Bolton and Davis were natural allies.

Religion in history and at the University of California was a touchy matter, as Stephens had learned when he proposed a joint appointment with the Pacific Theological Seminary of Preserved Smith, a leading authority on Martin Luther. "But I could not get the slightest encouragement. The *odium theologicum* is too strong." In order to keep everyone happy, Stephens had "to go around and speak once a year in Catholic, Episcopal, Presbyterian, Baptist, Methodist, and Unitarian churches." If he left one of them out, "some sect" would accuse him of "sectarianism."[62] Bolton's emphasis on Spanish Catholic history ran the risk of arousing sectarian concerns.

With the strong urging of Stephens and Davis, the Native Sons funded the first traveling fellowship, which provided $1,500 for research in foreign archives.

In 1911 the group added two resident fellowships. Davis publicized these fellow-ships in a popular magazine, suggesting that some California philanthropist should permanently endow the fellowships, but that was never done.[63] Thus the fellow-ships depended on a vote at the organization's annual meeting. The Native Sons continued to provide this essential support for historical study through World War II. In his plea for fellowship funding, Davis emphasized the singularity of the missions and the gold rush as forming a heritage that made California history and Californians unique in the annals of the United States. For Davis, the sup-port of historical scholarship was no less than a sacred patriotic duty. In one essay he piously concluded that California's history should be preserved so "that our fathers' high achievement in a later day shall not be unknown to their descendants. Let us go hence with hearts courageous and minds determined, each to make good his 'full measure of devotion.' Thus, may California's story become known to all Americans, and sink into the hearts of a grateful people."[64] Judge Davis knew how to appeal to local patriotism, and Bolton congratulated him for it.[65]

President Wheeler was also thinking about sources of funding for history. In 1913 Wheeler asked Bolton for a letter describing his funding needs.[66] The pres-ident hoped to interest Edward L. Doheny, the immensely wealthy California oil man, in Bolton's plan to publish southwestern and California history.[67] At Wheeler's direction, Bolton met with Doheny and explained his request. Doheny asked Bolton to draft a letter of agreement for Doheny's signature, which was sent in April 1914. It appeared to be all but certain that Doheny would provide $50,000 over five years for collecting and publishing documents from the archives of Spain and Mexico. Bolton's former student Eddie Dunn was already on his way to Spain to head a team of American copyists.[68]

A month passed with no response from the oilman. Bolton sent a letter to Doheny ostensibly asking for information so that Wheeler could announce the gift at commencement. He signed off, "trusting that nothing will happen to pre-vent you from carrying out what would be the greatest undertaking in Western history."[69] But something had happened: the revolution had spilled on to Doheny's Mexican oil fields. "All of the American employees have been driven . . . away . . . with the result that our properties are now at the mercy of any Mexican vandal or American hater," Doheny replied. He estimated his losses at $250,000 per month. Doheny hoped for better times when he would again consider aiding Bolton.[70] Bolton would hear from Doheny again, but with a very different sort of proposal.

The revolutionary period was not a safe time for Americans to be in Mexico. Bolton family tradition includes an incident when Bolton was in an "archive near

Juarez, when Pancho Villa's Army arrived."[71] The townspeople fled, but Bolton stayed at his work. Villa's officers questioned Bolton, who responded with an appreciative lecture on the glories of Mexican history. According to the perhaps apocryphal story, the Villistas put Bolton in charge of the archives. This family account may have been somewhat embellished in the retelling, but it seems true to Bolton's character. He could speak endlessly with high enthusiasm about his subject and was always willing to work cheerfully with whomever happened to be in charge, whether it was Porfirio Díaz or Pancho Villa.

In his first few years at Berkeley Bolton established a pattern that he would maintain for decades. He kept to his rigorous schedule of research and publication and quickly established himself as the most productive member of the history department. Likewise he became the wheelhorse in the doctoral program, though Teggart no doubt thought that Bolton gained quantity by sacrificing quality (as in the case of Chapman). The production of publications and new doctors marked the University of California as an increasingly important research university, just as Wheeler and Stephens had intended. Numbers mattered, but Bolton did not invent the metrics by which institutions and professors were measured. To advance in the professional and institutional pecking orders, the university and Bolton had to keep those numbers up. For better or for worse Bolton was creating a PhD mill in Berkeley.

In late 1913 the Boltons' seventh and last child was born, the only boy. "His only handicap seems to be that they have given him my name," he informed Fred. "I wanted to give him yours, but the matter lay rather outside of my jurisdiction."[1] Now with children who ranged in age from infancy to sixteen years old, the Bolton home must have been a bustling habitation. The demands on Gertrude were especially great. Bolton's letters to his brother sometimes mentioned her ill health and general weakness.[2] The strain of bearing seven children, the last one born when she was forty-one, had taken a physical toll.

Gertrude was by no means an invalid, for she continued to run the densely populated Bolton home with the assistance of a cleaning woman. Herbert Jr. recalled his mother as a vigorous woman who was more than a match for her husband. "Dad's domesticity was limited to dressing himself." Years of living on Bolton's modest earnings had made Gertrude a careful manager of the household treasury. She used seven-and-a-half-watt lightbulbs, and resisted turning on even these dim bulbs, in order to save money. The children often wore clothes that their mother made rather than store-bought goods. "Dad was at the university so much," Herbert Jr. recalled, "that nearly all of the task of raising us fell to our mother." She settled quarrels, allotted chores, and oversaw music lessons, practice, and homework. Young Herbert remembered his father standing at the head of the dinner table carving meat: "That's a fine roast, Mama. A little more Herbert? . . . it's good. More potatoes, and peas Tootie? [sister Gertrude] Here, pass your plate."

While he served his family, Bolton incessantly spoke about history and ate heartily and quickly, usually finishing before anyone else. Then he would ask, "Mama, have I had my pie?" Within the family the Boltons were known as Big Papa and Big Mama. Bolton loved to have his family around him, "but he was always the center of attention, as he talked on-and-on."[3]

His family enjoyed, or at least humored, Bolton's long evening lectures over the carving board. They knew that he was completely engrossed with his work, though Herbert Jr. later insisted that he was an attentive father who gave each child personal attention. Nevertheless, his unusual work habits often extended to Thanksgiving and Christmas even with large family gatherings on hand. He would work at his office until dinnertime, when one of the family would pick him up. After eating and visiting for a while, Bolton would become restless. Then he would ask someone to drive him back to the university. "I've got to get back to work," he would explain. Off he went, returning home at midnight or later. He was something of an insomniac. Eventually he established his own bedroom so that he could read without disturbing Gertrude. "And so it was," young Herbert wrote, "day after day, year after year, Saturdays and Sundays and holidays included."[4] Bolton sometimes set aside time for family outings on the weekends (although he probably inwardly chafed at losing precious time in the library). Usually the trips involved a heavy dose of history. There were missions to visit and old explorers' trails to drive over.[5]

Bolton's obsessive work habits conditioned his family life, but nothing suggests that this arrangement caused unhappiness in the Bolton marriage or maladjustment in the children. Letters between Herbert, Gertrude, and the children give a picture of a busy, contented, middle-class family (if one somewhat strapped for cash and a little overeducated in history) that was headed by a strong, though somewhat distracted, father. Herbert described his father as "in charge . . . master of the house," but the most striking word he used to describe him was "gentle." The letters that passed between Herbert and Gertrude bespoke a close relationship and the sort of mutual dependency that marks a successful marriage.[6]

Still, brief family outings aside, Bolton spent most of his time at the university or on the trail of some Spanish explorer. Bolton's regimen was obsessive, almost compulsive, a work routine that might have shortchanged his family. They did not see it that way. Yet it is fair to say that Bolton's work meant more to him than anything *but* his family. His devotion to research and writing was extraordinary by any reasonable standard. The Bolton clan was proud of the family patriarch. His admiring family's complete support of his prodigious labor is one of the chief reasons Bolton was able to do so much. However, Bolton's great reputation may have taken a toll on young Herbert. A successful, commanding, and famous father can be a fearful legacy. "To live up to his example," the son observed at the age of fifty-seven, "would have been a task for a giant or a saint."[7]

When Herbert Jr. recalled his father, he looked back over a lifetime of accomplishment, recognition, and public acclaim. But during those first years in Berkeley Bolton was not yet the imminent figure he would become. Nor was he an entirely free agent. While he worked diligently on his own research and teaching, Bolton cooperated with Stephens and friends of the university and its history department. The Native Sons of the Golden West were at the center of this group. In addition to providing research funds for Cal's graduate students, the Native Sons were interested in preserving the documentary basis for California's history. Under the guidance of Judge Davis the organization lobbied the state legislature for the establishment of a California Historical Survey Commission that would identify and preserve historical sources throughout the state, especially official records in the county offices.[8] Bolton complied with Davis's many requests for letters to the legislature and governor, and the bill authorizing the commission was duly signed into law.[9]

The legislation provided for three commissioners appointed by the governor. One was to represent the Native Sons; the second would be nominated by the University of California Board of Regents; naming of the third commissioner was entirely up to the governor. Not surprisingly, the Native Sons named Judge Davis chairman. The regents recommended Bolton. The governor appointed James M. Guinn, secretary of the Southern California Historical Society, thus providing balance in a state often split along regional lines. The commission named Bolton's doctoral student Owen C. Coy as secretary and archivist.[10] Under Bolton's guidance Coy produced guides to county records that are still of value today.[11] Davis constantly goaded them to work harder and faster.[12]

In 1915 Henry Morse Stephens became the first AHA president from west of the Mississippi River. This was not only a great personal achievement but a signal that the University of California's history program should be taken seriously. His presidency coincided with the Panama-Pacific International Exposition in San Francisco, so Stephens organized a concurrent meeting of the specially created Panama-Pacific Historical Congress, which was also declared to be a special meeting of the AHA. The congress showcased the Bancroft Library, the University of California, and Pacific Coast historical scholarship. Stephens and Bolton edited a volume of essays from the Congress, *The Pacific Ocean in History*.[13] The lion's share of the editorial duties for the conference volume fell to Bolton.[14] As might be expected, the writings of Cal faculty and students dominated the book. Stephens's essay on European conflicts in the Pacific was the lead article, while Bolton contributed two articles on California and New Mexico. The volume included papers from six of Bolton's students, whose topics ranged from New Mexico to San Francisco Bay. California faculty and other participants examined the Philippines and other Pacific Ocean subjects.

The book well expressed the historical outlook of Stephens and Bolton. As Bolton explained to the dean of the graduate college, the University of California history department should emphasize the writing of the state's history. But this work "should not be interpreted too narrowly, for problems and interests are generally regional rather than intra-state." Just as Turner, who had "made one of the great advances of all time in the understanding of democratic institutions," had studied the Old Northwest at the University of Wisconsin, California should adopt a similarly broad sectional outlook. The Bancroft made it possible to study not only "California history in a limited sense, but . . . the whole American West with its Spanish and English backgrounds, and with its Pacific Ocean influences."[15] Bolton had learned well his lessons from Turner, Garrison, and Stephens. Beginning with local history and resources, historians at Wisconsin, Texas, and California widened their perspective to include ever broader historical vistas: Wisconsin and the Old Northwest; Texas and the Southwest; California and the Far West, Latin America, and the Pacific.

Turner was never far from Bolton's thoughts in his first years at Berkeley. Explaining his course on western history to his brother, Bolton wrote that he had "established a point of view which will cause a rewriting of textbooks, much as Turner's work did." Bolton thought his perspective was more expansive than Turner's. "I approach American history from a continental and European standpoint, instead of from the standpoint of England alone." Thus in Bolton's course the West got its "due prominence in the colonial period as well as in the national period."[16] He would eventually express this outlook as hemispheric history, also known as the history of the Americas.

Everything was in place for Bolton to advance in the historical profession. He had many publications, graduate students, a great library, an important position, and growing recognition, but he still stood in the shadow of Turner and the other "big men" of the profession. Bolton wanted to be on the same elevated plane with them, especially Turner. To break through, he needed two things: a signature piece of scholarship that would impress professional historians, and a popular book that would influence the general reading public. He realized both of these goals at about the same time.

His chance for a popular book came when Yale University Press announced the Chronicles of America, a series comprised of short interpretive books by leading historians. Bolton offered to write a volume on Spain, "like what Parkman did for the French."[17] The new series must have seemed the perfect opportunity for Bolton to do what Turner had suggested a few months previously, but he soon learned that it was no easy matter to write with Parkman-like grace.

Like most well-educated Americans Bolton had read Parkman, even selected his *Pontiac* for the tiny Fairchild school library when he was principal. Parkman was perhaps the greatest American narrative historian of his time or any other.[18] His ability to describe historical scenes and personalities has never been surpassed. Parkman was an obvious model for Bolton. The New England historian had written about the titanic struggle of France and England for possession of North America. Bolton's work suggested a parallel story on the English colonies' southern flank. The editors of the Chronicles series no doubt saw it that way.

Bolton wanted to write with Parkman's verve, but he did not wish to adopt the same interpretive stance. Parkman called Spain "the incubus of Europe," where a "tyranny of monks" employed "their racks, their dungeons, their fagots" to guide "the mind from infancy into those narrow depths of bigotry from which it was never to escape." Parkman's own bigotry stemmed from his origins. He was a Boston Brahmin, an upper-class New England Protestant through and through. It was only right, as far as he was concerned, to excoriate the Roman Catholic Church and the absolutist Spanish monarchy that "chilled the world with her baneful shadow."[19] Parkman's prejudices were the very ones that Bolton was determined to extirpate from American historical writing. It would not be easy. Parkman's prejudices were distributed well beyond the boundaries of New England.

The job of dealing with Bolton's Chronicles of America volume fell to series editor Allen Johnson. Johnson was the sort of "eastern and northern" scholar that Turner had in mind when he urged Bolton to write a popular account of his subject. Born in Lowell, Massachusetts, in 1870, Johnson had been educated at Amherst College, the University of Leipzig in Germany, and École Libre des Sciences Politiques in Paris before earning a PhD at Columbia University in 1899. Johnson was a professor of history at Yale University when he teamed up with publisher Robert Glasgow for the new series, which was modeled after Glasgow's successful Chronicles of Canada.[20] After the series was completed, he became the first editor of the *Dictionary of American Biography*, giving it the careful editorial attention that made it a classic reference work.[21] In sum, he was a fine writer and an able editor who would hold the Chronicles authors to the highest literary standards.[22]

When Bolton offered to write a book like Parkman's, the New Englander Johnson knew exactly what the Berkeley professor meant, and he expected Bolton to produce what he had promised. But Bolton was not an easy man to direct. He had a substantial ego and a keen sense of professional turf. Johnson, on the other hand, was even more arrogant than Bolton and not always diplomatic in his dealings with authors. Bolton would experience Johnson's withering sarcasm more than once before the book was done.

While Bolton was negotiating his contract with Johnson, he wrote an essay intended for a select scholarly audience, "The Mission as a Frontier Institution in the Spanish American Colonies."[23] This article became Bolton's signature piece, the essential distillation of fifteen years' research in the Mexican archives and the Bancroft Library. He read this essay as a faculty lecture in March 1917 and the next month sent it to Jameson for the *American Historical Review.* "It is entirely interpretative and contains no footnotes," Bolton explained. "I have the feeling, however, that it reveals the significance of the mission as no other treatment has done, and is worth publishing somewhere."[24] Jameson's 1907 AHA presidential address should have inspired confidence that the editor would want to publish Bolton's essay. Jameson had encouraged American historians to investigate the history of religion in their own country. "In every other period of recorded time, we know that the study of religion casts valuable light on many other aspects of history," Jameson wrote. "Why should it be otherwise with the religious history of America?"[25] Perhaps he thought that Bolton was just the man do it. Jameson had been prompting Bolton to send something to the *Review* for more than a year.[26]

Five weeks after Bolton submitted his essay Jameson accepted it, "with one proviso": Bolton had included "rather extravagant language regarding Professor Turner" that Jameson wished to tone down.[27] The editor suggested that the following words be substituted for Bolton's original prose:

> Professor Turner's study of the Anglo-American frontier has been richly
> rewarded. Scarcely less conspicuous in the history of the Western World than
> the advance of the Anglo-American frontier has been the spread of Spanish
> culture, and for him who should interpret, with Turner's insight, the methods
> and the significance of the Spanish-American frontier, there awaits a recogni-
> tion not less marked or less deserved.[28]

Bolton had been thinking of "just such a modification."[29] The change was published with only slight alteration.

It is remarkable that Jameson and Bolton would have published this special plea for the recognition of Bolton's contributions as being equal to Turner's. Bolton's name was not mentioned, but if the statement was not meant to apply to Bolton, then to whom? Why mention Turner's "rewards" at all? What could that word mean if not the professional status, popular acclaim, top salary, and Harvard professorship that Turner enjoyed? The meaning of the words is plain. At forty-seven years of age, Bolton still labored in the shadow of Turner and thought he deserved to be seen on the same level. Jameson, a close friend and deep admirer of Turner, thought so too, or at least he was willing to publish the words (his words) in the *Review*. There was nothing wrong in asserting the importance of Bolton's work, but the words are oddly importunate and personally comparative, more like something one would see in an extravagantly positive book review written about someone else's work. Yet there they stand, like a flag atop some newly discovered mountain emblazoned with "*I* did this!" Bolton's claim to the mountaintop was not empty rhetoric, as his essay made plain. All those years in the libraries and archives of the United States and Mexico had given him secure command of his subject. *Bolton*, with Jameson's imprimatur, was *the* authority on *this* subject.

Bolton's mission essay outlined the significance of one of Spain's frontier institutions and the pioneers who built them, but these American frontiersmen were not quite like mountain men and yeoman farmers, for their intentions were dramatically different. Missionaries intended to Christianize and acculturate, or "civilize" in Bolton's language, the American Indian population. Missionaries trained Indians in European occupations, the Spanish language, and Spanish mores as well as the Catholic religion. While admitting that the missionaries were not always successful, Bolton valorized and validated their methods and purposes. He gave no attention to what Indians may have wanted or to any negative effects that missions may have had on them. In the main, Bolton judged the missionaries to have been humane and effective exponents of European civilization and Christianity. The missionaries' goals invited comparison to Turner's frontier. "The missions were a force which made for the preservation of the Indians," Bolton argued, "as opposed to their destruction, so characteristic of the Anglo-American frontier."[30]

Not only did Bolton plead for professional recognition in Turner-like proportions, but he did it by praising a frontier institution that challenged Turner's Anglo frontier on moral grounds. At its heart, Bolton argued, the Spanish colonial experience was a religious enterprise that emphasized humanitarian values. In some ways, Bolton's frontier was the diametric opposite of Turner's. Unlike Turner's Anglo-American frontiersmen who destroyed or removed Indians, the Spanish authorities sought to incorporate native peoples in frontier communities. Bolton's frontier was racially inclusive and driven by the Spanish government as well as the Church; Turner's frontier was racially exclusive and driven by individuals. Turner saw Americans confronting challenges and abandoning or modifying European culture for a new, democratic, uniquely American way of life. Bolton found missionaries Europeanizing American Indians and America itself.

It was as if Jameson had set the stage for a discussion between Turner and Bolton about the nature and meaning of the frontier in North America. Such a debate could have been intellectually productive, but it never happened. Neither Bolton nor Turner attempted to rationalize or combine their ideas into a single coherent frontier theory. Rather, Bolton's work was regarded as a new field of study without direct connection to Turner's frontier, despite obvious temporal and geographic overlap in the region that ultimately became known as the Spanish Borderlands.[31]

The mission essay established Bolton as the unchallenged master of his field, but it did not demonstrate the relevance of his subject to U.S. history in general. His emphasis on the southern tier of states from California to Florida marginalized rather then centralized the mission story. He said that millions of Latin Americans counted former mission Indians among their ancestors, but could only identify Indians in New Mexico and California as evidence for the continuing significance of missions in the United States. Turner could easily ignore Bolton's Spanish missionaries and Indians because to him they were peripheral, but it was precisely the periphery that interested Bolton. The zone of Spanish occupation and exploration that he described required his reconnaissance on both sides of the border. He had become a border crosser, a transnational figure in a liminal space of his own design.

Jameson admired Bolton's essay, but he was astonished when Bolton requested six hundred reprints of the article. As a rule the journal provided the author with twenty-five reprints gratis but charged for additional copies. Six hundred copies was unheard of.[32] Bolton explained that Edward J. Hanna, the archbishop of San Francisco wanted five hundred, presumably for distribution among interested Catholics.[33]

Archbishop Hanna's interest in Bolton's article is not surprising. In an age when Catholics were only beginning to gain acceptance as Americans, Bolton's assessment of missionaries as "American frontiersmen, and magnificent examples of the breed," was welcome indeed.[34] Thus began Hanna's friendship and support for Bolton's work. Hanna sometimes invited Bolton to dinner in San Francisco.

"While you smoke we may catch a gleam of wisdom through the haze," Hanna wrote in one invitation. The archbishop also provided some financial aid for Bolton's work, though the extent is unclear. "This little mite," Hanna vaguely explained in a note that must have accompanied a check, "to help your great work in behalf of our South West." As far as the prelate was concerned, Bolton's history, "in a way so perfect," gave "true views of the past."[35]

Bolton's reputation had become big. His success attracted the attention of leading historians, who wondered if Bolton could be attracted to their institutions. Not long after Bolton's mission essay appeared, William E. Dodd sent out a feeler asking if Bolton might move to the University of Chicago. Bolton was interested and suggested an entirely new course, the history of the Western Hemisphere. Andrew McLaughlin of Chicago followed up. He thought that Bolton's proposed course—"*in the large*—would be very interesting." But the United States had entered World War I, and that stalled hiring at Chicago. Could Bolton come to Chicago for part of the year in 1919? If so, perhaps a permanent arrangement could be made once the war was over. Bolton replied that his situation was "so pleasant" at Berkeley that he could "with a fair degree of contentment await developments" in Chicago.[36] After Bolton consulted with Stephens and President Wheeler about a temporary assignment and the possibility of a permanent opening in Chicago, he decided against going on a temporary basis. He blamed the decision on wartime dislocations and left the door open for future negotiations.[37] The courtship between Bolton and Chicago went on for two years. It was reminiscent of Turner's dance with Cal and Stanford. McLaughlin was not able to come up with the money for Bolton, but eventually was able to hire one of Bolton's new doctors, J. Fred Rippy.[38]

Early during the war a tragic death gave Bolton an unexpected opportunity to extend his influence in the public sphere. He had sent Leslie Albright, one of his doctoral students, as a Native Sons Fellow to work in the archives in Seville Spain. Within a short time Albright contracted typhoid and died an agonizing death.[39] It fell to Bolton to arrange for the shipment of Albright's effects to his next of kin, Horace Albright, acting director of the newly created National Park Service.[40] Horace Albright was a Cal graduate (class of 1912), as were many other early park service officials.[41] "I want to know you better because you were my brother's teacher and friend," Albright explained, "and also because, in your own line of work, you are doing a great service to the West." The park service had charge of the national monuments, which had historical significance.[42] "For instance, Father Kino's old mission, Tumacacori, is under our jurisdiction. Also Morro Rock, or

'Inscription Rock' in New Mexico. I want to find out how we can fit our work in with yours."[43]

"You may be interested to know," Bolton replied, "that I am just now bringing out a two volume work on Father Kino in the Arizona and Sonora region."[44] During the early seventeenth century Eusebio Kino, a Jesuit missionary, had founded Tumacacori, San Xavier del Bac, and Guevavi and explored places within the jurisdiction of the park service. "It is quite possible that I could help you materially in some aspects of your work, and that, on the other hand, you might assist me." Bolton was working on other Spanish explorers associated with the national parks and monuments. Perhaps, he told Albright, "our interests could be combined."[45]

Bolton's correspondence with Albright was the beginning of a close working relationship with the National Park Service. Bolton sometimes received remuneration for advising park service personnel, and he got material assistance from, as well as special access to, the parks and monuments in the Southwest. In 1924 NPS director Stephen Mather appointed Bolton "Special Agent of the National Park Service in connection with your work in the Southwest."[46]

Bolton's relationship with the park service was important. It gave him quasi-official status when he investigated historic trails and sites on federal lands. Through his friendships with important people in the federal government, Bolton's work became widely known among officials who made decisions about historic sites. Bolton's interpretation of Spanish Borderlands is implicit in the national monuments today. His recommendations for employment were respected and often favorably acted upon. This gave him an important source of patronage for his students, especially during the Great Depression when academic employment dried up. As his students moved up the ladder in the federal bureaucracy, Bolton's reputation and influence grew accordingly. These relationships helped Bolton to forge a professional empire that extended far beyond academe.

Meanwhile, Bolton extended his reach within the university. The Bancroft Library was his research home, but the curator, Frederick Teggart, was its master. At first Bolton worked closely with Teggart. They even co-wrote an elementary-level history of California, which was rejected by the Board of Education in 1915.[47] Teggart was a difficult man to get along with. One source of contention was Teggart's control of the Bancroft. Bolton had placed his Mexican manuscripts there for convenience and safekeeping, but Teggart treated these papers as if they belonged to the library. He went so far as to make it difficult for Bolton to access them. One Saturday afternoon in 1915 Professor John Van Nostrand happened to overhear the rising voices of Bolton and Teggart in the history department offices. Teggart insisted that as curator he had the authority to keep Bolton out of the Bancroft whenever he pleased. Bolton threatened to knock Teggart's false teeth down his throat if he tried it.[48] Happily, the two men parted without exchanging blows, but this verbal fight no doubt put an end to thoughts of any further collaboration on a book for school children.

Feuding with Bolton was foolish. With the help of Judge Davis, Bolton was emerging as a public figure in the state. His academic accomplishments helped to elevate the reputation of Cal among academics throughout the United States. President Wheeler and Stephens would have no choice but to side with Bolton in any controversy with Teggart that came under their purview.

Without an advanced degree, Teggart represented an older generation of autodidactic university professors who were being steadily phased out of regular faculty positions at Berkeley and elsewhere. Realizing this, Teggart and Stephens agreed that the curator should obtain the doctorate so that he would have the bona fides required of professors in the modern era of academic professionalization. They also agreed that if Teggart published a book that satisfied the requirements for the PhD in history, the University of California would confer the degree under Stephens's mentorship. However, when Teggart published *Prolegomena to History: The Relationship of History to Literature, Philosophy, and Science* in 1916, Stephens reneged on his promise to approve Teggart's book as a dissertation. Many years later Mrs. Teggart said that nothing in forty years of marriage matched her husband's "fury and bitterness" at Stephens's treachery.[49]

By late fall Bolton replaced Teggart as curator, with Bolton's student Herbert Ingram Priestley continuing as assistant curator.[50] In 1917 Teggart was moved out of the history department. Although he continued to teach a history course, he was a man without a department. In 1918 he left Berkeley to help philosophers John Dewey and Arthur Lovejoy establish the American Association of University Professors at Johns Hopkins University. Of course, President Wheeler participated in these personnel decisions. Hoping that Teggart would find permanent employment in the East, he approved a one-year "nominal" appointment without pay.[51]

Stephens, following the time-honored pattern of strongly recommending a despised colleague for employment elsewhere, plumped Teggart to Jameson for a permanent job as a bibliographer in Washington. "I believe him to be the very best man in the whole United States to undertake a job of the kind he contemplates with headquarters in Washington," he wrote, adding that he was better trained for such a job than "for anything else." Alas for Stephens, Jameson was not optimistic about Teggart's chances for a post in Washington.[52] Jameson's assessment of Teggart's job prospects was not an accurate barometer of professional respect for Teggart's published work. The book that Stephens would not accept for a dissertation was widely admired on the East Coast and in Europe. The founders of the *New Republic* honored him with a luncheon, where (characteristically) Teggart criticized the editors for publishing a *"Journal of Opinion"* instead of "knowledge." Indeed, Teggart turned down offers to teach at eastern universities, including Johns Hopkins, because he preferred to return to Berkeley, where he was not wanted.[53]

Teggart's ouster occurred just as the United States was about to enter the world war. University enrollments declined because of military enlistments, while course offerings were reduced because faculty took military assignments or civilian war work. Even the forty-eight-year-old Bolton considered leaving the university to help the war effort in diplomatic service or for the National Board of Historical Service, a group that included Turner and produced propaganda.[54] Bolton finally decided to stay at Berkeley because he could not support his large family on the salary the board offered.[55]

Bolton got his share of patriotic work at home. The university formed the War History Committee, which Bolton chaired. The committee was supposed to gather and preserve the records of servicemen and civilian war workers who were associated with the university. He also served in the war cabinet of the State Council of Defense.[56] Bolton's war work brought him into contact with Edward A. Dickson, a hard-charging member of the Board of Regents.[57] Probably at Dickson's insistence, the War History Committee work was added to the California Historical Survey Commission, headed by Judge Davis and Bolton with Coy as their field man, and this brought Bolton into uncomfortably close contact with the regent. Born in Wisconsin in 1879, Dickson had been raised in California, graduated from Cal, and worked for the *Los Angeles Express*. He eventually acquired the *Express* and had important banking interests as well. Dickson cofounded the Lincoln-Roosevelt League, which was instrumental in the election of Hiram Johnson to the state governorship. In 1913 Governor Johnson appointed Dickson to the University of California Board of Regents. He was a primary moving force in converting the Los Angeles State Normal School into the full-fledged University of California campus now known as UCLA.[58]

Regent Dickson was imperious and insistent in his dealings with Bolton. As far as Dickson was concerned, he was Bolton's boss and the professor should act accordingly. He thought writing history was essentially a clerical task that any good secretary could do. Consequently he arranged for the appointment of Southern Californian Genevieve Ambrose, finagled office space for her at Berkeley, and told her to go to work. Dickson's meddling caused trouble. There was no provision in the state budget for Ambrose's salary, so Bolton and some members of the Native Sons actually had to arrange for a bank loan in order to carry on the war work.[59] Dickson wrote to Bolton demanding that Ambrose be placed "in charge of the historical department, giving her a change in status which will automatically carry a salary."[60] Such an arrangement would make Ambrose, who was essentially a clerk with no historical training, the supervisor of Coy and perhaps even Bolton as far as the war work was concerned. This seemed a bit high-handed (not to mention insulting), and Bolton resisted. It did not matter to Dickson that Bolton and Coy would be responsible for writing the history of California's participation in the war, or that it made no sense that with Ambrose in charge they would not be involved in the selection of historical materials on which they would rely. Ambrose, Dickson argued, would make more efficient decisions.[61]

This arrangement did not work out. The added war duties interfered with the commission's original obligation to preserve historical archives. The state legislature did not provide adequate funds to support the work that Dickson had envisioned. Ambrose proved incapable of writing some of the basic reports that had been assigned to her, so Dickson asked Bolton to put more of his time toward war work. The war project eventually died for lack of funding. In the meantime, however, Bolton was harassed on all sides. "You, with your kindly urgency regarding the Missions," Bolton drily explained to Judge Davis, "and Dickson's solicitude that I take the war work of the Commission under my personal charge, are highly flattering to an humble person like myself, but I hope you will not forget that I am Professor of History, Curator of the Bancroft Library, Chairman of several University Committees, Editor of two series of University Publications and Co-Editor of two Historical Magazines, and that there are only twenty-four hours in the average Berkeley day."[62] Eventually the war work went away, but Dickson did not. He remained on the Board of Regents until his death in 1956. In the 1940s Bolton and Dickson would find themselves working at cross-purposes once again.

While Bolton, Dickson, Ambrose, and Coy fought the war at home, Edward Doheny saw the conflict as an opportunity to forward his interests in Mexico. When the war was over, perhaps President Woodrow Wilson's interventionist thinking could be concentrated on the problem of Mexico and petroleum. Maybe

Bolton and other scholars could help. "For 30 years I have had association with Mexicans," the oil baron told Bolton. Most of them were "worthy people . . . capable of gradual development into industrious, self-governing communities." Doheny wanted "to see gathered by scientifically trained persons all the facts which have to do with the industrial and social life of Mexicans." The ultimate purpose of this enterprise would be to present "a comprehensive and interesting statement, which may be presented to the President of the United States, . . . together with practical suggestions as to the ways in which the people and government of the United States can best aid Mexico . . . to realize an orderly industrial state." Doheny's scholars would also produce a book for popular consumption and publish source materials. "I offer to provide $100,000 to conduct the work I have indicated," Doheny concluded.[63]

Doheny hoped at one stroke to co-opt academe, influence the federal government, and shape popular opinion. It was an expensive scheme, but if it all worked out, it would be worth it. While he claimed that he wished to safeguard Mexicans from exploitation and oppression, Doheny was primarily interested in protecting his own interests in Mexico through U.S. intervention. Nevertheless, President Wheeler approved Doheny's plan, and the Board of Regents provided office space at Berkeley for the Doheny Foundation. The reasons for the regents' enthusiasm are easily found in the agreement that enjoined George W. Scott, the head of the Doheny Foundation, "do all in his power to provide a fund for the development and maintenance of the Bancroft Library in order that it might be brought to the desired usefulness and efficiency."[64] Here was the potential source of the large private endowment that Stephens, Bolton, and Wheeler had been looking for. Bolton and Bernard Moses represented the university and served on the foundation's executive committee.[65] The university appointed twenty research associates (mostly from outside the university) and gave Professor Priestley a temporary leave to do foundation work in Los Angeles.

Nothing worked out as planned. Scott proved to be disorganized and made unwarranted demands on Priestley.[66] The hope that twenty academics from widely scattered places would work harmoniously proved illusory. Far from providing riches for the Bancroft, the Doheny Foundation funded only a few small projects for less than $3,000.[67] Out of spite, Scott even refused to pay one of the research associates for his work, a willful act that brought down the wrath of Professor Moses and the monitory attention of a university lawyer. With the war's end, it became clear to Doheny that Wilson would not undertake a new adventure in Mexico. The Doheny Foundation faded away, but Bolton remained hopeful. In

1920 he reminded Doheny of his promise to provide $50,000 for Bolton's work over a period of five years. "I trust that we can proceed at once with the first $10,000," Bolton wrote to his presumed benefactor.[68] But the money (or even a response) never came.

Doheny's failure to become a major donor to Cal came just when the university lost one of its greatest patrons. In April 1919 Phoebe Apperson Hearst died. A large group of faculty and administrators attended her funeral in San Francisco. Stephens, Bolton, and other historians paid their respects. Stephens had been in poor health for some time. After the services he sat with Dean Walter Morris Hart on the cable car to the ferry building. The two men chatted about the beauty of the words in the Episcopalian service conducted for Hearst. Suddenly Stephens swayed and fell away from Hart. He gasped a few times and then was still. Stephens was dead.[69]

Stephens had sensed that he did not have long to live. A few weeks before his death he had written instructions for memorial services to be held in Faculty Glade "without fuss and feathers, and as cheaply as possible." It was as he had wished. An academic procession entered the glade, where attendees heard the beautiful words of the Episcopalian rite that Stephens had so warmly admired a few days before. After a reading of selected psalms, someone read "Lead Kindly Light," which was then echoed by the carillon in the Campanile. A solemn recessional heralded the end of the ceremony. Henry Morse Stephens, founder of Berkeley's first nationally respected history department, a man of letters who circulated among California's elite, tirelessly advocating for the university and historical studies, the one who was most responsible for the acquisition of the Bancroft Library and the hiring of Bolton, was gone. He left a large institutional inheritance at the University of California. Bolton was the principal heir.

Thanks to Stephens the Bancroft Library and Cal were now synonymous with historical scholarship in California. Indeed, Berkeley was the only practical place to study history in the state, but this situation was about to change. Henry E. Huntington, formerly of San Francisco but reestablished in the Los Angeles area, had become a very serious collector of art, rare books, and manuscripts. Like his uncle Collis of the Southern Pacific Railroad, Huntington had made his money in railroads. Henry expected to take control of the Southern Pacific when Collis died, but other investors prevented it. Consequently Huntington sold his shares to E. A. Harriman, the SP's most determined rival. In Southern California Huntington invested his considerable wealth in interurban railroads and real estate development, a winning combination that further enhanced his fortune. Huntington used some of his money to purchase books—and not just books, but whole libraries. He dominated the world's rare-book market from 1911 to 1926. He was an Anglophile and his taste in books and art reflected his preferences. By 1919 he possessed one of the most remarkable collections of rare books in the world, and it was still growing. For several years he had been discussing the fate of the library with trusted friends. George Ellery Hale, the famous Cal Tech astronomer, convinced him to endow an independent research library at Huntington's ranch in San Marino that would be open to the public, at least to the select public of qualified researchers. In 1919 Huntington's lawyer drew up an instrument that provided for the creation and maintenance of a library, art gallery, museum, and park for the public. It was a grand idea, but making it so was not easy. Years would pass before the library was open to researchers.[70]

Bolton had hoped that Huntington would give his collection to the University of California, but at least the new library would be open to scholars.[71] Perhaps Huntington could aid the university in other ways. In 1919 Bolton visited Huntington at his mansion to explain the needs of the Bancroft. Huntington did not contribute money to the Bancroft, but he and his staff cooperated with Bolton and the Bancroft by granting access to Cal researchers and loaning rare documents. Occasional institutional conflicts were unavoidable when the two libraries competed for new acquisitions. The chronically underfunded Bancroft was almost always at a disadvantage.[72] So it was that the two libraries emerged as friendly competitors. In some areas their collections overlapped, but in other ways California's great libraries were quite different. One institution was public, underfunded, and devoted primarily to the Spanish Borderlands, Latin America, California, and the West. The other was privately financed, was comparatively rich, and specialized in England and Anglo-America, California, and the West. Just as the Bancroft was made for Bolton, the Huntington reflected the outlook and interests of Turner. In time the Huntington would lure Turner just as the Bancroft had attracted Bolton.

SEVEN

· Teachers and Students—
Worlds Apart

When Bolton took over the Berkeley history department, he was in the midst of a period of writing that began with *Athanase de Mézières* in 1914 and culminated in the publication of *The Spanish Borderlands* in 1921. During this highly productive time Bolton solidified his position as the preeminent historian in his field while developing hemispheric history as an undergraduate course that extended his thinking about borderlands and American history. He did these things amidst the multitasking environment of the department, the Bancroft Library, the university, and graduate mentorship.

"There was but one Stephens and no one can ever fill his place," Bolton wrote to Turner.[1] Nevertheless, President Wheeler gave Bolton a temporary appointment as department chair. As far as the history faculty were concerned, there was no question about who should get the position. The entire department had asked him to serve permanently. Bolton claimed that he did not care if he got the chairmanship, "because my position will continue to be the most important in the department, *as it has always been.*" Bolton had good reasons for believing that he was the top dog. With Teggart gone, he controlled the Bancroft and had the most graduate students. Eleven of the fourteen Berkeley history PhDs had studied under Bolton since 1911, and he had more MA students than the rest of the department put together. He was also chairman of the university board of research and of the editorial board of the university press, which published the monographic studies of the faculty as well as some graduate theses. He also served as coeditor of the

Southwestern Historical Quarterly and as advisory editor of the *Hispanic American Historical Review*. He claimed that his position was "the most important (in history) west of Chicago or even Columbia," a calculation that placed Turner just east of the meridian of demarcation. It did not matter who became the administrative head of the Berkeley department. "It is productive work and graduate students that count most, and here at California this tendency will be fostered more and more."[2]

Bolton, now forty-nine years old, considered himself one of the top history professors in the country. Given the standards that he used—active research, publications, training of graduates, influence in the university and the profession—it was hard to argue with his logic. Bolton perhaps overstated his national reputation, but his judgment about who ran things in Berkeley was undoubtedly correct. In August the regents made his appointment permanent. Now Bolton truly held the keys to the Bancroft and made it his personal research kingdom. As department head (or chairman) he appointed summer school teachers, recommended new faculty to the president, and controlled the history budget, curriculum, and faculty teaching assignments, not to mention the appointment and distribution of graduate assistants and fellowships. With only temporary interruptions for leaves he would head the department and direct the Bancroft until his retirement twenty-one years later.

Chairman Bolton immediately began to think about reorganizing the undergraduate history curriculum. During Stephens's regime he had taught undergraduate courses on Spain in North America, the Southwest under Spain, and the history of the trans-Mississippi West, as well as graduate seminars in these subjects.[3] Stephens had taught History 1, the popular broad survey of Europe that had been the freshman introduction to history. No one could match the verve and drama of Stephens's presentations, so Bolton eliminated History 1 and substituted a more restricted European survey. He added a new, two-semester class that he would teach, History 8, "a lower division course of wide sweep, covering the 'History of the Americas,' from pole to pole and from Columbus to now." History 8 would be "an entirely new venture in the country and in the world," he explained to Fred. "I shall probably have 300 students in it."[4]

The History of the Americas became Bolton's signature course at Berkeley. He had been thinking about it for a while, even proposed it when he considered moving to the University of Chicago. It was a logical outgrowth of his work on the borderlands, which required him to understand both sides of the border. Bolton subordinated national histories, including the history of the United States, to the general story of the Western Hemisphere—the same concept that Stephens had applied to Europe in History 1. At Berkeley national histories would be taught to upperclassmen after they had taken the basic hemispheric course. Bolton believed this idea made sense not only in California, with its Hispanic heritage, but also for every American university. It was a large, revisionist idea at the time, and Bolton thought his pedagogic rationale unassailable. His course was immediately popular at Berkeley. More than seven hundred students enrolled in the fall of 1919. The next semester, more than twelve hundred showed up in Wheeler Auditorium. There were not enough chairs for them. He continued to draw superenrollments for the rest of his career. It helped that the course was required for history majors until 1933, but its popularity extended across disciplinary boundaries. History 8 was a fundamental part of Cal students' university education for decades. Scores of Berkeley doctoral students learned how to teach the course by watching and assisting the master in the classroom. Bolton's History of the Americas was the core course that defined the California school of history, as it was commonly called, from 1919 through the end of World War II.[5] Bolton continued to teach the history of the American West for upperclassmen. Priestley and Chapman taught courses on Mexico, Latin America, and California.

The outlook of the California school was hemispheric, but it looked out from California. This prospect pleased at least some university constituents—local patriots like Native Son Judge Davis—because it placed the Golden State on the world stage. Thus Bolton's curricular administration yielded the bonus of enhanced local support. From a purely pedagogical perspective Bolton thought the curriculum offered fresh new insight into the history of the United States as well as the Americas; but some people thought that the California school simultaneously gave too much attention to Spanish America as well as California and regional concerns. Teggart had returned to Berkeley for a one-year appointment in 1921. His tenuous status did not keep him from attacking Bolton's plan for history at the University of California. Much trouble had arisen, he argued, "owing to the conflict of interest between 'History' as a University study, and 'History' as a representative of local patriotisms." The problem was that while thousands of students took history courses at Berkeley, they knew little about European history. "No one, I think, . . . would dream that any amount of 'Spanish-American' history would constitute a proper training in the subject known everywhere as 'History.'"[6] Teggart recommended the establishment of a local history unit separate from the history department that presumably would reemphasize Europe. Thus he would divide and diminish Bolton's empire.

University administrators heard Teggart's criticism and questioned Bolton's ideas about history department staffing and curriculum.[7] In the end Bolton had his way because the quantitative results were hard to argue with. In the early 1920s the University of California history department became the sixth-largest graduate program in the country behind Columbia, Chicago, Harvard, Pennsylvania, and Wisconsin.[8] Nearly three-quarters of Cal students studied American history, most of them under Bolton. It was easy for him to demonstrate that his department was a success on every level and to discount critics like Teggart.

The placement of doctoral students in professorial chairs was one of the marks of Bolton's growing professional power. His students were most successful in winning positions in the Southwest, as might be expected. They were especially popular at the University of Texas. Dunn, once he finished his degree at Columbia, took a position at Texas, where he had begun his studies with Bolton. Charles Cunningham, a Cal PhD, soon joined him. Cunningham was Teggart's doctoral student, but they had a falling out. Consequently Cunningham asked Bolton to recommend him for teaching positions, which he did.[9] A third Bolton student, Charles Wilson Hackett began teaching at Texas in 1919, but his unusual path to a Texas professorship revealed strains between teachers and students who were all striving to achieve professional success.

Hackett had begun his studies with Bolton in Austin, followed him to Stanford, and finished at Berkeley. He wanted a job at Texas, but Cunningham got it. In 1918 Bolton urged Hackett to take a position at the University of New Mexico, so in September Hackett bundled his wife and infant daughter into his old car and headed for Albuquerque—a daunting automobile journey across deserts and mountains on unpaved roads. Charles Hackett's first impression of Albuquerque and the university was decidedly negative. The worst thing was the prevalence of tubercular victims who lived in Albuquerque because of the climate's supposed recuperative qualities. He begged Bolton to find him another place.[10]

Before Bolton could act, Hackett abruptly resigned and fled with his family to Texas.[11] The department chair, Bolton's old friend Eugene C. Barker, liked Hackett and thought he was a good teacher, but could not give him a permanent position, because Dunn and Cunningham were already there. The university was recovering from a political crisis. Governor James Ferguson had attempted to fire several faculty who were not to his liking, thus creating a national uproar over security of tenure.[12] Ultimately the legislature impeached Ferguson and he was removed from office, but the episode thrust the university into a prolonged political fight that included considerations of faculty religious affiliation as well as their political leanings.[13] Under the circumstances, Barker simply did not know if he would have funds to hire Hackett.[14]

So Hackett hung on as a temporary instructor, resenting Dunn and Cunningham, whose position he thought he should have had in the first place. His resentment boiled over in a letter to Bolton. He claimed that Cunningham and Dunn were disloyal to Bolton. Dunn looked upon Bolton as "hopelessly provincial" because he had not personally researched the Spanish archives. Dunn "tried to knife you," Hackett claimed, in his recent review of Bolton's *Texas in the Middle Eighteenth Century,* because Bolton had not used Spanish documents that had recently become available.[15] Dunn's antipathy toward Bolton had led him to support the hiring of Cunningham instead of Hackett in 1917. Cunningham believed that Bolton's letter had landed him the job. "So as I see it your archenemy, Dunn, promoted a man who had no claim on the place, and you backed him at a time when I had no job." What could other Texas students hope for "if I, a Texan, after working and coming up with the goods, have to be skuttled *[sic]* for a boob like Cunningham." Meanwhile Dunn and Cunningham, who "hate you like a snake," enjoyed the fruits provided by good tax-paying Texans like Hackett. He went on in this vein for twelve handwritten pages.[16]

Bolton, who must have been taken aback by Hackett's vituperative letter, mildly replied that he had Hackett's interest at heart.[17] Of course, he could not tell him that Barker was keeping him informed of Hackett's prospects at Texas.[18] By January 1920 it was becoming clear that Dunn was going to leave the university for government or newspaper work. Cunningham too would leave the history department, so Hackett would finally get his chance for a permanent slot. "We will take care of Hackett in any . . . arrangement that we may finally make," Barker promised Bolton. In the meantime Barker had to figure out how to keep Hackett and another new instructor, who was "worth more potentially to the department than Hackett."[19] The instructor's name was Walter Prescott Webb, who would more than justify Barker's faith in him.

Hackett's claims about Dunn were not entirely a surprise to Bolton. Dunn, whose dissertation was on Spanish Texas, thought that he and Bolton were bound to become rivals in the field, but he had a plan to prevent this competition from becoming unfriendly. He suggested that he and Bolton divide the field between them and coauthor a documentary history of Spanish Texas. Such an arrangement would be fair to both parties, Dunn thought.[20] Dunn's letter must have come as a rude surprise to Bolton, who had done everything he could to help Dunn. Now his very junior protégé wanted to share Bolton's glory. Bolton tactfully declined to divide the field.[21] Dunn did not take the hint and continued to press Bolton on a cooperative project. Finally, Bolton agreed to work with Dunn, perhaps because he had thousands of documents from Seville that Bolton wanted for the Bancroft.[22] Whatever the case may have been, the projected work never came to fruition, but Bolton got his documents.

The conflicts among Bolton and his graduate students were in themselves insignificant, but they illustrate the stresses of graduate study and graduate teaching and mentoring. Bolton had considered Dunn one of his most promising students and a good friend. Yet their relationship was inherently unequal. Bolton was the patriarch of a growing academic empire; Dunn, one of Bolton's many minions. Just as Bolton dared to be regarded as Turner's equal, Dunn wished to reconfigure his relationship with Bolton on a basis of equality. Mentor–graduate student relationships are often fraught with disparities of power, knowledge, ambition, and accomplishment. Such relationships can be ambivalent and volatile, as in the cases of Dunn, Cunningham, and Hackett.

The Turners and Boltons of the world were the great role models for graduate students. Ambitious students sought to match the accomplishments of their academic patriarchs. Dunn's solution for the Oedipal dilemma was to share Bolton's kingdom. His directness was extraordinary, but the problem that Dunn described was the common one. How does one break free and establish a professional identity that is not merely a function of one's teacher? Given his relationship with Turner, this was an issue that Bolton must have understood implicitly. In the end he decided to patch things up with Dunn by agreeing in principal (however insincerely) to divide the kingdom by coauthoring a book with him. They did not write the book, but to the credit of both men, they restored their friendship, which lasted for the rest of Bolton's long life.

Hackett and Bolton also remained friends, but in 1920 he was not the only graduate student of Bolton's who was unhappy with his mentor. In 1920 Bolton published *The Colonization of North America, 1492–1783* with his former student Thomas Maitland Marshall, who taught at Washington University in St. Louis.[23] Although not intended as a complete text for History 8, it was organized along the lines of the Americas course. All the European colonizing nations were presented. British colonial and United States history was presented as one experience among many, although the Revolution turned out to be the crowning moment in the Bolton and Marshall volume. The collaborators disagreed over matters of style. Marshall preferred a "pleasing presentation" over excessive detail. Whatever literary shortcomings the coauthored book had, Marshall strongly believed, belonged entirely to Bolton. One of the first reviews knocked the book for its turgid style. "It is a bit nasty to say that I told you so," Marshall wrote, "but such is the case." They had planned a second volume on South America, but Marshall was not convinced that they should go ahead. "I am giving you the opportunity of severing the connection," he explained. "Compromises are seldom satisfactory, as is shown by the criticisms of the first volume," which were "along the very lines where we disagreed." Aware that his letter had a disagreeable tone, Marshall closed by assuring Bolton that he "didn't have cactus for breakfast."[24]

On the whole the book was well received by reviewers, but placing the colonial history of the United States in the context of the multinational history of North America was new and unfamiliar. One of Bolton's peers, Frederic Logan Paxson, who occupied Turner's old chair at the University of Wisconsin, summed up the strengths and weaknesses of the book. "I think you are well within the truth in saying that the book gives a 'shock to some old traditions,'" Paxson admitted to Bolton. While the book succeeded "admirably" in revealing United States history through a wide-angle lens that incorporated all of the European powers and their colonies, Paxson was not certain that it met the needs of college teachers. "You have created a new subject rather than elaborated a subject already taught in American universities." Paxson doubted whether most universities would "teach the whole field of colonial history, interesting and valuable as it is." He also worried that from the standpoint of U.S. history "the thing we are driving at" would be "broadened and changed in its proportions." As far as Paxson was concerned, the elaborate treatment of Latin America was "somewhat aside the mark."[25]

Paxson's reservations revealed the essential problems that many history professors had with Bolton's Americas concept. The broad comparative courses that Bolton envisioned necessarily made the British colonies and the United States less central in the general scheme of things. Professors would have to retool by learning more about Spain, Portugal, France, Sweden, and the Netherlands. There was something vaguely subversive about insisting that the United States should be seen as one among many former European colonies. What was Paxson "driving at?" While he had trained under McMaster at Penn, Paxson was a thoroughgoing Turnerian. It was a large enough revision of American history to incorporate western states and territories in the national narrative. Adding Spain and all the rest was too much. It would be better to concentrate on the true engine of American development, free land and frontier institutions.[26] Years later, when Bolton was considering adding Paxson to the Berkeley faculty, he would have done well to reread Paxson's letter from 1920.

The literary criticism from Marshall and substantive criticism from Paxson were not markedly different from that of Chronicles of America series editor Allen Johnson, who had rejected Bolton's early drafts for the series. Bolton disappointed Johnson not only on matters of style but on punctuality. Even though Bolton had promised to give priority to the Chronicles series, he was working on several other projects, including *Kino's Historical Memoir of Pimería Alta*, the *Colonization* book with Marshall, plus nine articles.[27] All of these publications came out during the years when Bolton was working on his still-unnamed contribution to the Chronicles.

The Kino volume was the most troublesome of Bolton's other publishing ventures. He quarreled with Arthur H. Clark, the publisher, who eventually sued Bolton for costs incurred due to delays and Bolton's ceaseless revisions. Eventually the case was dropped.[28] All of this took time away from the Chronicles.

In the meantime Bolton seemed to lavish time and attention on *Kino*, which involved archival and trail research. For the rest of his life Bolton would combine exhaustive documentary work with personal inspections of historic sites and explorers' routes. As Bolton stated in his biography of Kino, he "retraced nearly all his endless trails and identified most of his campsites and water holes—all this in an effort to see Kino's world as Kino saw it."[29] In following the trails of Kino and others, sleeping on the ground at their campsites, eating trail rations, and smoking by the campfire, Bolton came to fully identify with his subjects. His perspective won many admirers, but it would also mark his work as a kind of hero worship that would not ring true in the post–World War II era.

As with *Athanase de Mézières* Bolton drew an oversized map with remarkable ethnogeographical details. Like the Texas chart, his "Map of Pimería Alta" implied a transnational and multicultural history. It identified general tribal areas and dozens of specific Indian communities as well as the locations of Spanish missions and *visitas*, places where Kino occasionally preached. Bolton traced the routes for thirty-six of Kino's journeys out of Mexico north to the Gila River in Arizona and west to the Colorado River. The trails make a pattern like a gnarled ironwood tree spreading across the Sonoran Desert. Bolton did not bother to include the international boundary between the United States and Mexico, a lapse that reinforced the impermanence of national borders even though Kino's travels spanned modern national boundaries and, in Bolton's point of view, perhaps transcended them. By following and interpreting Kino's trails, Bolton himself became a transnational figure—a historian of Native America, Spain, and Mexico as well as the United States.

But Bolton had not forgotten the interpretive devices of the United States. He marked an east-to-west line of "Frontier Settlement When Kino Arrived in 1687," which illustrated Kino's contribution to the spread of European civilization, as Bolton described it—or Spanish colonial conquest, as it is understood by others. The line of settlement declared Bolton's loyalty to Turner's concept of a moving frontier. Turner's line moved west; Bolton's line moved north. Eventually the lines would converge.

Bolton's boots-on-the-ground history set him apart from Turner. Turner loved the outdoors and could write about the environment in beautifully descriptive, emotive language, as when he described the Grand Canyon for a friend. "We saw the world made at sunrise yesterday," he wrote. It was nothing less "than the unfolding of the dark chaos into the form and color of the Grand Canyon's gigantic occupants."[30] But Turner reserved these word pictures for his personal letters. For him outdoor life was about recreation, not academic work. It is doubtful that Turner influenced Bolton's trailside history; perhaps McMaster was a source of inspiration. McMaster's early career as a surveyor of Civil War battlefields and a Princeton bone hunter in the West may have crept into his teaching and casual conversation at Penn in the 1890s. If so, Bolton never mentioned it in his letters.

The most likely model for Bolton's fieldwork was a man he never met, Francis Parkman. Parkman was not only a great narrative stylist but a devoted field researcher who examined every scene of historical action in his books. "In short," Parkman explained, he studied his subject "as much from life and in the open air as at the library table."[31] Parkman's field research enabled him to reconstruct stirring scenes of the struggle between France, England, and Indians in North America with almost "novelistic perfection," as historian Wilbur Jacobs put it.[32]

Parkman sometimes used his personal adventures as a basis for describing the acts of historical figures. Once he made a dangerous climb up a rocky canyon and then used that experience to describe the British assent to the Plains of Abraham in *Montcalm and Wolfe*. Parkman performed other feats of derring-do that found their way into his writings. Jacobs perceptively characterized Parkman's extension of his own experiences into his descriptive prose as a form of narcissism. Thus Parkman became the historian as hero.[33]

Bolton aspired to Parkman's artistic prowess and to the supposed authenticity that the Brahmin's field research gave his work. He did not go to Parkman's extreme of self-modeling, but Bolton did put himself in the picture by emphasizing that he had replicated the exploits of his heroes, an achievement diminished only slightly by the fact that Bolton was often in the seat of a Hupmobile rather than a saddle. Like Parkman, Bolton portrayed himself as a man of action who was a match for the physical environment. In Bolton's retracing of Kino's trails, Bolton also became the historian as hero.

As important as Kino and his other projects were to Bolton, they were entirely extraneous as far as Johnson was concerned. After several times putting off sending a manuscript to Johnson, Bolton had the bad judgment to send his editor two offprints of freshly published articles. Johnson coolly acknowledged them and added that he would rather see Bolton's manuscript. "Pray when may I expect that long-delayed document?"[34] Bolton at last sent Johnson two manuscripts, a long and a short version. Neither pleased the editor. Although he appreciated Bolton's expertise in his subject, he wanted "an impressionistic picture of these Spanish adventurers and borderers." As it stood, Bolton's book was too detailed and boring. "To inflict dry tomes on the public after promising interesting literary volumes," he added, "would make us a laughing stock."[35] "The average reader wishes graphic pictures and human interest, not an account of a shadowy individual traveling so many miles on one day and so many the next, with so many horses and so many goats, reaching a place with an unpronounceable name, after so many days of travel." And then he gave Bolton an elegant piece of advice. "I wish that I could shut you up in a room without your books and your notes, with only a pen and paper, and bid you write a book for us out of your memory." Then perhaps Bolton could "set down large impressions and paint pictures on a big canvass, against that wonderful atmospheric background of the Great Southwest—and the result would probably be the book we want."[36]

Bolton worked on revisions for more than a year—when his other projects did not interfere. In April 1919 he sent a revised manuscript to Johnson.[37] Neither Johnson nor the publisher, Robert Glasgow, liked Bolton's revised manuscript. As Glasgow loftily put it, "Professor Bolton has not the artistic faculty sufficiently developed to write one of our books." The publisher believed that the only salvation for Bolton's work was to hire someone to rewrite it.[38] Johnson assured Bolton that the practice was common. The editor himself had taken a large role in rewriting one of the Chronicles volumes. He praised Bolton's skill as an investigator, but insisted that he had not yet developed "the artistic gift."[39]

Bolton read Johnson's letter when he was just beginning his term as head of the history department, so the idea of a ghostwriter had some practical appeal. While accepting Johnson's proposal, he demanded the right to approve the manuscript for historical accuracy.[40] Once Bolton had agreed to accept a reviser, Johnson and Glasgow decided to edit the manuscript in house. Then Bolton would not have to acknowledge another writer at all. Most important, Johnson assured him that Bolton's judgment of facts would be final.[41]

Johnson assigned Bolton's manuscript to Constance Lindsay Skinner, a gifted writer with an unusual background. She was born in the trading village of Quesnel, British Columbia, the daughter of a Hudson's Bay Company trader. Formal education in Quesnel was limited, but Skinner read widely in her parents' large library. At age fourteen she went to a private school in Vancouver where she became a newspaper journalist. After gaining experience, Skinner moved to Los Angeles and went to work as one of William Randolph Hearst's "sob sisters." Skinner ran with California's Bohemian crowd. She counted writer Jack London among her friends and lived for a summer on stage actress Helena Modjeska's Southern California ranch. Determined to become an independent writer, Skinner published verse, magazine articles, and two plays, one of which was produced in New York in 1917.[42] She was a vivid personality on the New York publishing scene. One of her friends described her as a "mountain of a woman, dressed in fantastic red plush, with dyed hair and mascaraed eyes, with gaudy costume jewelry jangling on her arms." She possessed "an incisive wit" that put "the fear of God into the various writers who worked with her." Skinner had no respect for academic credentials and was thankful she had never attended a college.[43]

Skinner wrote one of the first Chronicles volumes, *Pioneers of the Old Southwest: A Chronicle of the Dark and Bloody Ground,* under her own name. Turner liked the book and asked Johnson about her. "I hope you will appreciate the subtle compliment," Johnson wrote to Skinner, "from one of the foremost historians of the United States."[44] Johnson, of course, could also feel flattered at Turner's indirect compliment to his judgment in choosing Skinner—who had published no history previously—to write the volume. Johnson was so taken with Skinner's first effort that he asked her to write a volume on the fur trade for the series, but that project had to wait until Skinner was finished with Bolton's manuscript. "It is an awful mess," Johnson warned.[45]

Part of the problem, Johnson acknowledged, was that the story of Spain in America was apportioned among Bolton and three other writers. There was some overlap, but Johnson understood one thing with regard to Bolton's contribution: "Clearly, it is highly desirable to link the Borderlands with Spain and with the rest of New Spain," he explained to Skinner.[46] Johnson's line of thought may have led to the eventual title for Bolton's book, *The Spanish Borderlands.* It would become more than a title. Along with his conception of hemispheric history as embodied in the Americas, the borderlands idea would be forever associated with Bolton. Just as important, Bolton's confrontation with Johnson and Skinner convinced him that it was necessary to emphasize the significance of Spanish-American history. This led him to sometimes make extravagant claims about Spain and its heroes.

In January 1920 Bolton received the revised manuscript from Johnson. Johnson did not want Bolton to edit the manuscript, but to give a "verdict on the work of the reviser in general."[47] The editor reminded him that he had promised "to do for Spain in America what Parkman did for New France; that is, to write a book totally unlike your other books and designed to interest the ordinary reader." Then he urged Bolton to "make the book your own." Johnson refused to reveal the name of the ghostwriter but assured Bolton that he could "trust his [sic] literary sense as well as his sense of historical values."[48]

But Skinner's work did not reassure Bolton. First, there was the matter of perspective. Skinner (and presumably Johnson) wanted Bolton to tell the story of Spaniards in the territory that became the United States, and "why Spain isn't here now." Everything that was not "at least relatively important today" ought to be excised. Skinner's sense of contemporary importance was far different from Bolton's. The latter, for example, wished to emphasize in the story of Florida the "constructive" efforts of the Spanish commander Pedro Menéndez de Avilés in founding St. Augustine. Skinner, on the other hand, thought that telling about the short-lived French Huguenot settlement at Fort Caroline was the main thing, even though Menéndez slaughtered the Protestants like sheep and forced France to abandon designs on Florida. What did St. Augustine matter, Skinner argued? Spain did not expand its settlements from there, and a few years later England founded Jamestown and its people spread "to the mountains and beyond and down into Georgia." Moreover, "the Huguenot-Spanish fight . . . ought not to be ignored in any American history," because it "was prophetic of the power which would break Spain." "Spreading Protestantism . . . foiled Philip II's ambition" and "raised against him his antagonist Elizabeth and Drake's guns." "This book should not be written from the Spanish standpoint but from the American," Skinner concluded. "The 'conservative movements' of Spanish exploration may be interesting to antiquarians, but they are not vital to the ordinary reader."[49]

Skinner had presented in a few words the Anglophilic prejudices that, in Bolton's mind, constituted what was wrong with standard interpretations of American history. Protestant England prevailed; Catholic Spain failed. The prospect of such ethnocentric bigotry appearing under his name was intolerable to Bolton. "I am not of that school of writers who speak traditionally of 'the dark shadow of Spain,' or supposes the 'Spanish institutions in the New World crumpled like a house of cards at the touch of the Anglo-Saxon,'" he explained to Johnson. "There is no excuse for another book written in the old spirit of ignorance and prejudice," he wrote without referencing Parkman as the author of such books.[50] Bolton was willing to accept Skinner's stylistic changes, but "after your complete annihilation of any slight literary pride which I may have had[,] the only refuge for my self respect [sic] lay in still daring to hope that I might venture to have some historical opinion with regard to your revision."[51]

Bolton was also concerned about Skinner's reorganization of his book. "X," as Bolton called the still anonymous Skinner, had folded the chapter on Texas into the one on New Mexico and, in similar fashion, had combined material on Kino and other Jesuit missionaries into a chapter titled "The Missions" that covered only the Californias and Arizona.[52] Bolton insisted on restoring separate chapters on Florida, New Mexico, Texas, Louisiana, and Alta California and on the Jesuits in Arizona and Baja California.

While Bolton revised the Skinner manuscript, Johnson made clear that Bolton's concerns about interpretation were not uppermost in his mind. "What a job you had!" he wrote to Skinner. "My fear is that he wont [sic] know the difference between your work and his own," he added, although Bolton's letters made plain that he had a perfect understanding of the dissimilarity of Skinner's interpretation of the borderlands. Johnson condescendingly explained that Bolton was one of those professors who had an excessive reverence for facts. "The more of these sacred things you can amass the bigger man you are." Johnson supposed that "Bolton would turn a handspring which would land him across the continent, if he had any inkling that a mere woman had revised his manuscript."[53]

In the end, Glasgow and Johnson had the good sense to give Bolton his way on large matters of organization and interpretation, but they kept much of Skinner's language, which gave *The Spanish Borderlands* its distinctive literary quality. Bolton retained full authorial credit and acknowledged Skinner's "able assistance" only in a single prefatory line. Most important, Bolton won the bigger battle by insisting on his interpretation of the continuing significance of Spanish colonial history. Despite Skinner's and Johnson's insistence that Bolton's story should make Spain fade away so that Protestant England and the United States could take over, he emphasized the permanent stamp of Spain and Mexico on the region. His preface sketched the influences of Hispanic culture, language, religion, law, institutions, and people, which were "growing stronger," especially in the Southwest. "In short," he concluded, "the Southwest is as Spanish in color and historical background as New England is Puritan, as New York is Dutch, or as New Orleans is French."[54]

The origin of the title is uncertain, but it most likely came from Johnson, whose letters mention the words "borderers" and "borderlands." In Johnson's mind the terms may have emphasized the marginal nature of Spanish history in the Chronicles series. And Bolton may have suggested the term as a convenient and obvious way to refer to those places "belonging to the United States, over which Spain held sway for centuries."[55] Whatever the case, *The Spanish Borderlands* presented Bolton's point of view with his name indelibly imprinted on it.

The success of Bolton's little book helped him to teach and promote History 8. Yale University Press brought out an inexpensive textbook edition that Bolton and other professors—especially those who trained under Bolton—assigned to students.[56] In 1928 the director of Yale University Press concluded that the Chronicles volumes sold especially well in California and Texas because of the presence of *The Spanish Borderlands* in the series. Bolton attributed this success to the spread of his course, History of the Americas, throughout California and the Southwest. Not surprisingly, *The Spanish Borderlands* was one of the "interesting little books" he recommended for the course.[57] Thus, the Chronicles series gave Bolton a large audience and a core text for his broad course on the Western Hemisphere.

Bolton received something from *The Spanish Borderlands* in addition to recognition and his royalty: a writing lesson. His acknowledgment of Skinner was perfunctory, but her influence on his style was lasting. All of his subsequent books displayed a muscular and romantic style that owed much to her and to Johnson.

The editorial controversies associated with *The Spanish Borderlands* quickly faded, yet these exchanges reveal much about the prevailing perspective on United States and American history in Bolton's day. Johnson's arch criticism and his desire to convert Bolton's Hispanophilic story into a standard Anglocentric narrative shows how little impact Bolton could have on bedrock historical prejudice that had become naturalized as conventional wisdom among historians. Johnson gave in to Bolton's perspective perhaps because he was tired of the long-running project and wanted to be done with it, or maybe because he thought Bolton's points were trivial in the larger scheme of the Chronicles. Whatever the case, Bolton's book laid out a basic narrative that has influenced historians and organized the study and teaching of borderlands history for many decades. It is true that the book contains many passages that display the author's propensity for glorifying Spanish pioneers. However, Bolton's interpretive stance was in part the inadvertent product of the publisher, editor, and unacknowledged coauthor, who pressed their own prejudices on Bolton. In combating the anti-Catholic and Anglophilic views of history common to his time, Bolton produced a Hispanophilic record of heroicized soldiers and missionaries. He emphasized the positive and lasting accomplishments of Spain, but ignored the terrible costs of European conquest for American Indians and Africans.[58] Yet, with all of its shortcomings, his book became a foundation work that widened readers' angle of ethnic vision. Thus Bolton helped to open American minds to the religious and cultural variety of the American experience.

And what did Turner think about Bolton's Americas and borderlands ideas? If anyone could help shift the American historical perspective it was he. Turner never specifically mentioned *The Spanish Borderlands,* but his letters to Bolton stated that his writings offered a new perspective on American history that supplemented Turner's work.[59] "You are not only adding valuable historical criticism to the Spaniards in the [southern] region of the United States," Turner observed, "but you have really opened up . . . a new field."[60] "Your study of the advance and retreat of the Spanish frontier" he added, "is one that admirably fits with my own studies of the ~~truly~~ American advance, and makes it possible to understand the meaning of that advance more clearly."[61] The word "truly," whether struck by Turner or someone else, shows that Turner's first impulse was to privilege Anglo over Hispanic activities.

Still, Turner said that Bolton's work fit "admirably" with his own. How so? The most likely places to look for Bolton's influence in Turner's work are his essays on sectionalism.[62] Turner intended these articles to add regional nuances and specificity to his broad frontier interpretation of American history. He thought that each distinctive section developed as a result of particular frontier influences on the pioneering populations that occupied them. While the history of the frontier explained the past, sections explained the continuing uniqueness of American history—its exceptionalism compared to Europe—and perhaps foreshadowed the future. Each section bore the imprint of its frontier past, but unlike Europe, which had broken into separate nations, American regional conflicts were resolved politically under a common constitution rather than by warfare, the Civil War being the dramatic exception.[63] When Turner considered the Pacific Coast and arid regions of the Southwest, he thought of the impact of the environment on Americans who came from the East.[64] He did not consider any lingering influence of Hispanic and Indian people, whom he considered mere relics of an irrelevant past. Turner mentioned that the Southwest was a section, but he did not describe its salient qualities or any continuing Hispanic influences. In a discussion of culture in the Far West Turner noted that literacy rates were "worst" where "Mexican stock abounded," but said nothing more about Mexican or Spanish cultural contributions to the region.[65]

Turner's *The United States, 1830–1850: The Nation and Its Sections*, published posthumously, paid slight attention to the Hispanic past.[66] He admitted that along the Gulf Coast "a special form of society developed from the meeting of the Spanish and American frontiers and the different habits, institutions, and purposes of the two peoples," but did not describe this hybrid society or give it any importance. His chapter on Texas and the Far West featured Anglo-American incursion, invasion, and conquest and transformation of northern Mexico into an Anglo-American province. As he put it, "The formation of society did not become characteristically American and influential until well toward the end of the forties," after Anglos had overwhelmed the Hispanic population.[67] For Turner the "~~truly~~ American" frontiers, sections, and history were Anglo-American.

Despite Turner's private praise for Bolton's work, nothing in Turner's writing indicates that Bolton had even the slightest impact on his thinking. Nevertheless, Bolton believed that his scholarship fit well with that of Turner's. "My own work," Bolton wrote of an essay on sectionalism that Turner published in 1926, "confirms your generalizations. Indeed," he continued, "they go beyond national lines, and I have come to regard the Western Hemisphere and not the United States as the area within which we must study European expansion." And then Turner's "imitative disciple," as Bolton had once called himself, asserted that Caribbean development was "much the same whether Spanish, French, Dutch, Danish, or English." The historical similarities were "determined largely by geographical forces." "Prairie," he continued, "does not change essentially across the forty-ninth parallel. British Columbia probably has more in common with Oregon and California than with Ontario."[68]

In his eagerness to ingratiate and associate himself with his mentor, Bolton misconstrued Turner and ignored the main points of his own work. When Turner wrote that U.S. history must be thought of "in continental, and not merely in national terms," he was speaking about the continental scope and environmental divisions that made for political and economic sections in the United States. He was not iterating a small version of Bolton's hemispheric vision of history. Turner's "glacial invasion of humanity . . . modifying but not obliterating the older landscape" was not an acknowledgment of the continuing influence of Indian and Spanish cultures but a description of Turner's idea about successive patterns of Anglo settlement and development.[69]

Of course there were environmental similarities of the sort Bolton mentioned to Turner that crossed national boundaries, but there were cultural differences that should not be ignored. We may assume, for example, that if Spain had colonized

British Columbia, Catholic missions would have played a part in the process. In his "Mission as a Frontier Institution," Bolton argued that history and culture made a difference. Had he abandoned that position? Probably not, but in corresponding with Turner, Bolton was insisting on their common identity as American frontier historians, not on their differences. Still, one must conclude that while Turner was trying to make finer distinctions about the development of the United States, Bolton was intent on blurring differences with ever broader historical generalizations. Bolton would march farther down this road even while immersing himself in exhaustively detailed research and writing. Turner was "glad to think" that he "had any influence upon [Bolton's] career as accurate scholar and as interpreter of the large field which you have made your own."[70] Tellingly, he did not explain to Bolton *how* he had been influenced by the work of his student. Turner was a great teacher; he was not always an avid learner.

Between 1917 and 1921 Bolton's conception of hemispheric history, "The Mission as a Frontier Institution," and *The Spanish Borderlands* emerged as the essential foundations of his historical thinking. His hemispheric concept was a broad-gauged and broad-minded attempt to unify more than four centuries of American history. He established fieldwork as an integral part of his research method. His work on Spanish Catholic missions and missionaries valorized and validated a group that was seeking wider acceptance in American society. Yet his efforts to associate this work closely with Turner's reveals Bolton's willingness to ignore troubling inconsistencies. Withal, he was more inclusive than most of his contemporaries, many of whom rejected or, perhaps like Turner, merely ignored him. Bolton believed that he was leading a movement to reorganize and revitalize American history on a broader, sounder basis. His hope was not realized during his lifetime.

The presidency of the American Historical Association symbolized the pinnacle of professional achievement to which Bolton aspired. By 1922 five of Bolton's teachers and patrons had been elected to that high office: McMaster (1905), Jameson (1907), Turner (1910), Stephens (1915), and Haskins (1922). If Stephens could reach the pinnacle from Berkeley, why not Bolton? There were signs that the AHA leadership thought he might be made of presidential timber. Two months after publishing his mission article in the *Review,* Bolton was elected to a three-year term on the AHA Council.[1]

The nominating committee controlled elective offices in the AHA. Each year the committee placed a slate of nominees before the membership for election. The elective offices included the second vice presidency, first vice presidency, and presidency. Unlike nominees for the nominating committee and council, the vice presidents and president ran unopposed. The second vice president was routinely nominated for the following year's first vice presidency, and the first vice president was normally tapped for the succeeding presidency. In 1921 there was a movement to nominate Bolton for the second vice presidency.[2] As Bolton told the story, fate stymied his chances. He claimed that he stepped aside in favor of the ailing Woodrow Wilson, who did not live out his AHA term of office.

The story of the 1921 nomination is essentially true, but there was more to it than Bolton's gracious declination in favor of Wilson. It was considered bad form to mount an actual campaign on behalf of any particular person, although one suspects that campaigns were indeed carried on. In 1921 Victor Hugo Paltsits spear-headed a campaign to nominate Bolton for the second vice presidency. Paltsits was not a subtle man.[3] When Paltsits's active politicking on Bolton's behalf became too obvious, Frank C. Hodder, Bolton's friend on the nominating committee, alerted Bolton, who claimed to have no knowledge of the campaign on his behalf.[4] Bolton asked Hodder to drop his name from consideration in order to avoid making a bad impression on the AHA membership.

Hodder thought Bolton's withdrawal prevented a potentially nasty fight that would have damaged Bolton's reputation. If he had remained in the race, some would have suspected Bolton of approving the campaign. Besides, Hodder thought it was only a matter of time before Bolton became president.[5] One month later Wilson's name was being mentioned, and Bolton "heartily" endorsed him for the second vice presidency.[6]

While AHA officers considered and reconsidered Bolton's executive qualifications, the University of California was undergoing a presidential crisis. During the hysteria that accompanied the world war, President Wheeler had been attacked as pro-German on the frivolous (but nonetheless inflammatory) grounds that he had studied in Germany when he was a young man. At about the same time his health began to fail. It became clear that Wheeler's days as Cal's president were numbered. In the last few months of his crippled presidency an ineffective committee consisting of a regent, Ralph Merritt, literature professor Charles Mills Gayley, and law school dean William Cary Jones ran the university. Unhappy faculty called the committee the Triumvirate.

Not all professors were unhappy with the prospect of committee rule. While still on leave in the East, Professor Teggart proposed the elimination of the office of the president in all universities. No one had defined what the qualifications for the office should be, Teggart argued, yet the successful candidate was given a free hand and an indefinite term of office. The remedy, he thought, would be a board of deans of the university schools.[7] Teggart did not explain how a such a committee would interact with boards of regents, state legislatures, governors, or any of the universities' constituencies, but that was not his main concern. Teggart, whose tenure at Cal hung by the slimmest of threads held by President Wheeler, had experienced unchecked presidential power firsthand. He wanted to weaken the office of the president (especially Wheeler's office), by asserting that it was obsolete and subject to abuse. While he worked in the East to establish the American Association of University Professors, he published fourteen articles in national magazines and professional journals on topics that ranged from university administration to world peace.[8] Two years in Washington had made Teggart a national figure in intellectual circles, instead of a has-been who was looking for work. When read in the light of Teggart's publications, his impending termination looked like a peremptory abuse of presidential power.

In July 1919 the enfeebled Wheeler resigned and was replaced by Bolton's friend David Prescott Barrows. Teggart was one of the beneficiaries of the change in Berkeley administrations. Wheeler had intended to fire him, but Barrows demurred.[9] Whether out of fear of a national protest or because of respect for Teggart's considerable intellectual horsepower, President Barrows recommended him for a permanent faculty appointment as associate professor of social institutions. In 1923 the Board of Regents established a department of social institutions with Teggart as its sole member. Professor Teggart had finally found congenial company.[10]

Bolton despised Teggart, but the ousted librarian had plenty of support from faculty in other parts of the university.[11] While Teggart had sojourned in the East, an influential group of professors known as the Kosmos Club had worked to give the Academic Senate more power. Frederick Teggart was elected president of the Kosmos Club in 1920. Club representatives circumvented the Triumvirate and then president Barrows by talking directly with the Board of Regents, which granted extraordinary powers to the Academic Senate, whose members were elected by the faculty. This arrangement substantially reduced the powers of the university president, including control over hiring and promotion, admissions, approval of courses, degree programs, and allocation of research funds. The Academic Senate distributed its new powers and responsibilities through a faculty committee structure. The president and his deans were left to manage the physical plant and to handle noncurricular and other nonacademic matters. The power of the Berkeley faculty, especially prominent professors like Bolton, was unique in the American academic world. However, these changes made it hard for President Barrows, who accepted the presidency under one set of rules and expectations but had to govern under entirely new conditions.[12]

President Barrows's tenure in office was not long. The Academic Senate and Barrows differed on administrative matters. When there was conflict, the regents ultimately sustained the president, but the continuous need to negotiate and make adjustments wore on Barrows. In May 1922 Barrows announced his resignation to be effective the following year.[13] Thus Teggart, whom Barrows had saved from termination, helped to prematurely end Barrows' term as university president. Wheeler, Stephens, and Bolton had pushed Teggart out of the Bancroft Library and history department. Seemingly bereft of support, Teggart had forced his way back into the university and bent it to his purposes. It was a stunning reversal of fortune that Teggart engineered with intelligence and craft.

Bolton now had an implacable enemy on the faculty. Teggart extended his bitter grudge against Bolton to the history department and Bolton's students on the Berkeley faculty. In 1923 Teggart was evidently behind decisions by the Committee on Courses and the Executive Committee to quash the history department's offering of year-long upper-division courses in colonial Latin American history, taught by Professor Priestley, and the Latin American national period, offered by Professor Chapman. Committee interference in history department curricular matters was unwarranted, Bolton complained to lame-duck president Barrows. There was no historian on the executive committee, he reminded the president, "only one [presumably Teggart] who might claim to be" a historian, who "has made a conspicuous failure of several professorships in different fields and in my opinion has no fitness to pass judgment upon the work of any Department of History or of any person in any Department of History."[14]

Teggart may have been behind an attempt in 1923 to deny a promotion to Chapman, his former graduate student who had defected to Bolton. When Bolton learned that some faculty objected on the grounds that Chapman did not merit promotion because the history department was "over-developed on the side of Western and Spanish American History," he understood that the attack was on Bolton's history department as well as on Chapman. Bolton defended Chapman and the department.[15] Such attacks, whether inspired by a vengeful Teggart or from other faculty, did not affect Bolton's control of the history department and the Bancroft Library. The criticisms, however, did not go away, and there was some truth in them. Bolton had loaded the department with his own people and shaped the curriculum along lines suggested by his own work.

Bolton was not involved in the faculty revolt against Wheeler or Barrows. "The university is in the throes of reorganization on 'democratic' lines," he wrote brother Fred. "Personally . . . I am not convinced that it is all to the good." Faculty committees were "made up on the Jacksonian principle that one man is as good as another and that rotation in office is sacred; why should not shoemakers legislate for doctors?" he sniffed.[16] It was not that Bolton did not participate in university politics. He simply preferred to politick on a personal level by appealing to the powerful people who controlled his world. He made every effort to accommodate governors, legislators, wealthy benefactors, regents, and university presidents whom he served. Throughout his life Bolton successfully negotiated with university presidents using personal charm and the influence of his scholarly reputation.

Bolton respected institutional authority and the officers who wielded it. Insofar as he possessed power within the system as department chair, director of the Bancroft, and chair of the research committee, he happily used that power for the benefit of himself, his faculty, his students, and his projects. Bolton's decisions about the distribution of resources were not always to the liking of his colleagues. One graduate student reported seeing Priestley dissolved in tears after Bolton had spent the entire annual acquisition budget for an item that he needed for one of his projects.[17]

Bolton consolidated his power in the history department by hiring historians who would support him. The presence of his students Priestley and Chapman on the history faculty was helpful, but he could not fill the ranks entirely with Bolton men. When he added medievalist Louis Paetow to the department in 1921, Thomas Maitland Marshall assured him that Paetow knew "which way to jump" and would be "loyal"—qualities that would ensure Bolton's domination of history in coming years.[18]

Student placements on important faculties bespoke Bolton's professional influence outside the university. The University of Chicago called J. Fred Rippy.[19] Arthur Aiton went to the University of Michigan, and John Lloyd Mecham joined the Columbia faculty.[20] These prestigious appointments demonstrated Bolton's clout and the growing visibility of his California school of history. As these young professors marched up through the ranks, they would acquire position and influence in the profession, but the success of one Bolton student did not always please the others who wanted plum positions. Marshall had wanted Aiton's spot at Michigan and complained when he did not get it.[21] Like race horses jostling out of the gate, each man strove to move to the head of the pack. They all needed Bolton to get them there.

Professional recognition came to Bolton in other ways. In 1922 he lectured to Hispanic-American historians at the annual AHA meeting; in "Two Types of Courses in American History" he argued for a general hemispheric course like the one he taught at Berkeley. "My position seemed to be approved quite generally," Bolton concluded. "No one took issue with me."[22] At the luncheon conference on the general course in American history, Bolton sat at the head table next to Turner. Again Bolton argued for his Americas course, but most of the other professors merely wanted to add "a little more detail here, or a little more drill without changing the scope of the course one whit." Turner smoked his cigarette and made no comment. As usual Bolton believed that silence and assent were synonymous.

Nevertheless, the meeting reminded Bolton that Turner and other older historians still controlled the historical profession. Most of the leaders in Turner's cohort were only about seven to ten years older than Bolton, but to him they seemed far more senior and deeply entrenched. "Jameson, Turner, Haskins, [Charles McLean] Andrews, and . . . the rest of the Old Guard still look old to me." Bolton understood that younger historians regarded him as one of the older generation. "Now I find myself surrounded in the hotel lobbies by young instructors and assistant professors who apparently regard me as quite venerable, or perhaps antique." If Bolton was a bit wistful about the tender regard that comparative youngsters had for him, he was also a little jealous of the "Old Guard" who were "like a sore thumb, 'always on hand.'"

The 1922 meeting also encouraged Bolton's ambition to be AHA president. His old mentor Charles Homer Haskins was president that year. He mentioned Bolton in his presidential address as one of "his 'boys' who had reached the top of the profession," Bolton recalled. Haskins's boys called him the Duke. When Bolton congratulated him on the presidency, Haskins replied, "Well Bolton, I expect to take part in such an affair for you some day. Your students are already scattered all over the country." Bolton was flattered, but Haskins's comment merely reflected the political reality of ascending to the highest office in the profession. Connections mattered. Numbers mattered. "He perhaps knew," Bolton observed, "that my students are my most precious professional 'jewels.' Long live the Duke!"

Now in his early fifties, Bolton's academic reputation was secure even without the AHA presidency. But other presidencies were available to a successful academic, especially one with administrative experience. Early in Bolton's career he and his brother had been courted for small-college and normal school presidencies. They had chosen to head programs at universities as smaller fish with a much bigger pond to swim in. In 1912 Fred moved to the University of Washington, where he became dean of the school of education.[23] Fred still had the presidential bug and asked his brother to keep an eye out for opportunities in the West, but Bolton's love of his borderlands field seemed to have entirely driven out the presidential itch.[24] Then in September 1923 came an unsettling event in the form of a natural catastrophe. The summer heat had parched the Berkeley hills to a sere brown when a broken power line caused the dry grass to ignite. Fire blazed up and roared down the hillsides chasing Berkeley's inhabitants towards the bay. The inferno missed the university but in only a few hours devoured block after block of homes north of campus. News of the disaster flashed around the country.[25]

Bolton had been on campus when his neighborhood was engulfed by flames. Gertrude and the children were safe, but the Bolton home on Scenic Avenue was a total loss. Before fleeing, she had managed to load their Hupmobile with their clothes and silver service, but Bolton's personal library of several thousand books lay in ashes.[26] Unfortunately, the home had not been fully insured. Letters from concerned friends came from around the country. "I hope I know the worst when I see that your house is listed as lost," wrote Guy Stanton Ford, Bolton's old fraternity brother and now dean of the University of Minnesota graduate school. Hackett sent a check for thirty dollars, as "a sort of second wedding present."[27] Bolton put a bold face on his family's traumatic loss. "Yes, we were in the path of the flames," he told to one well-wisher, "and they cleaned us up nicely."[28] His sister Grace complimented him on taking the "loss in a most beautiful spirit," but it must not have been easy to lose all of the personal things the Bolton family had accumulated.[29] The impact of the fire on Gertrude must have been immense. For the next ten years the Boltons would move from one rented house to another.

In one sense the fire had been liberating. The destruction of the Bolton house meant that there was one less tether to Berkeley. In early 1923 Robert Vinson resigned the presidency of the University of Texas in order to head Western Reserve University in Cleveland.[30] Vinson's resignation immediately raised the specter of political influence in the selection of the next president. Texas governor Pat M. Neff, who was rumored to want the presidency, made recess appointments to name seven new members of the Board of Regents.[31] Eventually the legislature would have to confirm the governor's designees, but in the meantime Neff's regents controlled the board. If Neff wanted the presidency, he could have it.

The Texas faculty, of course, wanted a new president with academic credentials. "Don't be surprised if our offer drops on your door step some day," Barker told Bolton, "and don't kick it off without careful consideration." Barker predicted that the regents would authorize a salary of $10,000 to $12,000 with an official residence thrown in. He promised Bolton the unanimous support of the faculty, at least in the beginning.[32] He even told his old friend, perhaps too optimistically, that he could devote half of his time to research and writing.

It is difficult to gauge Bolton's interest in the Texas presidency in the summer of 1923. Several of his students nominated him for the job, possibly at his request.[33] Perhaps he thought of using the offer as a lever to advance his salary at Berkeley. One suspects, however, that the incineration of his home caused Bolton to seriously consider the prospect of moving back to Texas. The projected salary was handsome; the provision of a presidential residence might have seemed downright providential. As the search process in Austin developed, Bolton became a very interested observer.

Bolton had two trusted sources of Texas intelligence: Barker and Hackett.[34] Given the political situation, Hackett was not sure whether congratulations or condolences would be in order if Bolton got the position. The university was likely in the future to become rich from oil revenues derived from its two-million-acre West Texas tract. At the moment, however, retrenchment and meager salaries were the rule, and the Texas regents ran roughshod over faculty and the acting president.[35]

Other worrying news came from Hackett's pen. The University of Texas owned the García collection, which included a Hernán Cortés document that Bolton reckoned was worth $100,000. The university had decided to sell it for $50,000. Would Bolton be interested in acting as agent for a 10 percent fee?[36] Perhaps oil wealth would come to the university eventually, but in the meantime the library might have to sell its archival riches.

As the situation developed, Barker continued to advise Bolton about his prospects. "If you ever have a meeting with [chairman of the Board of Regents J. Lutcher] Stark," Barker advised, "act as if you really respected his opinions." Barker hoped the regents would select Bolton, though he knew they were concerned about the religious beliefs of presidential candidates. He hoped that Bolton was not "a sincere pagan."[37] Bolton was probably not exactly a pagan, but he had long since sworn off church attendance. At Berkeley his Sunday services were in the Bancroft.

The regents did not act as quickly as Barker had hoped. In May they offered Governor Neff the presidency, but he turned it down. Neff recognized that there was substantial opposition to his appointment from the faculty and the influential university alumni organization, the Texas Ex-Students Association. The Texas-exers included some of the state's most prominent and powerful people. Even though Neff did not accept the offer, faculty and students were outraged that the presidency would be treated in such a cavalier way. Two regents immediately resigned in protest. The remaining regents, who were overwhelmed and surprised at the depth of the anger directed at them, turned to a respected academic nominee, but it was not Bolton. His friend Guy Stanton Ford got the nod because of his impressive administrative credentials as dean of the Minnesota graduate school.[38] Ford could read the Texas political situation as well as anyone and instantly declined.[39]

Events were now moving swiftly. On May 19 Barker and another professor called on regent Joe Wooten and made the case for Bolton. Wooten disclosed that the regents "had gotten the impression that" Bolton was "sort of a sissy." How or why this rumor got started is anyone's guess. Perhaps ascribing effeminacy to Bolton was a form of negative campaigning. Barker argued that nothing could have been further from the truth, and assured Bolton that he had "described [his] masculine qualities." He also trumpeted Bolton's administrative experience as department chair and as adviser to Wheeler and Barrows, and his position on the California Historical Survey Commission. Wooten was convinced. He called Stark, and the regents offered the presidency to Bolton. The board would be "carried away by any constructive plan," Barker advised Bolton. "Any vision of possibilities will beget a glow." The alumni would flood the regents with petitions for Bolton's appointment. He also told Bolton that the Texas-exers planned to unseat the board by stymieing their confirmation in the legislature. He assured Bolton that he did not have to worry about the removal of the board that elected him, but also admitted that "it will be no holiday task for the first year."[40]

The Texas faculty and alumni were desperate to get Bolton. If he turned them down, after Ford's quick refusal the regents were unlikely to look outside Texas again. And Neff was not entirely out of the picture. He could still exercise a controlling influence over the board. On May 28 the regents unanimously elected Bolton president with a $10,000 salary and a residence. "I know the man who gets it will for a time have a little taste of Hell," Barker frankly stated, "but if he's the right sort I'd want him to take it." "You can come here & virtually dictate your terms," Hackett wrote.[41]

Barker had prepared a brief résumé for the edification of the regents. After stressing Bolton's scholarly attainments and administrative talent, Barker added this short paragraph: "He is a Democrat, a Christian, and, we believe, a church member. Certainly he is in hearty accord with the church as a great uplifting social force."[42] "There may be some question of the propriety of this," Barker apologized to Bolton. Religious and political association "ought to have nothing to do with the matter, but it has with the Board, and on careful reflection I put it in." In truth, Bolton's California political affiliation in 1924 was "Declines to State"; he registered Republican in 1916, 1922, 1926, and 1934. Except for 1918, when he registered as a Progressive, in all other years he declined to state a party affiliation.[43] Gertrude and the eligible children consistently registered Republican. It seems likely that Bolton's political views fell somewhere on the progressive side of the Republican spectrum but that he preferred not to publicly affiliate himself with the party. As with religion, Bolton believed that the less said about politics the better, but he was a practical man. Had he taken the Texas presidency, he might well have registered as a Democrat and joined a church simply to satisfy Texans who thought such things were important.

Brother Fred's advice was emphatic: "I hope you accept and believe you will." Fred assured his brother that he would not have to abandon his scholarly work as long as he had an adequate staff. In Texas Bolton would be able to "control the situation," in contrast to California, "where there are apparent mean jealousies."[44] It all looked good to Fred, who would have accepted the Texas presidency had it been offered to *him*. Fred's career had been all about educational administration, but Herbert's commitment to active scholarship was deeper than his older brother's. Early in Bolton's career the journey from farm boy to college president seemed the logical narrative arc for the story of Bolton's life, the attainment of the pinnacle of professional success that would punctuate his rise in society. In 1924, with the Texas presidency in his grasp, it was no longer so simple. Bolton worked nights, weekends, and holidays in the Bancroft, not because he needed to, but because he wanted to. The events and characters of the past completely consumed whatever time was not required for other matters. Bolton's only complaint was that there was not more time to devote to his missionaries and explorers. Family considerations also mattered. Gertrude was not in the best of health. Moving would be hard on her and she did not like the Texas climate.

Not everyone was enthusiastic about the prospect of a presidency for Bolton in Texas. When the news got to Santa Barbara, Bolton's old friend Father Engelhardt wrote, "I hear you are going to leave California for Texas, K.K.K.dom!" The good father feared that history would lose "a valiant knight," because President Bolton would be preoccupied with university affairs.[45]

Bolton was wise enough to seek counsel from someone who knew what it was like to be president of a university in turmoil. David Barrows at first encouraged him to consider the position, but after thinking it over for a few days, wrote him a letter. "I want to express to you my final advice, not to accept this presidency nor any other." Barrows's main reason for this conclusion was Bolton's research agenda. Barrows assured Bolton that he would neither have time for scholarship nor be able to recover the intellectual ground that he would lose while serving as president. Bolton had created "a school of Western American History and your leaving it will mean its dissolution." As for the rewards and burdens of the presidency itself, Barrows gave a succinct summary based on his own experience:

A university president has little or no personal freedom. He can not count his time his own, nor can he make his own arrangements, [or] choose his own associates. These are all done for him by the interests of the institution which he serves. There is practically no spare time. One has to abandon reading, reflection, the intimacies of family and friends and give a hundred per cent of time, energy, and devotion to a task that after all is mainly a mere resolution of minor difficulties. I do not believe that you would find that it would pay.[46]

Barrows thought that the University of California could not afford to lose Bolton. He was not alone. The Native Sons of the Golden West issued a resolution commending Bolton for his contribution to California history. It would be an "irreparable loss to the cause of Pacific Coast and Southwestern American History" if he went to Texas.[47] After fifteen years in California Bolton had become a fixture, almost an institution in the state. Texas, he perhaps realized, was a part of his past that he had romanticized. He had built an almost ideal situation for himself in California, including a library, faculty, graduate students, and a significant amount of institutional power within and outside the university. Why should he give it up for what Barker called "a little taste of Hell" in Texas?

Bolton turned down the Texas presidency, citing his "reluctance to leave scholarship for administration—it would cost me the struggle of my life." But that was not the end of it. Barker, Hackett, and his other friends urged him to reconsider. A swarm of Texas telegrams descended on Bolton's Berkeley residence. They begged him to come to Austin to save the university. He could not resist the temptation. Bolton agreed to go to Austin to advise "the regents and ex-students what I think to be the great needs of the Texas University," as he told a reporter for the *Austin Statesman*.[48] Bolton may have thought he was going to Texas to offer salutary advice, but the regents and everyone else thought he was there to negotiate the terms of his appointment to the presidency.

The notes that he made—there were three drafts—suggest that Bolton gave the regents a stirring speech.[49] "Texas is the University of Destiny," he jotted on a telegram blank. There followed a lesson in borderlands history that described Texas as the keystone from its Spanish beginnings up to the Civil War. Then he outlined some problems. Changes had to be made. Religion and politics should not be injected into university matters, he indicated on one draft, though not on others. Security of tenure and academic freedom found their way into his notes. Texas had an opportunity to be a great university, but the legislature had to increase support, "not *niggardly*, but *big*," he added. New buildings, higher salaries, library support, more graduate assistants were all needed. "*Will you do it?*" he asked the regents? A new medical school and a university press were needed. The wealthy people of Texas had to step up and fund buildings, fellowships, professorships, and a press to the tune of a million dollars. Draw a line on a map from Baltimore to Berkeley, he told the regents. There was not one great university south of that line. Texas had the opportunity to be the first great university in the southern region. It was all very uplifting stuff, especially to the alumni and faculty. After his one-day visit to Austin, they wanted Bolton more than ever.

Bolton and the University of Texas would have been better off if he had simply declined the position and said no more about it. Going to Austin merely to give advice about how to do a job that he had refused to take showed poor judgment on Bolton's part. When he addressed the regents, there was no doubt in anyone's mind, except Bolton's, that he was dictating the terms of his contract.[50] He wanted (presumably for himself) a larger salary and expense account, an end to political interference, academic freedom for faculty, subsidies for graduate work, more graduate assistantships, and campus improvements. The regents agreed to everything.[51]

Still, Bolton seemed reluctant. Someone suggested that Bolton might consider taking the presidency on a temporary basis, perhaps during a one-year leave from Berkeley. Born of desperation, the one-year proposal was doomed from the start. Had Bolton accepted, he would have done all the heavy lifting required to get things moving in the right direction. Then, having made a huge personal investment in the university, he would have packed up and left. Perhaps the regents believed that Bolton would decide to stay rather than abandon all of his Texas accomplishments. Bolton could not have taken this proposal seriously, but he did not forthrightly reject the offer, perhaps to avoid offending his Austin hosts. Whatever the case, the Texans who waved goodbye as Bolton's train left Austin believed there was a good chance that Bolton would be back.

A gulf of misunderstanding separated the "maybe" that the regents inferred from the "never" that Bolton intended. A new blizzard of telegrams and letters fell on Berkeley. The regents would be glad to have Bolton if he stayed "a year, less than a year, or more than a year," wrote Hackett. He could tell "the Legislature, the Board of Regents, and the whole University to 'go to hell' at any old time." If Bolton did not go to Texas, it was "an absolute fact" that the presidency would go to Walter Splawn, former Texas economics professor and member of the state railroad commission.[52] Because Splawn was a friend of Governor Neff, the appointment was widely regarded as political, despite Splawn's educational credentials, which included degrees from Yale and the University of Chicago.

Barker held out hope that his old friend would finally give in to the pressure from Texas. One year's vacation from Berkeley might do him some good. "Go ahead now and accept," Barker wrote. "Get to Texas as soon as you can," he concluded. This time Bolton would not budge, although he did not give what Texans understood as a Shermanesque absolute, final, and unmistakable "no" to their continuing importunities. Believing that he had turned them down several times, Bolton ceased to reply to begging telegrams from Texas. This left some of his supporters under the impression that he had not finally declined the presidency. Still believing that Bolton might come, Hackett wired Bolton that higher education in Texas would perish without him. "How can you remain indifferent?" Hackett wondered.[53] The Ku Klux Klan's endorsement of Splawn made his appointment even more distasteful to Hackett and others who opposed the politicization of the university.

The earnest pleading of Barker and Hackett included information that would have discouraged Bolton even if he had been seriously considering the Texas offer. One of Hackett's telegrams revealed that some Baptists associated with the governor were opposed to Bolton. "Pay no attention to a few disgruntled Neff Baptists," Hackett wired. "University churches have endorsed you." Barker, explaining away opposition, wrote that it was "just a part of the damned political slough that we are bogged in. It doesn't amount to anything and will not trouble you after you accept."[54] Who would believe such assurances?

Bolton had always avoided being drawn into political controversies, but Austin was a minefield of potential trouble. During his Texas visit, he had refused to discuss a fund drive to build a memorial stadium at the university, but Harry Moore, the publicity director for the stadium, now wanted his views about the building's value. Moore imagined that Bolton was "a real red-blooded man" who supported athletics and the new stadium. Moore wanted to use a pro-stadium statement from Bolton for fund-raising purposes, but assured him that anything Bolton wrote would "not appear in a false light."[55] Even if accurately quoted, Bolton's opinion about the stadium was bound to make someone angry. The regents and faculty supporters said he would have smooth sailing as president, but the reality of Texas politics, which involved religion, sports, and the Ku Klux Klan, argued very differently.

The regents finally realized that Bolton would not take the presidency. They elected Splawn. Barker and Hackett were disappointed. Another member of the

Texas faculty, Frederic Duncalf, wondered if the new president was "the sp(l)awn of the Devil."[56] The future of the University of Texas seemed uncertain at best, but Barker was hopeful that President Splawn would respect the faculty. Wanting to be certain that Splawn understood their position, the faculty asked Barker to speak for them at Splawn's inauguration. The Texas professor stood and made a speech that stressed the importance of academic freedom for professors and political independence for the state's university. It was a brave thing to do and deserves to be more widely known.[57] What did Splawn think of Barker's strong words? There is a hint perhaps in Splawn's recommendation to eliminate advanced courses in the field of Latin American history. The history department had made a large investment in this field, which began with Bolton and was primarily in the hands of his student Hackett. Barker saved the day again with a forceful argument for maintaining a well-established program and against micromanagement from the president's office. Splawn resigned in 1927. Some Texans thought that Barker should be the next president of the university, but he did not want it. Some faculty feared Barker's fierce honesty. When it was reported that a new president had been appointed, Barker received a news clipping about it from an anonymous sender. Scrawled at the bottom were the words, "Hee! Hee! Ha! Ha! Ha! Not you, Thank God!"[58]

The Texas episode snuffed any of Bolton's residual ambitions to be a university president. If nothing else, he had received an education about the political realities of the job. Bolton had many qualities that fitted him for such a position, including a deep understanding of and dedication to the university's mission, a pleasing personality, a commanding presence, and tact. In his mid-fifties, Bolton had made himself into the person that he had wanted to be—an imposing figure imbued with authority who was deserving of respect and positions of great responsibility.

Yet Bolton's response to the Texas offer revealed some traits that argued against his placement in such a difficult executive post. He disliked political controversy, but a university president deals with it constantly, though perhaps not to the extent of controversy-plagued Texas in 1924. Bolton wanted to please, but a president cannot please everyone. To avoid giving offense, Bolton was sometimes unable to speak directly to friends or to those in power. He sometimes dithered, as in the case of the Texas presidency, in which he at first agreed to visit Austin and consider the offer, then withdrew, then agreed to go to Texas to give advice, and then departed Austin leaving the impression that he might be persuaded to take the job. Bolton lacked the decisiveness that good executives need. Perhaps most telling, Bolton's ego drew him back to Austin, where friends, students, and alumni were clamoring for him to save the university. He believed that he could say some words and do some good, but that was a vain and misguided hope.

None of Bolton's disqualifications for the presidency made him a bad person. Indeed, in other settings those same personal traits served him and others well. In some ways they remind us of the ambitious fatherless farm boy—diffident toward authority, ambitious to rise, polite, believing that hard work could accomplish anything and would be appreciated by those who gave out the rewards.

After his Austin visit Bolton must have realized that his future was in the Golden State. Now he was truly all for California, as he had once told Morse Stephens. But another presidency still beckoned. In 1924 Bolton's friends made a second serious effort to nominate him for the second vice presidency of the AHA. Seventeen members recommended him for the post, more votes than any other prospective candidate received. But the nominating committee discounted Bolton's supporters because most of them lived on the Pacific Coast. Perhaps there was a lingering memory of Paltsit's campaign for Bolton or a suspicion that Bolton was campaigning for the office.[59] Bolton would have to wait for his presidency.

Bolton's decision to stay in California did not mean that he had escaped the vicissitudes of local patriotism and widely held prejudices concerning race, religion, politics, and history. He did not record his personal beliefs about religion, but his scholarly work on Catholic missions had moved him away from anti-Catholic prejudice to an uncritical admiration for pioneer priests and the Church that they served. Bolton's ideas about other religious and racial groups are more difficult to track, because he carefully avoided making controversial statements that might reflect adversely on the university.

Bolton employed a simple tactic when discussing subjects that might be unfamiliar, discomforting, or even offensive to Anglo-Californian audiences: he raised the discussion to a more general category of analysis. For example, when explaining Spanish colonization, he emphasized that like the English, Spaniards were Europeans. Spanish missionaries were Catholics, yes, but the important thing was that they were Christians. Europeans all, Christians all—that was the main thing. Bolton's easy generalizing elided the centuries of conflict between Spain and England, Protestants and Catholics while making all European Christians march toward the same great brotherly goal—a free and democratic Western Hemisphere. Not everyone was able to see history in the happy light of Bolton's ecumenism.

Belief in eugenics was widespread in the United States and had gained a particularly tenacious hold on some Californians who feared that the pure "white" race might be polluted by intermarriage with blacks, Mexicans, Jews, Asians, and Indians, who were thought to be a lesser order of humans. Golden State eugenicists were especially concerned about Mexicans, whom they racialized as dark-skinned, mixed-blood mongrels who should be kept south of the border. The Human Betterment Foundation in Pasadena advocated sterilization of people deemed unfit to procreate. Eugenics enthusiasts included respected intellectuals like botanist Luther Burbank, Stanford's David Starr Jordan, and Cal's Benjamin Ide Wheeler.[1]

Bolton wrote little about his racial ideas, and there is little evidence to suggest that he was influenced by the eugenicists. Nevertheless, it must be admitted that his racial views included some of the common biases of his age. An examination of Bolton's ideas about race must begin with his early work on free blacks in the South before the Civil War.[2] Bolton's history of the antebellum origins of the free-black class was rooted in contemporary racial questions. "People everywhere in this age of national expansion," he explained, "are interested in the problems of racial contact." Bolton expressed dismay that there was racial conflict in the land and that whites and blacks did not live in harmony. He believed that an understanding of the historical causes of racial conflict would create "an additional basis for . . . the formation of present day policies." This was an important question because the Spanish-American War had added "new millions of ~~an inferior~~ alien people" that had "greatly increased the magnitude of our race problem." Whether Bolton or an anonymous editor struck the words "an inferior" and interlineated "alien" is unknown, but both choices show Bolton's discomfort with people of color, perhaps even a eugenic strain of thought. It is clear, however, that Bolton thought it important to avoid the past mistakes of American race relations in the antebellum South, which had created a racial underclass subject to discriminatory laws. Frequently characterizing blacks with the language of their white governors, Bolton uncritically accepted the notion that free blacks were shiftless people who constituted a menace to white society. He argued, however, that black behavior resulted from the appalling conditions that he described. Racial friction in the antebellum South led to violence, and white elites believed that "blacks and whites, all free, could not exist side by side in peace. ~~That they were wrong has not yet been fully demonstrated.~~" Who was the editor? Was it an ambivalent Bolton or someone who was more hopeful about race relations in the United States at the turn of the century? Bolton censured laws that put blacks on an unequal legal footing, but he did not speak out against de jure racial segregation in his own time—certainly not when he was in Texas.

Had Bolton continued to think and write about African Americans, he would have left a more fully developed body of work that would be easier to judge, but he completely abandoned the topic for his work on the Spanish Borderlands. However, he did leave one bit of personal writing that illuminates his racial views in 1923, when he was traveling through the South. "It is the land of Darkies," he wrote.[3] At each railroad station, he saw "the usual motley mob of Negroes." At one stop, Bolton got off the train so that he could surreptitiously listen to their "ludicrous chatter. Young Sambo greets a middle-aged woman with 'D'y'all want some money?' rattling the small change in his pockets." She replied, "Gawd man, y'all haint got nuthin' but *nee-ickels*. Ah's got 'nuff one dollah bills to make y'all a shirt! Yuh! Yuh! Yuh! Yuh!" To him, the exchange was merely "typical of [blacks'] carefree banter." He did not look for deeper meanings in a conversation about money between poor people, even though he saw poverty all around him in the form of "dilapidated farm houses and Negro shacks." Perhaps Bolton's own past had inured him to rural poverty. Or maybe he thought that African Americans were bound to be poor and were content with their condition. This was the sort of thoughtless racism that infused American society in Bolton's time, and he was not immune to it.

Bolton discovered in Mexico a strikingly different model for race relations. In the Spanish missions, Bolton found an institution that ameliorated racial conflict through a program of religious and cultural assimilation. When in 1917 Bolton referred to the mission as "an industrial training school," it was hard to miss the implicit comparison with Reconstruction-era efforts to educate freedmen, Booker T. Washington's Tuskegee Institute, and the system of Indian schools that the federal government had established in the late nineteenth and early twentieth centuries.[4] He no doubt had these latter-day institutions approvingly in mind when he wrote about missions. It is ironic that when Bolton was worrying about the racial complications of national expansion in the 1890s, he fretted over "alien" people whose ancestors had been products of Catholic missionary activity. By 1917 Bolton's racial outlook had become assimilationist, not eugenicist.

Perhaps that is why Bolton was willing to speak up for Native American legal equality. In 1916 he was at work on a case before the California State Supreme Court concerning Indian citizenship.[5] The Lake County clerk had refused to register to vote Ethan Anderson, a Pomo Indian. With the assistance of a reform group, the Indian Board of Cooperation, Anderson brought suit against the county.[6] Evidently Anderson's lawyers asked Bolton for his opinion in the matter.[7]

Bolton argued that "all Indians living within the territory ceded by Mexico to the United States in 1848 . . . became citizens of the United States; and that all such in California and their descendants are now by virtue of our present Constitution, entitled to vote, if they have the proper educational qualifications."[8] Indians had become citizens under the Republic of Mexico by virtue of the Plan of Iguala, he reasoned, and the Treaty of Guadalupe Hidalgo had guaranteed U.S. citizenship to all Mexicans in the Southwest if they wanted it. Thus, Indians residing in the Mexican cession became citizens.[9] Bolton cited Mexican law, several relevant U.S. court cases, and the 1849 California constitutional debates to strengthen his claim. Anderson's counsel accepted Bolton's reasoning and asked the court to decide the case on that basis. Ultimately, the court decided in favor of Anderson but on narrower grounds.[10] Nevertheless, Bolton's participation in this case demonstrated his support for Indian citizenship and voting rights, while furnishing a striking contrast with Turner, who had described no place for Indians after the frontier era had passed.[11]

Bolton's many trips to the Southwest inspired comments on the Indians who lived there. In the summer of 1922 he toured New Mexico with an Indian guide and visited several Pueblo towns as well as prehistoric ruins. He was particularly taken with Zuni, "a city of terraced houses ranged in streets" that he found "interesting beyond expression." He was glad to see the Zuni Pueblo before it was "too late," Bolton explained, for he believed that it would not be long before all of the Pueblo towns would be entirely deserted. Bolton viewed recent developments in Pueblo country with mixed emotions. While he lamented the passing of old ways, he seemed glad to report the existence of Indian schools, the YMCA, and the widespread use of English. Still, he recognized that assimilation was not wholly successful among the Pueblos. "Americanization goes on rapidly," he observed, "but many go back to their blankets even after graduating from Carlyle [sic]."[12] Like many Americans of his time, Bolton was ambivalent about the assimilation of Indians into the dominant society. He believed in Indian citizenship and civil rights, but he also assumed that assimilation meant the destruction of Indian culture. Like most Anglo-Americans, Bolton failed to recognize that Indians were able to adapt to changing circumstances while maintaining their distinctive identity as Native Americans.[13]

Six months after visiting the Pueblos, Bolton learned about the Bursum Bill, a proposed federal law that would have permitted white squatters on Pueblo lands to secure valid titles and water rights to the detriment of the Indians. The reaction of the Pueblos and their supporters was so strong that Congress scrapped the original bill and passed a more evenhanded law, the Pueblo Lands Act. In the meantime, opposition to the Bursum Bill invigorated the Indian reform movement that ultimately found expression in the Indian New Deal during FDR's administration.[14]

Bolton, outraged by the Bursum Bill, joined the rising wave of resistance to it. "All of us ought to join in a protest against the grave injustice to that remarkable people of the Southwest," he wrote to anthropologist Edgar Hewett. He thought circulating a petition would be a good idea. "If I can help in the cause in any way," Bolton offered, "let me know."[15]

Bolton's reaction to the Bursum Bill was in line with the interest in Indians that he had expressed earlier and that surfaced in his graduate teaching as well. By 1921 Bolton had supervised ten master's theses and doctoral dissertations that covered U.S. Indian policy in all of the southwestern states and northern states west of the Rockies. Bolton also directed work on Oklahoma Indians, the fur trade, southwestern tribes, and the Nez Perce, Iroquois, and Cayuse Indians. In all, his graduate students wrote thirty-six theses on Indian topics.[16] For most other mentors, these figures would have represented the graduate teaching of a lifetime, but with more than four hundred graduate degrees to his credit, Indian topics accounted for less than 10 percent of Bolton's students' graduate work. Nevertheless, the fact that his students completed ten studies of federal Indian policy between 1914 and 1921 suggests Bolton's interest in this topic at that time.

But no one in 1921 would have argued that Indians were the main subject of Bolton's interest. Spanish missionaries occupied his attention more than anything else. Bolton's consistent praise of Catholic missionaries put him in the forefront of academics who wished to cast Catholic history in a positive light. Bolton was not alone in a crusade to rehabilitate Catholic friars, as Archbishop Hanna's request for hundreds of offprints of his 1917 mission article suggests. Bolton's friend Judge Davis had a special interest in preserving the missions, which was perhaps inspired by his own Catholic heritage.[17] Davis considered himself a peer of Charles Fletcher Lummis, author of many articles and books, including *The Spanish Pioneers*. Although Lummis was not himself a Catholic, his book was distributed to every council of the Knights of Columbus in the United States.[18] Davis described Lummis as "one of your 'here-to-defend' men," while characterizing his relationship with Bolton as that of "fellows in the same regiment, you know!"[19] Evidently Davis believed that he, Lummis, and Bolton were jointly involved in refurbishing the historical image of the Catholic Church and the Spanish Empire.

Catholics were not the only religious group subject to prejudice in the United States. Bigots and eugenicists excoriated Jews on religious and racial grounds. Indeed, college fraternities like Bolton's blackballed Jews as well as Catholics. Nor did the academic world welcome Jews.[20] Professors often inquired about the race of candidates for professorships, and Bolton routinely provided the information. Bolton described an applicant to his brother as a small man who "looked like a Jew," but did not reveal if he actually was a Jew or merely resembled one.[21] Someone else asked about the ancestry of Charles Coan, whose last name raised a doubt. Bolton assured her that Coan was "not a Jew, and his personal appearance would remove any suspicions."[22]

While Bolton evidently believed that Jewishness—or its absence—was apparent in a person's physical characteristics, he did not believe that Jews should be barred from graduate school or academic employment. Bolton trained Jewish students and worked hard to place them, although this was not an easy task, as the case of Abraham Nasatir shows. Nasatir was a gifted student who received the bachelor's degree from Berkeley at age seventeen. He was interested in the history of the Rocky Mountain fur trade, so Bolton asked his former student Thomas Maitland Marshall to direct Nasatir's MA thesis at Washington University.[23] Marshall refused, so Nasatir remained in Berkeley with Bolton, where he finished the MA (1922) and PhD (1926). Marshall met Nasatir while he was in St. Louis doing research. He characterized Nasatir as "a smart but very obnoxious Jew. When he leaves we hope the Jefferson Memorial will be left to us. We hope that we will not see his like again." Bolton coolly replied that if he had refused to work with "a man of ability" because he was "obnoxious . . . half of my men would have been sent elsewhere."[24]

Marshall's vicious comments about Nasatir foretold the difficulty that Bolton would have in placing him. He wrote strong letters that recommended Nasatir as his "most brilliant student," "a real scholar," with "a very fine spirit," though he was "youthful," and "good naturedly egotistical." Because of his youth and enthusiasm, Nasatir needed the "kind guidance of some one who really likes him." If he got the right kind of treatment, he would "almost certainly prove to be a great man."[25] Nasatir landed a one-year job at the University of Iowa, but Bolton's glowing recommendations failed to obtain permanent employment for him. Professor Arthur P. Whitaker explained that Nasatir's "race was against him" in the competition for a job at the Florida State College for Women. Bolton bristled at Whitaker's mention of race: "Such a thing would be inconceivable in another community."[26] Bolton knew better than that. Finally Nasatir landed a job at San Diego State Teachers' College, where two of Bolton's students, Charles B. Leonard and Lewis B. Lesley, already were teaching history, but barriers existed even there. At first Leonard objected to Nasatir and another Bolton student, Clarence DuFour, took the job. Nasatir at last got the San Diego position when DuFour resigned in 1927.[27]

In the 1920s anti-Semitism in academe was common throughout the country. In 1922 Harvard president Abbott Lawrence Lowell, who worried that the proportion of Jews enrolled at Harvard had risen from 7 percent to more than 21 percent, proposed a quota on Jewish admissions. Lowell was surprised when Jews and others attacked his plan, which he thought would benefit Jews and gentiles alike. Harvard's gentility would not be adversely affected by association with unassimilated Jews, Lowell reasoned, and Jews would not be subjected to the increased anti-Semitism that would inevitably result if there were too many Jews at Harvard. To mute the criticism, Lowell appointed a committee to recommend a new admissions policy. The committee restated Harvard's commitment to admissions criteria "free from discrimination on grounds of race or religion." It also recommended a plan to admit more students from the South and West, which was another way of limiting Jewish enrollment.[28]

Even professors who wrote favorable recommendations for Jews were careful to let the readers know that the Jew in question would be socially acceptable, as when Carl Becker wrote to Bolton on behalf of Hans Rosenberg, "Neither in appearance nor in manner does he strike one as particularly Jewish." Rosenberg was "likeable . . . polite and cultivated and modest, in no way aggressive or boastful."[29] Of course, simply disclosing that Rosenberg was a Jew would have been enough to disqualify him for employment in most universities at the time. Berkeley did not hire Rosenberg, but we do not know why.

There is every reason to believe that Bolton was sincere in his condemnation of anti-Semitism, but he had practical reasons to curry favor with the Jewish community. At about the time that Nasatir was working on his master's degree, a Jewish lawyer from San Francisco, Sidney M. Ehrman, began to support Bolton's work with generous contributions. Ehrman had graduated with the Cal class of 1896 and had become a prominent San Francisco attorney. He had also joined the Native Sons. Every year Bolton went before the Grand Parlor meeting of the Native Sons to explain the work of the history department, the accomplishments of fellows whom the organization had funded, and the continuing needs of the history department. In 1922 Bolton declared that Californians ought to be ashamed that they had not published the first history of California, written by the Franciscan missionary Francisco Palóu, *Noticias de la California*.[30] Afterward, Ehrman, still a stranger to Bolton, touched his arm and asked how much it would cost to publish Palóu's work. Bolton said, "Well, $5,000." "All right, the money is yours," Ehrman replied.[31]

From that moment Ehrman underwrote the publication costs of most of Bolton's books. He also gave to Bolton a substantial cash gift—an honorarium, he called it—when Bolton published *Fray Juan Crespi, Missionary Explorer of the Pacific Coast*. In all, Ehrman may have given as much as $50,000 to subsidize Bolton's work. Bolton and Ehrman became personal friends. The Boltons crossed the bay to keep dinner and opera dates with the Ehrmans in the city. In summer they were guests at Ehrman's Lake Tahoe lodge, and Bolton invited Ehrman along on some of his southwestern expeditions to retrace the routes of Spanish explorers.[32] Bolton must have been pleased when the governor appointed Ehrman to the University of California Board of Regents in 1930.

By the standards of the time Bolton's ideas about race and religion were tolerant, and the history he wrote was inclusive, though not universally so. He believed that it was his duty to convert narrow-minded people to a broader view of the past. The Native Sons of the Golden West seemed to be an appropriate audience for Bolton to work on. Some of Bolton's presentations pandered to his listeners' interests in Anglo history, as in 1922 when he extolled Chapman's work on Spanish California, which was funded by the Native Sons. Chapman's "most impressive thesis" was that "Spain's hold on California, weak though it was, made it possible for the United States, when the time came, to absorb California." Otherwise, "our country today probably would be bounded on the west by the Rocky Mountains." The logic was tortured, but the meaning was clear to listeners who heard with Anglo ears. Hispanic history was a prologue to the United States' amoeba-like and presumably benign absorption of California. This sort of pap prepared the way for Bolton to dun his listeners for money to transcribe, translate, and publish Spanish documents and to restore the ruined missions for the edification of California's citizens and tourists. "It seems almost ungracious" to ask for money, "but we are all working together," he said. "You are not working for your own glory, nor for the glory of your Native Sons' fellows," Bolton assured them; "you are working for the glory of California, and so are we."[33] Applause erupted in the room.

After making his pitch for funding, Bolton moved on to somewhat more contentious ground. "I wonder how many of you realize that this ... very week we are celebrating the 100th anniversary of the beginning of representative government in California." Democracy did not begin in California with the raising of the Stars and Stripes in 1846, he explained, but with Mexican independence. First, there was the Revolution in the British colonies, and that event eventually inspired democratic revolts in Spanish America. Thus, California was "the heir of two great struggles for freedom." Not satisfied that he had made his point, Bolton added that "one might say that some of the results of the revolution of 1776, which gave birth to the stars and stripes, coming by way of Mexico beat the flag to California by a quarter of a century."[34] He struck out a sentence explaining that Indians were a substantial part of the electorate in Mexican California.

Bolton also informed the Native Sons that the University of California school of history was embarked on a revisionist course of great importance. In praising the work of the Native Sons fellows, he said that Cal was creating "a new synthesis of American history." "I say," Bolton declared, "American history as it generally has been written, has not been American history," but a provincial story told from an East Coast perspective. Californians had "a higher vantage point and we are trying to show that American history is made up of many national streams."[35]

Bolton's appeal to the Native Sons for an enlarged view of American history enlisted well-educated, broad-minded men like Judge Davis, Sidney Ehrman, and other Native Sons, at least for the time being. Davis's and Ehrman's status as religious minorities may have nurtured their willingness to enlarge American history from the "higher" perspective of California, as Bolton put it. But Bolton's appeal also drew in California boosters who liked the idea of their state's university leading the nation to a new view of history that cast California in an important role. Bolton's new history would not be merely a story of California and the nation, but California and the world. Bolton's borderlands and Americas history appealed to westerners for the same reason that Turner's frontier history did: it made their region important and by extension it made *them* important.

Yet Bolton understood that his appeal for a larger, more inclusive sense of American history must not unduly challenge those Native Sons who had a narrower, more filiopietistic sense of the past than the Davises and Ehrmans among them. He balanced lessons about Mexican democracy and multinational history with praise for those whom he called "the first Americans in this state," which meant immigrants from the United States who had begun to filter into California late in the Spanish era. In 1923 he sketched the pre–gold rush American pioneers who settled in various parts of the Mexican province. Bolton mapped California's Anglo-owned land grant ranchos and explained them as a precursor to the Bear Flag Revolt, but did not bother to mention that most of these men had become Mexican citizens and that few of the Bear Flag rebels—a small minority of Anglos in California—owned land in Mexican California.[36] No one should be shocked that Bolton elided some of the inconvenient details of California history in a series of fifteen-minute talks to a general audience. Anyone who has lectured understands the tyranny of the clock. The relentlessly ticking second hand can change more history in a minute than Napoleon's army did in a year. Yet Bolton understood what to leave in and what to leave out. By carefully choosing his words and topics, Bolton won the favorable opinion of the Native Sons, as well as a steady source of funding for himself and his graduate students. It would not always be so.

Some important subjects in Anglo-California history were so sensitive that Bolton sought the opinion of Judge Davis. His comments on Mary Floyd Williams's thesis about the 1851 San Francisco Committee of Vigilance well illustrate this point. The manuscript had originally been written under Teggart's guidance, and Bolton edited the final version for the University of California Publications in History series. Then he sent it to Davis, perhaps sensing that this delicate topic should be vetted by someone of the judge's stature and sensibilities before printing it for the world to see. Californians had long debated whether the hangings that the vigilance committee had carried out were justified. Many believed that the executions were lynchings dressed up as justice that blotted the character of the Anglo founders of San Francisco.[37] Some of the sons of the founders—Judge Davis, for example—were now numbered among San Francisco's elite and belonged to the Native Sons of the Golden West.

As it happened, the thesis in question portrayed the San Francisco vigilantes as upstanding men who put the safety of the community above strict adherence to formal law. When law failed to protect them, Williams—or perhaps Bolton—wrote, "they did to the outlaws among them the things that seemed right in their own eyes." These actions, in her view, were in the American "spirit" of things and were necessitated by the general lawlessness that prevailed at the time.[38] The vigilance committees, according to Williams, were a form of direct democracy that supplanted corrupt and ineffective (but duly elected) officers and regular courts.

And what did the judge think of this line of reasoning? Splendid! Publish it as soon as possible and with no further editing, which might ruin the book. Not only did the manuscript make early San Franciscans look good, but there were other reasons to publish it as well. "Certain things are transpiring in the world, including the United States," the judge hinted darkly, "which may make us all realize before long that some of these problems of . . . law and order . . . will be present with us soon again."[39] The judge, it seems, advocated the use of vigilantes to stave off Bolsheviks and Wobblies. And so the book was published as part of the ongoing search for a useable past, as well as a celebration of Anglo pluck and resourcefulness in the face of a crime wave.

Not all extralegal activities of the 1850s were regarded as fair game, however. In 1927 the dean of the graduate division complained about the MA thesis of Richard Mitchell, a study of Joaquín Murieta, California's legendary Mexican bandit. The dean thought that the topic was not very uplifting and that it contained no heroes. Bolton snapped back that the thesis had merit as a study of social conditions in frontier California. Then he compared it with Williams's study of the vigilance committee, in which he had found no great heroes but which seemed to serve a useful purpose anyhow.[40] The Murieta thesis was approved and Mitchell eventually became principal of Beverly Hills High School.[41]

Bolton's determination to broaden the perspective on American history without offending Anglo sensibilities is perhaps most apparent in his school text, *California's Story*, coauthored with his former colleague from Stanford, Ephraim D. Adams. The textbook was an important part of Bolton's comprehensive influence on history education at all levels in the state.[42] Bolton's interest in elementary and high school teaching grew naturally out of his experience as a teacher and his brother's field, educational training. Bolton had teamed with Barker to publish their own school text in Texas. Soon after arriving in Berkeley, Bolton had partnered with Teggart on a California history text, but his estrangement from Teggart doomed their project. Adams was a more congenial collaborator. Authorial responsibilities were divided neatly in half. Bolton contributed the story of the Spanish and Mexican eras, while Adams wrote about everything that followed. Bolton took editorial responsibility for the entire text.[43]

Bolton and Adams did not risk alienating California patriots with their textbook. Their preface fulsomely declared that "the authors have emphasized those qualities of courage, self-sacrifice, and service which have been typified in the State's great men. The devotion and heroism of the early [Franciscan] Fathers, the boldness of the Vigilantes, the initiative of the pioneers, the generosity of men prominent in later years—all contribute to that type of citizenship toward which it is hoped all users of this book will strive as an ideal." Leaving aside any criticism of childhood aspirations to vigilantism, which normally have to be tamped down a bit in the school yard, one must acknowledge the forthright manner in which the authors promoted the worship of California's heroes. Bolton and Adams singled out modern-day Californians who exemplified admirable qualities, including Hubert Howe Bancroft, David Starr Jordan, Benjamin Ide Wheeler, and the brilliant botanist (and leading eugenicist) Luther Burbank, as well as industrialists, entrepreneurs, scientists, artists, and contemporary public figures such as Hiram Johnson and Herbert Hoover.[44]

The substantive chapters follow the well-worn trail of Bolton's work. Missionaries, especially Father Junípero Serra, were explorer heroes. The Mexican-American War came and went without apparent cause, but with a good effect—

the U.S. acquisition of California. There were a few interesting twists in the gold rush story. So many men went to California that some people feared that the Eastern Seaboard would lack a sufficient number of workers to staff its industries. Luckily, failed revolutions and famine drove German and Irish immigrants out of Europe and into America. "Thus, the east got these new immigrants," the authors explained, "while California got the pick of the energetic, daring, young Americans." There was no question about who got the best end of that deal. California's Native Sons and nativists alike could cheer the Bolton and Adams narrative.

As promised in the preface, the book portrays the San Francisco vigilantes in the best possible light, which is to say that it follows the reasoning of Mary Williams's thesis. The leaders of the first and second vigilance committees are presented as disinterested men who wanted only to restore good government to chaotic San Francisco. After hanging several bad men and whipping and banishing others, "San Francisco was a quiet, orderly city." Thus salutary hangings and floggings were merely illustrative lessons in American civics. As Bolton and Adams explained, the only way to "have good government all the time was to be on the watch all the time against evil doers."

In addition to cultivating Anglo pioneer sentiment, Bolton intended his little textbook to instruct children in the fundamental facts of California's Hispanic history. More than one hundred heavily illustrated pages tell the story of the Spanish and Mexican influence on California, from the time of Cortés to the coming of Frémont. Watered down it may have been, but Bolton gave the children of California a positive history of the state's Hispanic past. It was the juvenile version of *The Spanish Borderlands,* complete with a hemispheric perspective.

By the mid-1920s Bolton had become a familiar and respected figure in California and an asset for the university. Nevertheless, he was still an employee of the institution in an era when university presidents had immediate authority over the faculty and impressed a personal stamp on daily campus life that would seem extraordinary at today's large institutions. Even trivial transgressions by the faculty could attract the attention of the president. In 1926 President W. W. Campbell made clear Bolton's place in the Berkeley pecking order. It had come to Campbell's attention that Bolton had led his class in a football cheer during the week before the big game with Stanford. In Campbell's opinion, this was "an unjustified use of academic time and opportunity."[45]

Bolton was then fifty-six years old, the department chairman, a full professor with twenty-seven years of college teaching experience. During the 1926 academic year alone, he had published three books in six volumes, and he would be knighted by the king of Spain. Some senior professors might have given an impolitic response to President Campbell's reproach, but not Bolton. He waited a week, and then explained that the problem began when the previous class ran over its allotted time because of an examination. The air in the hall was "very bad," and because of the lateness of the previous class, Bolton's students were slow getting to their seats so "the psychology of the class was very . . . disturbed." He had prepared a difficult lecture that would require the full attention of his students, who suffocated in the fetid and perturbed atmosphere. What was he to do? Professor Bolton drew on his many years of teaching experience. He asked for someone to lead a cheer while his assistants held the doors open, thus clearing the air and improving student psychology in one masterly pedagogical stroke. The whole episode took only five minutes and the lecture was a great success. "I have written the above in order to explain and not to argue." He had attended only one football game in his entire career (a Stanford game), because he was too busy with "writing to find the time."[46] In the end President Campbell agreed that a "reasonable amount of student cheering and singing" once in a while was all right.[47]

This minor incident reveals Bolton's way of dealing with criticism from those who sat in judgment over him. Even as Bolton adroitly explained himself to the president, he insisted that he was loyal and obedient. This was more than a ploy. Bolton moved at the highest levels in the university and had no desire to alienate Campbell.

The skirmish with Campbell preceded a controversy that could have had been more serious because it involved the Native Sons. In 1927 the state legislature with the advice of the Native Sons voted to place statues of Junípero Serra and Thomas Starr King in the national Capitol. Bolton and Davis had strongly supported Serra, but there was a vigorous debate over who should be California's other representative. Eventually a consensus formed among the Native Sons for King—a Protestant minister who supported the Union and raised money for the Sanitary Fund during the Civil War. A newspaper reported that Bolton opposed the selection of King, and this came to the attention of President Campbell and Governor C. C. Young, who had already signed the legislation naming Serra and King. Campbell asked Bolton to explain his views so that he could share them confidentially with the governor.[48]

Now here was some dicey business. If California's leading historian came out against King, then the governor, the state legislature, the Native Sons, the university, and President Campbell would be embarrassed. Bolton, of course, depended on the goodwill of all of these people, and he had just recommended some Berkeley students for Native Sons fellowships. Moreover, the controversy happened to come, Bolton explained, at a moment when there was "a pretty strong feeling on the part of some . . . Native Sons that more work should be done on the American period of California history and less emphasis placed on the Spanish period."[49]

Considering all of this, Bolton answered Campbell carefully. The newspaper had misquoted him, he said. Actually, Bolton had told the reporter that he "had not given the matter sufficient attention to have a personal opinion." Now, Bolton was pleased to report, he had studied King's life and found that "he was a much larger figure than I had supposed." Bolton went on to characterize King as "a worthy representative of California." But he hedged a bit, saying that it would require further study to determine whether King, "next to Serra," was "the *best* representative of California." Nevertheless, he added, two legislatures and the Native Sons had thoroughly considered the matter. Bolton also warned Campbell that some aspects of the question were "not altogether historical. I do not need to commit these to paper, but . . . could tell you better such things as I have learned in a personal conference."[50]

Whatever Bolton might have said privately to President Campbell, some things seem obvious. If Serra, a Spanish Catholic missionary, was to represent California in Washington, D.C., then a New England Protestant minister like King would provide religious and ethnic balance that would mute anti-Catholic sentiment against Serra. At Campbell's request Bolton wrote to the governor expressing his support for Serra and King.[51]

But by then, Bolton had formed an opinion of King quite different from the one he had given to Campbell and Young. When the controversy over King erupted, Bolton asked a former student, Professor Joseph Ellison of Oregon State College, about King's role in the "saving of California for the Union."[52] Under Bolton's direction Ellison had written a dissertation about California during the Civil War. "To say that King 'saved California for the Union' seems to me a great exaggeration," Ellison replied. "It is a myth." King preached to the converted, who received "an extra dose of loyalty making some of them perhaps hysterical." Bolton responded to Ellison on the same day that he wrote the governor. "My opinion of King coincides quite closely with yours."[53]

Bolton's shrewd negotiation of California's cultural fault lines helped to make him the most important historian in the state. Bolton was not only a leading academic historian with an international reputation but also a well-known public figure in California. His rise to public prominence was no accident. He worked at it. By the 1920s Bolton had become the face, the voice, the embodiment of history to Californians—a leading spokesperson for the university as well as the history department and the Bancroft Library. He represented the university's history program before the regents and the state legislature. Newspapermen asked his opinions about historical topics and he provided them, usually without the sort of repercussions that resulted from his comments on Serra and King. Bolton was famous—very famous by academic standards. There are several cartons of newspaper clippings about him in his papers at the Bancroft.[54]

For the most part, Bolton told his public audiences what they wanted to hear, even when that meant ignoring complicated and contradictory evidence. If his supporters in the Native Sons wanted heroic tales about their Anglo forefathers, Bolton provided them. Yet he simultaneously argued in favor of an inclusive, multinational, and multicultural historical view that suggested a new way to envision American history. He had the canny ability to wrap these ideas together in a narrative that washed over his audience without alienating them. When Bolton did disturb his listeners, they let him know about it and he adjusted accordingly. Bolton served many masters, including the university, the Native Sons, and private benefactors. As he saw it in the 1920s, it was his job to keep them all happy. He believed that by serving the university and its friends, Bolton's California school of history would produce a narrative that would stand alongside or even supplant the established story with its northeastern biases. But to do that, Bolton had to cultivate public and private support in a world where history was politicized along ethnic and religious lines.

FIGURE 1.
Bolton as a high school student. Courtesy of the Bancroft Library.

FIGURE 2.
Bolton the school teacher.
Courtesy of the Bancroft Library.

FIGURE 3.
Bolton and his roommate at the University of Wisconsin.
Courtesy of the Bancroft Library.

FIGURE 4.

Charles Homer Haskins and Frederick Jackson Turner at Johns
Hopkins University. Courtesy of the Huntington Library.

FIGURE 5.

Benjamin Ide Wheeler, president of the University of California.
Courtesy of the Bancroft Library.

FIGURE 6.
Henry Morse Stephens at Bohemian Grove. Courtesy of the
Bancroft Library.

FIGURE 7.
University of California Faculty Club, 1902. Stephens is fourth
from left. Courtesy of the Bancroft Library.

FIGURE 8.
Doe Library under construction at about the time Bolton was
hired. Courtesy of the Bancroft Library.

FIGURE 9.
The Bolton Family, c. 1919. Courtesy of Gale Randall.

Bolton and Father Zephyrin Engelhardt at the Mission Santa
Barbara, c. 1915. Courtesy of the Santa Barbara Mission Archive.

FIGURE 11.

Bolton with knights and a few ladies at his round table in the 1930s. Courtesy of the Bancroft Library.

FIGURE 12.

Bolton with one of his gigantic maps for the Americas course.
Courtesy of the Bancroft Library.

FIGURE 13.
Bolton atop an Anasazi ruin. Courtesy of the Bancroft Library.

FIGURE 14.

Bolton and a Navajo guide survey the Grand Canyon. Courtesy of the Bancroft Library.

FIGURE 15.

Bolton salutes his companions (and rides on). Courtesy of the
Bancroft Library.

FIGURE 16.

Bolton taking notes in Mexico, c. 1940. Courtesy of the Bancroft
Library.

FIGURE 17.
Somewhere in Mexico with George Hammond on his left and
Aubrey Neasham on his right. Courtesy of the Bancroft Library.

FIGURE 18.
Bolton (at the head of the table on the left near the windows)
in the Great Hall of the Faculty Club, c. 1948. Courtesy of the
Bancroft Library.

FIGURE 19.
Frederick Jackson Turner at the Huntington Library. Courtesy
of the Huntington Library.

FIGURE 20.

"Captain" Reginald Berti Haselden at his microscope in the
Huntington Library. Courtesy of the Huntington Library.

FIGURE 21.
The final Bolton residence on Buena Vista. Courtesy of the
Bancroft Library.

FIGURE 22.
The Boltons' living room. Courtesy of the Bancroft Library.

FIGURE 23.
Bolton in the 1940s, working in the Bancroft with his assistants
Virginia Thickens and Margaret Walker. Courtesy of the
Bancroft Library.

TEN · Exploration, Empire,
and Patrimony

Bolton wanted to know the ground that his Spanish explorers had covered. His keen interest in mapping and historical geography was apparent as soon as he arrived in the Southwest. For the rest of his life Bolton either would be on the trail in search of Spanish explorers or planning a new expedition. He loved these trips more than anything else he did.

Personal examination of the trails of Coronado, Kino, Anza, and Escalante was as important to Bolton as minute examination of their manuscripts. Bolton conducted his trail research in roadless, rugged, desert terrain that stretched for many hundreds of miles and across an international border. When on horseback, he carried transcripts of the originals in a briefcase looped over the saddle horn in order to accurately map the route and (just as important) to detect inaccuracies, lapses, and elisions in the manuscript. Cross-country travel in the desert could be dangerous, especially in the summer. A few hours in the desert without water in July could kill the unprepared sightseer. Winter days were mild, but nights could be bitterly cold. Bolton's desert treks were not for people who required creature comforts.

By the 1920s the topography of the Southwest was as familiar to Bolton as the card catalog of the Bancroft Library. He liked to call himself an explorer, a title that associated him with the last wave of European and Euro-American discoveries from the poles to the mountains and jungles of Latin America, Africa, and Asia.

Any other scholar working on the exploits of early Spanish adventurers probably would have toured at least some of the territory he had traversed. Few historians would have explored the country as comprehensively as Bolton did. Indeed his name became synonymous with personal exploration of western trails and terrain. His maps remain important sources for the study of northern Mexico and the Southwest. Maps and mapmaking delighted Bolton. "He would work for days and days," recalled Bolton's doctoral student William Henry Ellison, "with large detailed maps spread over the floor . . . on his hands and knees with documents . . . trying to figure out whether Anza passed on one side of a certain hill or the other." Ellison and most of Bolton's other graduate students admired his attention to cartographic detail. A few dissenters thought that his minute attention to explorers' routes and campsites amounted to a trivial pursuit. One of his graduate students boldly murmured during a Bolton lecture that he did not care on which side of the arroyo Jedediah Smith had urinated.[1]

It is safe to assume that only a minority of Bolton's listeners shared such sentiments—and even safer to assume that they would not dare to utter such heresies within Bolton's hearing or within earshot of some of his more loyal students. Indeed, Bolton's students and friends regarded travel on the trail with him as a rare privilege to experience history firsthand, with Bolton's running commentary on historical figures, history, and geography as sound track. Bolton's expeditions to the borderlands were famous. A retinue of guides, National Park Service employees, and friends accompanied him. The cast of supporting characters changed over time, but Bolton was always the star of these desert traveling parties.

On occasion Bolton sought fresh companions for his trail trips. In late 1927 Frank C. Lockwood, a dean at the University of Arizona, invited Bolton to serve on a committee to promote the erection of a statue of Jesuit pioneer Father Eusebio Kino. Bolton enthusiastically accepted Lockwood's assignment. He invited Lockwood to join him on the trail of Juan Bautista de Anza, who had led two expeditions across the Colorado Desert to California between 1774 and 1776.[2] Lockwood jumped at the chance and hired two automobiles and drivers for the occasion.[3] Bolton and Lockwood quickly became fast friends.

Dean Lockwood was the sort of muscular scholar that Bolton appreciated. After a stint as a Methodist minister Lockwood earned a PhD in English literature at Northwestern University in 1896. He taught at Allegheny College, but his political activism and his wife's membership in the Unitarian Church combined to force his resignation.[4] He took a position at the University of Arizona in Tucson. The desert and its history appealed to Lockwood. He switched from studying Wordsworth and Coleridge to writing about Kino and Geronimo.[5] Bolton's work inspired Lockwood to travel in Mexico to see historic sites. On one such foray he hired a guide to go to Cocospera, an isolated mission in the state of Sonora. Once they reached that remote place, the guide attempted to rob Lockwood at knifepoint while they were climbing the stairs in the ruined bell tower. Instead of forking over his cash, Lockwood shouted, "You unmitigated reprobate!" and knocked his assailant down the stone steps.[6] The dean was neither a sissy nor a cusser. One has to admire a man who would not resort to coarse language even while engaged in a knife fight.

The professors' trek through Arizona and Mexico in 1927 and 1928 was typical of Bolton's trips through the region. After arriving in Tucson by train, Bolton met Lockwood and his drivers and headed south. He used Anza's diary to trace the Spanish soldier's route down into Mexico and then turned northwest toward the international boundary at Sonoita, Arizona. The trip took nine days. They ate canned beans, slept in their blankets, and let their beards grow. The cars' high clearance enabled them to drive unimproved roads and across country over sagebrush and cactus, but not always without incident. When they became mired in deep sand, a Mexican boy with a team of horses pulled them out. Then a vacuum tank failed on their Dodge delivery truck. The professors found someone with a similar car, who sold his good part to them. That was lucky, as the closest place to obtain a new part was hundreds of miles away in Phoenix. In Sonoita Bolton hired a local vaquero to guide them, but he could not save them from all trouble. When a spring broke on their Studebaker, the drivers transported it in the Dodge to Yuma for repairs. Meanwhile, Bolton and his guide hiked the fourteen-mile round-trip to Heart Tank, a natural spring where Anza had watered his horses. The Spaniards had called the route "el camino del diablo," and with good reason. The trail must have been hell on men and horses in the eighteenth century, but Bolton and Lockwood thought it was great fun. They supposed that they were the first to cover that rough trail by automobile.[7]

One detail remained. Bolton and Lockwood had crossed back into the United States by way of a mere desert track, instead of going through a port of entry on a regular road. Thus Bolton asked Lockwood (whom he addressed as "Maestre de Campo") to get in touch with the Mexican consul in Tucson. "Since you and I both shall wish to make other trips into Sonora," Bolton sensibly advised, "we must not get into the rogue's gallery."[8]

These desert expeditions were among Bolton's most treasured memories. When he published *Anza's California Expeditions*, Bolton thanked his American and Mexican companions and drivers, including his wife, who drove "the stretch from

Berkeley to Antioch and through the Coast Range to Coyote Creek."[9] Gertrude deserved the tribute. Retracing the Spanish trails in California was a common Sunday outing for the Bolton family. On one of these trips Bolton was driving while Gertrude sat in the passenger seat of their Hupmobile. A short circuit in the wiring gave her a rude shock, and she pled with her husband to stop, but he "stubbornly clung to the wheel," his son recalled, "with a heavy foot to the throttle."[10] He finally stopped—in the nick of time. Gertrude jumped out and the seat burst into flames. What price scholarship?

Bolton photographed his trips, scattering the images through his books with the credit line "Photo by Bolton." He included maps with the information that had been won at the cost of broken springs, failed vacuum tanks, long walks, and nights spent wrapped in blankets on stony ground and tile floors. "Compiled from original data and personal explorations by Herbert E. Bolton," the map captions read.[11] They were among his proudest accomplishments. The Berkeley professor's exploration, maps, and photographs gave his books an air of authenticity as well as the stamp of scholarly authority. Bolton was no mere ivory tower scholar. He conceived of himself as a scholarly explorer, not unlike the studious Kino, who abandoned his academic studies for a life of exploration and evangelism in the wilderness. And, of course, Bolton the explorer-historian was very much like Parkman.

No one who was training graduate students in American history was quite like Bolton. A growing number of graduate students went to Cal to work with him. J. Franklin Jameson's compilation of history dissertations in progress in 1926 show interesting data that Bolton passed on to graduate dean Charles Lipman. With thirty-nine dissertations under way, Berkeley ranked sixth behind Columbia (104), Chicago (99), Harvard (75), Pennsylvania (54), and Wisconsin (49). The only other western universities with an appreciable number of doctoral candidates were Stanford (13) and Texas (12). Most of Cal's history dissertations were on the western United States or on "America south of the United States," Bolton explained.[12] Priestley and Chapman may have guided a few of these projects, but Bolton directed the lion's share. By the spring of 1926, 31 doctors and 164 masters had completed their degrees under Bolton, far fewer than half of his career output of completed graduate degrees.[13]

The staggering number of Bolton's students highlights his contribution to the development of graduate education at the University of California. Building a graduate program at any university requires a critical mass of students—enough people to regularly fill seminars, staff graduate assistantships, and hold fellowships. If these positions had gone unfilled, the university and the Native Sons would likely have withdrawn their support. A large part of Bolton's job was to attract resources to the history program and to annually demonstrate that those resources were being well used by showing that graduate students were getting good jobs and were publishing.[14] Thus the California school—or the Bolton school of history, as it was sometimes called—was an enterprise that demanded constant recruitment of fresh graduate students, replenishment and expansion of public and private funding, and successful placement of finished masters and doctors.[15] The greatest share of responsibility for these efforts fell on Bolton.

The sheer number of Bolton's graduate students raises the question of his attentiveness to graduate teaching. Burdened with administrative work, dedicated to completing his enormous publishing agenda, anxious to get out on the trail, how could Bolton give more than cursory attention to his graduate students? Former students gave dissimilar but compatible answers. When Lockwood queried Bolton's students about their experiences with him as a teacher, they responded with uniform praise about his ability to introduce a spirit of cooperation in the seminar. Often there were more applicants for admission to the seminar than there were seats at his round seminar table. Bolton therefore interviewed prospective students in groups and quickly established who was prepared and who needed more work. Nevertheless, sometimes as many as twenty-five people were admitted to the seminar, so many that the overflow had to sit behind the lucky ones who had a seat at Bolton's table.

The students who admired Bolton's seminar teaching praised his technique of asking questions that revealed to the student the shortcomings of his paper. Bolton always avoided humiliating criticism, they said. Rather, he believed that it was his role to encourage and support graduate student research. Any student's shortcoming in knowledge could easily be remedied, Bolton thought, but the damage done by public humiliation might never be repaired. If they worked hard—which to Bolton meant hard digging in primary sources—graduate students would ultimately produce good work if they had any talent. He taught by example. He seemed to be always at work in the Bancroft Library. When he took a break, he sought conversation among the graduate student night owls in the Bancroft barn. Thus, among his grateful students Bolton earned a reputation as a gentle, knowledgeable critic and a mentor who invited them to collaborate with him on a grand historical adventure.[16]

For most graduate students the combination of avuncular advice and kindly support was irresistible, coming as it did from one of the most important historians of the day. For most of them, Bolton's gentle ways confirmed his greatness as a teacher. For most, but not all. Some thought he was just inattentive, perhaps even lazy in a selfish sort of way. The time that he did *not* spend reading and marking up papers could be used to further his own projects. Earl Pomeroy, who studied at Berkeley in the 1930s, later criticized Bolton for being lax in his oversight of graduate students, making light writing assignments, and sometimes requiring mere reports on research rather than full-blown research papers. Bolton seldom marked up or returned student papers, but even Pomeroy—definitely not a Bolton fan—felt obligated to point out that "he encouraged them, by example and general exhortation, to publish" their work, including some seminar papers. "He liked to speak of his students as . . . 'knights of the round table,' giving them the impression that they were members of a trailblazing fellowship."[17] And, of course, Bolton dispensed patronage to graduate students in the form of graduate assistantships and Native Sons fellowships—not to mention countless letters of recommendation for jobs. To Pomeroy (who completed his doctoral degree under the direction of Frederic Logan Paxson), it seemed that Bolton's students got all the advantages, that Bolton promoted his field above all others, and that he gave a disproportionate share of departmental and library resources to his students and his research interests. Sixty years later Pomeroy still thought it was unfair.

Other graduate students thought Bolton was a savior. Irving B. Leonard went to Berkeley to study Spanish and taught in the language department as adjunct faculty. In the early 1920s, as Leonard recollected, Leslie Byrd Simpson (who was then a young adjunct faculty member) schemed to force Leonard out of the language department so that Simpson's job could be preserved. Leonard, with a wife and two babies to feed, was desperate. Bolton stepped in to make sure Leonard did not lose his teaching job and then took him as a student in the history program.[18] Like Pomeroy, many decades after the fact, Leonard recalled with amazing clarity the controversies that occurred in his graduate days. Leonard was eternally grateful for Bolton's help; Pomeroy (who frankly acknowledged that Bolton had helped him too) thought of himself as being outside Bolton's golden circle and keenly recalled the inequalities that existed under his aegis. Both men doubtless were accurate in their recollections of Bolton, if somewhat selective because of their personal perspectives. Their memories testify as well to the peculiar pressure of graduate school when real and imagined slights are magnified and remembered forever.

Bolton's laissez-faire style of mentoring graduate students seemed to become more apparent as time went forward. In the early days Bolton's close personal association with students like Hackett, Dunn, and Marshall meant that he also spent a good deal of time editing their essays and dissertations so that they could be published in the *Southwestern Historical Quarterly* or by the University of California Press. He was relatively close in age to that first generation of graduates, who felt that they should share professional recognition and success in equal measure with Bolton. That closeness also meant that Bolton's graduate students from the early period felt free to criticize him as their peer, or at least to speak frankly to him. By the 1920s the age difference was much greater. The twenty-something student who arrived at the round table then saw a fifty-something, chain-smoking, workaholic academic powerhouse who controlled everything they needed at Berkeley but the air supply. He spoke generously about sharing a great adventure, but the students of that generation did not expect to share anything with him in equal measure. By then Bolton was too large a figure, too important to their own prospects—and getting too old—for them to comprehend him as anything but a grand and (they hoped) benign and beneficent patriarch.

Bolton's consistent and effective support for Cal's graduate students in history helped them to get academic positions. His job as recommender-in-chief was made somewhat easier because by the 1920s he could recommend his new doctors to former students who were already established at all levels of academe, such as J. Fred Rippy at Duke and Chicago and William Henry Ellison at the State Teachers College in Santa Barbara.[19] During the course of his career Bolton's students held at least ninety-eight jobs in sixty-five colleges and universities. This figure does not count graduate teaching, part-time, or temporary positions. The students who landed these professorships deserve at least as much credit for the accomplishment as Bolton, but placements demonstrated the demand for his students.[20]

Bolton's students taught in twenty-three states and the territory of Hawaii, but they were not hired uniformly across the United States. Eighty doctoral placements were made in colleges west of the Mississippi; eighteen were to the east. Southwestern states accounted for the bulk of the hiring, as might be expected. From the Sabine River to the Pacific Ocean there were sixty-six placements. California institutions alone accounted for thirty-seven, but Texas and Oklahoma together hired fifteen Bolton students. Just as one would expect interest in borderlands and Latin American specialists to have been highest in the Southwest, institutions in the Pacific Northwest and northern plains were least interested in Bolton's students.

The center of gravity for Bolton's placements rested on the border with Mexico, but he placed some of his PhDs east of the Mississippi River, as well. Illinois and Michigan schools hired ten Bolton students. Five of them were priests and nuns who taught at Loyola University in Chicago and Barat College of the Sacred Heart in Lake Forest, Illinois. Prestigious placements came at the University of Chicago and the University of Illinois. The University of Michigan appointed two Bolton students. Before World War II, Vanderbilt, Duke, Ohio State, and Princeton hired Bolton's doctors.

Bolton's influence was strongest in California, especially at Berkeley, where soon after his arrival he had added two of his men, Priestley and Chapman, to the history faculty. He was not finished. In the 1930s and '40s Bolton added even more of his doctoral students to the Berkeley department. Critics thought he went too far.[21] Another two of Bolton's men went to the UCLA faculty. Seven more Bolton students held positions in California state colleges, and eight taught in private institutions. Nine teachers in junior colleges rounded out the list of home-state placements in higher education. In addition to these college placements, Bolton's graduate students filled scores of high school teaching positions. Ninety-two junior high and high school teachers were identified in a 1945 festschrift that listed his students and their employment if known.[22] This figure no doubt understates the proportion of Bolton's master's students who taught school. There was no employment information for 162 of his graduate students (about 40 percent), but it is safe to assume that a substantial number of them taught at some time. Add to the identifiable teachers and professors the unknown number of other students who took his graduate and undergraduate courses, and the true extent of his influence may be roughly estimated. Hundreds of Bolton's students taught history in California at every level from kindergarten to graduate school. Bolton also directly influenced teaching in California as an official university representative to public schools. From time to time he toured high schools and junior colleges, reviewed their history programs, visited classrooms, and evaluated teachers.[23] By the 1920s Bolton had built a teaching empire that spread from Berkeley to the remote reaches of the West and beyond, far beyond. Few history professors have had as much influence on teaching as Bolton.

With 104 doctorates and 323 master's degrees to his credit, the size of Bolton's graduate corps was formidable. The number of women among Bolton's graduates is likewise impressive. Most of Bolton's female graduate students were master's students. In fact, 52 percent of all graduate degrees earned with Bolton were taken by women. When the figures are adjusted to account for people who took two graduate degrees with Bolton by counting them only once, female representation rises to 57 percent. From 1909, when Bolton's first master graduated, until 1944, when he hooded his last PhD, an *average* of nearly six women per year earned a master's degree with Bolton having directed their theses (see table, pp. 168–69).

A phalanx of seventeen women stood among Bolton's doctoral students. On average, Bolton hooded a woman doctor every two years. The first woman to earn the doctorate with Bolton took the degree in 1925, but most of them earned their degrees after 1930. In an age when women were not encouraged to take the PhD, seventeen was a big number. According to oral tradition, Bolton discouraged women from taking the doctorate.[24] It was probably true that Bolton advised women against taking the ultimate degree, but this may have been because he fully understood and frankly explained the difficulty of placing women in university positions. Women's colleges were the exception to the general rule of hiring men exclusively—or at least as the first choice.[25] Four of his doctoral students were nuns who taught at Catholic institutions. None of Bolton's women were placed at comprehensive universities. Capable women historians, such as Adele Ogden, taught high school, or they went into other fields of employment, as did Marian Lydia Lothrop, who worked for the U.S. Civil Service Commission. Whatever their employment destiny may have been, one thing is clear about Bolton's Knights of the Round Table: most of them were ladies.

While women formed a solid majority of Bolton's graduate students, they did not get a fair share of the resources Bolton distributed. Assistantships and fellowships for women were in short supply everywhere. Frederic Logan Paxson asked if Bolton would take a woman from Wisconsin and whether there might be a fellowship or assistantship for her.[26] The woman in question did not take a degree with Bolton—perhaps did not even enroll at Berkeley—but Bolton did see to it that a few of his women graduate students received fellowships and assistantships.[27] The number of women so favored was very small and not in proportion to their numbers in Bolton's history program.

Bolton's gender discrimination, however, should not be understood as a lack of confidence in women's intellectual ability. He consistently relied on women for assistance in Spanish translation. Department secretaries May Corcoran, Helen Carr, and Ellen Fessenden and her sister Josephine assisted in the preparation of his manuscripts.[28] Mary Ross, one of his MA students, took an especially strong role in the writing of *Arredondo's Historical Proof of Spain's Title to Georgia*. "The actual writing was done by myself, but so great has been her aid," Bolton acknowledged, that the 110-page introduction was published separately "under joint-authorship" as *The Debatable Land: A Sketch of the Anglo-Spanish Contest for the Georgia Country*. Bolton's willingness to credit Ross as coauthor infers that she, perhaps like Skinner, had an important influence on his writing.[29] In the 1920s Ross returned to Georgia, her native state, but then went back to Berkeley, where

Bolton's Graduate Degrees by Year and Gender, 1909–1944

Year	Total Degrees	Total MAs	Total PhDs	Number of Women MAs	Number of Women PhDs	Women Graduates (%)
1909	3	3	0	2	0	67
1910	1	1	0	0	0	0
1911	0	0	0	0	0	0
1912	4	4	0	4	0	100
1913	6	6	0	4	0	67
1914	11	10	1	7	0	64
1915	5	4	1	3	0	60
1916	10	6	4	4	0	40
1917	14	13	1	10	0	71
1918	9	7	2	3	0	67
1919	9	7	2	6	0	67
Totals, 1909–1919	72	61	11	43	0	60
Average/Year, 1909–1919	6.5	5.5	1.0	3.9	0	n/a
1920	7	4	3	2	0	29
1921	8	8	0	3	0	38
1922	15	14	1	9	0	60
1923	22	15	7	9	0	41
1924	15	12	3	10	0	67
1925	27	24	3	19	2	78
1926	21	18	3	13	1	67
1927	25	21	4	13	0	52
1928	24	16	8	14	0	58
1929	14	11	3	9	0	64
Totals, 1920–1929	178	143	35	101	3	58
Average/Year, 1920–1929	17.8	14.3	3.5	10.1	0.3	n/a
1930	13	10	3	6	1	54
1931	31	29	2	18	2	65
1932	19	15	4	9	0	47

Year	Total Degrees	Total MAs	Total PhDs	Number of Women MAs	Number of Women PhDs	Women Graduates (%)
1933	17	12	5	5	0	29
1934	17	9	8	4	1	29
1935	12	8	4	3	1	33
1936	15	11	4	5	0	33
1937	12	8	4	4	0	33
1938	8	5	3	2	1	38
1939	9	4	5	2	2	44
Totals, 1930–1939	153	111	42	58	8	43
Average/Year	15.3	11.1	4.2	5.8	0.08	n/a
1940	12	5	7	1	4	42
1941	2	0	2	0	0	0
1942	6	1	5	1	1	33
1943	2	2	0	1	0	50
1944	2	0	2	0	1	50
Totals, 1940–1944	24	8	16	3	6	38
Average/Year, 1940–1944	4.8	1.6	3.2	0.6	1.2	n/a
Total for All Years	427	323	104	205	17	52
Adjusted Total*	378	274	104	198	17	57
Yearly Average, All Degrees (1909–44)	12.2	9.2	2.9	5.9	0.5	
Yearly Average, PhDs (1914–44)			3.5		0.6	
Yearly Average, Women PhDs (1925–44)					.85	

SOURCE: Data from Ogden, Sluiter, and Crampton, *Greater America*, 549–672; and Bannon, *Bolton*, 283–90.

*Arrived at by counting only once people who took two degrees with Bolton.

she supervised student teachers of social studies at the University of California experimental high school—yet another reinforcement of Bolton's influence on California's history teachers. Ross said that she continued to assist Bolton in research and editing.[30] If so, he did not acknowledge her help in the prefaces of his books except for proofreading his biography of Kino.[31] However great Ross's contribution may have been, in the 1920s his style took on the romantic tone that characterized his work ever after.

Professional limitations for women were more than an academic concern for Bolton. His sixth daughter Gertrude was a history teacher with a master's degree in modern European history. She enrolled in the doctoral program at Cal, but dropped out to teach at the Kamehameha School for Girls in Honolulu.[32] After two years she wanted a college teaching job in California. Her supportive father wrote twenty-six letters to the presidents of every junior college and state college in the state. Bolton assured them that she was capable of teaching courses in modern Europe as well as U.S. history, civics, and of course, Bolton's history of the Americas.[33] After Bolton recommended his daughter for a position at San Francisco Junior College, he wrote a second letter insisting that it was imperative to hire someone who could teach his Americas course at the new junior college. Gertrude got the job.[34]

The placement of so many students at all levels of the educational system enabled Bolton to spread his core idea for revamping the way history was taught—the Americas. Bolton's two-semester course was well established at Berkeley, but the lack of a text held back the adoption of the course at other institutions. In 1928 he published an elaborate syllabus for the course.[35] Bolton assigned it to his students and hoped that the book would provide the needed pedagogical tool for professors who taught the course elsewhere.

Of course, Bolton sent the syllabus to Turner, who had retired from Harvard and was living in Pasadena. Turner's acknowledgment of the Americas syllabus was positive but perfunctory. A quick perusal convinced him that it would have "a real and important influence upon the study of American history."[36] "You of course recognize it only as a pioneer effort," Bolton responded. He planned to write a two-volume work on the Western Hemisphere, but in the meantime his syllabus would have to do. "I may never get it done," he accurately predicted. "I would not do you the injustice to claim that I have in any satisfactory way expounded or applied your views of the frontier[;] nevertheless they are, in my mind at least, one of the underpinnings of the framework which I have constructed in my crude way," he acknowledged. "I am not sure that you would be able to recognize them."[37] Once again, the student asked the master to engage his ideas. Once again, Bolton was disappointed. Turner's failure to intellectually debate or critique Bolton's work was perhaps understandable. The elder scholar was getting on in years and his health was fragile. Did Turner believe that Bolton had carried on and perhaps expanded Turner's ideas about frontiers and sections, or that he had merely added peripheral material to the main story of U.S. history? Turner never said.

Turner had retired from Harvard, but he continued his research in the newly opened Huntington Library in San Marino, California, which his old friend Max Farrand directed. Farrand, who had tried to hire Turner at Stanford and Yale, believed that Turner could offer sound advice and speed development of the new research library. Thus the preeminent historian of the American frontier (and a pretty good fly fisherman) finally moved to California. "It was with great delight that I learned . . . that you were coming to California," Bolton told Turner. Bolton's enthusiasm was sincere. "Everybody here on the coast realizes what a great thing it is for us to count you as one of the Far Western group of scholars."[38] Bolton was still top gun in California, but Turner's presence on the coast might have reminded him of the joke he had made about Turner at the American Historical Association meeting a few years previously—like a sore thumb, always on hand.

In 1928 Bolton once again seemed to have a serious chance at the AHA presidency. The Nominating Committee chair was Bolton's student and friend Charles Hackett. Hackett greatly admired Bolton, but conditions kept him from pushing Bolton for the second vice presidency, despite the fact that he had twelve nominations, which placed him in the top rank of potential candidates. Ephraim D. Adams, Bolton's friend and coauthor, was one of the other leading candidates. Adams suffered from an apparently terminal case of tuberculosis, so there was strong sentiment for his nomination. In addition to these sad circumstances, the punctilious Hackett did not want it to appear that he was unduly pushing his mentor at the expense of other deserving candidates. Bolton supported Adams's nomination and actually wrote on his behalf. The ailing Adams got the nod.[39] It was beginning to look as if Bolton would never reach the AHA presidency.

In 1928 two University of Colorado professors who had studied with Turner planned a conference on the history of the trans-Mississippi West to meet in Boulder the following year. Bolton and Turner agreed to attend.[40] There would be roundtable discussions and individual papers meant to provide a broad perspective on western history. Turner did not want to speak formally but wished to provide advice and a friendly presence.[41] Bolton agreed to speak after dinner. His address had the promising title "Defensive Spanish Expansion and the Significance of the Borderlands," which echoed Turner's "Significance of the Frontier in American

History."[42] Even though Turner would have only an informal role perhaps the conference at last would provide a forum to contrast and compare the ideas of Turner and Bolton.

If Bolton had hoped that his address would engage Turner, he was disappointed. Turner's health prevented him from going to Boulder. Even though he was not in the banquet hall, Turner was still an important presence. Before Bolton gave his address, someone suggested that the conference send salutations. The entire assembly rose to salute Turner.[43] Then Bolton stood to address his audience. His speech was one of his most important statements about the meaning of borderlands history. "The old Spanish Borderlands were the meeting place and fusing place of two streams of European civilization," he averred, "one coming from the south, the other coming from the north."[44] The borderlands were "a zone of contact, the scene of a long series of conflicts, ending in territorial transfers." In spite of these changes in national sovereignty Spanish culture was a continuing presence in the southern tier of states. "It is we of the borderlands," Bolton said, "who have the strongest historical bonds with our Latin neighbors." Bolton's contemporary borderlanders appreciated Latin Americans' "brilliant minds, their generous hearts, and their delicate culture." He concluded with this ringing call: "It would be only fitting if we of the borderlands should be foremost in a fair-minded study of our common historical heritage, foremost in a study of our common problems, and foremost in making closer and stronger bonds of true international understanding." Bolton found in his study of the borderlands not only a unique and romantic heritage (which his address also illustrated) but a meaningful history that informed the present and lit the path to a cooperative future with Latin America.

Bolton thought he had found a useable past strikingly different from Turner's jeremiad about American history. Turner wondered in his frontier essay what the future might hold for the United States now that the frontier was closed. If the particular conditions that promoted national development and fostered the emergence of American character no longer existed, what now? In Bolton's mind, history pointed to a hopeful future because Spain had left its imprint on the borderlands, thus making the region's residents more sensitive and open to Latin American culture. He thought modern borderlanders and Latin Americans could work together to solve common problems. Turner saw barriers to civilization and dead ends in non-Anglo cultures; Bolton saw cultures that mixed and fused. Turner worried about a frontier that had forever closed once free land was gone; Bolton saw the borderland frontier as an opening for a cooperative future.

What did Turner think of all this? "The Conference was a very real success,"

Turner's student James F. Willard wrote him. "The papers were excellent, especially one by Herbert E. Bolton," he added, and promised to send Turner a copy of the proceedings.[45] If Turner read Bolton's address, he did not mention it to Bolton.

Turner was silent, but Bolton was not. In the 1920s Bolton continued to publish documentary volumes much like his translation of Kino. His edition of Francisco Palóu's *Historical Memoirs of New California* was meant to be a foundation document for California history. It was also marked by the romantic gloss that appealed to Californians "who have lived to enjoy the fruits of the civilization whose seeds" Palóu planted. The padre was "one of the great figures" of "the heroic days" of California's mission era.[46] Bolton had no reservations about the goals of Palóu and his missionary companions, who brought "Faith and civilization to the wilds of America, both North and South." While Bolton emphasized the historical value of Palóu's writing, he also made clear that the friar had recorded "heroic deeds."[47]

By now, Indians, who had taken a leading role in Bolton's early work, had become mere objects of missionary attention. In his edition of Fray Juan Crespi's account of Spanish exploration and settlement in California, Bolton described the Indians as "heathen" and "rude neophytes," while Crespi was a "splendid wayfarer."[48] Like Kino and Palóu, Crespi was no mere recorder of facts, but a hero whose "Christian teachings" to the native people would "never die." Crespi's diaries contained "the adventures, the thrills, the hopes, the fears" of Franciscan missionaries, but little of the Indians' motivations. Bolton sometimes included notes to anthropological literature, but allowed statements such as Crespi's "thievishness is a quality common to all Indians" to stand without comment.[49]

There was no venom in Bolton's decision to allow missionaries to speak for themselves, ethnocentric stereotypes and all. His intention was not to vilify Indians, but to glorify his heroic friars. He was writing for an appreciative audience—local patriots and Catholics who loved the positive history that Bolton published.[50] Had the Native Sons included a substantial number of California Indians, Bolton might have given more thought to the friars' language and biases. But in the 1920s and '30s Bolton did not have to worry about a constituency that was critical of damage caused by missionary zeal and colonial conquest. These voices would rise later. For the time being Bolton preached to the converted. Neither Bolton nor his admirers realized that in later times Bolton's editions of missionary writings would be one of the important sources of evidence for ethnohistory that was critical of the men and events that he sought to valorize.

Scholars should be grateful for the great care that Bolton took in translating and editing these important documents. His meticulousness in the archives and on the trail gave his publications lasting utility. However, in retailing the accounts of missionaries and soldiers while characterizing them as heroes, Bolton gave his stamp of approval to a conquest that was sometimes brutal and frequently disastrous to Indian society. In due time this criticism would be laid at Bolton's door, an unexpected patrimony.

ELEVEN · The Grand Patriarch

The 1930s were challenging years for the University of California. In July 1930 Robert Gordon Sproul became president of the university. No one was surprised. As university vice president and secretary of the regents, Sproul was in effect the "operational president" from 1920 on, according to Clark Kerr, Sproul's successor.[1] Bolton, of course, knew Sproul well and worked closely with him. Sproul assumed the presidency during the Great Depression, a time when his legendary attention to budgetary detail was most needed.

Hard times for the country meant hard times for the university. Yet there was a glimmer of hope. In the midst of the depression Bolton would have plenty of money to fill two new and much needed senior positions. In 1930 university benefactors provided endowments for two new history professorships, the Margaret Byrne in American history and the Sidney H. Ehrman in European history. The Ehrman endowment grew out of a family tragedy, the untimely death of Sidney Hellman Ehrman, son of Bolton's benefactor. Like his father, young Ehrman had an interest in history. After taking the baccalaureate at Berkeley, he studied European history at Cambridge University, where he contracted a horrible infection in 1929. His parents rushed to Sidney's side, but to no avail. The Ehrmans endowed a chair for European history at Cambridge and another at Berkeley in their son's memory.[2] Shortly after his son's death Sidney Ehrman was named a regent of the University of California.[3]

In 1930 death came to one of Bolton's important friends, Judge John F. Davis.[4]

The judge, domineering though he was, had been one of Bolton's most important allies among the Native Sons, his colleague on the State Historical Commission, and a savvy navigator on the choppy political waters of state politics. No one could entirely replace him as an effective advocate for the Native Sons' fellowship program.

Hoping that Davis was a good Catholic, Father Zephyrin Engelhardt said an RIP for him. Alas, he would have done the same for Charles F. Lummis, who had died in 1928, but he was not a Catholic. "He jumped into eternity with both feet without examining whether there is a bottom to it," so the Franciscan priest would not sing the mass for him. Engelhardt, motivated no doubt by the most kindly intentions for Bolton, went on to explain that it was "stupidity" not to act to save one's soul. "The Lord save us, but we must want to be saved and must save ourselves, too," he explained.[5] Engelhardt's not-so-subtle message was clear: Bolton knew "the Truth" and should act accordingly. The message could not have been lost on Bolton, but he remained silent on his religious beliefs, even to well-meaning priests who were his friends. He continued to believe whatever he believed as quietly as possible.

In 1930 Bolton published one of his major works, *Anza's California Expeditions*, consisting of four volumes of translated diaries and correspondence, plus a fifth (separately published as *Outpost of Empire*) containing Bolton's history of events based on the documents. Bolton's narrative covered Juan Bautista de Anza's leadership of two expeditions to California and the founding of San Francisco between 1774 and 1776. *Outpost* was Bolton's first full volume of history since publishing *The Spanish Borderlands* in 1921. Since then, his many other publications had been edited documents with long introductions that were sometimes reissued separately.[6] Bolton's introductions had given him practice in presenting his Spaniards in a grand heroic light. Under Bolton's pen Anza's deeds were comparable—indeed superior—to those of Lewis and Clark. Anza he characterized as "a man of heroic qualities, tough as oak, and silent as the desert from which he sprang."[7] One sees the archetypal western hero—quietly strong and determined to do the right thing. But there was something more here than mere hero-mongering (though there was plenty of that). Bolton had learned how to construct a lively historical narrative that captured the reader's imagination. He had assimilated the writing lessons that Johnson, Skinner, Turner, and Parkman had offered him. Bolton's prose was now sprinkled with memorable imagery, as when he briefly described Anza or the conquest of New Mexico: "Now, like an athlete, gathering force for a mighty spring, the frontier of settlement leaped eight hundred miles into the wilderness." He was not Parkman, but he had become an engaging narrative writer.

In this book Bolton saw the Indians as his Spanish friars and soldiers saw them—as fitting subjects for improvement by religious instruction, or perhaps as sly and dangerous opponents. But in one case Bolton found an Indian personality worthy of extended treatment: Palma, a Yuma chief. The helpful Palma wanted baptism and longed for a mission in his Colorado River homeland. His story thus became a minor theme that reinforced Bolton's positive larger story of Spaniards bringing civilization to America. He titled the concluding chapter "Palma Before the Cathedral Altar." Bolton's use of Palma as a foil for his European protagonists was a literary trick that he could have learned from Parkman.[8]

Not everyone appreciated Bolton's prose or his Spanish hero-mongering. Constance Lindsay Skinner reviewed *Anza's California Expeditions* for a New York paper. She thought Anza a "typical product of the Spanish-American frontier," but rejected Bolton's claim that Anza's exploits were greater than those of Lewis and Clark. "One blinks, hardly believing such arrant nonsense can really be on the page," she wrote. Anza's travels were not heroic, but the common stuff of "frontier folk." Skinner thought that the value of the book lay not in Bolton's "deductions and interpretations," but in the documents that he presented.[9] The critique was rooted as much in her Anglophilia as it was in Bolton's literary excesses. Yet she grudgingly admitted that students of the frontier owed Bolton a debt of gratitude for publishing the documents.

There is much truth in Skinner's review, but she missed some things. Of course there was the large, folded map, "Anza's Routes through Pimería Alta," which showed his trails crossing the international border, Bolton's usual symbol for inferential transnational meanings.[10] But this time Bolton's final words on the founding of San Francisco went beyond cartographic inference. San Francisco developed "on the borderland of competing powers and varied civilizations." Spain, Mexico, Russia, England, and the United States competed for California and the town that Anza founded. "One flag followed another" until the United States won the prize. But even then, "an astounding medley of races" converged on California during the gold rush. In the twentieth century San Francisco was still "a borderland community, an interpreter of diverse faiths, a nexus between Nordic and Hispanic cultures, a Western Hemisphere outpost toward the vast world that lies beyond the Pacific, a link between the restless Occident and the patient, mighty Orient."[11] Here Bolton explicitly used the borderland motif to tell a national story with transnational dimensions. And because San Francisco was still a borderland community, its future was open to new transnational possibilities. Whereas Turner's frontier ended, Bolton's borderland frontier lived on with the continuing invigoration of new national and cultural contacts.

There was more to Bolton than hero worship. He had been giving short takes on the borderlands since his 1917 mission essay, but his thought remained general, inchoate, asserted rather than argued. He seemed to be working up to a big statement about the significance of the borderlands in American history. Perhaps he was waiting for the right moment.

In 1930 the right moment appeared on the horizon. Ephraim Adams was in a Pasadena sanitarium for advanced tubercular victims. In January Adams came down with pneumonia. Then his heart began to fail. Bolton arranged for Adams to receive an honorary degree from Cal in May, but he was not well enough to make the trip north to receive it. "It is very much like you to have thought of this," Adams told his old friend. They were giving him the "rest-cure" in Pasadena, and Adams hoped to be teaching at Stanford in the fall. Adams returned to Stanford, but not to teach. His funeral was held in the Stanford crypt.[12]

Adams's death left a vacancy in the chain of succession to the AHA presidency. In 1931 Bolton was named to fill the empty slot for the first vice presidency, which meant that he would finally become president in 1932.[13] His presidential address would be the perfect moment to develop his ideas about the American borderlands. Or would it?

As only the second president from west of the Mississippi Bolton felt obligated to represent the interests of the West. The Pacific Coast Branch had been founded to provide an opportunity for Far West members of the AHA to enjoy some of the benefits of the parent organization without the expenditure of time and money required to go to meetings in the East. On rare occasions the AHA meeting ventured to the Midwest or the South, but most meetings were on the Eastern Seaboard. With the exception of the "special" meeting in the Bay Area in 1915 during Stephens's presidency, the AHA had never met on the West Coast. This was a matter of concern to the growing contingent of western historians who belonged to the AHA. Before the Toronto meeting Bolton told one of his friends at Princeton that he might propose that one year out of four the AHA meeting should be held west of the Mississippi River. He supposed that such a proposal would be regarded as "radical" by eastern members.[14] This issue and other western complaints would continue to fester during the 1930s.

More than regional changes were afoot in the historical profession. During the 1930s Bolton's generation took over. His immediate predecessor as AHA president happened to be Carl L. Becker, Bolton's Wisconsin fraternity brother. Finally the "old guard" whom Bolton had complained about in 1922 was being replaced. Of course, the new leaders of the profession were not youngsters. Bolton and the others were in their sixties when they assumed the AHA presidency.

Bolton's tenure as president probably convinced President Sproul to add to the historian's prestige by naming him the Sather Professor of History. The much loved Henry Morse Stephens had formerly held the Sather professorship, but it had remained unfilled since his death in 1919. In 1930 Bolton's salary was $7,500, and he had not had a raise since 1924, the year when he turned down $10,000 and the Texas presidency.[15] With the Sather professorship, Sproul gave Bolton a raise to $8,000.[16]

The raise was nice, but the effects of the depression could not be denied. The state legislature cut the total university budget by 26 percent between 1931 and 1939.[17] Faculty, including Bolton, adsorbed some of the fiscal pain in the form of salary reductions, but his was restored after two years. Some of his colleagues did not see their 1932 level of compensation again in the 1930s.

The honor of the AHA presidency and the Sather professorship no doubt meant much more to Bolton than the temporary pay reduction. New honors came to him in 1931 when the king of Italy made him Knight Commander of the Crown, a recognition that went nicely with his 1926 Spanish knighthood.[18] Bolton's appreciative studies of Catholic missionaries had made him an international figure.

Bolton's importance was recognized at home as well as abroad. For years Bolton had made annual recommendations to the Native Sons of the Golden West for two traveling fellows funded at $1,500 each. The fellowships had been invaluable to the graduate students, to the Bancroft Library, and to Bolton. After making recommendations in 1930, the Native Sons told Bolton not to bother referring any names for the following year. He no doubt figured that the depression had taken its toll, but the Native Sons had a plan. Instead of funding graduate students, they gave Bolton $3,000 for a research trip to Europe in the summer of 1931.[19] He had long anticipated such a trip, but the demands of work at the university and the cost had prevented him from going. Now he planned a whirlwind tour of archives in search of material for a biography of Kino.

Bolton was in Europe less than three months. It would prove to be his only trip to the Old World.[20] He spent most of his time in Spain, but also went to France, Italy, Belgium, Holland, and England. As usual, he regarded his research as a glorious adventure—an exploration in search of his hero that rivaled Henry Morton Stanley's search for David Livingstone in Africa. He had "ransacked the repositories of America and Europe," he revealed in his introduction, aptly titled "An Adventure in Archives and on the Trail." "Equally intriguing . . . has been my odyssey on Kino's trail," a sentiment reminiscent of Parkman's claims about research in the open air.[21]

Bolton returned from his barnstorming tour of European archives excited and refreshed, but he still had to attend to the mundane details of his job. Filling the Byrne and Ehrman professorships with top-notch people would be important to the university, the department, and Bolton. The university wanted to attract senior professors who would become new jewels in the Berkeley crown. One of the two new faculty would likely succeed Bolton as department chair. At Cal, retirement was mandatory at the age of seventy—in 1940 for Bolton. He wanted to bring in someone who would secure his legacy at Berkeley. For that reason the Byrne professorship was the most important because the Americanist would likely have the most influence on the program that Bolton had created.

Bolton developed a list of four prominent historians as candidates for the Byrne: James Truslow Adams, Frederic Logan Paxson, Eugene C. Barker, and Arthur M. Schlesinger. Adams and Paxson quickly moved to the top of the list. Adams, a man of independent means who had never held an academic appointment, was probably a straw candidate as far as Bolton was concerned.[22] Paxson appealed to Bolton for several reasons. He had won the Pulitzer Prize for his *History of the American Frontier* and had studied with Bolton under McMaster at Penn.[23] Wisconsin had hired Paxson to replace Turner. As Turner's heir at Wisconsin, Paxson had the name most clearly associated with the history of the American frontier, but his interests were varied. His dissertation, and first book, examined U.S. recognition of Latin American republics.[24] We can imagine Bolton thinking that Paxson was a historian who would fully understand and sympathize with Bolton's broad Americas concept. Consequently, Sproul offered Paxson the Byrne chair. Bolton promised to throw his hat in the air and cheer if Paxson agreed to come. He hoped that Paxson would be "sympathetic toward the larger aims" of the Berkeley department, especially "Hispanic America" and "the Western Hemisphere (such as I am developing in my History of the Americas)." Paxson accepted the offer.[25]

Now Bolton turned to the Ehrman chair. He recruited James Westfall Thompson from the University of Chicago for the professorship that Ehrman had endowed with $250,000—an immense sum in the midst of the depression. (The Byrne endowment was only $150,000.) A prolific writer, Thompson was perhaps the most important medieval historian in the United States at the time.[26]

The Paxson and Thompson hires were home runs. Both men were stars who had been raided from top-flight universities. Each was at the top of his game and would add luster to the University of California for years. The university's ability to come up with big money for major professors during the depression spoke to Cal's growing power and prestige. Bolton's ability to recruit such men made him a hero at home and increased his professional clout. The president-elect of the American Historical Association could accomplish big things in the history profession—there was no doubt about that. Paxson's acceptance was probably most important to Bolton's peace of mind. The big man from Wisconsin seemed simpatico with Bolton in every way and would help to secure Bolton's legacy, or so it seemed at the time.

While Bolton was recruiting new professors, Frederick Jackson Turner toiled in the congenial atmosphere of the Huntington Library. Since moving to California in 1928, Turner had taught occasional courses at Cal Tech and worked on the "Big Book," as his long-awaited project in American history was called (now with a bit of derision from historians who felt they had waited too long for it to appear). Turner's health was failing. His heart was weak, and he developed other infirmities. On March 14, 1932, he suffered a heart attack that he knew would be fatal. "Tell Max [Farrand] that I am sorry I haven't finished my book," he told the doctor.[27] He died that evening in his home. The funeral was in Farrand's residence on the grounds of the Huntington Library. Turner was cremated and his ashes were sent to Madison for interment.[28] He had lived for seventy-one years, a full life by the standards of the day. Yet it seemed impossible to his friends and students that he was gone. Guy Stanton Ford was stirred when he read Farrand's memorial for Turner. Sitting at his desk in Minnesota at the end of the day, Ford kept thinking, "Is Turner really dead? Did he grow old, become deaf, halt in his springy stride?" Ford could not accept it. "It is strange how I cannot associate age or failing powers with Turner. They do not belong with him any more than rust on a Damascus blade." Turner's death reminded Ford of his own mortality. "If Turner grew old we must all be growing old," and "what came to such an embodiment of eternal youth, is even more inescapable for all the rest of us."[29]

Bolton had written occasionally to his other mentor, John Bach McMaster, but he had never been as important to him as Turner.[30] In 1932 McMaster was in frail health but still labored at his memoirs. "Time was plentiful," he wrote, but never completed the sentence.[31] A heart attack took him on May 14, 1932.

Bolton had seen Turner several times at the Huntington Library and even visited him at his Pasadena home shortly before his death. Farrand's memorial notice moved Bolton to comment on Turner's qualities as a professor.[32] "Turner was not only one of the great scholars but also one of the great teachers of his generation." It was a loss to the world that Turner had not been able to finish his long-anticipated book. "However," Bolton philosophized, "I suppose that nobody ever finishes his job. Turner would have done enough if he had never written anything but his essay on the significance of the frontier." Late in his own life Bolton still referred to Turner as the Master.[33]

Eight months after Turner's death Bolton rather thoughtlessly remarked to Farrand that "I might drop dead and never finish my book."[34] But Turner reached out from the grave and published two volumes posthumously. Or rather, his constant friend Farrand published them for him. The first was a collection of Turner's essays on sectionalism compiled by Farrand, which won the Pulitzer Prize.[35] Three years after Turner's death the "Big Book," *The United States, 1830–1850*, finally appeared, with the concluding chapters completed by Farrand.

While Bolton always praised Turner's work on the frontier and sections, his geographical perspective was far broader than his mentor's. In 1931 John Parish announced the Pacific Coast Branch's new journal, the *Pacific Historical Review*, and Bolton made a few suggestions to its editor. He was "disappointed in one particular." As announced, the journal would be about the western United States, which Bolton thought too narrow because that region was "not an historical unit, or at least never was until relatively recent times." The "entire Pacific Coast area from Panama to Alaska was a unit down to the middle of the eighteenth century," and Bolton doubted "if any worth while study of the western portion of what is now the United States has been or can be made for this earlier period without keeping in mind the entire region." Indeed, Bolton would have preferred that the journal include "the entire Pacific Coast area of the Western Hemisphere," although he admitted that there might be practical reasons to place more modest geographic limits on the new journal. Nevertheless, Bolton was "not writing this note merely to register a difference of opinion, but am doing it in the hope that it may have some influence" on the "scope of the publication, which ought to mean much for the history of the Western Hemisphere," he insisted. The journal would "miss its part and lose its opportunity if too narrowly conceived."[36]

Professor Parish, who was on the UCLA history faculty, got the message. The new journal should express Bolton's concept of hemispheric history, the hallmark of the California school. When the first number of the *Review* came off the presses, Parish declared, "The Basin of the Pacific was an entity. Its history was a unity." Therefore the new publication would be "a medium of expression for this unity." The *Pacific Historical Review* would welcome articles about the western states "of both North and South America, on the islands of the seas, and on the new and old countries of Australia and Japan, China and Asiatic Russia."[37] Because the annual PCB conference was a mini-AHA with all fields represented, editor Parish allowed that occasional articles from other regions would also appear in the pages of the journal. Pushed by Bolton, Parish conceived of an even broader publication than the Berkeley patriarch had imagined. Bolton's hemispheric outlook was there, but so was the echo of Stephens's Pacific Coast history that reached out across the sea to Asia. Thus the distinctive transnational perspective of the *Pacific Historical Review* was born.

Bolton's advice about the new journal may have crystallized his thinking about his AHA presidential address. When he was notified of his election, he groused that he would "be in misery" for two years racking his brain for something to say.[38] His address would have been a matchless opportunity to develop his ideas about borderlands history, but as his letter to Parish showed, hemispheric history was never far from his mind. At first he planned to speak on a narrower topic, Jesuit missionaries in Latin America—a lecture that would have offered a counterpoise to Francis Parkman's classic account of the Jesuits in French Canada. The choice of subject seemed especially appropriate for a meeting in Toronto, but as the meeting drew near, Bolton completely changed his topic. Perhaps James Truslow Adams's 1931 book, *The Epic of America*, changed his mind.[39] Adams had written only about the United States, rather than "America," as the title promised. This was one of Bolton's pet peeves. Whether in response to Adams or for some other reason, Bolton would deliver his famous and much criticized address "Epic of Greater America."[40] He would use his presidency as a bully pulpit from which to preach the need for American history that transcended petty national perspectives.

Bolton had come to believe that what he called traditional national histories, taught without a broader context, were not only narrow but misleading and destructive. In announcing the appointment of Paxson and Thompson to their professorships, Bolton observed that the University of California had already become one of the nation's leading graduate schools in history with students (mostly Bolton's) who occupied important academic positions throughout the land. The new professors would add to the importance of Berkeley as a center for research and graduate training. Then he declared that although it was "customary to say that it is a greater achievement to make history than to write it," that depended on "how history is made, and how it is written." Historians participated "in the making of history, and their influence may be good or bad. Somebody has bungled things badly in recent history making," he wrote without making clear exactly what had been botched. He averred that bad historians "whose interpretations were not only influential, but unsound and therefore vicious" were partly responsible for an unnamed turn of events (perhaps meaning the rise of European fascism). Paxson and Thompson would add to California's ability to produce "well trained historians" who were "as important to the world as well trained scientists, doctors, or lawyers."[41] Surely Bolton believed that he was making history as well as writing it, that his hemispheric view corrected unsound and perhaps vicious interpretations, and that his work and that of his students would have far-reaching effects.

When Guy Stanton Ford asked about Bolton's historical "points of view," he replied that "the most expansive idea which interests me is the presentation of American history as Western Hemisphere History instead of Brazilian History, Canadian History, or United States History." It was "absurd to assume that the Western Hemisphere has developed in isolated chunks," he continued, "yet we in the United States have proceeded on that assumption."[42] The coincidence of Bolton's presidency and the Canadian meeting must have seemed almost providential. The Canadian city would give Bolton an appropriate stage on which to proclaim his hemispheric point of view.

As the date of the AHA meeting approached, University of Toronto authorities informed Bolton that they would confer an honorary Doctor of Laws degree on him at the time of the conference. This was Bolton's fourth honorary degree, the first three having come from Catholic institutions: Catholic University of America, Saint Ignatius College (now the University of San Francisco), and Saint Mary's College in Moraga, California. More honorifics would follow, but the Toronto degree, combined with the AHA presidency, elevated Bolton to a plateau that few historians ever reached. The boy from Tomah who wanted to rise in society had indeed risen.

Bolton's presidential address was the view of a man who was seeing it all from the top. Ten years previously he had lectured the AHA about the need for a hemispheric course. Then he was well established; by 1932 he was the top dog. His address struck all the familiar themes of his hemispheric Americas course. United States history that was taught from the perspective of only the thirteen British colonies that formed the United States had "helped to raise up a nation of chauvinists." Because of the growing importance of inter-American relations and "from the standpoint of correct historiography," it was time for a change to a synthetic general course on hemispheric history that would provide a foundation for national courses. His footnote to that sweeping statement said merely that "this point is so patent that it hardly needs demonstration," adding that "a movement in this direction is well under way."[43] The movement, of course, was centered at Berkeley and carried to other campuses primarily by Bolton's students. "The Epic of Greater America," enunciated at Toronto, Bolton no doubt believed, would accelerate and broaden the trend that he had begun in California.

Bolton devoted the bulk of his speech to a history of the Western Hemisphere from the age of Columbus to modern times. While recognizing the competition among European nations for colonial resources, he stressed what he regarded as broad commonalities of historical development. Spanish, English, French, and other European colonies were organized around a system of mercantilism. The British North American colonies were only the first to revolt against the mother country; Latin American colonies followed suit not long afterward. All the newly independent countries eventually established democracies that were more or less successful. Every new country experienced periods of conflict and instability. The frontier had reshaped European institutions everywhere, just as Turner had explained for Anglo-America and the United States. All people yearned for freedom and prosperity and had achieved a good deal of it. The world war had even demonstrated "emphatic Western Hemisphere solidarity," because, "of the twenty states to the south, eight joined the Allies, five broke relations with Germany, and seven remained neutral."[44] This seemingly happy agreement among the American nations was now threatened because, Bolton said, European capital and people were moving rapidly to South America. He worried about a proposed colony of one million Germans planned for the Upper Amazon Basin. These developments were potentially troublesome because "fundamental Western Hemisphere solidarity" had existed since independence. "European influence today far outweighs that of Saxon America," as he called the United States and Canada, and "Europe is bending every effort to draw the southern continent more and more into the European circle and away from its northern neighbors."

Bolton was not blind to conflict among the American nations. He explained "manifest destiny" as a "madness for conquest" that was "the other side of the Monroe Doctrine." The Mexican-American War resulted in Mexico's loss of the northern half of its territory. Nevertheless, the Mexican cession and the Oregon boundary settlement with Great Britain gave the United States and Canada Pacific ports and unsettled lands that attracted European immigrants while keeping "both nations young with continued frontier experience," prolonging "opportunity for social experimentation" and perpetuating "American and Canadian characteristics." Saxon America's southern neighbor came under the rule of "one of the remarkable men of all time, Porfirio Díaz, half-breed Zapotec Indian, and soldier hero," Bolton explained. Bolton saw Díaz's regime as a "Golden Age" of Mexican development; poor Mexicans saw Díaz differently and rebelled. The aims of the revolution were socialistic and nationalistic. "In so radical a program vested interests have suffered," he said. "The Church has been involved," Bolton observed, but he did not say how.

In his conclusion, Bolton turned to the borderlands. Bolton explained that he did not mean borderlands to be exclusively geographical regions. "Borderline studies of many kinds" would be fruitful. "Borderland zones are vital not only to the determination of international relations, but also in the development of culture. In this direction," he continued, "one of the important modifications to the Turner thesis is to be sought," though he did not suggest what modification might be needed.

Bolton tossed off his borderlands observations in a brief paragraph before returning to his major theme. He called for broad synthetic studies of the Western Hemisphere that would include such themes as environmental, economic, and religious history. And he rhetorically asked who had stated "the significance of the frontier in terms of the Americas?" The eighth and final footnote to the published address stated that the proposed syntheses were not "a substitute for, but . . . a setting in which to place, any one of our national histories." Then Bolton took a parting shot at James Truslow Adams. "A noted historian has written for us the *Epic of America*," Bolton said, but for Adams "America" meant the United States. "We need an Adams to sketch the high lights and significant developments of the Western Hemisphere as a whole." Such a synthesis "done with similar brilliancy" would produce "the 'Epic' of *Greater* America," he concluded.

Bolton outlined broadly shared historical patterns that transcended national boundaries but spent little time explaining exceptions to the general trend of common development that he perceived. Perhaps much should be forgiven in a speech that covered more than four centuries and an entire hemisphere. Given such lordly parameters, the address was bound to be general and short on particulars. But Bolton's willingness to ignore almost entirely the important differences among American nations is surprising. He had made his reputation by examining the minute details of Spanish exploration and colonization. In his mission essay he had noted significant differences in Anglo and Hispanic Indian policy. But in "The Epic of Greater America" religion and Indians scarcely merited a mention. Troubling details were lost in a fog of general assertions about shared experiences in a progressive hemispheric history. In time his critics would have a field day with Bolton's smooth elisions and confident generalizations.

The problems with Bolton's address became so painfully obvious that when his admiring student and biographer John Francis Bannon published Bolton's important essays, he put the "Epic" speech in a special section called "The 'Other' Bolton," in which it was the only essay.[45] Yet it was the same Bolton who for years had been preaching—that is the best word for it—about the Americas and hemispheric history. The AHA address was simply a convenient collection of the thoughts that had been spread in many letters and uncounted lectures before uncritical undergraduates and public audiences. He had carried his crusading message to the loftiest pinnacle in the profession, where it would enjoy the closest professional scrutiny.[46]

The most severe critics of the "Epic" would rise in the future, but before leaving Bolton's presidential address, it is worth returning to his very brief concluding statement about the borderlands. While Bolton approvingly mentioned frontier influences on hemispheric history, as Turner might have done, he took the opportunity to mention that a consideration of culture in borderlands regions provided a basis for the modification of Turner's frontier thesis. Once again, Bolton stopped short of carefully analyzing the ideas of his now dead mentor. Perhaps Turner was too recently in the grave for that. Whatever the reason, Bolton missed a chance to put some intellectual flesh on the borderlands bones in a setting where it would have mattered. Eighty years after the event one wonders if a thoughtful lecture about the significance of the borderlands in American history might not have been more useful and appreciated in the long run.

Bolton's students presented a gift to him at the Toronto meeting. George Hammond and Charles Hackett had organized the production of *New Spain and the Anglo American West*, a festschrift consisting of two volumes of his graduate students' essays. Volume one covered New Spain, and two the Anglo-American West. The collection was an impressive testament to Bolton's influence as a teacher of specialists in Hispanic and Anglo-American history—indeed, of his hemispheric interests. Bolton was deeply moved by the presentation, but the process of compiling the festschrift revealed that some less happy forces were at work. Initial plans called for Arizona dean Frank Lockwood to write a biographical sketch of Bolton. After corresponding about the matter with several of Bolton's students, Hackett warned Lockwood that he should avoid including too much praise of Bolton in the biography. Some of Bolton's Berkeley colleagues accused him of courting publicity, and he was "somewhat sensitive to the charge."[47] He even canceled a dinner his students had planned to honor his twentieth year at Cal, saying that "certain people" would think he "was seeking too much glory."[48]

It is not difficult to imagine that some of Bolton's colleagues were jealous of him, and not only because of his election to the AHA presidency. He had great influence within the university. In the department his power was nearly absolute. He wielded authority with a smile on his face, but it was authority nonetheless. Outside the department Bolton had enemies. Chapman believed that there was a "legion of those who [were] envious of his reputation and achievement in scholarship."[49] He still sat on committees with Teggart, who had never forgiven Bolton for his part in shoving him out of the library and the history department.[50] Chapman described a committee incident that probably involved Teggart, although he did not mention him by name. During a meeting "Bolton was being insulted, as usual, by a certain other member of the committee." Bolton said that he resented the remarks and would take them up after the meeting. Later, as Chapman watched, Bolton approached the man "and offered to settle the question then and there, 'as man to man.'" Watching Bolton's tormentor back down, Chapman "got somewhat of a thrill" out of the proceedings, although the spectacle of two sixty-something professors grappling in a committee room would have been horrifying to most observers.[51] Whether the chastened bully was Teggart or some other professor, the essential point remains: not everyone on the Berkeley faculty liked or admired Bolton.

Was he a glory seeker, as some of his critics thought? Bolton's personal style was self-effacing, but he retained a news clipping service that sent items about him from papers around the country.[52] He received extraordinary news coverage, especially from Bay Area papers. Who would doubt that this attention caused jealousy among some of his less noticed colleagues?

A certain amount of resentment of Bolton in the Berkeley faculty was to be expected, but the festschrift also exposed rivalry among Bolton's students. A few months before the Toronto meeting the editorial committee named William Binkley to present the volumes to Bolton in Toronto. J. Fred Rippy objected and instead proposed that all of the contributors should elect the Toronto presenter. Rippy wanted Lockwood to tally the votes.[53] Aside from a zealous regard for democracy Rippy's agenda can only be surmised. It seems most likely that he considered the presentation assignment as an honor in itself. Who but Bolton's most respected student should hand him the volumes? Perhaps Rippy hoped to be designated as the presenter. Whatever the case, Lockwood refused to be drawn into the controversy, and Binkley made the presentation as planned.[54]

One other controversy arose among the editors. Hackett had warned Lockwood to avoid writing a sketch too eulogistic, but the publication committee decided that his essay was too laudatory. The Arizona dean had asked Bolton's graduate students to assess him as a teacher.[55] Lockwood incorporated their responses in his essay, and, ironically, it may have been the unstinting praise of Bolton's students that made Lockwood's sketch into a panegyric, at least in the minds of the committee. Lockwood's biography of Bolton did not go to waste. He published it in the *Catholic World*.[56]

The early 1930s seemed a culminating period in Bolton's professional life. In 1933 the National Park Service appointed him to the National Advisory Board of the Historic American Buildings Survey (HABS).[57] Bolton's work with HABS was a natural outgrowth of his lengthy association with the park service, his scholarly interest in missions, and his exploration of historic trails and places.[58]

Bolton's increasing activity with the federal government meant that he had more power to assist his graduate students in obtaining federal employment. Academic jobs became less plentiful as the depression dragged on, but there were possibilities for temporary and permanent federal employment in the field now called public history.[59] Two of his graduate students, Phillip Brooks and Vernon Tate, found important positions in the newly created National Archives. Brooks became associate director of the archives and then director of the Truman Library in the 1950s.[60] Tate earned a reputation as an authority on the microfilming of records.[61] Several of Bolton's students moved into the National Park Service. Vernon Aubrey Neasham became a regional historian for the Park Service in Santa Fe and went on to an important career as the state historian for California's Division of Beaches and Parks.[62] After leaving the University of Texas, Eddie Dunn had a varied career dealing with Latin America in private enterprise and public service including stints with the Department of State and Department of Commerce. When Bolton was president of the AHA, Dunn was financial advisor to the government of the Dominican Republic.[63] Bolton used all of these connections to find employment for his students and to forward his own work.[64]

As Bolton's professional influence expanded, his family life was evolving. His children grew and left home. By 1932 four of his daughters (Frances, Helen, Laura, and Eugenie) were married, Bolton told Eddie Dunn, but "they all still talk of Dunn and Hackie [Hackett]." Daughters Jane and Gertrude were in the teaching profession. Herbert Junior was "six feet high and a sophomore in the University." Mrs. Bolton's health was "not good," but she was "wiry and plucky." His wife was "just as efficient as she always was . . . but I wish that her health might improve," he added.[65] Gertrude suffered from Parkinson's disease. Mild tremors plagued her but she carried on her household routines.[66]

The Bolton household was shrinking, but Bolton picked this moment to move into a large new home that emblematized his status as one of the most famous historians of his day. He hired the Bay Area architect Edwin Lewis Snyder to design a home at 2655 Buena Vista Way, about eight blocks north of campus.[67] Everything about the Boltons' new home (even the name of the street it sat on) was appropriate to Bolton's interests and station in life. It was large. He wanted enough bedrooms so that all of his children could come and visit. The home incorporated architectural elements of the Spanish colonial revival style. The first floor of the two-story structure is built of painted white brick, while the second story is board and batten with a roof of terra cotta tile. In a manner suggestive of some Mexican California adobes a projecting second-floor balcony makes a covered porch for the ground-floor entry. Jutting westward from the main building was a large one-story living room that terminated in a bay window with a view of the Golden Gate. The living room interior with its rough beams and cathedral ceiling could have been modeled after a mission chapel. Stained-wood floor, smooth plaster walls, a heavy wooden lintel, southwestern art, and colorful curtains suggestive of Mexican serapes made the place look exactly like what it was: the fitting home of Herbert E. Bolton, the Spanish Borderlands historian, or rather, *the* Spanish Borderlands historian.

Everything about Bolton's life bespoke a man who was a great success. He had risen to the top of his field, and he possessed all of the things that symbolized his arrival: many publications, hundreds of graduate students, excellent salary, titles, authority, national and international acclaim, respect, a fine family, and a beautiful residence. If some of his colleagues were jealous, there is no need to try to puzzle out the reasons. They were all on display at the university and at his home.

In the early 1930s a few clouds marred this otherwise serene vista. For decades the Native Sons of the Golden West had funded graduate studies in history at Cal, but in 1933 "advocates of rigid economy" slashed the fellowship budget from $3,000 to $1,000. For the rest of the decade the Sons would not give more than that amount per year.[68] Monetary deflation made the cuts less severe than they appeared, but the reduction showed that Bolton's influence among the Sons was on the wane.

In the mid-1930s Bolton's substantial professional reputation was intact. Thus when Carl Becker's school text came under attack, the beleaguered author turned to Bolton for help.[69] "I have been charged . . . with being a communist and with advocating the Russian soviet system," he telegraphed. "If so disposed please wire your opinion whether I am a communist writer and whether my books advocate communism."[70] Bolton forcefully defended Becker. He found "no basis for the charge" of communism and declared that Becker was "one of our most brilliant and soundest historians" who was "truly patriotic to our American institutions." "The charge against you is, of course, absurd," he told Becker. Nevertheless, he added, "I fear that it is indicative of some of the troubles in which historians may find themselves in this country."[71]

Bolton did not elaborate on his belief that historians might face trouble from red-baiters. Perhaps he sensed that in the midst of the New Deal, conservative forces were slowly gathering strength. In the future such forces would eventually emerge within the Native Sons organization, much to Bolton's dismay. In the meantime, Bolton continued to use his palliative tactics with the Sons and California Anglophiles, but his urge to please local patriots would soon embroil him in controversy.

TWELVE

· Bury My Heart
at Corte Madera

Bolton took great pride in discovering long-lost historical sites and documents, but high-profile announcements of newly revealed historical treasures entailed an element of risk. An error could damage Bolton's hard-won reputation. There was little chance of his making a mistake with Spanish colonial writings. He knew the geography, environment, and mission architecture of the Southwest as well as anyone in the world, so it was unlikely that he would go wrong there. But Bolton was willing to make pronouncements about matters that were on the margins of his well-established, internationally recognized scholarly competence.

In the mid-1930s Bolton's part in the mistaken identification of supposed Spanish mission ruins in Georgia became an embarrassment. In 1925 he had collaborated with Mary Ross in the publication of two books about Spain in Georgia.[1] Ross had written a master's thesis at Berkeley on Anglo-Spanish conflict in North America.[2] Bolton's cooperation with Ross was in keeping with his long-established practice of working with women graduate students, usually as translators. In this case, Ross took an important role as amanuensis and investigator.[3]

As usual Bolton acknowledged Sidney M. Ehrman for his financial support of both volumes. "I have received a number of very flattering comments on the Georgia books," Bolton informed his patron, "thus throwing bouquets at both you and me."[4] Bolton's work on Georgia was a sideshow compared to his work on California, Texas, and the Southwest. Perhaps that is why he left so much of the work to Ross, a native Georgian. Perhaps it was Ross who provided the unattributed illustration used as a frontispiece in *Arredondo's Historical Proof of Spain's Title to Georgia*, "Ruins of Santa María Mission, near St. Mary's, Georgia," which showed a fuzzy photograph of a roofless structure made of tabby, a sort of primitive concrete. Bolton included two maps in *Arredondo* that located Santa María and other supposed missions near extant tabby ruins on the Georgia coast.[5] From 1923 to 1930 Ross published articles in the *Georgia Historical Quarterly* on Spanish settlement in Georgia, including an essay that pled for the restoration of the old Spanish missions.[6] In 1934 the *New York Times* reported that the Mission Santo Domingo would be restored with public funds and that Bolton would "advise the builders."[7]

Some Georgians, however, questioned the Spanish origins of the crumbling tabby walls. The Georgia Society of the Colonial Dames of America, perhaps with a touch of wounded Anglocentric pride, sponsored a careful documentary and archaeological investigation confirming that the old walls were abandoned nineteenth-century sugar mills. Subsequent archaeological investigations have found physical evidence of Spanish settlement, but no actual buildings or ruins have survived from the Spanish mission era.[8]

Bolton and Ross did not invent the myth about Spanish mission ruins. Georgia real estate developers had used the misidentified "mission" ruins to boost tourism and property values. As Marmaduke Floyd, the principal author of the Dames' report, put it, "The extraordinary publicity that California gave to the remains of the Spanish occupation of that state influenced the taste of the nation during the 'gay nineties' to mission furniture" and all of its "abominable imitations." After the Great War "California Spanish mission affectations decorated hot-dog stands and synagogues, filling stations, hotels, and," Floyd dryly added, "houses of every use."[9]

Ross evidently told Bolton about the "mission ruins," but that does not excuse him from responsibility for carelessness. He wrote that one set of "Spanish" ruins was "known as 'The Old Sugar House,'" so he was aware of conflicting views. Bolton's failure to investigate the ruins when he was in Georgia in 1923 contrasts tellingly with his tireless travels in the U.S. Southwest and northern Mexico. Instead of visiting the ruins while he was in Georgia, Bolton was content to rely on Ross's opinions about them.[10]

The Historic American Building Survey asked for Bolton's opinion about restoring Mission Santo Domingo in Georgia, a state historic park.[11] By this time Bolton was receiving newspaper clippings about archaeological investigations of Georgia's ruins. Still, he referred the park service to Ross because he had "more pressing obligations elsewhere."[12] When *Georgia's Disputed Ruins* issued from the press in 1937, the authors were much harder on Ross than they were on Bolton.[13] He continued to promote her work on the Georgia missions to the park service as late as 1939.[14] Bolton made no public retraction or correction of the errors in his book. While he did not originate the mission myth, he was certainly the most important scholar to lend it credence. If nothing else, the Georgia mission episode demonstrated that once errors crept into the public's historical consciousness, they were difficult to remove. It also showed that once Bolton took a position, he did not readily change it.

It was perhaps fortunate that Bolton's error was made in Georgia rather than in California and that he shared the responsibility with Ross. Had he been caught with a misidentification in California, Bolton's embarrassment would have been greater because of the local publicity that would have resulted. Even so, it is likely that word of the Bolton-Ross faux pas got around. Earl Pomeroy, a Berkeley student in the 1930s, was aware of the Georgia flub, though he may have heard about it later.[15]

Plenty of people would have relished the prospect of seeing Bolton with a red face. Several of them decided to play a practical joke evidently meant to do just that. The plan was to fabricate a brass plate presumed to have been left by Francis Drake when he visited the Pacific Coast in 1579. The names of the perpetrators of this hoax were not revealed until 2002. In the meantime the joke evolved in unexpected ways. While most of the essential facts are now known, some details remain shrouded in mystery.[16]

The prank was the brainchild of George Ezra Dane, a prominent member of E Clampus Vitus, a fraternal organization that flourished in California during the gold rush.[17] Known familiarly as ECV, the lodge was, as a historian frankly stated, more of "a joke, a sort of parody of the solemn and mysterious fraternal orders then so popular in the states." ECV membership dwindled after the gold rush, but was revived in 1931 by several Bay Area writers and professors from the University of California.[18] The members elected officers with absurd titles like Grand Clampatriarch, Grand Noble Recorder, and Noble Grand Humbug that parodied the exalted titles given out in other lodges. Assiduous research by learned Clampers, as members were called, showed that the first Clamper was Adam (yes, *that* Adam), that St. Vitus was their patron saint (also patron saint of coppersmiths, among other groups), and so on and so forth. ECV was devoted to the welfare of widows and orphans, "especially the widows," who were somehow aided by an instrument called the "staff of relief." The organization held Clampbanquets, where it was rumored that substantial amounts of alcohol were consumed. Occasional Clamproclamations were made. Sometimes the organization placed commemorative bronze plaques at legitimate historic sites, but the main object of the organization was to cause general hilarity and to poke fun at everything and everyone, especially swells who took themselves too seriously. The Clampers, it seems obvious, were the fun-loving alter ego of the Native Sons of the Golden West.

Just when the pranksters made the fake Drake plate is not known, but it was probably inspired by the spectacular hoax of Harry Peterson, curator of Sutter's Fort State Historic Park. In 1936 ECV met at the fort, where Peterson told the story of the 1846 Bear Flag Revolt, which established California's short-lived Bear Flag Republic. The assembled Clampers well knew that the original Bear Flag had been destroyed in the 1906 San Francisco earthquake and fire, but Peterson now revealed that he had saved the hallowed artifact. In the eerie light of a flickering lantern Peterson held up the tattered flag. Even among the impertinent and irreverent Clampers, who by the time the holy flag was hoisted were pretty well lubricated, "there was a moment of silence, for here was something historically stupendous."[19] The flag and story, it was soon revealed to the credulous audience, were both fabricated, but Peterson had demonstrated that a good story with a convincing prop and a little stagecraft could fool otherwise skeptical people.

The lesson was not lost on Dane, who would become the Grand Noble Humbug of the Yerba Buena (San Francisco) chapter of ECV in 1937. By all accounts Dane was a remarkable man. He had been associate editor of the *Harvard Law Review* and specialized in admiralty law. Dane had a sharp wit that reminded Clampers of Mark Twain. Indeed, Dane was a published Twain scholar.[20] He had all of the qualifications needed to perpetrate a great hoax. He intended to top Peterson's gag by forging the Drake plate, which claimed California for England by virtue of a concession from the Indians. Then to complete the joke, he would have the California Indians revoke the title with a second plate of brass. He assembled a band of co-conspirators: George Haviland Barron, George C. Clark, Lorenz Noll, and Albert Dressler, none of whom were Clampers. Dane probably involved outsiders so that Clamper cognoscenti would not leak word of the prank.

Barron, retired curator of California history at San Francisco's De Young Museum, purchased a piece of brass from a ship chandlery. According to Noll, Barron hated Bolton, although he gave no reason for the curator's animosity. Barron gave the metal to Clark, an inventor, art critic, and appraiser, who inscribed the brass with a hammer and cold chisel. "BEE IT KNOWN VNTO ALL MEN BY THESE PRESENTS IVNE. 17 . 1579," the inscription began, and continued on to claim "NOVA ALBION" for England in the name of "HERR MAIESTY QVEEN ELIZ-ABETH," concluding with the name "Francis Drake." Clark also made a hole that was supposed to have held a silver sixpence bearing the queen's image. He even put his initials on the plate's face, a C with an enclosed G, a signature he believed would easily reveal that the brass was a fake. The maker then belabored the plate with a ball-peen hammer to make it look old and gave it some other treatment to produce what looked like an antique patina. On the back of the brass someone wrote ECV in florescent paint that would be invisible until exposed to an ultraviolet light. Then Clark planted the plate on a hill near Corte Madera.[21] Either the pranksters intended to persuade Bolton to go to the site, where he would "discover" the plate, or some other finder would show it to Bolton. Burying the plate in the ground would have the additional advantage of giving it some added weathering.[22]

Bolton was an easy mark for Dane's prank. He was a Clamper who held the illustrious title Grand Royal Historian of the Yerba Buena chapter. For years he had urged his students to keep an eye out for the plate that Drake had left behind. In 1921 Bolton had participated in a commemoration of Drake's landing at the bay named for him.[23] He agreed to speak about Drake at the February 1937 meeting of ECV, where the fake plate would have a starring role. But events did not transpire according to plan.

On February 6, 1937, the Yerba Buena chapter of E Clampus Vitus met in the Hall of Comparative Ovations at the Wells Fargo Museum. Clampers freely consumed libations as usual. At particularly solemn moments a Clamper sounded the hewgag, the sacred horn of the ancient and honorable order. New members, called suckers, were initiated to the call of "Bring on your poor blind candidates," who then saw the light of day. The initiates included William Fuller, chief of the Miwok ranchería in Tuolumne. Fuller generously announced that the Miwok round house in Tuolumne would be used as the Hall of Comparative Ovations when the Clampers met there in May, which was part of Dane's elaborate prank. After the induction ceremony Brother Herbert Bolton "expostulated at some length on Drake."[24] Historian Robert Chandler suspects that this was the moment when Bolton or some other Clamper was supposed to reveal the newly found plate. Then after a moment of reverent silence Dane would have exposed the fake with ultraviolet light, making Bolton and everyone else who was taken in the victims of his harmless prank. But there was no plate, no ultraviolet light, and no joke—at least not the one that Dane had intended.

What had gone wrong? In the summer of 1936 Beryle Shinn, a young Oakland department store employee, was driving in the Marin countryside. Near the hill where the plate was stashed, Shinn had a flat tire. Before fixing the tire, he decided to go up the hill, where he amused himself by rolling some rocks down the slope. "As I pulled a rock from the soil," Shinn recalled, "I saw the edge of a metal plate which was partly covered by the rock."[25] He took the plate to fix a hole in the floor of his car but deferred the repair for several months. When he finally set to his task, he noticed some crudely engraved writing and the word "Drake." Acting on the advice of some unnamed Berkeley student, Shinn telephoned Bolton about his find. Or so Shinn said. It is possible that Shinn was the vehicle that Dane and company used to transport the plate to Bolton sometime before the ECV meeting. Oddly, Bolton did not record the date in February when he first met Shinn. Or perhaps Shinn did accidentally find the plate just as he said.

Whatever the case, Bolton was completely taken in. "I surmised its identity even before seeing it," Bolton said. "My mind leaped to the conjecture at once, because for years I have been telling my students to keep an eye out for Drake's plate." Shinn, he added, had not been one of his students.[26] Bolton evidently checked the text of the plate against the published sixteenth-century accounts of Drake's voyage. The close agreement with one of the texts and the apparent antiquity of the artifact in his hand convinced him that it was truly the object that Drake had left behind in 1579. There was even a hole, evidently meant to hold the sixpence mentioned in the sources.[27] Seeing and touching the artifact convinced Bolton that Shinn had made an important historical find. Bolton's almost instantaneous, if not a priori, authentication of the brass tablet came also with the realization that the thing must be priceless. Of course he wanted to obtain it for the Bancroft Library, but how?

Bolton's papers include a carelessly scrawled but unsigned note that offered Bolton 10 percent of the plate's sales price for his help in authenticating it. The note raises many questions, but two things are certain. First, Bolton kept the note in a folder with a copy of the bill of sale for the plate that Shinn subsequently executed.[28] So Bolton attached some sort of significance to the note, if only as a record of his involvement in what he believed was an important historical discovery. Second, the note casts doubt on Bolton's public assertion that Shinn's "chief interest in the plate was to have it preserved for the public, and he never asked nor would he discuss a price for it."[29] Perhaps Shinn did not immediately put a specific price on the plate, but the note shows that he recognized that the plate had substantial monetary value and that he might sell it. These were important considerations in his dealings with Bolton.

Thus Bolton, convinced that the plate was genuine, and perhaps having a pecuniary interest in it, enlisted Allen L. Chickering, president of the California Historical Society, to purchase the plate for the University of California. Chickering began to solicit donations from society members and other prominent Californians, citing Bolton's unqualified belief in the plate's authenticity.[30]

On February 28, 1937, Chickering met Bolton and Shinn in the shadow of the campus campanile; the three piled in a car and took the Richmond ferry to Point San Quentin.[31] They retraced Shinn's summer excursion and, after some difficulty, found the discovery site. The record Chickering kept of the trip described the commanding view of the countryside and the bay. Although bad weather obscured the scene at the time, he imagined that on a clear day one could see the "snowy Sierras." Real or imagined, the vista that he conjured inspired "the thought . . . that it might be the place where the plate had been set up, but this is another story." What other story? The location where Shinn found the plate was plain enough, was it not? Would it not have been reasonable for Chickering to conclude that if the plate was genuine, and if it was found under some rocks in this rural location, then Drake had left it there? But as we shall see, the fake plate had more tales to tell, as Chickering was perhaps already aware.

The trip to Corte Madera left Chickering and Bolton more deeply convinced that the plate was Drake's and that it must be obtained from the young finder. On the ferry ride back to Richmond they ate lunch and the two men began to work on Shinn. Such an important historical relic ought to be on public exhibition, they argued, but arriving at a fair price would be a difficult matter. There was no telling what such an artifact was worth if a wealthy man wanted to get it for the Smithsonian Institution or the British Museum. Chickering thought he could raise $2,500 as a "finder's reward" for Shinn. The buyers would assume the risk of the plate's genuineness and "possible legal complications."[32]

On the following Monday, Shinn appeared in Bolton's office, saying that he wanted to show the plate to his uncle. Shinn promised to return it the next day. He did not. This was worrisome. On Wednesday Bolton telephoned Shinn, who said he would bring the plate to Bolton's office at 8:00 that evening. Bolton and Chickering waited until 8:45, when Shinn showed up without the plate, but with a lot of problems. Shinn was "frightened to pieces" because his uncle said that he might be prosecuted in connection with the plate, though he did not explain why. Shinn threatened to ship the plate out of the state in order to get rid of it and the worries that it caused. Chickering soothed Shinn by explaining that if he sold the plate to them, Bolton and Chickering would deal with troublemakers. Chickering agreed to pay Shinn $3,500, "taking the risks of genuineness and of any claims."

Shinn agreed to the deal immediately. He went to retrieve the plate from his uncle but returned without it because the house was locked. He promised to bring it the next morning, Thursday, but again the plate failed to appear. Finally, on Friday morning, Shinn exchanged the plate for $3,500.[33]

The documents that describe these negotiations can be read in several ways. In one view, two wily and powerful older men were determined to have the plate and put enormous pressure on an innocent young man who was beyond his depth. In another view, Shinn, a shrewd negotiator, set the trap, presented the bait, got his quarry to commit, withdrew the bait, drove up the price, limited his liability, and sold.

We do not know if Shinn was part of Dane's elaborate joke, but Bolton's immediate, intuitive (and wrong) authentication sent the prank spinning off in an entirely unexpected direction. Instead of being merely funny, the joke turned into a windfall for Shinn, who received what amounted to one year's salary for an associate professor of history at the University of California in 1937. Perhaps it all happened just the way Shinn said it did, but by art or by accident, he walked away from the plate with a nice sum of money. He bought a house and got married.

The buyers wasted no time in conveying the plate to the University of California. On the same day that the plate and money changed hands, Bolton told President Sproul that he and Chickering had managed to get the article with the assistance of historical society donors and prominent Cal alumni, including a member of the Board of Regents, who happened to be Sidney M. Ehrman.[34] Bolton assured the president that he would "make every investigation necessary to demonstrate the genuineness of the treasure," but he did not say precisely what those investigations would be.[35] Indeed, it appears that Bolton did nothing but compare the text of the plate with the texts from the published accounts. Nothing in the record shows that he sought expert advice from anyone before he announced the discovery to the world.

The California Historical Society announced that Professor Bolton would give a luncheon address on April 6 titled "Newer Light on Drake and the Location of His Anchorage in California." The title of Bolton's talk was modest enough, but the brief preview in the announcement thrilled the imagination. "Dr. Bolton will make the most astounding revelation yet made respecting Drake and California. Members who miss this meeting will have cause to regret it."[36] By this time Dane must have known about Bolton and the plate. The society was putting out a special publication about it, and Dane was chair of the publication committee. Bolton would astonish his listeners at—where else?—the Sir Francis Drake Hotel in

San Francisco. By the time Bolton read his paper, the title had become "Drake's Plate of Brass."[37] The draft of his essay shows that he interlineated words like, "it seems," and "apparently." He substituted "surmised" for "decided," and "evidence" for "proof." Evidently he was having second thoughts about what the plate had to say about Drake's anchorage. He crossed out the concluding sentence which predicted that a monument would be erected where Shinn had discovered the brass, and penciled in at the foot of the page, "*New Data* doesn't change anything." In making these changes, Bolton was not abandoning his commitment to the plate's authenticity—this he made abundantly clear in his presentation; however, he softened the tone of certainty in his original essay and backed away from the Corte Madera discovery site.[38]

Bolton likely had been warned about a new revelation concerning the plate. Within days of Bolton's announcement, William Caldeira publicly claimed that he had found the plate near Drake's Bay in late 1933, an impossibility given what is now known about it. Nevertheless, many people at the time accepted Caldeira's story at face value. In 1933 Caldeira was a chauffeur employed by Leon Bocqueraz, a member of the California Historical Society.[39] Advance word of Caldeira's revelation could have come to Bolton from Chickering, who happened to live across the street from Caldeira's new employer, John Brockway Metcalf (son-in-law of Henry E. Huntington).[40] Caldeira claimed that he did not recognize the plate's importance but kept it in his employer's car for a while before tossing it out near Corte Madera, not far from where Shinn found it. Chickering formally interviewed Caldeira on April 9, three days after Bolton's lecture and one week before newspapers printed the chauffeur's claim.[41] If Chickering warned Bolton, it was not in time to keep Bolton from embarrassing himself in print. The original version of his essay went to press as a special commemorative issue of the *Quarterly of the California Historical Society* and was laid upon the tables at the Sir Francis Drake Hotel.[42] It was too late to turn back; Bolton pulled some punches and prepared the audience for the possibility that Drake might not have erected the plate above Point San Quentin.

The chauffeur's story was questionable at best. Nevertheless, Bolton and Chickering satisfied themselves that Caldeira was truthful and that his account only made the plate's authenticity more convincing. As far as they were concerned, Caldeira's story eliminated the possibility of fraud on Shinn's part—a point that Chickering was quick to emphasize with doubters.[43] In this case, as in all others, Bolton and Chickering converted confounding evidence into positive proof for the plate's validity.

In May the Ancient and Honorable Fraternal Organization, E Clampus Vitus, met in Tuolumne, California. Brother Bolton entertained the Clampers with another talk about Drake. After explaining to his fellow members that the plate had to be found to resolve the differences between variant accounts, he said, "I did so," and then held aloft a facsimile of California's choicest archaeological treasure.[44]

Bolton's replica was not the only brass plate at Tuolumne. Outside the Miwok round house (now transformed as the ECV Hall of Comparative Ovations), stood a post with an inscribed plaque that looked very much like a newer, less weathered version of the one that Bolton had authenticated. This one, however, was signed by Miwok chief William Fuller and had been made by Berkeley geologist and paleontologist (and Clamper) V. L. VanderHoof. The text said that Drake had "seduced" the ancient chief and therefore revoked the grant of 1579 "ON GROUNDS OF DECEIT, FRAUD, AND FAILURE TO OCCUPY SAID DOMAIN."[45] In the place of a sixpence the maker had mounted an Indian head nickel on the plate.

Shortly after the Tuolumne meeting the Clampers published *Ye Preposterous Booke of Brasse*, which was amusing, ironic, sarcastic, and full of hints about the true nature of the plate. Charles Camp, a well-known California historian and Clamper, wrote the parts of the *Booke* that dealt with the fake plate. Camp was not a part of the original conspiracy, but he was evidently in the know by the time of the Tuolumne meeting. According to Camp's parody a Clamper expert had made various tests of the plate, including "ultra-violet fluorescence and infra-red illumination" that would show "three letters . . . E.C.V." The test also revealed that the plate appeared to have been beaten "with the round end of a machinists hammer." The absence of weathering was merely testimony "to the mildness of the California climate." Camp concluded that the plate proved that Parson Fletcher, who accompanied Drake in 1579, was an Elizabethan Clamper. Therefore, the ECV should reclaim the artifact "as the rightful property of our ancient Order."[46] The Clampers' reputation for poking fun at one and all should make any reader wary of taking the *Booke* at face value. Yet its description of specific testing, mention of the florescent ECV brand, and the declaration of ownership along with the new, similar plate at Tuolumne should have raised an alarm in Bolton's mind. Yet, if he realized the implications of the Tuolumne meeting and the *Booke of Brasse*, he did not act on them.

Doubters began to cause trouble. During a visit to UCLA, President Sproul dined with several prominent people in Pasadena. They told him that "a reputable historical magazine" would soon carry a "'blistering' attack on the genuineness of the Drake Plate," evidently referring to Reginald Berti Haselden's soon-to-be-published article.[47] Captain Haselden, as he was called, was a specialist in Elizabethan literature on the staff of the Huntington Library. Sproul also reported that the respected historian Henry Raup Wagner, who had published a book about Drake's voyage to California, had given speeches "ridiculing" the plate because the spelling was "not Elizabethan and . . . the brass . . . not the kind that was being made in . . . Drake's time." The renowned astronomer Edwin Powell Hubble told Sproul that the plate should be chemically analyzed "in order to be prepared for the onslaught." On purely historical matters, Hubble believed that Bolton could "hold his own" against the plate's critics, "a conclusion with which I find myself in complete agreement," Sproul added.[48]

Bolton was now in a tight spot. On his word bankers, lawyers, corporation presidents, distinguished alumni, the California Historical Society, a university regent, and the University of California had committed their money and prestige to the plate. If the plate proved to be a fake, more than a historian's reputation was at stake, as President Sproul made plain to Professor Bolton. Accordingly, Bolton told the president that he had already taken steps to involve three Berkeley scientists in the question. "Every new Fact noted or discovered regarding the Plate," Bolton told the president, "strengthens our belief in its genuineness." Bolton's bluff assertions notwithstanding, the president continued to hear that the university had been hoaxed and was "just a little nervous about the situation."[49]

In those days, when a university president became a little nervous, the faculty became anxious, and Bolton no doubt understood that he was expected to save the university from embarrassment. The Huntington's Captain Haselden spurred Sproul's case of the jitters with a relentless attack on the plate. The captain was not a man to be taken lightly. He oversaw a staff of women who stood for inspection at their desks every morning.[50] Haselden was interested in the problems associated with authenticating manuscripts. He took special pride in exposing frauds. In 1935 he published *Scientific Aids for the Study of Manuscripts*, in which he used three examples of forgeries that he had discovered in the Huntington Library collections. Haselden adamantly recommended the use of the latest scientific tools, some of his own invention, to examine manuscripts, "whether stone, wood, wax, papyrus, vellum, . . . paper"—or brass, one would suppose. He considered ultraviolet lamps and fluorescence particularly useful tools.[51] In a perfect world, Bolton would have collaborated with Haselden to determine the plate's authenticity or, at the very least, would have used Captain Haselden's methods to reveal the telltale initials of the Clampers on the plate's reverse. But alas, Bolton relied only on the published texts and his own hopeful intuition.

Bolton's optimism was not enough to satisfy Captain Haselden, who was convinced that the plate was a hoax that should be exposed as a fraud. Just as quickly as Bolton had concluded that the plate was genuine, Haselden knew in his bones that the thing was a fake. If the amount of Drake correspondence in the captain's files is any indication, the Drake controversy must have consumed much of his time.[52] He wrote to experts at Oxford University and the British Museum, both of whom summarily rejected the plate's legitimacy.[53] Armed with the British Museum's opinion, Haselden sent copious advice to Bolton concerning what ought to be done to test the plate. Bolton responded that he would consider "worthwhile" suggestions but public discussions were "pointless" until there was a "clear understanding of problems."[54] Haselden believed that his understanding of the key problem was perfectly clear. He thought that Bolton had authenticated a fraud and that a proper investigation would reveal it. Now it was obvious that Bolton did not intend to cooperate in exposing a hoax that made him look foolish.

In September 1937 Haselden's article "Is the Drake Plate of Brass Genuine?" moved the controversy along. Haselden questioned the relic's authenticity on the grounds of form and orthography and insisted that scientific tests of the metal must be done. He also questioned the veracity of the chauffeur's tale. "Until further evidence is forthcoming," Haselden concluded, "judgment on the authenticity or otherwise of this discovery must be suspended."[55] The same issue of the *California Historical Society Quarterly* that printed Haselden's essay carried "Some Notes with Regard to Drake's Plate of Brass," by Allen L. Chickering. While professing not to be an expert, Chickering produced many examples of variant spellings from Drake's day that seemed to refute the arguments of the Elizabethan expert Haselden. He also vouchsafed the character of the "manly and straightforward" Shinn, who "neither made the plate nor was a party to any hoax in connection with it."[56] The chauffeur Caldeira made his statement "only in the interest of truth, for he had no possibility of financial gain from it." (It is worth noting, however, that Caldeira wanted some money for finding the plate and got "a little reward from the ... California Historical Society," according to his former employer Bocqueraz.)[57]

To build his case against the plate (and Bolton's rash judgment), Haselden corresponded with Earle Caley, a metallurgical chemist with the Frick Laboratory at Princeton University who had published work on ancient bronzes.[58] Caley gave

Haselden advice about the scientific investigation of purportedly ancient relics that the captain forwarded to President Sproul. Haselden also forwarded an unpublished essay that he had submitted to the *California Historical Society Quarterly* that criticized the plate on stylistic, linguistic, and orthographic grounds. "I feel very strongly that this matter should be cleared up," he declared. Haselden feared "the enormous amount of harm to scholarship" that a forgery could do. The plate, he suspected, had been "made as an amusing and ingenious joke, which got completely out of hand (no doubt much to the surprise of the perpetrators thereof)."[59]

Sproul passed Haselden's letter along to Bolton, who defended the plate on every count. In Bolton's mind, the plate's very unusualness argued for its authenticity. Every error and oddity meant that it was genuine. As far as Bolton was concerned, only the problem of dating the metal remained to be addressed, and he was "earnestly trying" to find some qualified person to do it. "The sponsors [of the plate] have never declared the plate to be genuine," he wrote. "They have expressed their belief in its authenticity, but always with an *if.*"[60]

The "if," however, was often covered with Bolton's dense overburden of superlatives extolling the importance of the plate and its discovery, while minimizing or entirely ignoring evidence that called it into question. Bolton and Chickering had begun this approach even before the plate's discovery was officially announced, when they were trying to raise money, and it was plainly evident in Bolton's California Historical Society address. On that occasion, Bolton noted the discrepancies about the plate in the two published accounts of Drake's voyage—Richard Hakluyt's and Parson Fletcher's in *The World Encompassed*. Bolton declared that there was only one way to determine which account was correct, and that was to find the plate. Then, he said to the crowd: "Here it is! Recovered at last after a lapse of 357 years! Behold, Drake's plate—the plate of brasse! California's choicest archaeological treasure!" He continued, in more measured prose, that "the plate, assuming its authenticity, completely vindicates Parson Fletcher."[61] Thus Bolton's occasional qualifiers got lost in thickets of grand pronouncements about his wonderful discovery. Equally important, Bolton used the plate to validate the contestable account of Parson Fletcher instead of the other way around.

The arrangement for scientific tests of the brass remained an unresolved and nettlesome problem until late in 1937. Chickering was at first opposed to tests that would physically damage the plate, and was particularly wary after Berkeley scientists told him that there was no point in having it analyzed.[62] It was difficult to argue against making a scientific study, but chemical and physical tests were a high-risk venture. If tests did not show that the brass was from Drake's time,

Haselden, Wagner, and other critics would have a field day. If it was old brass, the plate's authenticity still was not proven, as a clever forger might have used old metal for his fake. Even so, Sproul thought tests would help to put the university "in a much better position before the scholarly world," and Chickering came around to this view as well.[63] So it became necessary to find a scientist who had experience with antique metals. Bolton consulted with Berkeley chemist Joel Hildebrand and two other university scientists. While these professors generally agreed that the plate was authentic, Chickering complained that they had not been cooperative. In October Sproul officially asked Hildebrand and a philologist to aid Bolton. They, of course, "generously agreed" to help, as the president put it. "Obviously," Sproul explained to Bolton, "neither of them will do much, because they do not desire, in the slightest degree, to take matters out of your hands."[64] It was apparent, however, that Sproul thought Bolton needed help.

After accepting the president's courteous invitation to assist Bolton, Hildebrand took a leading role in identifying Colin Fink of Columbia University to examine the plate. So, early in 1938, Bolton shipped the brass to Columbia and waited for results. He could not have been happy about sending the plate for scientific study, especially if he took seriously either the Clampers' warnings or Haselden's sharp criticisms. Indeed, he may well have feared the worst.

Professor Fink had a few questions about the plate even before it arrived. He was curious about its patina because he was certain that he could tell if the coating was very old or recent.[65] The patina presented a problem, because the front of the plate appeared to be a burnished golden color. Chickering confessed that his son had asked the Wells Fargo Bank for advice about making reproductions of the plate. Bank employees had sent him and the plate to the Western Newspaper Union in San Francisco, where the good guild members had cleaned the plate with kerosene. They were about to scrub it with lye when Chickering Junior weakened and retrieved the plate.[66] After Captain Haselden learned about the cleaning, he gleefully wrote to Caley. Sit down and prepare for a "horrible shock," Haselden warned the scientist. "The brass plate has been so carefully and thoroughly cleaned that you can shave in its reflection. It glitters! I will not harrow your feelings with any more details."[67]

Once Fink had the plate, new questions arose. "Frankly," he wrote, "I know of no brass plate which we could set up on the Pacific Coast and expect to find in such good condition after 350 years." Fink also wondered why there was no corrosion in the hole that supposedly had held a sixpence. There should have been evidence of some electrolytic reaction between the silver and the brass, but there was none, and curiously, a sixteenth-century sixpence still fit perfectly in the hole. Fink assured Bolton that he had raised these questions "to fortify ourselves against any attack" and to assemble "all the proof possible supporting the contention that the plate is genuine." Bolton easily provided answers for Fink. The Indians did it. They might have taken the plate from its post and knocked the sixpence out of the hole. The plate was exposed when Caldeira and Shinn found it, but perhaps it had not always been so.[68]

While raising some questions about the plate, Fink also made clear that he believed it was his job to defend its genuineness, even before he had completed scientific tests. As Bolton told Chickering, "Professor Fink . . . has just about arrived at the place which we had reached several months ago." Already Chickering had learned that Fink was "impressed with the sanctity of the plate."[69] So it seems that the plate itself convinced Doctor Fink of its antiquity and authenticity, just as it had first seduced Bolton. After Fink's work was completed, Chickering lunched with him in New York. Fink remained "deeply interested in the Drake plaque," Chickering explained. "He was so impressed with the importance of his job and the secrecy which he believed that it involved, that he did not even show it to his wife. In fact he showed it to no one except President Butler of Columbia, and to him only just before it was sent back." These revelations confirmed Chickering's "very high opinion of him as a man and a scholar."[70]

Several months passed before Fink and his coauthor, E. P. Polushkin, completed the tests and filed the final report, but it was all that Bolton, Chickering, and Sproul could have hoped for. The report, published in the *California Historical Society Quarterly,* found that the brass was undoubtedly from Drake's time. The examination of the patina now showed that it accounted "for the good condition of the plate even after more than three centuries' exposure (whole or partial) on the shore of the Pacific."[71] Fink and Polushkin also suggested that the many irregular indentations on the plate were made by Indians "who were afraid of a mysterious or hostile power . . . and tried to destroy the plate by striking its surface with their tomahawks; they were not familiar with the toughness of metals." By this time the scientists had found microscopic evidence of corrosion products, though they did not say that these resulted from a reaction between silver and brass. Fink and Polushkin went far beyond confirming the antiquity of the brass material, writing "that the brass examined by us is the genuine Drake Plate referred to in the book, *The World Encompassed by Sir Francis Drake,* published in 1628." So the Columbia scientists—like Bolton—found that the plate vindicated Parson Fletcher. And like Bolton, they were willing to use negative evidence to support the plate's authenticity. For example, the patina that the printer's union staff had so easily wiped away with a kerosene-soaked cloth became an invincible armor against the salt air. While maintaining the language and stance of objective scientific inquiry, the Fink report gave unqualified support not only to the plate's antiquity but also to its documentary validity and authorship. Thus the historical conclusions of Fink and Polushkin extended far beyond the scientific evidence.

Captain Haselden, who had put his faith in scientific examination, was flabbergasted. He wrote to President Sproul. "I think it was in very bad taste for the gentlemen who examined the plate" to state that it was the "genuine Drake Plate," Haselden wrote. To him the scientists seemed "very naive." Haselden was not "going to let the matter rest," he told Sproul, until he was satisfied that the plate was "genuine or a fraud.". Sproul's response was not encouraging. "I wonder if your own attitude toward the matter is strictly scientific?" Sproul asked the captain. "It seems to me that you show signs of becoming a 'crusader.'"[72] Haselden had insisted on a scientific examination, and there had been one. The case was closed as far as Sproul was concerned.

Haselden was all the more disappointed that the editor of the *Quarterly* had decided not to publish his own essay containing "very vital evidence against the plate," as he put it. "I refrain from speculating . . . on the reason for this," he added.[73] His Princeton friend Caley disagreed with the Fink and Polushkin findings, but he was philosophical. "I am very much afraid that the sponsors of the plate now have the weight of authority on their side and that it will be difficult if not impossible to cast any slurs of suspicion on the plate," he informed Haselden.[74]

Caley proved to be correct. While some skeptics remained suspicious, the plate was proudly displayed in the Bancroft Library and generally accepted by the public. In 1977 renewed controversy about all things Drake in California reached fever pitch as the quadricentennial of the mariner's California landing approached. In 1977 the university conducted new tests, which revealed the plate had been made from modern brass. By then Bolton had been dead for nearly a quarter of a century, so he did not have to deal with the humiliating revelation that he had been duped.

One wonders why Bolton could have been taken in by what seems in hindsight such an obvious fake. In some ways the Clamper forgery was more convincing than its makers could have imagined. It looked ancient to the untrained eye. Once Bolton lent his authority to the forgery, others easily believed in it. There was another reason why Bolton, Chickering, Fink, and a host of others believed that the plate was a true artifact of Drake's voyage: they *wanted* to believe in it. For them, the plate was not just a metal document or a valuable antique. It was the holy grail—a venerable Anglo-American, Protestant religious relic.

As such, the Drake plate figured in a struggle for California's cultural high ground, and afforded Bolton a unique opportunity to ingratiate himself with a California elite that identified with the state's non-Hispanic pioneers. For decades, Bolton had publicized the Spanish and Catholic founders of the Golden State— Serra, Crespi, Garcés, Anza, and all the rest. He had emphasized the religious motives and humanitarian goals of the Franciscan missions. His books gave scholarly recognition and respectability to California's Spanish colonial roots and academic weight to the romantic myth of Spanish California that evolved in the early twentieth century. Drake's plate offered a powerful counterweight in this cultural and historical balance because it testified to an ancient English claim to California and spoke to Protestant religious primacy as well. Bolton made this point explicit when he revealed the plate to the California Historical Society and explained the Indians' fascination with Parson Fletcher's religious services and Drake's fervent prayers. "As an evangelist," Bolton said, "Father Serra himself could hardly have been more zealous than was Drake."[75] He also told his audience that Drake had looted and desecrated a Catholic Church in Guatulco on the Pacific coast of New Spain. Bolton was well aware of the spiritual significance of Drake's plate and the religious conflict that it symbolized.

Had Bolton forgotten about these sectarian matters, his correspondents would have reminded him. When Caldeira's story became public, one local fellow wrote to Bolton that the story was "rather fishy." He thought that "certain ones" desired that "the Jesuits . . . supplant Sir Francis Drake in the great honor" of discovering San Francisco Bay. "Make your name famous," the correspondent went on, "by words and writings that will not perish with time. The higher patriotic thots [sic] bring one to the hearts of mankind."[76] Evidently, patriotic thoughts were highest when they praised England's heroes over Spain's. A more subdued letter came from a member of the Mill Valley Episcopal Church. He wanted Bolton to confirm that Drake's divine services were the first Protestant services held in the New World, or at least on the Pacific Coast. What historical significance did Bolton attach to these divine services, he asked?[77] Bolton's vindication of Parson Fletcher gave additional heft to the conviction that Protestant England had just as good a spiritual claim to California as Catholic Spain—and perhaps better.

Bolton's announcement of the discovery of the plate inspired a San Francisco paper to publish a poem the next day. Bolton kept a typescript of this poem, which praised Drake:

Here for the Queen her courtier courted death
Gambled warm life for England's deathless fame
Signed, "Francis Drake," and from the golden page
We take his message, and our heritage![78]

Bolton understood this verse quite literally, as one of his letters to a Canadian woman revealed. She wanted him to give the plate to George VI, whom she regarded as the plate's rightful owner. Though Bolton was not willing to relinquish the plate, he assured her that he had only the most friendly feelings toward Canada and "Mother England," as he put it. "You will be able to understand my sentiments regarding this matter when I tell you that my ancestors were nearly all English, that my father grew to early manhood in Leeds, and that I am of the first American-born generation in my family."[79] The golden page was *his* heritage.

After three decades of fighting on the Spanish Catholic side in California's culture wars, Bolton could strike a blow for his people, his hero, and his religious roots. At last Bolton could extol English heroes whose blood and beliefs he shared and whose exploits he saw reflected in the golden sheen of the plate of brass. In the case of the fake Drake plate, Bolton's promotion of a California hero clouded his critical sense. "Higher patriotic thots" may bring historians "to the hearts of mankind," as Bolton's correspondent put it, but they led Bolton into error.

Critics of Bolton's part in the Drake plate affair should not lose sight of the fact that he was a victim of fraud, not a perpetrator. Bolton's mistakes were errors of enthusiasm and carelessness, not willful falsification. Fink's unqualified declaration no doubt quashed any lingering doubts that Bolton may have had. His correspondence does not hint that he realized the plate was a fraud, so he cannot be held to account on the charge that he wittingly allowed a fake artifact to bamboozle the public. But the makers of the phony plate knew, and they kept quiet. Perhaps they were unwilling to expose the university, Bolton, and their state to ridicule. Maybe they feared criminal prosecution or a civil lawsuit. Surely Bolton should be criticized for his reckless endorsement of the plate; but the full blame for the Drake plate fraud rests squarely on the men who authored it. For decades the forgery illustrated schoolbooks, graced the rooms of the Bancroft Library, misled historians, and caused needless controversy about where Drake landed. All the while, guilty men kept their secrets. The perpetrators are all dead, but even now their perfidy prevents a full understanding of the many mysteries surrounding the Drake plate fraud.

While Bolton fought to vindicate the Drake plate, the professional world of history stirred with new developments. J. Franklin Jameson, who should justly be regarded as one of Bolton's chief professional benefactors, died in 1937. Charles Haskins, Bolton's favorite teacher at Wisconsin, also passed away that year. But the deaths of the last of the Old Guard were not the most salient changes shaking the professional foundations of history in the 1930s. The new generation of historians who replaced Jameson, Turner, and Haskins were making their presence felt, while professors from western institutions were bringing regional matters to the forefront of AHA politics. These demographic shifts influenced a general revolt against the administration of the AHA.

The generational and regional bases for the rebellion were linked. During the 1930s Bolton's fraternity brothers from Wisconsin in the 1890s became AHA presidents: Carl Becker (1931), Bolton (1932), and Guy Stanton Ford (1937). Bolton and Ford, who was dean of the Graduate School in the University of Minnesota, both served at western and midwestern institutions. AHA presidents Lawrence M. Larson of the University of Illinois, Frederic Logan Paxson at Berkeley, Max Farrand of the Huntington Library, and James Westfall Thompson, who taught at Berkeley, assumed the office in 1938, 1940, and 1941, respectively. (Larson died in 1938, so First Vice President Paxson served out his term that year.) From 1932 to 1941 there were six AHA presidents from midwestern and western institutions; seven if one counts Ephraim Adams who died as Second Vice President. From

1884 to 1931 there had been five presidents from these regions. The shift reflected the growing importance of western universities as well as the reputations of the men elected. Recognition of westerners seemed to indicate that the AHA was not a closed corporation that rewarded only professors from a few elite eastern institutions. However, westerners, including some who became AHA presidents, did not see things in this pleasing meritocratic light.

Even though Bolton was a colleague and friend of many of the 1930s rebels and presidents, he was not a key figure in the revolt. This was to be expected. Bolton always avoided overt political controversy. He was looking toward retirement and had already held the presidency, so why go looking for trouble? But Bolton's old friend Ford would spark the revolt, and two of Bolton's colleagues, Paxson and Thompson, would become involved. The Pacific Coast Branch would likewise become embroiled, and the fallout from the controversy would have lasting consequences for the AHA and the PCB.

There was a need for change in the AHA. In 1929 the association had undergone an awkward reorganization that had provided for a secretary and an executive secretary. Most of the important duties devolved on the executive secretary. To make matters worse, neither of these officials lived in Washington, D.C., the AHA headquarters. In effect, there were three AHA offices. Patty W. Washington, the longtime office secretary in Washington, handled many routine matters. The secretary, Dexter Perkins, was on the Cornell faculty, and the executive secretary, Conyers Read, taught at Rochester. Conyers and Read were Harvard men, a fact that made the AHA leadership seem a bit clubby. The fact that the AHA leadership occasionally met at the Harvard Club in New York City reinforced this notion. Members were often perplexed about whom to contact, so Perkins, Read, and Washington often redirected correspondence to one another. They worked well together, but the organization was quite opaque to outsiders who thought they were getting the run around.

In addition to the council, there was an Executive Committee of four plus the two secretaries. Only two councilmen were members of the regular council, but the executive group often made important decisions that shaped the debate of the council. The Executive Committee was meant to streamline operations of the AHA because the council was too large, dispersed, and unwieldy to act quickly. It was not intended to be a semisecret closet government, but it is easy to understand why some AHA members thought it was. Westerners, of course, were effectively closed out of the Executive Committee because they lived so far away. Thus geographical circumstances helped to reinforce the conviction of some westerners that the eastern establishment meant to close them out of influential AHA offices.[1] Even historians who had strong eastern connections understood the situation in regional terms once they took positions in western universities.

In 1937 Guy Ford, having lived with the three-headed AHA beast as vice president and president, proposed a committee to consider reorganizing the AHA. Ford and President Paxson appointed a Committee of Ten, which was chaired by John D. Hicks, professor at the University of Wisconsin and Paxson's former graduate student. The Committee of Ten labored for about two years. During that time the PCB tried to use the committee to advance its own agenda. While early relations between the PCB and its parent organization were cordial, festering resentment had been building for several years. As far as westerners were concerned, Read and Perkins treated the PCB and its council representatives with cavalier indifference. A PCB representative was supposed to report to the AHA council; however, from 1931 to 1937 PCB delegates were not invited to attend the council meeting.[2]

During this period the AHA withdrew financial support for the PCB. Until 1926 the AHA appropriated fifty to seventy-five dollars per year to defray costs of the PCB's annual meetings. From 1927 to 1933 the AHA provided four to five hundred dollars per year, an increase intended to help establish the new *Pacific Historical Review*, which began publishing in 1931. After 1933 the AHA council reduced the appropriation until the PCB received nothing in 1938.[3] The removal of AHA support was a matter of deep concern to the PCB, which received no direct dues from AHA members. It did not help matters that the PCB leadership learned indirectly that the AHA planned to permanently end its annual subsidy. Some PCB members predicted that westerners would leave the AHA and form their own organization.[4]

PCB representative James Westfall Thompson attended the 1937 meeting in Philadelphia to present to the council the PCB's case for the restoration of funding. Unfortunately, he was not informed that the meeting was to take place on the day before he arrived. Then Read accused the PCB of failing to send the required branch report. Thompson, who was about to be elected as second vice president of the AHA, was livid at what he regarded as high-handed treatment. When Read asked for the PCB report (which had been sent to Washington rather than to Read in Rochester), Thompson criticized the "imperfect articulation" of the various AHA offices.[5] "Where is the [AHA headquarters] situated?—in Washington, Philadelphia or Rochester?" Thompson asked. "It seems as if Guy Ford was right," he continued, "in contending that the administration of the

AHA is a tangled skein of conflicting and concurrent jurisdictions, with unnecessary duplications and financial statements that will bear elucidation." When Read complained that the PCB report was "not exactly a friendly gesture of filial affection," Thompson retorted that the AHA treated the PCB "more like a step-child than as a legitimate offspring."[6] We should suspect that Thompson had a great deal to say about this to his colleagues Bolton and Paxson, who was the sitting AHA president.

The procession of western AHA presidents from Cal in the 1930s were also PCB members. With a Berkeley historian presiding over the AHA, and the Committee of Ten hard at work, some westerners thought the moment had arrived for the PCB to assume a larger role in the national organization. Therefore, the PCB submitted a report to the Committee of Ten suggesting that the AHA stood to lose much of its western membership if the PCB separated from the AHA. The report pointed out ("threatened" might be a better word) that an independent PCB would become "a far western rival" of the AHA. But this sorry turn of events need not come to pass, the report said. Most PCB members preferred to remain with the AHA if a mutually satisfactory arrangement could be made. If the PCB was to be a part of the AHA, the branch should receive a share of its members' AHA dues. The report also proposed reorganizing the AHA along regional lines with several new branches like the PCB.[7] The stepchild now presented itself to the Committee of Ten as the very model for AHA reorganization. All that was required was for the AHA to hand over money, power, and respect. It did not happen.

Instead of accepting the PCB's proposals, the Committee of Ten initially recommended permanently discontinuing a PCB subvention, but ultimately agreed to a small sum to help pay for the branch meeting. Hicks and his committee relented because they recognized that many PCB members thought that the 1903 AHA resolutions establishing the PCB constituted a contract with the parent organization. Committee chairman Hicks argued that the PCB existed only because of the "unsolvable geographic problem of the distance to the Pacific Coast." "We are opposed," Hicks wrote for the committee, "to the formation of additional branches or the further subdivision of the Association into semi-autonomous groups of any sort or kind."[8] The PCB would remain a stepchild of the AHA.

Despite the unchanged status of the PCB, by the end of the 1930s it looked as if western historians had achieved a substantial professional victory. A string of western presidents and other AHA officers had broken the grip of the East Coast Old Guard. The most optimistic historians in western universities could imagine themselves rising to the highest levels of professional prominence, if their professional achievements rose to the level of a Bolton, Paxson, or Thompson. The PCB was a different story. It simply did not figure into the calculus that determined who was and who was not important in the AHA. Argue though they might, PCB members could not change that. National recognition of PCB members came not from their association with the PCB, but flowed primarily from the importance of their scholarly work. Insofar as an institutional connection was important, one's university affiliation (whether as an alumnus or a professor) was most important. In the 1930s Berkeley had come into its own, not the PCB. Bolton had built the Berkeley history department's reputation through his own work and by hiring two men who became AHA presidents.

While the western revolt festered, Bolton continued to push his ideas about hemispheric history. His work had attracted the attention of Secretary of State Cordell Hull, who thought the professor might be useful to Roosevelt's Good Neighbor Policy. In 1935 he gladly accepted Hull's invitation to serve on the National Committee to Cooperate with the Pan American Institute of Geography and History, while noting that four of the other men appointed to the committee "were trained in my seminar," having earned the doctorate at the University of California.[9]

Such honors were regarded as routine matters in the Bolton household. Paul Johnson, Eugenie Bolton's fiancé, happened to be at dinner the evening that Bolton received Hull's invitation. Johnson described Bolton's manner as "offhand greatness." Presiding at the table, Bolton struck Johnson as "an electric sort of person, full of energy and idiot humor." Bolton casually mentioned that he had "received an invitation from FR." The children were "mildly interested," and Gertrude merely murmured that it was "quite an honor."[10] Bolton thought he might go to the conference if President Sproul would fund the trip, but he did not. Consequently Bolton regretfully declined to attend.[11]

Bolton was happy to give optimistic speeches that fostered better U.S.–Latin American relations. His perspective on hemispheric history fit neatly with FDR's Good Neighbor Policy. In 1937 Secretary Hull appointed Bolton to the National Committee on the Columbus Memorial, to be erected in Santo Domingo. "Any gesture which emphasizes the unity of the history and interests of all the countries of the Western Hemisphere," Bolton replied, "I consider desirable."[12]

In 1938 Bolton's reputation and connections gave him the opportunity to see South America for the first time. He had been invited to attend the Seventh Pan American Conference, scheduled to meet that December in Lima, Peru. He wanted to go, but money was an issue. He explained the Lima conference situation to his former doctoral student Irving Leonard, who was on the Rockefeller Foundation staff. "If I knew where I could raise the money to cover expenses I should very much like to go"; this may be the shortest successful application for Rockefeller funds on record. A few weeks later the foundation provided $1,000 for the trip.[13] At about the same time, President Sproul authorized $1,000 from university funds, so Bolton had enough money to attend the eighteen-day conference and to travel extensively afterward.[14]

On December 2 Bolton began the long journey to Lima aboard a Pan American airliner. The flight to Mexico City retraced some of the travels of his Spanish explorers. He picked out the trail of Eusebio Kino. "The whole map lay before me in one eye-full—a vast region which cost him months to traverse on horseback, and we . . . covered it all in an hour."[15] After a long day with many stops en route the airliner finally deposited Bolton in Mexico City, where he met with the Pan American Trade Committee. In the Mexican capital there was time for entertainment that included a bullfight after lunch and a fine dinner at El Patio, "a high-class night club" where Bolton "heard fine music, saw expert stunt dancing, and a most orderly, well dressed and civilized company of patrons, half of whom [were] wealthy." The following morning Bolton met more Mexican dignitaries, including "several ex-presidents of the Republic and other worthies," before flying on to Lima.[16]

Bolton had little specific to say about the Lima conference, although he was impressed with the people he met. Cordell Hull topped the list of U.S. officials who were in Lima, but once the formal program was concluded, Bolton traveled with Dr. Ben M. Cherrington, chief of the State Department's Division of Cultural Relations. They crisscrossed the Andes, visiting each of the southern republics. The two men liked each other and cultivated a friendship that served professional as well as personal purposes. Bolton promised to write Secretary Hull about Herrington's work on cultural relations between the U.S. and Latin America.[17]

He saw old friends as well as new ones. Irving Leonard was at the conference. In Buenos Aires he met Eddie Dunn, who was the U.S. commercial attaché there. Perhaps it was Dunn who arranged for an article about Bolton in the *Buenos Aires Herald*.[18] Bolton parted company with Cherrington in Caracas and flew to Puerto Rico, Santo Domingo, Haiti, and Cuba, where he made short stops before flying on to Miami. In Los Angeles a freak snowstorm forced the plane to land "seventy-five miles outside the city. Sunny California!"[19]

As usual, when Bolton returned to Berkeley, he faced a mountain of unanswered correspondence that took him weeks to deal with. While he restored order to his desk—insofar as his desk was ever in an orderly state—the subject of Latin American relations was never far from his mind. President Sproul asked him to speak at UCLA on Pan American Day in mid-April.[20] "Would a talk on the Lima Conference be suitable for the occasion?" he asked his former doctoral student, history professor John Walton Caughey. Indeed it was. While in Los Angeles Bolton had taken the opportunity to speak with UCLA faculty and a Rockefeller Foundation representative about Cherrington's plan to visit the Pacific Coast in the summer. Then, on July 6, he delivered an address on "cultural cooperation with Latin America" to the National Education Association meeting in San Francisco.[21] Indeed, Bolton was willing to speak on this subject whenever called upon. The preeminent historian of the Spanish colonial frontier had become a spokesman for friendly relations among the American nations in the twentieth century.

Bolton's promotion of the Good Neighbor Policy was entirely consistent with his interests and thinking about Latin America. As far as he was concerned, the Roosevelt administration was promoting *his* hemispheric point of view. He had noticed, as he told historian Fulmer Mood, that Roosevelt had "adopted the phrase 'the Americas,' which will help the good work go on," meaning Bolton's good work. He added that he had been "summoned to Washington by the State Department" for a conference in November.[22] His service to the State Department convinced Bolton that his Americas concept was taking hold throughout the nation and at the highest levels. In fact, the Good Neighbor Policy did not spring from a careful reading of Bolton's work but from the evolving recognition that the United States should treat other American nations with tact and respect.[23] In Bolton's view, however, the national and international recognition he received was evidence of the far-reaching impact of his ideas. He was not entirely wrong to believe this. As he informed the director of the Hispano-American Education Bureau in New York, his syllabus on the history of the Americas was "used in more than a hundred colleges from which I judge it has been well received."[24] By 1939 he was a towering figure in American letters and one of the leading academic voices in Latin American history. The Good Neighbor Policy and his minor role in it gave him reason to hope that the world was moving in his direction.

Bolton's trip to Washington in November convinced him that the future for Latin American specialists was wide open. When a prospective graduate student inquired about the prospects for the field, he replied that there was "just now a very definite increase of interest in Latin American affairs which I am confident will result in the establishment of new courses and a broadening of programs for the study of Latin American history and allied subjects." His experience in Washington convinced him that there would be "a call for fifty additional teachers of Latin American subjects." "This may be too optimistic," he added, but Bolton was an optimistic man. "Most men have to create a market for their services," he counseled the inquiring student, but "the opportunities are unlimited."[25]

Bolton's essential optimism made him popular with graduate students, but he could be deaf to less cheerful dissenting voices. When Bolton spoke at the State Department, a local reporter called him the "Boss Debunker." While in the capital, Bolton indulged "in the pastime of debunking history," the newsman wrote. Bolton went through his usual litany of criticisms, chiding historians for neglecting Latin America, calling George Washington a "father by adoption" in some parts of the United States because the Southwest owed "its independence not to Washington, but to . . . Mexican forefathers." He went on to explain that the American Revolution lasted not for seven years, but for fifty, that Harvard was not the oldest college in the New World, and that all of the sixteenth-century colonial homes were in Latin America, not Boston, Jamestown, or Charleston. "It was the English who killed the Indians," the journalist learned from Bolton; "Latin Americans treated them kindly and preserved them." These secondhand statements are easily recognized as a truncated version of Bolton's "Greater America" essay. They did not have the desired effect on the reporter. "All this is very interesting, but it won't get anywhere," he wrote with his tongue planted firmly in cheek. "We have been told too long all the things the professor says are wrong are right. We do not want to unlearn the facts that have been taught us."[26]

The little article was a bit of a send-up, and Bolton no doubt thought it very funny, as it was intended to be. Accordingly, he saved the clip. Nevertheless, the unnamed writer used humor to make a point. Bolton's hemispheric perspective and his critique of "American" history did not go down as well on the East Coast as it did on the West Coast. Easterners had no need of it. Westerners could embrace a history that diminished Boston, New York, and Washington while elevating their comparatively ancient Spanish origins. Bostonians, New Yorkers, and Washingtonians felt otherwise. Nevertheless, Secretary Hull and Cherrington found in Bolton a useful academic voice that was happy to utter a positive hemispheric message. Bolton continued to speak on these themes for the rest of his life.

The southwestern borderlands were the geographical and intellectual foundation for Bolton's broad outlook on the history of the Americas. Accordingly he continued to work on the Spanish explorers whom he credited with discovering the region. In October 1939 Bolton explored the vast terrain covered by Fray Francisco Silvestre Vélez de Escalante and his companions in 1776.[27] The Escalante expedition traversed a great circular route from Santa Fe to the Utah basin and back. Bolton was determined to see it all with several companions including his former doctoral student George P. Hammond (then a dean at the University of New Mexico) and Jesse Nussbaum, a National Park Service archaeologist. The twelve-hundred-mile trip passed through New Mexico, Utah, and Arizona and ended at the Grand Canyon. Bolton and his friends then searched a remote part of the Navajo reservation for a purported Escalante inscription. Next, they followed the part of the Escalante trail accessible by automobile to the south rim of the Grand Canyon where they continued with horses and mules. Nussbaum reckoned that this was "the most difficult trip" he had "ever taken with saddle and pack animals in 35 years of exploration in remote parts of the Southwest." The stock was without water for more than a day. Bolton and his companions had a little water but no food during that period. Bolton never complained. He slept in his tent with his glasses and a light on so that "he could pick up a manuscript and study during the night should he awaken." In Nussbaum's opinion, Bolton was a "splendid and courageous companion."[28]

If Nussbaum's description of Bolton's heroic trail riding seems a little overdone, it is perhaps because the letter was written to impress the reader with Bolton's vigor. Bolton had asked the archaeologist to send the letter to an insurance company so that it could ascertain whether Bolton was insurable.[29] He was approaching his seventieth birthday. Insurers were more interested in actuarial tables than in testimonials. In a few years Bolton would declare that he was uninsurable because of heart trouble. His request of Nussbaum may have sprung from the first manifestations of health problems that developed not because of strenuous days on the trail, but from decades of sedentary living while enveloped in a cumulus cloud of cigarette smoke.

In 1939 Bolton had many years left to live, but only a matter of months before retiring from the university at the mandatory age of seventy, which Bolton would reach in July 1940. His looming retirement exposed three important questions for the university to answer. First, and most obviously, who would replace Bolton? He was by far the most important history professor on the faculty whether measured by public renown, professional reputation, publications, or graduate teaching. Who would—who could—replace him? The university would also have to appoint a new director of the Bancroft Library. Bolton's retirement inevitably opened the question of the future of the history department. Would it continue along the lines of the so-called California school, which was based on Bolton's hemispheric concept? Or would some new area of emphasis be found? There was no doubt in Bolton's mind about how that question should be answered. Cal should maintain its preeminence in the field he had pioneered. That conviction conditioned his solutions for the other problems.

Bolton had a great deal to say about the future of the Berkeley history department, but other opinions mattered, as the discussions about a replacement for the retiring James Westfall Thompson showed. Bolton proposed two candidates: Crane Brinton of Harvard and Robert J. Kerner, who was already a full professor of modern European history on the Berkeley faculty. Frederic Paxson thought that Brinton was "a clever historical essayist" but had not yet proved that he was worthy of the Ehrman chair. On the other hand, the appointment of Professor Kerner would release his salary so that additional new junior appointments could be made.[30] Paxson also thought it important to reward people who had served the department well. Thus Paxson recommended his colleague, Bolton concurred, and Sproul turned the matter over to a university committee to make a recommendation.

Paxson's advice about hiring senior professors from the inside to reward performance and avoid morale problems would be echoed in the discussion of Bolton's replacement. Paxson's financial argument is also worth noting. By appointing Kerner, Sproul would have two salaries (a total of $16,500) to divide among the new Ehrman chair and one, perhaps even two, junior appointments. Assistant professors of history at Berkeley were getting $3,000 per year or less. In other words Sproul could give Kerner (who had been making $6,500 per year) a $1,000 raise, hire two assistants at $3,000 each, and save $3,000 per year, which is apparently what Bolton recommended.[31] This was the sort of arithmetic that shaped the future of the history department.

The recital of these prosaic budgetary details sheds some light on the accusation that Bolton refused to hire Jews for the Berkeley history department, an allegation still heard today. Part of the savings from Thompson's retirement was taken up by the one-year appointment of the medieval historian Ernst Hartwig Kantorowicz, a German Jew. Kantorowicz had immigrated to the United States after losing his professorship at the University of Frankfurt because he was a Jew.[32] He was an assimilated Jew and a strong German nationalist with decidedly right-wing views. After World War I he had taken up arms against communists. Even his biography of Frederick II was meant to serve a nationalist agenda. Although Kantorowicz was an early critic of the National Socialists, he would later be accused of being a Nazi in all but his Jewish heritage. The Nazis certainly did not recognize him as someone fit to teach German youth, so like other Jewish faculty, he was forced out of his professorship.[33]

Kantorowicz's early work was in some respects idiosyncratic, but he is now recognized as a major figure in medieval historiography. He would have been a fitting candidate for the Ehrman chair. There is no reason to think that he was considered as a replacement for Thompson, but Bolton asked Professor Ferdinand Schevill of the University of Chicago about Kantorowicz's fitness for a position at Berkeley. Schevill judged Kantorowicz as neither a "great scholar or a superior intellect," concluding that "a less than major position in your university is quite compatible with his attainments."[34] Bolton forwarded Schevill's remarks to Sproul without comment.

The Chicago professor's comments about Kantorowicz's book were harsh but not unique. The Frederick biography had been published without footnotes and included a lot of mythology and folklore about the medieval emperor. Critics attacked his work accordingly. Kantorowicz subsequently published a volume of documentation intended to disarm his detractors, but it did not silence them.[35] Despite Schevill's unsupportive assessment Bolton invited Kantorowicz to join the Berkeley history department as visiting professor of medieval history for the 1939–40 academic year. He assigned Kantorowicz the standard course load of two undergraduate courses and one graduate seminar per semester and allowed him to pick the topics for each course. Bolton promised the Jewish refugee "a friendly welcome by all the members of the History Department."[36] Whether Kantorowicz was hired because Sproul insisted over Bolton's objection remains an open question.

If Bolton objected to Kantorowicz, anti-Semitism would not have been his only motive. Bolton was a critic of the German system of higher education. World War I propaganda had probably hardened his views. In 1920 he had observed that "among older university men" there was a "strong predilection toward" German university training. However, "it had become generally recognized that . . . American university degrees stood for much more than German degrees."[37] In the same year he answered "No" to four questions asking his opinion about the proposed establishment of a federal Department of Education. At the foot of the questionnaire he scrawled "Keep Federal hands off! *Don't Prussianize education.*"[38] Bolton may well have objected to Kantorowicz because of his German training.

Exposure to Kantorowicz seemed to eliminate whatever reservations Bolton had about him. In the spring of 1940 Bolton attended the visiting professor's illustrated public lecture on Charles the Bold. Kantorowicz made a very good impression on Bolton and the rest of the history faculty who were present. He thought that Kantorowicz would "be a real scholarly asset to the University" and an effective graduate teacher. Therefore, he unequivocally added, "I recommend that he be made Professor of History on permanent appointment."[39] The permanent appointment did not come until after World War II had ended, but that was not Bolton's doing. If anti-Semitism was the reason for keeping Kantorowicz as a temporary instructor in the history department, the fault must be found elsewhere.

But Bolton did have reasons for being reluctant to hire Kantorowicz in 1939. He was keen on hiring his own students for the history department, which already had three of them in Priestley, Chapman, and Lawrence Kinnaird, an assistant professor. Kinnaird was very much a borderlands historian in the Bolton mold, having written a dissertation on Spanish Louisiana.[40] He had begun his teaching career at Davis, which was then the university's agricultural college. For administrative purposes the small history program there was considered to be part of the Berkeley department. In 1937 Kinnaird transferred to the Berkeley faculty. He taught the Americas course, and thus Bolton regarded him as a key asset.

In August 1939 Bolton recommended Engel Sluiter, another of his doctoral students, for an instructorship to begin in September. Bolton raved about Sluiter, who had "a superior mind" and was "glowing with zeal for research and writing." His special interest in Dutch colonial American history would expand the department's Americas offerings and allow an additional section of History 8.[41] Yet Sluiter's fate was embedded in the shifting sands of other departmental hiring decisions. Foremost was the Ehrman professorship, which was still up in the air. The university search committee had decided to recommend an outsider, William E. Lunt, a historian of medieval England. Bolton did not concur, because Lunt's field was very similar to that of other Berkeley professors.[42] Consequently Bolton continued to recommend Kerner for the position, which went unfilled for the time being.

Bolton recommended Priestley for the Sather professorship because his scholarly interests were so close to Bolton's. He also recommended Priestley to succeed him as the director of the Bancroft Library. Looking to the field of U.S. history, Bolton thought that someone senior should be added to supplement the work of Paxson in the post–Civil War period. Bolton thought that Avery Craven of the University of Chicago or Professor Hicks from Wisconsin would be suitable.[43]

In the spring Bolton revised his recommendations for new hires. Having changed his mind about who should get the Sather professorship, he now recommended longtime Berkeley professor William A. Morris instead of Priestley. Morris was a "sound scholar," in English constitutional history—hardly a ringing endorsement for a named professorship. Bolton still recommended Priestley as director of the Bancroft Library. If Bolton seemed to vacillate in his guidance on appointments, it was due to his desire to redistribute the salary savings from his and Thompson's retirement so that new faculty could be hired and at least some old hands would be rewarded. Bolton wanted to parcel out "whatever honors and emoluments may be attached to my titles," as he put it.[44]

Bolton's notions about heirship and entitlements extended to the possibility that the university might decide to bring in a distinguished scholar to carry on his own work. Predictably, he believed that the best men in the country were his students Arthur Aiton at the University of Michigan and J. Fred Rippy at the University of Chicago. The relations of the American people had "become matters of major concern . . . to our Government" and would become more important in the future. Now that Berkeley was established as the leading center for the study of the Americas, "it is a matter of wisdom to maintain that leadership," he argued. "I cannot be too emphatic in presenting this aspect of the matter."[45]

Bolton's logic was clear enough, but if a senior appointment would vouchsafe the reputation of the Americas program, why had he waited until the eleventh hour to tell Sproul? Why had he recommended the preferment of lesser-known, less accomplished, junior people (who in time did not prove to be major figures) instead of one nationally recognized historian? Bolton must have believed that there was strength in numbers. Four of his "boys" on the faculty would carry the Americas program forward. Consequently Bolton, like King Lear, divided his kingdom— his "honors and emoluments"—and with results that he did not foresee. It was a great mistake.

When the establishment of the new Morrison professorship was announced, Bolton continued to advocate for Hicks or Craven in U.S. history.[46] Bolton's unwavering support for these two historians no doubt reflected Paxson's constant encouragement as well. By bringing in Hicks (who turned out to be the choice for the Morrison professorship), Paxson added an ally who was not only his student but a senior professor with national stature. The strength of Paxson and Hicks would balance the weight of Chapman, Priestley, and any number of junior professors. Perhaps Bolton hoped that the power of local patriotism would prove to be a decisive factor in the affairs of the Berkeley history department. Sidney Ehrman, other California patriots, the Native Sons, the California Historical Society, and perhaps even the Clampers would provide political and financial support for Bolton's vision of history while the young professors established their reputations. If this was his plan, he hoped in vain.

Sproul followed some of Bolton's recommendations but not others. Priestley became the director of the Bancroft Library. Sluiter got his permanent appointment. Kinnaird was promoted. But the big prizes, the two professorships, did not go to Bolton's nominees. Kerner, rather than Morris, became the new Sather professor. The Ehrman professorship went to Raymond Sontag, an outsider specializing in nineteenth- and twentieth-century European diplomacy. The university began to court Hicks, but he turned down the first offer and did not come until 1942. Perhaps that is why in 1941 the university hired a new instructor in U.S. history, Walton Bean, who had studied under Paxson. Thus Paxson began to establish his own stable of students alongside Bolton's. From the standpoint of financial rewards and university laurels, little of Bolton's estate went to his students. Almost all of the salary savings and titles went to men in other fields.[47]

Nevertheless, as Bolton approached retirement, his influence seemed to be well established in the university. In retirement Bolton would remain a fixture on the Berkeley campus. As a revered emeritus professor he would occupy a box seat from which to view the dismantling and dissolution of his empire.

Like King Lear, Bolton imagined a retirement that would be as full of honor and accomplishment as his life had been when he undisputedly ruled his empire. He also expected his successors to administer his realm much as he would have done. His old friend and fellow Penn alumnus, Paxson, would head the department. Priestley would guide the Bancroft Library, while Chapman, Kinnaird, and Sluiter would carry on the Boltonian tradition of the Americas and borderlands history. Bolton believed that these men would defend the empire that he had built.

It all began well. In February 1940 Bolton learned that the University of Pennsylvania would confer an honorary doctorate on him at the spring commencement.[1] This was the seventh such degree for Bolton.[2] Additional honors came from near and far. The Native Sons of the Golden West feted him in April.[3] The California Historical Society followed suit in May. Paxson explained his admiration for Bolton to the society: Some mountains seemed to shrink as the traveler approached them, "but Bolton grows into nobler proportion as one draws nearer to him." Then, perhaps with unintended candor, Paxson added that Bolton's retirement would change the University of California because he would "have no successor."[4] This was meant as a graceful compliment to Bolton's life of unparalleled scholarly accomplishment, but Paxson's words suggested something else as well. Bolton's students on the Berkeley faculty, singly or as a group, could not replace the old man. They could only teach his courses.

In May the president of the Dominican Republic bestowed on Bolton the

Heraldic Order of Cristóbal Colon. "It is a signal honor to be associated in this way with the name and deeds of the great discoverer," Bolton wrote when he acknowledged the award.[5] Who would doubt that Bolton, who thought of himself as an explorer and discoverer, admired and identified with Columbus as much as he did with Anza, Kino, Coronado, and the rest of his Spanish frontiersmen?

The honors were satisfying memorials to a long and distinguished career, but they would not pay the bills. Bolton's university retirement paycheck would not match his university salary. Consequently he looked into public lecturing to fill the gap. He offered to lecture in Southern California for $100 per engagement. After paying his own expenses and giving the lecture bureau 20 percent of the fee, he would clear $50 or so. But Bolton had larger ideas in mind. He was thinking about lecturing to the general public "anywhere in the country," for a "considerably larger fee."[6] Bolton had been lecturing for forty years. Why not capitalize on all of his experience on the platform? Despite its initial appeal, the itinerant lecturer's life proved less permanent and profitable than he had hoped.

Bolton did not plan on spending all of his time on the lecture circuit. Retirement finally gave him the opportunity to get back into the desert in search of his heroic explorers. He had two large projects on the drawing board, a study of Francisco Vásquez de Coronado's exploits, and a book about the explorations of Fray Francisco Silvestre Vélez de Escalante. In January and February he managed to trace Coronado's route through Mexico from Compostela to the U.S. border.[7] The year 1940 marked the quadricentennial of Coronado's exploring expedition, and many observances and activities were being planned on both sides of the border, including the erection of an international monument dedicated to Coronado and friendship between Mexico and the United States. This project was right up Bolton's alley, combining exploration, scholarship, and the Good Neighbor Policy. The U.S. Coronado Exposition, New Mexico and Arizona Coronado commissions, National Park Service, and the universities of California, Arizona, and New Mexico organized an expedition to locate Coronado's trail. The trail followers included three of Bolton's former doctoral students, Aubrey Neasham (southwestern regional historian for the National Park Service), George P. Hammond (University of New Mexico), and Russell Ewing (assistant professor of history at the University of Arizona), as well as several other men. The trip took twenty days of automobile travel, a journey made difficult by rain, flooded streams, and mud-clogged roads. Despite the difficulties Bolton and his companions established where Coronado had crossed into the United States, "at least to our satisfaction," as Neasham put it.[8]

Once Bolton concluded his final semester's work and received his Pennsylvania degree, he returned to Coronado's trail north of the border. Mid-August (not the best season to make a pilgrimage to the desert Southwest) found him at the La Fonda Inn in Santa Fe, where he met Neasham. Every three or four days Bolton would write a long letter to Gertrude, or "Mama," as he called her. He used the letters, which described his travels in some detail, as research notes when he returned to Berkeley. Equipped with a government car, Bolton and Neasham drove over Glorieta Pass and then down the Pecos River to Antón Chico.[9] Bolton described the farmers as "old-time Spaniards (not Mexicans) descendants of the sixteenth century pioneers.

Bolton and Neasham motored back to Albuquerque, picked up Hammond, and headed west to Gallup, which was then hosting the annual Indian fair. Representatives of thirty-nine tribes were there, dressed "in their brightest finery," he told Gertrude. Then they "set forth south for Zuñi, which was Coronado's objective—the Seven Cities of Cibola." From Zuni Bolton's route swung southwest through the eastern Arizona towns of St. Johns, Concho, Show Low, Lakeside, and McNary. "From McNary south we were again on the Coronado Trail," Bolton wrote, "and nobody has had it right before." Bolton thought the determining factor was a *barranca* (gorge) then called Post Office Canyon, "which forced Coronado to . . . cross at a shallower point." He judged the ford to be an important discovery, because it could be used to test Coronado's route for many miles in both directions.[10]

From the deep defiles of eastern Arizona Bolton and company traveled southward to the Gila River, into the Aravaipa Valley and thence down to Bisbee on the Mexican border. Bolton shot off another letter to Gertrude. "The Park Service is paying all my expenses," he assured Gertrude, who worried about money. In addition, Bolton expected to get "$10.00 per day as collaborator." For Bolton this arrangement was the best of all possible worlds. "I'm having a vacation with pay and all expenses."[11]

After consulting with Arizona archaeologists, the trio returned to Santa Fe by way of Tucson, Phoenix, and Globe. "We have been strenuously on the move," he told Gertrude. He was not exaggerating, and he was not finished yet. Bolton and Hammond left Neasham and went on to west Texas, Oklahoma, and Kansas. The trip convinced him that the "two canyons visited by Coronado were Tule Canyon and Palo Duro Canyon, both being parts of the same great network of barrancas."[12]

Bolton would have been satisfied to stay on the road for the rest of his life. Whether he traveled by plane, train, automobile, horse, jackass, or foot, it seemed not to matter to him. A soft bed in a luxury hotel or blankets on rough ground were all the same. For nearly one year Bolton was intermittently on the trail. When he finished the Coronado trail, off he went looking for Escalante. Again he found trail companions in Neasham and Hammond. Other comrades came and went along the way.

The lecture circuit was less appealing than the trail, but it paid well. In January his friend Ben Cherrington, formerly of the State Department but then on the University of Denver faculty, arranged for Bolton to speak about the Good Neighbor Policy in Colorado, Wyoming, and Utah.[13] For about two weeks Bolton hopped from state to state, often speaking at several venues per day. The schedule was exhausting, and Bolton was not certain that the lecturer's life was for him. "This talkie-talkie business is pretty silly," he complained to Gertrude, "and I don't know how long I would be able to stand myself—or the people stand me!" But the money was good. Cherrington arranged for a $500 honorarium while one of the other universities paid his expenses.[14] In March Bolton made another well-paying lecture tour "barn-storming on Inter-American Relations in what we used to call the Middle West," he told Wisconsin historian Curtis Nettels.[15] He combined his speaking with a trip to St. Augustine for a National Park Service Advisory Board meeting.[16] One way or another, Bolton was making retirement pay. As he explained to park service administrators, "I still have to earn my living."[17]

In May 1941 a substantial new source of income appeared on the horizon. The centennials of the gold rush and California statehood were looming on the horizon. Edward A. Dickson, Los Angeles newspaper publisher, university regent, and UCLA booster, proposed a ten-volume centennial history to be published in 1950. Two decades previously, Dickson and Bolton had worked together on the California Historical Survey Commission. Bolton had resisted Dickson's attempt to redirect the commission toward chronicling the California contribution to World War I, but now the Southern Californian was making an offer that Bolton could not refuse.[18] He wanted Bolton to be general editor with a salary of $6,000 per year. Dickson proposed an elaborate scheme with an editorial board, state advisory board, and county advisory boards that would have involved hundreds of people. Dickson's ideas about history had not changed: he thought that any competent clerk could compile historical facts. In each county fifteen to twenty people would "assemble historical data" for the editorial board, which presumably would direct the writing of the decade-by-decade chronicle that Dickson had in mind.[19] The project would be expensive—about a quarter of a million dollars, which the legislature would have to provide. In the meantime he advocated the use of university endowment funds already in hand.

Bolton was willing to head up the project and to enhance his annual retirement income for a few years. But he must have been horrified at Dickson's unworkable scheme. Instead, Bolton proposed that well-known scholars be paid to write individual volumes on specific topics. He pared down the editorial committee structure and limited its authority to supervising and facilitating the authors' work. As for Dickson's vast committee network, "it should be enlisted only in a manner consistent with the dignity of the University," Bolton advised President Sproul.[20] Once again, Bolton and Dickson were in conflict over the nature of history and how a big historical project should be administered. Their differences would sharpen in coming months as historical events overtook both of them.

But for the time being, Bolton continued his round of lecturing and Spanish trail research. In May he delivered the University of California's fourth annual Bernard Moses Memorial Lecture, which he titled "El Dorado: The Coronado Expedition in Perspective."[21] In June he went looking for the spot where Escalante crossed the Colorado River in the bottom of the Grand Canyon. The only practical way to reach the crossing, Bolton hypothesized, was by boat down the San Juan River and into the canyon. Bolton engaged a river guide at Mexican Hat, Utah, which Bolton judged to be "the most isolated place in the United States, being two hundred miles from telegraph and railroad and fifty miles from telephone."[22]

Bolton's party spent "seven and a half days," he recalled, "floating down the river, running rapids, getting soaked, drying out, [hiking] to Rainbow Bridge, racing with mountain sheep which were running parallel to us on the cliffs, and generally having a good time."[23] He thought it all "real sport." "All you have to do is sit, occasionally riding a twelve-foot breaker." Amidst the excitement Bolton found what he was looking for. "I reached the Escalante Crossing and it all opened out as plain as day."[24] The place is now known as the Crossing of the Fathers. It was a good week for the retired professor with the bum ticker.

Retirement seemed to be all that Bolton had hoped it would be. The heavy teaching and administrative responsibilities were gone. He was free to pursue his field research, usually at government expense. Accolades came from everywhere. Speaking engagements were frequent and paid well. In November he was confident enough to request $200 plus expenses for a two-day appearance at Drake University. And there was the prospect of the editorship of the centennial history of California. The history business was paying off.

There were some clouds on the horizon. Even though the United States was not yet a belligerent, war blazed in Europe and Asia. The economy was improving as the country's industrial plant produced goods for other countries. Congress had instituted a military draft, which took some of his students, while others found positions in a State Department attentive to fascist inroads in Latin America. He promised to send a list of people who were eligible for State Department positions to Philip Powell, a State Department official who had finished his doctorate at Cal under Priestley.[25]

Of course, Bolton continued to plump his students for academic jobs. They were in demand. James King had an offer from Tulane but turned it down for a position at Northwestern. Bolton recommended Woodrow Borah for the Tulane position. "He is one of the most brilliant graduates we have ever had," Bolton offered, "quite the equal of King." Bolton expected "a notable output of scholarly work by him in years to come." The glowing recommendation included details about Borah's work in colonial Mexico. He added that Borah "was born in Mississippi of Jewish parents," a statement perhaps intended to aid Borah's candidacy by highlighting his southern roots while alerting Tulane authorities to his ethnic and religious heritage. Borah did not go to Tulane; instead he took a one-year position at Princeton University.[26]

In late 1941 everything changed. November began routinely when Bolton participated in a Latin American conference at the State College of Washington in Pullman.[27] Then he headed for the University of San Francisco, where he spoke about "Bases of Western Hemisphere Understanding." Suddenly cascading disasters struck. On November 18 Charles Chapman, star athlete, baseball scout, and professor, died from a heart attack.[28] Almost simultaneously Priestley suffered a stroke.[29] Bolton thought it unlikely that the sixty-seven-year-old Priestley would return to teach in the spring semester. On December 7 the Japanese imperial navy struck Pearl Harbor, and the nation was at war. Professor Kinnaird was called to Washington and was dispatched to South America on a government mission. Only Sluiter was left to replace these losses. For a time Bolton thought that he might also go to Latin America.[30]

These unexpected developments must have dealt a stunning blow to Bolton, especially the death and disability of Chapman and Priestley, which surely reminded him that his remaining days were limited. His mortality was brought home again in February when his older brother Alvin died at age seventy-four.[31]

Even though Bolton was still vigorous, his carefree days of exploring the desert whenever he wanted were over for the time being. The university called him back to run the Bancroft Library and teach his old courses. As Bolton feared, Priestley did not return to his post. He died in 1944.[32] In ordinary times Bolton would have served only for a semester until new people could be hired, but the war emergency changed everything. Young men (some professors as well as students) were leaving the university for military service. Kinnaird would be gone for the foreseeable future, so Sproul invited Bolton to teach his courses in the 1942–43 academic year. "I am glad of the opportunity to continue in the work in which I am happiest," he told the president.[33] He was happy also to have the income that teaching afforded, now that wartime travel restrictions and renewed university duties curtailed Bolton's fieldwork and lecturing. So everything fell on Bolton's shoulders, except for the chairmanship, which Paxson still held.

Where most men saw calamity, Edward Dickson saw opportunity. Not long after the torpedoes slammed into the hulls on Battleship Row, Dickson moved to modify his plans for the centennial history. Dickson wished to assemble "historical matter connected with the War," he wrote Bolton one week after Pearl Harbor. Sproul approved of the temporary use of endowment funds for a six-month trial of Dickson's plan. The regent asked Bolton to reconsider his plan for a statewide committee network.[34]

Dickson meant his proposal to be understood as a command.[35] He believed that the county committees would "collect historical material" that would be deposited with the university, but Dickson's proposed budget provided nothing for training or oversight of the volunteers. Nor did he give any indication of what classes of materials would be collected or how they would be authenticated and evaluated. Somehow the new sources would be converted into the "profusely illustrated" ten-volume centennial history, but Dickson provided no details about how that would be done aside from hiring Bolton, a second historian to assist him in Southern California, and two secretaries.

Dickson's plan could not bear critical scrutiny, as Bolton at once understood. Getting it approved by the regents had been a feat of political legerdemain that Dickson had accomplished by making Sproul the sponsor of the plan that went before the board. Once the proposal was approved, Dickson kept referring to it as "your plan" when he corresponded with Sproul. Furthermore, he directed Sproul to order Bolton to carry out the plan that Dickson had in fact authored. In 1919 Bolton and Judge Davis had resisted Dickson's attempt to shanghai the California Historical Records Commission for his war records program. That would not happen again, not if Dickson could help it. Now Dickson thought he had a way to control Bolton through Sproul. Bolton had ideas of his own.

Dickson was going to cause trouble, but early in 1942 Bolton was most concerned about addressing the enormous gap that the departure of Kinnaird, Chapman, and Priestley had created. It was now clear that his recommendation to hire young men and allow them to develop would not meet the circumstances. Now Bolton advised Sproul that a "mature man" would be best. He thought the most suitable candidate was J. Fred Rippy.[36] In March Bolton (with the approval of Sproul and Paxson) urged Rippy to "consider a call to California."[37] Bolton directed Rippy to reply by airmail if he was interested.

Bolton's letter gave the impression that the job was Rippy's if he wanted it, but the matter was not so simple. After Rippy expressed interest in the position, the Cal search committee raised questions about him. Bolton asked Rippy for reviews of his books, a list of his doctoral students, and his plans for future research.[38] Rippy gave a snappish, perfunctory response to Bolton's queries. "Does someone question my capacity and the soundness of my product?" Rippy claimed to have more graduate students than most of his Chicago colleagues. "I have never lost the inspiration that I received from you and the California group," he confided. "I shall carry on until the Great Reaper stills my hand." Bolton did not make clear who had raised an objection to Rippy, but enthusiasm for moving Rippy to Berkeley had cooled and the feeling appeared to be mutual.[39] The Great Reaper would not find Rippy in Berkeley when his time came.

While Bolton fought to pry Rippy out of Chicago, he was also dealing with Dickson's demands for the centennial history. "Under the circumstances, I think that it is up to you to proceed with our plans as expeditiously as possible," Dickson informed him. Dickson still insisted on the county committees, which he thought the university comptroller should organize.[40] He also directed Bolton to appoint Dickson's friend Grace Somerby as secretarial assistant for Southern California. She wanted to write a volume of biographies and to compile one of California statistics. "I think that both of these activities should be authorized at once," he advised Bolton.[41]

Dickson's behavior was a reprise of his peremptory, insulting, and outrageous actions in 1919. He treated Bolton like a hired hand and expected his orders to be carried out in the name of Sproul and the regents. As in 1919, he appointed a clerical employee to whom he gave important editorial responsibilities, a decision as unfair to her as it was to Bolton. By April Bolton considered resigning as editor.[42] But he soldiered on. Perhaps Sproul convinced him that it was necessary to humor Dickson for the good of the university. Sproul had recently announced that Bolton would receive an honorary degree at spring commencement. Withdrawing from a project that a regent and the president supported would be embarrassing to all concerned.[43]

Instead of retreating, Bolton proposed a new plan for the centennial history, one very different from Dickson's. Bolton projected a number of interpretive volumes that would be written by established scholars who would receive $2,500 each plus a royalty. As editor, Bolton would select the authors subject to approval by Sproul.[44] Bolton's reasons for staying on are not difficult to fathom. He could use the money as editor of the series. Sproul, who must have realized that he had been manipulated by Regent Dickson, probably gave Bolton some assurances of support for his position. In the spring of 1942 Sproul needed Bolton, a fundamental fact that may have finally occurred to Bolton as well as Sproul. The lines were drawn.

Even though Bolton and Dickson had not yet agreed on the overall design of the centennial history, Bolton moved ahead. Dickson might issue orders, but Bolton controlled the budget. He appointed his longtime secretary and friend Maxine Chappell as his assistant who would be in charge of "requisitions and bills," including those of Somerby.[45] In July Bolton outlined his plan for Dickson and sent Chappell to Los Angeles to confer with Somerby.[46] He hoped to present his proposal to the Centennial History Advisory Committee, consisting of Sidney Ehrman, Sproul, Dickson, and a third regent—an assemblage that seemed to be stacked in favor of Bolton. "I was very greatly impressed with your suggestion of a series of topical histories," Dickson admitted, "but upon reflection I am convinced that the original plan [Dickson's] should be carried out."[47] Flexibility was not one of Dickson's strong points. The two would wrangle over the series for months to come.

Not all of Bolton's collaborations were as disagreeable as the centennial history. Father Maynard Geiger, successor to the Franciscan historian Zephyrin Engelhardt at the Mission Santa Barbara, asked Bolton to participate in the Serra Cause, the effort to canonize Junípero Serra, California's first Franciscan missionary. Bolton accepted and was duly appointed to the Diocesan Historical Commission. His role on the commission was to gather and authenticate all of the written sources concerning Serra. The Historical Commission consisted of Bolton (styled "DOMINUM HERIBERTUM EUGENIUM BOLTON" in the appointment letter) and two priests, Geiger and James H. Culleton, chancellor of the Monterey-Fresno Diocese, which would oversee the cause.[48] The Serra Cause vice postulator, Father Eric O'Brien, would make the case for Serra before an ecclesiastical hearing. Bolton's contribution to the cause was limited to the evaluation of historical documents, but there should be no doubt of Bolton's enthusiasm for Serra.[49] The deliberate pace of the Vatican and wartime exigencies delayed the canonization proceedings for years.

Bolton's work on the Serra Cause must have been especially pleasing compared with the sometimes onerous nature of his service on the California centennial history project. Dickson rejected Bolton's plan for a series. Bolton talked it over with Paxson and John Walton Caughey, one of Bolton's doctoral students who was a professor at UCLA, and submitted a new plan to Dickson, who at first seemed pleased. Then, the day before a meeting of the Advisory Committee where Bolton was scheduled to present the new plan, Dickson told him to propose Dickson's original scheme instead. Bolton informed Sproul that he would not attend the meeting in order to avoid an open conflict.[50] Dickson smoothed over the dispute, claiming that Bolton was modifying his plans before reporting to the committee.[51]

But Bolton had had enough. He bluntly informed Dickson and Sproul that he would not serve as editor of the series as Dickson had conceived it. If the centennial history went ahead as Dickson proposed, "you have my best wishes," but "I shall be far from optimistic about the outcome."[52]

Dickson's response was characteristically unbending. He gave Bolton a lesson in California historiography, listing about three dozen books that in the regent's opinion already covered the topics that Bolton had proposed. "Why not merely check off twenty from the above lists and call it a day?" he asked. "So to repeat," Dickson insisted, "what is wanted is a Ten-Volume, Chronologically arranged, History of California, to which we can turn readily for information of an historical character." He concluded by asking Bolton to make "one more final effort to adjust your views so that we can go ahead along these lines."[53]

Dickson seems to have won the day, for in November Bolton was still in the editorial saddle cooperating with him.[54] Was he giving the "final effort" that Dickson had asked for? Perhaps Sproul had convinced Bolton that Dickson's goodwill was indispensable to the university. So Bolton gave in—or did he? In November 1942 he held two private meetings with historians in Southern and Northern California to discuss the series. We do not know what was discussed at these secretive meetings, but subsequent developments are suggestive. Sproul had provided funding for a half year, but the money was running out. It is possible that Sproul and Bolton decided to defeat Dickson's plans by supporting them to the maximum extent possible—by asking the state legislature for a sum of money that seemed extravagant during the war. Without consulting Dickson, the president requested $250,000 to fund the entire centennial project instead of asking for smaller amounts over a period of years. The appropriation did not even get through the legislative committee process. Then Sproul dropped support from university moneys that he controlled. "I wish that he had consulted me," Dickson complained.[55] He thought that it would have been wiser to request only $40,000 from the legislature. Dickson was down, but not defeated, not yet. He urged Sproul and Bolton to support new public and private funding initiatives. The university men dutifully supported Dickson's proposals, but they did not succeed.[56]

As soon as the quarter-million-dollar centennial history appropriation failed, Bolton fired off a letter to Sproul. "Perhaps not all is lost," he dryly observed. He then proposed a substitute plan that "would cost relatively little and in some ways would be better than the plan on which we were proceeding."[57] Bolton's plan was substantially the same as his former proposals. The series would be called the Chronicles of California. It would require "no fanfare [or] propaganda," and would not cost much. The books would be published by the University of California Press in the usual way, so no new appropriations would be needed.[58] Authors would not get a big fee but would receive a generous 15 percent royalty. Bolton relinquished the fat editor's salary and asked only for funds for his secretary, Maxine Chappell. Sproul approved the plan.

Dickson must have realized that Sproul and Bolton had outmaneuvered him. Dickson's centennial history faded away, but Regent Dickson would not. In a few years he would be a key figure in one of the university's most traumatic episodes, the loyalty oath controversy. His regard for Sproul at that time may well have been conditioned by his experience with his ill-fated history project.

In the meantime Bolton's economies helped the new series move forward, but only a few of the volumes were published as originally planned. Some authors published their books with other presses, and some titles never appeared. Bolton suggested that Dickson (or his friend and fellow regent Chester Rowell) write the volume on California Progressives. Fortunately, historian George Mowry wrote that volume, which remained the standard work on the subject for many years. A volume called "The Boom of the Eighties" that was projected under the name of Lindley Bynum did not appear in the series, but came out with the Huntington Library Press under the authorship of Glenn S. Dumke. Caughey had planned to contribute "California Victorians" to the series, but published *Gold Is the Cornerstone* instead. The list of these changes and evolutions could be extended, but the important point is this: most of the books that were published under the guidance of Bolton and coeditor Caughey were important and lasting contributions to historical scholarship. Similar results under Dickson's scheme would not have been likely.

Whether by clever intrigue or the unanticipated actions of the state legislature, Bolton had prevailed in the clash with Dickson. Now he could return to the problem of hiring a Latin Americanist. After failing to get Rippy, Bolton recommended a young man, James Ferguson King, who had taken the degree under Bolton in 1939. After donning the doctoral hood, King went to the State Department before taking an assistant professorship at Northwestern University. In the fall of 1943 Bolton recommended King to Sproul. While King's "removals to the State Department and . . . to Northwestern" had "somewhat retarded his writing," he was now "well on the way." "I should have preferred to see Rippy brought here," Bolton admitted, but "of all the young men . . . I put King in the first place."[59] King duly returned to his alma mater.

Bolton hoped that King would be a lynchpin in Cal's Americas program, and in one sense he was. He ably taught the Americas course and mentored many graduate students. However, King was not the big publisher that Bolton had hoped for. His main influence in the university was through his service in various administrative posts.[60] While it is unfair to judge King solely on the basis of the number of his publications, it is clear that he did not measure up to the task that Bolton had set for him. The same could be said about Kinnaird and Sluiter.

In 1943 Bolton thought that he had shored up Latin American history at Berkeley, but developments on the national scene undermined one of the cornerstones of Bolton's empire, his hemisphere-wide Americas course as the foundation for United States and other national histories. On April 4 the *New York Times* published a report on the results of a test on U.S. history given to college and high school students. Their ignorance was alarming, especially in the midst of a bloody war. If young men were marching off to die in some foreign land, they ought to at least know the history of their country and the ideals that they were fighting for, or so said critics of secondary and college curricula. The previous year AHA executive secretary Ford had established a committee on American history teaching at the college level. He wanted to get ahead of the "super-patriotic" forces whose "loose thinking and loud talking" about "what should be taught and how" might have some unfortunate influence because of war hysteria.[61] The *Times* article spurred the AHA and other educational groups to action. The AHA, the Mississippi Valley Historical Association, and the National Council for the Social Studies formed a joint Committee on American History in the Schools and Colleges, while similar state and regional committees formed throughout the country.[62]

The war hysteria that Ford feared was well represented by Richard Lloyd Jones, publisher of the *Tulsa Tribune,* who had been a Wisconsin student with Ford and Bolton.[63] After reading Bernard DeVoto's call on the AHA to make citizens of college students in the July *Harper's* "Easy Chair" column, Jones wrote to his old friend Ford. "It has long been an editorial thesis and crusade of mine that education for citizenship has been neglected by our universities and colleges" where academic cynics "inspired contempt for the principles and practices of the founders of this Republic." This was true, in Jones's estimation, in every state institution, including Ford's University of Minnesota. "You have too few Americans. You have Swedes, Norwegians, Poles, Finns, Germans who have come here to pluck the feathers out of the American goose and to remain foreigners."

Wisconsin was no better. Jones had gone to Wisconsin to work with Robert La Follette, only to become disenchanted when the "great progressive" named a state ticket based on ethnic considerations. After La Follette as leader of the Republican Party picked Swiss, German, and Polish candidates for state offices, Jones exploded. "Well for God's sake," he said to La Follette, "is there an American to fill an office in Wisconsin and have you got any Americans who will cast an American vote?" "My strength is with the people who speak foreign languages," the irritated La Follette replied, and that was the beginning of the end of Jones's relationship with him. Jones railed against the University of Wisconsin, on whose Board of Regents he served. Turner and Paxson were great teachers, Jones wrote, but they did not teach citizenship. Only Carl Fish measured up to Jones's patriotic standards. During World War I, Jones discovered that Wisconsin "was a German propaganda college" where courses in the German language were the only classes required of all undergraduate students.[64] The publisher went on in this vein for more than five single-spaced typed pages.

The U.S. Office of Education Wartime Commission, reacting perhaps to the sort of views that had been expressed in the *Times, Harper's,* and Jones's letter, asked for a series of reports "on how the content of college curriculum" could "be adjusted" to meet wartime exigencies. The University of Chicago responded with a report categorized by general fields: ancient and medieval history, modern Europe, the United States, the Far East, and Latin America. Professor Rippy was on the committee that wrote the report. The thoughtful section on the United States allowed that college surveys of U.S. history gave too little attention "to the hemispherical and world setting of our history," a nod in the direction of the Americas for which Rippy may have been responsible. But the one-year survey that the Chicago report proposed contained none of the breadth that Bolton had been urging on the profession for more than thirty years. The outline of the colonial and early national period emphasized "English heritage." Spain and Mexico were mentioned only in the context of U.S. expansion "at small cost." The Chicago World's Fair was mentioned, but the Spanish-American War was not.[65]

The section on Latin America, which Rippy presumably had much to do with, would have disappointed Bolton. It contained nothing about the hemispheric ideas

Bolton had espoused. The report ignored the colonial era and emphasized themes of Latin American economic development fostered by the United States and Great Britain since independence. "Collaboration between Anglo-Saxons and the Latins of America must continue; it should be made to contribute to their mutual welfare and satisfaction," this section concluded. The suggested readings included three titles by Rippy but nothing by Bolton.[66]

In August California historians under the leadership of Edgar E. Robinson of Stanford University considered the American history curriculum. The meeting was attended by representatives from the University of California's Berkeley and Los Angeles campuses, as well as other colleges and universities throughout the state. Junior college faculty held their own conference at Stanford a few months later. Robinson, who had studied under Turner, opened the conference with a keynote that explained the problem. Critics believed, with little reliable evidence at hand, that too little "American history" was being taught. There was not even any agreement on what American history was, Robinson noted, perhaps referring to Bolton's insistence that the term referred to the entire hemisphere, not just U.S. history. "Publicists," as Robinson styled the critics, were "always saying 'history teaches' and again, 'history repeats itself,'" nostrums that were generally believed, but these were not for Robinson. "Let the publicist on the radio and in the national magazines [call this] Americanism!" Historians knew better than to accept such easy generalizations, because of their detailed specialized studies, but Robinson observed that the history professorate could not go on teaching only specialized courses, or "history at random," as he called it. "Unless we are freer than seems probable, we will be forced to define the subject matter as well as its value before many years more have passed by."

Then Turner's ghost spoke through Robinson. "The roots of American civilization lie deep in American geography, [in] our unusual history in building a nation where none existed, in wealth of man-power, in use of machines, and most of all in the liberation of the mind of man during the nineteenth century." Robinson built to his conclusion. "American democracy is economic, social, *and* political, and our history for the first time in the annals of mankind reveals how man—a pugnacious animal at best—can live at peace and build for security and prosperity." Historians could help. "Perhaps we ought to teach that story of Americanism, and . . . perhaps it would be well if colleges and universities made it a requirement for graduation."[67] Robinson's message to his colleagues was clear: if we do not establish a required survey of U.S. history, someone else—"publicists" perhaps—will do it for us.

With the overwhelming influence of the University of California and so many of

Bolton's students teaching in California colleges, one might have expected strong support for the Americas course as the basis for curricular adjustments. Such was not the case, however. The twenty-six-page summary of the two-day conference mentioned the Americas course only once in passing. None of the Berkeley faculty in attendance, which included Paxson and Hicks, as well as Lawrence Harper and Eugene I. McCormac, mentioned the Americas, pro or con. Bolton's student-professors in attendance, Cardinal Goodwin (Mills College), Charles B. Leonard (San Diego State), Peter Matsen Dunne (University of San Francisco), Theodore Treutlein (San Francisco State College), and Donald W. Rowland (University of Southern California), said nothing about the Americas course. Of Bolton's students only John Caughey suggested the history of the Western Hemisphere as a substitute for the U.S. history survey course under discussion. No one took up Caughey's suggestion.

New voices were heard. "We have got to face the fact that history has suffered a good deal in public esteem," said Professor Hicks, adding that "we need to appeal over the heads of our students to their parents." A young C. Vann Woodward (Scripps College) said, "We should make it plain that the humanities did not develop altogether in Europe or in Greece," and referred to "American Civilization" in terms of the life of "the sections of the country and the peculiar regional and national situation." Paxson, as chair of the Berkeley history department, worried over problems of staffing a required U.S. history survey, but he already knew the solution to that problem. Bolton and Henry Morse Stephens had lectured to hundreds, sometimes a thousand students, with graduate assistants helping in smaller sections. There was no mystery about how a new U.S. survey would be done at Berkeley. In the end the conference recommended that every college and university in California require students to take a one-year survey of U.S. history before graduation.[68]

The near-silence concerning the Americas, Bolton's iconic course, was astonishing. Not only were the participants silent on that matter, but the discourse revealed that they consistently used the term "American history" to mean U.S. history. No one raised an objection, as Bolton surely would have if he had been there. It was as if the work of his lifetime of teaching, writing, lecturing, and cajoling anyone who would listen had been swept away in a moment. Had Bolton been at the conference, he might have changed the discourse, but he probably would not have changed the outcome of the meeting. Bolton quite suddenly was running against the historical tide.

Bolton's influence on college curricula in California prior to 1943 should not be underestimated. The junior college teachers who met at Stanford in November included in their report an analysis of history courses taught in thirty of their institutions. Twenty-six of them offered the Americas.[69] Nineteen of them offered the Americas and no courses on U.S. history. Only seven of the colleges offered courses in U.S. history. The junior college figures probably reflected the state of affairs at four-year institutions. Yet, like the university professors, the junior college history teachers in 1943 resolved that their institutions should henceforth require a course in U.S. history.[70]

The Stanford meetings had a lasting effect in Berkeley and throughout California. Professor Hicks began to teach the new required one-year lower-division U.S. history survey, History 17. The course, which drew up to a thousand students, immediately influenced staffing requirements, which Paxson described to President Sproul in a projection of the department's ten-year needs in 1944. History 17, "long needed," Paxson wrote, would be in even greater demand after the war. The Diplomatic History of the United States, which had been taught by Priestley, should be reinstated. "Every day it becomes more desirable" to increase offerings in U.S. history, Paxson reported. "The United States group badly needs permanent strengthening" by the hiring of an additional junior professor plus "additional recruiting" in the postwar era.[71]

Hispanic-American history, "upon which much of the reputation of the Department" had been built, had suffered "crushing loss" because of death and retirement. Kinnaird (who was expected to return from his State Department assignment), Sluiter, and King would have to fill the gap, as it was "unlikely" that there would be "early need for additional strength in this field," Paxson predicted. The university would "have to wait hopefully for these young men to gain prestige through their own performance."[72] Hicks became department chair a few years later, but he saw things exactly as his mentor had. "As a result of Bolton's emphasis on all the Americas," he wrote, "Latin American history was about the only field in which we believed ourselves to be adequately staffed."[73]

Bolton's hemispheric course would continue to be taught at Berkeley and elsewhere, but it no longer had a privileged place in California's college curriculum. It would remain as an artifact of Bolton's attempt to revolutionize the teaching of American history and to place the United States in a broader context. As Bolton's students died and retired, the course would be dropped from college catalogs.[74] Bolton's empire was in retreat.

Bolton retired permanently in March 1944. His student and biographer John Francis Bannon believed that Bolton's return to the lecture hall had been an invigorating tonic.[1] Perhaps, but it had also taken two precious years from the active retirement that Bolton had wished to fill with exploring and writing. Such time could never be reclaimed. While Bolton maintained that enthusiasm was the essential ingredient in successful teaching, his own performance may have become a bit stale.[2] One student recalled that his wartime classes were filled with bored GIs who dozed in their seats. That many of them were awaiting overseas assignments may have accounted for their lack of interest in Bolton's timeworn lectures.[3]

Two years of teaching and managing the Bancroft Library did not make Bolton younger, stronger, or healthier, but he kept up his strenuous schedule. Seven days a week he arrived on campus at 9 A.M., worked until noon, lunched at the faculty club, returned to the library, and went home to dinner just as he had always done. "I return to the university every night about 8 p.m., and go home at 11 or 12 p.m.," he related. It was the same old Bolton, almost. Wartime rationing meant that Gertrude could not drive him to campus, so Bolton applied for a larger gasoline allotment. Otherwise, he would have to take the streetcar and walk a quarter-mile uphill to reach his home, which was "contrary to my physician's orders," he explained. "I am uninsurable on the ground of what they call heart trouble." He did not explain his symptoms, but high blood pressure and angina are likely guesses. Bolton probably would have been better off to have quit smoking and climbed the hill, but he got the enhanced "B" card and continued to work at his heroic pace, sedentary though it was.[4]

The war had caused a shortage of cigarettes as well as fuel, but in Bolton's case, friends came to his aid. "Thank you for the Lucky Strikes and the matches," he wrote a San Francisco donor. "I now can blow a smoke screen that will protect San Francisco from any Jap raid and build a fire big enough to burn their fleet to the water's edge if they come." Another savior sent Bolton smokes from Albuquerque.[5]

Heart trouble or no, Bolton gave every indication that he intended to pick up exactly where he left off in 1942.[6] In the spring of 1944 he went to Palo Duro Canyon and the Big Bend country in Texas under the auspices of the National Park Service.[7] The Palo Duro excursion helped him to nail down Coronado's route through Texas, although his projected book about the Spanish explorer was not finished. He continued to consult with Father Geiger on the long-delayed Serra Cause.[8] His work on the Chronicles of California series continued apace. The State Department still wanted Bolton's services and invited him to give a course of lectures in Mexico City in 1945.[9] He accepted.

Bolton had one more chance to reinforce the faculty with a historian sympathetic to his view of history. Someone would have to take over as director of the Bancroft Library. Early in 1945 he began to recruit George Hammond for the job. Bolton and Hammond had been working closely on the Coronado project. Bolton had promised to publish his Coronado manuscript in a University of New Mexico Press series that Hammond edited. Bolton's manuscript was, as usual, long overdue, and Hammond was anxious to get it. He had already raised $1,000 in New Mexico for Bolton's uncompleted book.[10]

In the fall Hammond agreed to join the Berkeley faculty and to head the Bancroft.[11] A senior scholar with administrative experience and a strong record of publications in Spanish Borderlands history, Hammond was an excellent selection for the post. Bolton must have breathed a sigh of relief when Hammond arrived in Berkeley. Perhaps now his beleaguered empire was safe. The Bancroft was in good hands, but under Hammond's aegis the director's position would become a full-time administrative post. The age of kings who ran both the department and the library was over.

While Bolton returned to his vigorous version of retirement, his friends arranged for new honors. They realized (even if Bolton did not) that at seventy-five the time for such recognition was limited. The University of Wisconsin conferred the Doctor of Letters, an honorific especially dear to Bolton because it came from his alma mater.[12] The occasion must have prompted memories of Madison in the 1890s, his teachers Turner and Haskins, and his fraternity brothers Ford and Becker. And perhaps he recalled that hopeful young man Herbert, the Wisconsin farm boy determined to rise and to make something of himself in the world. Well, he had done that, hadn't he?

Several of his students prepared a second festschrift, with essays by Bolton's graduate students who had finished after 1932. The volume was meant to be completed in time for his first retirement in 1940, but the project was delayed until 1945. More than two-dozen essays by Bolton's last cadre of doctoral students make up *Greater America*, which was presented to Bolton at the Saint Francis Hotel in San Francisco.[13] The volume included a list of Bolton's graduate students and their publications that fills 123 pages, persuasive evidence of Bolton's influence as a teacher. Bolton's old friend and constant benefactor Sydney Ehrman helped to underwrite the book and presided over the gathering.[14] More than two hundred people, including President Sproul, attended the event, which was covered in San Francisco newspapers.[15]

With the end of the war, Bolton's students began to reemerge from government service. Woodrow Borah had served in the Office of Strategic Services (OSS, the precursor to the CIA). In 1946 he wrote Bolton a long letter summarizing his experiences. Borah had been in Europe with another of Bolton's doctors-cum–OSS agent, Albert B. Thomas. Borah set up OSS offices in Italy and Germany that scoured the archives for intelligence about Latin American relations with the Axis. Now Borah wanted to reenter academic life. Would Bolton help him?[16]

By the late 1940s there was probably no chance that Bolton could muscle another of his students into the history department, but he still had friends in other parts of the university. He recommended Borah for a spot in the department of speech. Bolton described Borah as "one of the most brilliant and scholarly men we have had here in History." He praised Borah's "great clarity of thought" and his "gift for forceful and cultured expression." "Frankly," Bolton noted, "I would prefer to see him in History."[17] In contrast to his 1940 letters, Bolton's recommendation mentioned nothing about Borah's Jewish background.

Borah got the job in the speech department and was grateful to Bolton. "Four people have written about the fine letter you sent the committee, and its great value in getting the appointment approved," Borah acknowledged. He taught in that department until 1962, when he transferred to the history department.[18] Bolton no doubt would have criticized the 1962 move as too long delayed.

The University of Texas engaged Bolton to teach in its Mexico City field school in the summer of 1946.[19] Bolton, who was back on retirement pay, was glad to get the money and equally happy about going to Mexico at the university's expense. Summer teaching in Mexico also afforded him the opportunity to make an active contribution to what he called Pan-Americanism. "True Pan-Americanism," he wrote, "consists in an appreciation by each part of the Hemisphere of the culture and common interests of all other parts, and a friendly effort of each to promote the best interests of each and all."[20] His thinking had come a long way from that of the provincial Yankee greenhorn who in 1902 marveled that Mexico City compared favorably with Milwaukee.

As always, Bolton worked on many tasks at once. He got some help with the Chronicles of California when John Caughey accepted an appointment as coeditor.[21] Bolton handled the authors in the north, while Caughey dealt with Southern California historians. An editorial board approved projects and made general policies for the series. On June 17, 1947, Bolton called a snap meeting of the editorial committee in Berkeley. It was announced on such short notice that Bolton did not bother to invite Caughey, who would not have had time to get there from Los Angeles. "We missed you and hope you will approve what we did," Bolton wrote.[22]

Caughey knew when he was being brushed aside and would have none of it. A full professor and editor of the *Pacific Historical Review* with books and articles to his credit, Caughey was well established in the historical profession and at UCLA. He was no more inclined to accept overbearing treatment from Bolton than Bolton had been to accept it from Dickson. He was especially chagrined because the committee had approved Bolton's proposal to accept manuscripts by unproven authors, including a master's thesis by Bolton's secretarial assistant Maxine Chappell.[23] Her thesis and proposed book had the rather unpromising title "Bodie and the Bad Man: Historical Roots of a Legend."[24] Bolton also had gained committee approval for an expanded undergraduate paper and a doctoral dissertation for inclusion in the series.[25]

"I do not approve the action taken," Caughey bluntly informed Bolton. "I believe the series must start with . . . the ranking California historians." If the series included "monographs on such limited subjects as Bodie," Caughey thought, it would surely fail. He also wondered what his role as coeditor truly was. He had no part in administering the budget or in signing new contributors. "I do not want to be a mere figurehead," he concluded.[26]

Samuel Farquhar, the manager of the university press, also had reservations about the direction that Bolton was taking.[27] Bolton put on a brave show and tried to make his case. He was especially keen on publishing Chappell's tome on Bodie, which he expected a mining company near Bodie would purchase in large numbers. "As a matter of business you may wish to make a memorandum of this," Bolton prompted.[28] He argued that Chappell's scholarship was as good as the established authors, who included such distinguished historians as Paxson, Hicks, Caughey, and Bolton himself. The "literary quality" of her manuscript was "much higher than is usual with professors," he wrote.[29]

Bolton failed to ram the new titles through. In his attempt to rein in Bolton, Farquhar demanded that Bolton's secretarial assistant for the series, Chappell, be moved to the press to do her work.[30] Chappell, of course did much more for Bolton than work on the Chronicles, so her removal would have been a real loss for him. Bolton got the message, dropped her from the series, and Chappell stayed put. "I am as anxious as you to have volumes in our series by ranking historians," he reassured Caughey, who had suggested some new authors. Bolton gave his former student authority to work directly with them. He made sure that Caughey had plenty of notice for the next meeting of the editorial board.[31] In short order, Caughey became the wheelhorse for the series both as author and editor.[32]

Bolton had shown very poor judgment by forcing on the editorial board a bunch of green writers who happened to have been Berkeley graduate students. The dustup between him and Caughey made a remarkable contrast to Bolton's dealings with Dickson just a few years earlier. He had justly objected to Dickson's dictatorial ways, but in the later situation, did not seem to understand that his manipulation of the editorial committee seemed like railroading to Caughey. This was the sort of blindness that came from having been indisputably in charge of history at the University of California for many decades. In the 1930s few faculty in the university (including UCLA) would have had the courage to challenge Bolton as Caughey did in 1947, when Bolton was seventy-seven with the clock ticking. Professor Caughey was not risking anything that the calendar would not put right. Bolton no longer had the horses to command the field, not even when he was on his home turf.

Yet he was not entirely bereft of power and influence, nor had he lost his ability to work a situation to his advantage. While the Chronicles contretemps was going on, Bolton was arranging for the publication of his Coronado manuscript, which was almost finished. For years he had promised Hammond the book for his University of New Mexico Press series, but when the editor-in-chief of Houghton Mifflin inquired about the book in 1946, Bolton replied that he would be pleased to publish with him. On the same day, he wrote, "I should be happy to have the book brought out by so good a house as Harpers," to an editor from that firm.[33] Bolton was shopping his manuscript to a more prestigious (and probably more profitable) publisher than the small and poor New Mexico.

In 1947 (at just about the time he was at cross-purposes with Caughey and Farquhar) a new suitor came to Bolton's door. Whittlesey House, a division of McGraw-Hill, was offering a $1,000 fellowship award and publication of the best manuscript with a southwestern theme. Bolton jumped on it. Within weeks he signed a contract with Whittlesey that provided for a $2,500 advance on royalties upon submission of the manuscript. Once the manuscript was in hand, the judges gave Bolton the $1,000 fellowship award and another $1,000 royalty advance.[34] All in all, it was a fine arrangement for Bolton, but there would be complications.

Bolton felt free to jump to Whittlesey, because he had never signed a contract with New Mexico. Still, there was no denying that he had promised the book to Hammond. Too, Hammond had raised $1,000 for the book, although it is not clear if the money went to Bolton directly, or if it funded trail research, or if it was in the nature of a publication subvention. Whatever the disposition of the money may have been, Hammond and Fred Harvey, the University of New Mexico Press director, had good reason to be aggrieved. Bolton could discount the wrath of Hammond, who as director of the Bancroft was in no position to make a stink. Harvey was another matter. He was hopping mad and enlisted the aid of Clinton P. Anderson, U.S. secretary of agriculture and future U.S. senator from New Mexico. The secretary had accompanied Bolton and Hammond on Coronado expeditions and was completely familiar with Bolton's gentleman's agreement to publish with New Mexico.[35] Anderson had used his good offices to outfit Bolton's Coronado excursions with federal equipment, personnel, and supplies. Now the secretary felt that he had been jobbed. Bolton sent him a meek letter. "I am greatly embarrassed at having caused you and Mr. Harvey such disappointment," he wrote. "It implies more importance than I have ever imagined might be attributed to my work," he disingenuously added.[36] Perhaps they could work something out that would be satisfactory to all parties, he added.

Harvey complained to William E. Larned, the director of the Whittlesey House division. Larned was taken by surprise and demanded an explanation from Bolton. Bolton relied on the letter of the law. There was no contract with New Mexico. He also argued that he had written a very different book than the one that he had agreed to write for Hammond and Harvey. Still, Bolton wished to avoid trouble, so he broached an idea for Larned's consideration. If New Mexico wanted a book, give it to them. "You print [Harvey's] large pages and sell them to him on satisfactory terms." Such an arrangement would "make him friendly and help promote your sales."[37] In the end, Harvey, Anderson, and Larned agreed to Bolton's plan for joint publication.[38]

There is no question that Bolton acted on naked self-interest in the *Coronado* controversy. He had reneged on his unwritten promises to Hammond in order to make more money and gain more honors. While this episode does not flatter Bolton, many an academic author might silently cheer him for taking control of his work so that Bolton, the creator, benefited as much as possible from his creation. Bolton, after all, had spent years researching, trailing, writing, and rewriting. Why should he not maximize his financial rewards? Now that he was in his second and permanent retirement from Berkeley, he needed the money. Even with royalties Bolton's retirement income fell considerably short of his former salary.[39]

So Bolton got his money, the Whittlesey House fellowship, and publication by two houses at once. In 1949 Whittlesey brought out the book as *Coronado, Knight of Pueblos and Plains,* while New Mexico titled its book *Coronado on the Turquoise Trail, Knight of Pueblos and Plains.* Under any title *Coronado* was Bolton's finest book. Although the *Time* magazine reviewer winced at Bolton's "neo-Rotarian style," everyone (including the *Time* reviewer) recognized it as the crowning work of a major scholar writing for a popular audience.[40] The book fully justified the immense amount of time and energy that Bolton had expended in the archives and on the trail. In 1950 General Dwight Eisenhower, then president of Columbia University, notified Bolton that *Coronado* had won the prestigious Bancroft Prize, an award that no doubt pleased Harvey and Anderson as well as Bolton and Larned.[41]

Bolton's *Coronado* was not his last book, but it may be regarded as the culmination of his writing style and historical perspective. As usual, Bolton paid special attention to the details of trail location, campsites, and topographical features. A map of North America printed on the endpapers shows Coronado's route stretching from Mexico City across the border to New Mexico and then to central Kansas. Two smaller maps illustrate some of the geographical details that Bolton had described in his letters to Gertrude. Still keenly aware of local patriotic pride, Bolton included an awkward paragraph about the California gold rush in his preface. Today it seems a stretch to say that "not altogether unlike that of Marshall's discovery in California, Coronado and his followers made known the great Southwest and contributed to its permanent settlement." In his by now familiar way, Bolton portrayed Coronado as a transnational hero, "an immortal link between the republics of Mexico and the United States."[42] Nor could he refrain from his habit of inflating the significance of certain events. For example, in introducing Pedro de Castañeda's description of the Grand Canyon, he wrote that "Castañeda's next paragraph is one of the most precious passages in all the writings ever put on paper with respect to discovery in North America," because it briefly recorded the first European attempt to reach the bottom of the great defile.[43] One wonders, if the Spaniards had actually succeeded in reaching the bottom, what super-superlative language Bolton might have employed to celebrate their descent.

Despite such excesses *Coronado* is a pleasure to read. Bolton tells the tale in high romantic style and creates a narrative arc that carries his hero from great expectations to a tragic end. The Pueblo Indians and other Native Americans are something more than mere objects. Bolton gives them names, motivations, and importance in the story. They too experience tragedy as result of Coronado's exploits. And as if to underscore their importance, Bolton included an appendix, "Pueblo Society," that described their towns, dress, irrigation, agriculture, and religion and other aspects of their culture. He gave special attention to the roles of Pueblo women. He thought they were "well advanced in many elements of civilization."[44] Bolton's statement inferred that other Indian societies were *not* as civilized as the Pueblos, but he meant it as a compliment. Perhaps in his old age Bolton was circling back to find a place for them in the borderland confluence of civilizations—Native American as well as European. Indian civilization was appended to *Coronado*, but at least Bolton was thinking about them.

Bolton's final retirement was not all about book writing. In 1947 he agreed to teach two courses at San Francisco State College—about two-thirds of the teaching load that he had carried at Berkeley. He reckoned that he would make $174.40 a month before taxes. He also taught summer school at Mills College in Oakland.[45] As Bolton explained to the secretary of the Carnegie Foundation, "retiring allowances fixed in pre-war days are altogether inadequate now, in view of post-war prices."[46] Bolton had no intention of teaching part-time until he dropped in his harness.

Despite his penurious situation Bolton continued his ambitious research itinerary with funds from several sources. Cal continued to give Bolton some support. The American Philosophical Society provided research funding beginning in 1947.[47] He received a grant for Spanish-American history from the Hurley Marine Works for research, editorial work, and travel support.[48] (Bolton generously used some Hurley money to assist young scholars' travel to Latin America.) He also expected to get a substantial royalty from the Escalante volume when it was published.[49] The National Park Service and State Department paid for official trips for Bolton's research. He therefore could draw on many different funding sources, each small on its own, but together enough to carry on his scholarly agenda.

Before completing Escalante, Bolton attended to the Serra Cause. He was enthusiastic about the project because Serra was the sort of pioneer missionary that Bolton had long portrayed in a heroic light. Serra was a bit of a guinea pig in a new canonization procedure that had been established by the Vatican.[50] The Church wished to introduce historical scholarship into the review process (as well as authenticated miracles, though these were not Bolton's concern).[51] In December 1948 an ecclesiastical court met in Fresno to hear the Serra Cause. Father O'Brien instructed Bolton to deliver the documents that the commission had and to comment on their completeness and reliability. Then Bolton would be asked to add any remarks that might be useful to the authorities who would review the case in Rome. The Fresno court was merely "a receiving station for information and documents," O'Brien explained. He sent Bolton the *articuli*, the reasons for Serra's canonization that O'Brien would attempt to prove from the documentary evidence. There was "no need for detailed discussion" of the *articuli*, but Bolton should familiarize himself with them so that "when the judges inquire . . . you can say that you agree or disagree . . . on the basis of your acquaintance with the documents."[52]

Bolton duly appeared in Fresno arrayed for the occasion in his scarlet Toronto doctoral robes. He delivered approximately two thousand documents *by* Serra. In January 1949 the court met at the Carmel mission, where Bolton delivered the documents *about* Serra and gave whatever additional testimony was required. Then the documents and testimony were shipped to Rome, where they would be minutely examined by the Sacred Congregation of Rites.[53] "Knowing the long memory of the Catholic Church," O'Brien told Bolton, "you can be sure that . . . your name will live on in the records at Rome." No doubt glad to know that his work would be enshrined in the Vatican, Bolton was also glad to receive a payment for his trouble. "The enclosed check, of course, is only a token of the debt of gratitude which the Franciscan Order in California owes to you."[54] The amount of the check was not stated.

The complete transcript of Bolton's testimony has not been released, but Bolton no doubt spoke positively about Serra at Fresno and Carmel. He claimed that the Devil's Advocate (the prosecutor who spoke against Serra's canonization) had subjected Bolton to sarcastic, "withering scorn."[55] Surely Bolton did not accept this dramatic treatment in silence. In a fragmentary typed response to the court's questions Bolton called Serra "the greatest of all [the] galaxy of Apostles to the heathen in North America."[56] As usual, Bolton hoped that superlatives would carry the argument. Such words seemed positive and harmless to him in 1948. Decades later his language would mark him as an unrepentant apologist for the missionaries who participated in Spanish colonial conquest, abuse, dispossession, and destruction of California Indians.[57]

There was no organized opposition to Serra's canonization in the 1940s, but a critique of the California missions and Serra was beginning to appear. Between 1940 and 1943 biologist and historical demographer Sherburne F. Cook, a member of the Cal faculty, published a series of detailed essays about California Indian population decline during the Spanish, Mexican, and Anglo eras.[58] Cook did not question the religious motives of the missionaries, but his work damned the secular results. He demonstrated that the missions were pestholes where Indians died in droves. Indeed, more Indians died than were born in the missions, which depended on a continuing influx of new Indian converts if the institutions were to survive. The original essays, published in the University of California Press series Ibero-Americana, were larded with statistics and testimony drawn from the Bancroft Library's vast holdings, some of which had been collected by Bolton and his students. Cook provided a stunning new ecological interpretation of the California missions that continues to be influential not only in California but also in world history.[59] In later years Cook teamed with Woodrow Borah to write their three-volume *Essays in Population History*, which extended Cook's original ideas to North America.

Cook did the heavy scholarly lifting, and Carey McWilliams provided a readily accessible popular account in 1946. McWilliams, editor of *The Nation*, used incendiary language to characterize the missions. Commenting on Cook's data on population decline, McWilliams wrote that "the Franciscan padres eliminated Indians with the effectiveness of Nazis operating concentration camps." "From the moment of conversion," he declared, "the [Indian] neophyte became a slave."[60] There was not much room for Catholic saints in the hellish vision of the missions that Cook and McWilliams limned.

Bolton likely knew about the sensational work of McWilliams. He certainly knew about his colleague Cook, who may have made copies of documents from the Mexican archives for Bolton.[61] Bolton coedited Ibero-Americana with Carl Sauer and Alfred Kroeber when Cook's essays were published in the series. Cook's work in historical demography may not have struck Bolton as being especially novel. Early in Bolton's career he had recognized the undeniable fact that Indian demographic decline had been a lamentable result of Spanish conquest. Describing early-sixteenth-century events in the Caribbean, Bolton observed in 1922 that "in a very short time the islands became nearly depopulated of natives." War, violence, and starvation were contributing causes, but "perhaps a greater number died of smallpox, measles, and other diseases brought from Europe." Consequently, Bolton noted, the native population of the island of Española declined from about 250,000 to an estimated 14,000, nearly a 95 percent decrease, with similar reductions on other islands.[62] Thus Bolton's sketch of the Spanish Caribbean prefigured Cook's thesis for demographic decline in California. Even the raw numbers were similar, except that the decline during the California mission era was not as drastic as the one Bolton had described for the Caribbean.[63]

Bolton never directly addressed this issue of California Indian population decline in print, and it is not known if he testified about it before the ecclesiastical court. However, his writings suggest that he would have argued that mortality from disease was unavoidable, that missionaries did what they could to treat the victims, and that Serra's intentions were good. He might well have added, as he did in his 1917 mission essay, that the Spanish missions were far preferable to the Anglo system of removal, reservations, and near-destruction.

Such ideas seemed humane and progressive before World War II, especially if the object was to valorize Hispanic-American Catholic history. However, Bolton's view of history would have less influence in the postwar era. The Holocaust had shocked Americans and caused some of them to reassess racial and ethnic prejudices. African Americans struggled for equality and were making gains, especially in the realm of higher education. American Indians were beginning the long march toward tribal sovereignty, a trek that included a radical reassessment of the meaning of Native American history. Throughout the world colonialism was on its last legs. Cook's work was in keeping with these developments. The "good intentions"–"it could have been worse" defense of the missions would find diminishing support among historians. After the war Bolton's views about missions seemed a mere apology for a destructive colonial enterprise.

The impact of the missions on Indians, Serra's still-unconsummated canonization, and Bolton's role in the Serra Cause continue to be matters of debate. The Vatican considered the Serra Cause with due deliberation. Thirty-six years after the court met in California, Pope John Paul II declared Serra to be venerable, the first of three steps to sainthood. In 1988 the pope beatified Serra, the second step. Then John Paul visited the United States, scheduling a stop at Serra's former mission in Carmel. In the United States the pope found substantial organized opposition to Serra. Protests by Indians and their supporters may have caused him to think again about the wisdom of sanctifying Father Serra, whose canonization remains on hold.[64]

The reaction against the Serra Cause lay in the future and would not affect Bolton when he was alive. Yet the evolution of the controversy clearly shows that in 1948 the earth was turning and that it was moving away from Bolton.

Bolton's world was changing. He was still a revered figure on campus but no longer had the clout that he had possessed before he retired. The university itself had been transformed by the war and its aftermath. Bolton's students taught his old courses, but the Bolton school was no longer the undeniable center of gravity in the history department. All these changes were plainly evident to the elderly gentleman who daily lunched at the history department's table in the Faculty Club.

More changes were on the way. In the spring of 1949 the University of California Board of Regents passed a resolution that would traumatize the faculty and have lasting effects: the loyalty oath. Because he was retired, Bolton was only indirectly affected, but his colleagues and students would be at the very heart of the storm.

The political climate in California reflected the concerns of the Cold War.[1] Many Californians feared that communists were plotting to overthrow the government. The sensational trials of Alger Hiss, Klaus Fuchs, and others convinced many that there were reds in high places who should be rooted out. A California state legislator submitted several anticommunist bills including a constitutional amendment that would have stripped the regents of power to determine the loyalty of university employees. All of these bills failed, but they illustrated the tenor of the times in California and throughout the country. University professors became the special targets of red-baiters. Just before the loyalty dispute at Cal, two communist professors were fired by the Board of Regents of the University of

Washington, where Bolton's brother Frederick was professor emeritus. At UCLA there was a controversy over whether to allow one of the fired Washington professors to speak on campus; permission was denied.

The developing crisis over communism was a particularly difficult one for President Sproul because it involved UCLA. As Clark Kerr (Sproul's successor) later said, "You can't understand the oath controversy without understanding the fact that there was already conflict between Sproul and the southern regents in general."[2] Believing that Sproul was too powerful and that the southern campuses (which by then included Santa Barbara and Riverside) did not get their fair share of state funding, the Southern California regents wanted to decentralize the administration of the university. Sproul opposed decentralization. Edward Dickson, as the longest-serving member and chairman of the board, was the most important southern regent. He had been instrumental in establishing UCLA and took a strong interest in whatever happened there.

The faculty response to the barring of communists from campus was temperate. The University of California had forbidden the hiring of communists since 1940. The faculty did not object. Likewise, for some time the university had required faculty and other employees to sign the oath of allegiance that all state employees signed as a condition of employment. Again, the faculty did not object. Sproul believed that professors would not balk at signing a stronger anticommunist oath that he believed would mollify southern regents and smooth the path of university appropriations in Sacramento.

When the regents met on the Santa Barbara campus in the spring of 1949, communism on campus was not on the official agenda but was a hot topic of informal conversation. Chairman Dickson was especially keen on barring communists from the university. He even called the board into executive session to discuss the subject. The concern of Dickson and other regents no doubt encouraged Sproul to submit an amendment to the standard state oath that Cal employees routinely signed. As amended, the oath affirmed: "I do not believe in, and I am not a member of, nor do I support any party or organization that believes in, advocates, or teaches the overthrow of the United States Government, by force or by any illegal or unconstitutional methods."

In the discussion that followed, Dickson was evidently the first to suggest that anyone who failed to sign the revised oath could be fired. He explained to the regents that the Los Angeles City Council had recently adopted a loyalty oath for city employees. "We had three members who refused to take the oath," he said, "and they were discharged immediately."[3] At that point no one expected a faculty revolt because of a revised loyalty oath, but Dickson's statement foreshadowed things to come.

Faculty concern about the new language developed as soon as they learned about it. Because the oath seemed to be associated with pending annual employment contracts, the faculty believed that signing the oath was a condition of employment that would have to be signed every year. In June the northern section of the Academic Senate met in Berkeley (UCLA and other southern campuses had their own section) and agreed to work with the regents in order to make satisfactory changes to the oath. Only a minority of the faculty present opposed the new oath on broad principles. One of them was Ernst Kantorowicz, who by then was a tenured professor of history. The Jewish refugee who had fought communists in Germany read a statement to the meeting that condemned the new oath. He had made a study of oaths, he said, and declared that while the present one appeared to be harmless, "all oaths in history that I know of, have undergone changes. A new word is added. A short phrase, seemingly insignificant, will be smuggled in." Recent history was a guide, he continued. "Mussolini Italy of 1931, Hitler Germany of 1933 are terrifying warning examples for the harmless bit-by-bit procedure in connection with politically enforced oaths." History demonstrated that it was unwise to yield "to momentary hysteria, or to jeopardize, for the sake of temporary temporal advantages the permanent external values." The regents were bullying the innocent professor to relinquish tenure or "his human dignity and his responsible sovereignty as a scholar."[4] These were soaring words, but few professors thought that the oath was more than a meaningless and disagreeable technicality, something to be signed and forgotten. They were wrong.

A complicated series of negotiations ensued between Sproul, the Academic Senate, and the regents. Eventually, each party felt that the others had acted in bad faith. The positions of the faculty and the regents hardened. In February 1950 the regents required that all university employees sign the oath as written in 1949 or, in lieu of the oath, sign an explicit affirmation that he or she was not a communist. Otherwise, nonsigning faculty would be fired on June 30, 1950. Professors believed that among state employees they were being unfairly singled out, because they alone were required to swear that they were not communists.

By this time everyone understood that the university was embroiled in a major controversy. "The situation here is approaching the proportions of a dangerous whirlwind," Dickson wrote Regent Sidney Ehrman, who was considered to be a voice of moderation. "Every civic and patriotic organization—such as the American Legion, the Parent-Teachers' Association, the Native Sons, . . . Knights of Columbus, Pro America, etc." supported the regents, and were "organized into a joint committee for decisive action" if the regents rescinded the oath. Dickson characterized faculty objections to the oath on principle as "the ugly utterances of those who seek to conceal their un-American views under the cloak of academic freedom." About one-eighth of the faculty had not yet signed the oath. "How many of them are Communists affiliated with subversive groups?" he wondered. "Somehow or other we must identify this unidentified minority."[5] The witch hunt was on.

Nonsigners who came within reach of Dickson were in for a hard time. He confronted Clark Kerr after he had publicly opposed the oath. "Dickson actually grabbed me by the coat lapels and shook me a bit, wanting to know why I would do a thing like that." Kerr explained that he was a member of the Society of Friends, which objected to oaths on religious grounds. He added that he had a right to speak as a private citizen and that his position was the same as Governor Earl Warren's.[6]

For a brief period a compromise seemed to give nonsigners the option of presenting their cases to the faculty Committee on Privilege and Tenure. If the committee found that they were free of communist taint, the regents would employ them. But after several faculty successfully went through this process, the regents reneged on the agreement by a one-vote margin (with the help of Dickson's tie-breaking vote), thus plunging the faculty and regents into a hopeless morass of fear and mistrust. The regents fired thirty-one nonsigning faculty, including Kantorowicz and John Caughey, who had been among the most determined anti-oath professors. The legislature attempted to solve the problem by requiring all state employees to sign a new oath that included a statement about membership in subversive organizations. It was hoped that this would eliminate the faculty complaint that they were special targets. But the state oath included new wording about whether signers had belonged to the communist party *in the past*. Faculty objections were stronger than ever. The parties went to court.

The University of California loyalty oath controversy absorbed the attention of the faculty, administration, and regents to the exclusion of almost everything else. George Stewart, professor of English, described the atmosphere at Berkeley: "We woke up, and there was the oath with us in the delusive bright cheeriness of the morning. 'Oath' read the headline in the newspaper, and it put a bitter taste into the breakfast coffee. We discussed the oath during lunch at the Faculty Club. And what else was there for subject matter at the dinner table?"[7]

The oath controversy quickly became a cause célèbre in academic circles throughout the nation. The AHA passed a resolution (thought by some members to be rather tepid) that emphasized the abrogation of tenure while ignoring the question of oaths. The Mississippi Valley Historical Association named a committee to draft a resolution about the Cal situation and appointed Professor Ray Allen Billington of Northwestern University to chair it. Billington queried Cal professors, including Caughey and Philip Powell, who was on the Cal faculty at Santa Barbara. Powell, a student of Priestley and Bolton who had served in the State Department and in the OSS during the war, was a very conservative man.[8] While he supported efforts to uphold tenure, he thought the question of oaths "a little more vague and the hardest one to get across to the general public." "The whole thing stinks," he concluded, "so I just keep away from it. There has been exaggeration and hysteria on both sides, so as friend [Dean] Acheson would put it, I'll just wait and let the dust settle."[9] Conservative or not, Powell probably reflected the attitudes of most Cal professors.

Even though Caughey had lost his job, he stuck to his ideals. He had received a Rockefeller Foundation grant that funded work at the Huntington Library for several months, but this would not keep the wolf from the door forever.[10] Caughey believed that the regents were imposing political conformity on the faculty. He hoped that the Billington committee's resolution would uphold academic freedom and condemn "thought control." Billington crafted a resolution that demanded the restoration of tenure and that forthrightly condemned oaths as a threat to academic freedom and a violation of American traditions of freedom and democracy.[11]

Well-intended resolutions had no effect on the regents or the courts. The state supreme court eventually decided that the state had the right to require the oath of its employees. The fired faculty were given the opportunity to reclaim their jobs if they signed the oath. Most of them did. John Caughey was one of them; it must have been a bitter moment for him. Ernst Kantorowicz did not sign. He accepted a position at the Princeton Institute for Advanced Studies, where he ended his days with the likes of Albert Einstein.

Bolton did not mention the oath in his correspondence, but it was impossible for him to escape discussions about the episode. He had an office at the university and lunched daily at the Faculty Club. Colleagues in the history department were actively engaged in the dispute, especially Kantorowicz and John Hicks.[12] Bolton's students on the Berkeley faculty, Lawrence Kinnaird, Engel Sluiter, James King, Woodrow Borah, and George Hammond, were at risk if they did not sign. And Caughey, Bolton's student and coeditor, became one of the loyalty oath martyrs. It is safe to suppose that Bolton would have signed the oath if he had been required to do so. He probably would have advised Caughey and the others to sign it if they had asked him. Bolton's point of view likely mirrored Powell's. It would blow over if everyone would just stay calm. But the Cold War had turned hot in Korea and few cool heads could be found. The scurrilous charges of U.S. senator Joseph McCarthy added fuel to the fire.[13]

The Native Sons of the Golden West were not immune to the hysteria that surrounded them. Bolton continued to be a liaison between the university and the Native Sons, who provided fellowships to Cal's history graduate students. L. Mario Giannini, president of the Bank of America, was a prominent member of the Native Sons and a member of the Board of Regents, as his late father had been, Amadeo Peter Giannini, the bank's founder. Mario Giannini, a staunch anticommunist, took a managerial view of the oath controversy: the inmates should not be allowed to run the asylum. Thus the regents' decrees must be upheld. When the regents voted to permit the faculty Committee on Privilege and Tenure to hear the cases of nonsigners (a procedure that the regents subsequently revoked), Giannini was the only regent who voted no and resigned in protest. "If the original loyalty oath were rescinded," he told the board, "the flag would fly in the Kremlin."[14] The Sons passed a resolution "commending Regent Gianinni [sic] for his stand and urging him to reconsider his resignation." So, when Peter Conmy, past grand president of the Native Sons, informed Bolton that for the first time since 1913 the Sons would not fund a history fellow, he cited the loyalty oath. The Native Sons believed that state university professors gave "a poor patriotic example to the state."[15]

Conmy enumerated three additional reasons for withdrawing funds. The Sons felt that the organization did not get sufficient publicity for its donations. Conmy was convinced that the university did not treat undergraduates well, because classes were overcrowded and professors were more concerned with research than teaching. Then he confessed that there was a personal reason for his objection to continuing the fellowship. Conmy believed that Cal had denied him a professorship in the history of education because he was a Roman Catholic. He went on to claim that there were no Catholic faculty in any important public university schools of education anywhere in the country. He consoled himself with the knowledge that he stood shoulder to shoulder with Catholics who suffered for their faith in communist countries, although he admitted that his sacrifice was "insignificant" compared "with the price paid behind the iron curtain."[16]

Bolton's jaw must have dropped when he read Conmy's letter. He had recently received the Serra Award from the Academy of American Franciscan History. Serra Cause advocates had given him a special silver medal for his work on behalf of the proposed saint. Pope Pius XII had knighted Bolton with the Equestrian Order of Saint Sylvester for the same reason. Bolton numbered many lay Catholics, priests, and nuns among his friends and graduate students. Many of the Native Sons traveling fellows (most of whom were Bolton's students) had collected documents in foreign archives relating to Catholic history in the Americas. For almost half a century Bolton had championed Catholic missions and missionaries. But in 1950 none of this was enough for the Catholic anticommunist (and personally aggrieved) Conmy. If it was true that education departments discriminated against him and other Catholics, what sense did it make to punish a department that had probably done more than any other non-Catholic history department to advance Catholic history in the United States?

Bolton did not respond to Conmy's bizarre combination of contemporary politics and personal animus, and probably that was best under the circumstances. He had known Conmy for more than thirty years and perhaps understood that it would be futile to argue the matter. Conmy had taken the History of the Americas course with Bolton as an undergraduate, but Bolton had refused Conmy permission to enroll in his graduate seminar. Instead Conmy enrolled at Stanford, where he eventually took the MA in history. From Cal he earned a master's in education, an EdD, and a library degree. He also took several law courses at Boalt Hall.[17] In 1939 Conmy asked Bolton for a recommendation to teach at San Francisco Junior College. "I think that you will agree that I have had enough work in history to teach same in junior college," Conmy wrote. Although Bolton may have agreed, a letter for Conmy has not surfaced. Perhaps Conmy believed that Bolton had not adequately supported him, though Bolton was under no particular obligation to do so. Conmy's general complaints against the university are hard to credit, but he doubtless believed that he had been a victim of religious prejudice in the academic world, as many Catholics had been. His grievances were not the product of a deranged mind, but one prepared to see slights where none existed. Conmy's complaint shows that bigotry, real or imagined, can be deeply wounding. Conmy sent copies of his letter to President Sproul and others, but there was nothing to be done. The Native Sons fellowships were gone and would never return.

Finding new sources for funding graduate research would have to be someone else's concern. Bolton redoubled his efforts to raise money for his many pending projects. He even tried to sell his own considerable collection of historical manuscripts.[18] Evidently there were no buyers, because after his death these papers became part of his collection at the Bancroft Library. In 1949 he sketched out a plan that he thought would attract donors. He wanted to edit and publish the great Venegas manuscript that he had acquired for the Bancroft Library. Then he planned to write a biography of Gaspar de Portolá, first Spanish governor of the Californias. He was obligated to write "Daughter of Spain" for the Chronicles of California series, and he listed several other projects. Even though he was approaching eighty years old, Bolton still hoped to secure funding for his projects. He thought he could "get *Big Money*," as he jotted at the top of his notes.[19]

Bolton wrote to Horace Albright and other wealthy people asking for donations to provide stipends, research assistants, and other support. He emphasized the need for a general synthesis of the history of the Western Hemisphere, "a vision which I first among historians conceived." The projected book was "vital to inter-American understanding," and if Bolton did not do it, no one else would. "I never expected to write such a communication to anybody," Bolton claimed, but the university was giving money to the "new sciences" and not to history, or at least not to Bolton.[20] As he explained in his letter to the American Council of Learned Societies, he wanted to give up teaching at San Francisco State so that he could continue his work unencumbered. He asked Guy Ford, who was still secretary of the AHA, where he might get "a fairly sizable research grant" to finish his hemispheric study. "I have a habit of delivering the goods," he reminded his fraternity brother, "and I was never more 'rarin' to go than right now."[21]

But money did not flow in Bolton's direction as it once had. In 1950 he resorted to teaching history at Contra Costa Junior College at $3.50 per hour, which was even less than he got at San Francisco State. He was required, of course, to sign the standard state loyalty oath affirming that he had not been a member of the communist party or other subversive organization for the past five years.[22]

Bolton's plans for the future no doubt struck potential donors as a bit unrealistic. He may have felt fit as a fiddle, except for his weak heart, but others understood that Bolton was an old man. Perhaps Bolton's projects were no longer the best investment in scholarship that a well-heeled donor could make. Still, Bolton tried to convince old friends that he was still up and at 'em. When he sent a copy of *Coronado* to Sidney Ehrman, he insisted that he was "still on the job."[23] The oath controversy was then raging, and Bolton might have taken the opportunity to express an opinion about it to his old friend and supporter. He did not.

Bolton was not exaggerating when he insisted that he was still working. The Escalante project was now his full-time concern. He had agreed to publish it with the Utah Historical Society, but the society president evidently got wind of Bolton's dealings with New Mexico and *Coronado*. "Any rumor that you may have heard that somebody other than yourself is to publish my *Escalante* is without foundation," Bolton averred.[24] As usual, Bolton the perfectionist was slow in completing the manuscript. He gave his usual reasons for delay—the complications of preparing an accurate edited translation and of drafting a detailed map based on meticulous research and personal observations of the trail. "Somebody said 'Scholarship is Hell on Manners,'" Bolton apologized to his editor in Utah. "You will probably say 'so are scholars.'"[25]

In early 1951 Bolton was pushing himself to put the finishing touches on the Escalante manuscript when something terrible and completely unexpected happened. Charles Hackett, one of Bolton's first graduate students at Texas and Stanford, was ill with cancer. Late in February, "Hackie" as Bolton's young daughters had once called him, shot himself.[26] Bolton was devastated. The two had been especially close. Hackett had lived with the Boltons when he was a student. "Mrs. Bolton and I loved him as a son," Bolton wrote, "my children adored him as a brother."[27] Such a loss could not be overcome.

On March 15 Laura Brower, Bolton's third daughter, drove her car on to the Golden Gate Bridge, stopped near the south tower, and got out. She ran to the railing and jumped to her death. Papers reported that she had been depressed because of a serious illness. She left a note for her family. "I am sorry it has to be this way, but there seems to be no answer. I love you." The *San Francisco Chronicle* carried the news on the front page under "UC Professor's Daughter Leaps from the Gate Bridge." Other Bay Area papers also carried the story.[28] One cannot easily imagine the impact of such a tragic and horrifying event on the elderly father and mother. The very public nature of the death, the spectacular means of accomplishing it, and the stigma that then attached to suicide must have made Laura's death infinitely worse for the Boltons to bear.

There are no letters from Bolton about Laura's death. Perhaps he simply could not bring himself to write about it. Bolton handled his daughter's death as he handled everything else. He buried his grief in work. He had promised the Escalante manuscript to his editor in May but was able to get it to him in April. He called it *Pageant in the Wilderness*.

Pageant would not have surprised any of Bolton's devoted readers. Explorer priests were the heroes of the story. Bolton likened one of them to "Daniel Boone in Franciscan garb" and gratuitously mentioned the Declaration of Independence because the expedition occurred in 1776.[29] The book included two folded maps in a pocket. One is a facsimile of a map from the time, richly detailed with place-names, topographical features, Indian territories and their communities, and Spanish settlements. The other map shows the route of the Escalante trail as established from Bolton's archival and field research. It was all vintage Bolton. But there is something in Bolton's tone and style that sets it apart from his earlier work. The prose is spare, and he emphasized the peaceful nature of the episode he described. "Unlike many chapters in the early history of North America," this expedition did not result in bloodshed. While he noted that there were some Indians who resisted Spanish colonization, these pages were filled with cooperative people. When Fray Escalante met with a friendly Havasupai, "the friar lighted a *cigarro*," he wrote. They "alternately puffed on it," and "then they smoked another."[30] This intimate, cooperative encounter resulted in a crude map of some of the country that Escalante and his companions would cover in their journey. Bolton's conclusion was hopeful: "Thus ended one of the great exploring expeditions of North American history, made without noise of arms and without giving offense to the natives through whose country they had traveled."[31] Historical outcomes were not as happy for Indians as Bolton's words suggested.[32] Even a quiet conquest can have bad results for the conquered.

But Bolton was in no mood to think about bad outcomes. He immersed himself in the details of an imaginary world of Spanish explorers and merged it with his own past. He reached far back into his memory to describe the sort of horse that Fray Francisco Garcés might have ridden. "From boyhood experience with Spanish mustangs used by the Winnebago Indians of Wisconsin," he recalled, "I have imagined that Garcés' horse was buckskin colored, with a dark stripe along his backbone."[33] We may wonder about the accuracy of Bolton's boyhood memories of Indian ponies in the Badger State, but it is no wonder that such memories were crowding in on Bolton's thoughts about his Spanish heroes. He seemed to be in a contemplative mood, brought on perhaps by personal tragedy as well as the turmoil of the oath controversy. Maybe his age had something to do with it. Bolton was eighty years old when *Pageant* was published. It was his last book.

With *Pageant* finished, Bolton turned to other projects and worked in his time-honored way—every day, all day, and part of the night. Gertrude drove him to campus and picked him up for dinner, but sometimes he would climb into a vehicle that resembled the family car without bothering to identify the driver. Forbearing neighbors drove him home, much to the chagrin of Gertrude, who waited for Herbert until finally returning home to find him there. He was the stereotypical absent-minded professor, totally preoccupied with his work; but old age may have impaired his ability to immediately recognize familiar faces. In 1950 his grandson Thomas Johnson, a student at Berkeley, met him on campus and said, "Hi, Big Papa," his family nickname. Bolton looked up and asked, "Who are you?"[34]

Perhaps Bolton's failure to instantly identify his grandson was simply due to his having been abruptly roused from deep concentration on one of his projects or even on the loyalty oath controversy. Yet there is no denying that old age takes its toll, and Bolton was not an exception, no matter how strenuously he denied it.

Impaired or not, Bolton spent his days working on projects and dealing with the voluminous correspondence that still came his way. When asked to write a foreword to a new book, he wanted to know how much he would be paid. The answer must not have been encouraging, because Bolton's contribution consisted of two sentences: "A good book needs no foreword by anybody but the author. This is an admirable book."[35]

Yet Bolton was generous to Wilbur R. Jacobs, a young professor at the Santa Barbara campus who wanted to know what Turner had been like as a teacher. Bolton wrote a long helpful letter with two supplements that Jacobs eventually published.[36] He thought that Turner was a great historian "not because of voluminous writings, but for the freshness of his ideas," which "gave significance to the history of every township, county, territory, or state." Bolton read his own ideas about the Americas into Turner's frontier thesis. While the Master's frontier essay "appealed to local patriotism everywhere across the Continent, from Plymouth to San Francisco," he wrote, it now illuminated "the history of all the other Americas—British, Spanish, Portuguese, French and Dutch. No wonder Turner is worshiped as a prophet."[37] A grateful Jacobs visited Bolton in Berkeley, where he found him working at his desk, wreathed in tobacco smoke.[38] Jacobs called him the "master" of the "Bolton School."[39]

Many people asked for Bolton's help, and they usually got it if it was within his power. An anthropologist wanted to know something about the shells that Bolton had described in one of his early books (probably *Kino*). "Whatever I may have said . . . was more reliable than what I remember about them now." Then, oddly, he quoted the Bible: "When I was a child [I] spake as a child, etc."[40]

Someone sent him a battle-ax that he found "very interesting indeed." The relic might have been left on the coast by that old sea dog Francis Drake. Bolton hoped to have it examined by "the very best authorities in the United States. That is what we did with the Drake Plate and the result is that all specialists are convinced that it is genuine. I hope for a similar opinion regarding the axe."[41] Evidently the ax did not pan out, for Bolton said no more about it. Allen Chickering sent Bolton a facsimile of the Drake Plate that he greatly appreciated.[42] Bolton continued his usual work routine, but some of the juice had gone out of him. Then came another blow. Early in 1952 Helen Schneider, his second daughter, underwent surgery. Postoperative complications took her life. "She is a very dear child," he had written many years previously when baby Helen had been desperately ill. She was "beautiful in temperament and feature. We can't spare her."[43] But now she was gone.

Despite these crushing personal losses the eighty-two-year-old Bolton made the effort to keep up his daily regimen. In June he attended the Baccalaureate Mass for Catholic graduates of Cal. He told the priest, "Old age is just an illusion."[44] Some illusion. One afternoon not long after the mass, Bolton was working at his Bancroft desk. When it was time to go home, his legs would not work. Friends took him to the hospital, where doctors determined that Bolton had suffered a stroke. They sent him home to recuperate.

Letters and visitors descended on the Bolton home. Horace Albright was in Glacier National Park when he heard about Bolton and his daughter Helen. "You are a great hero to us here by these two pieces of grievous news, and we are saddened more than we can express in words."[45] In August his friend John Bannon wrote him a letter that Bolton's assistant, Virginia Thickens, read to him. Bolton still could not read and found it difficult to speak but "was most emphatic in asking me to tell you that he 'received it with great pleasure,'" Thickens wrote.[46]

He recovered his speech and seemed to rally somewhat. He enjoyed visits from his children and grandchildren, but his mind drifted. One day when his daughter Eugenie and her daughter Gale were visiting, he began to speak to no one in particular about his childhood in Wisconsin. He had a second stroke that confined him to his bed for good. More small but debilitating strokes followed. He could not remember the recent past. As his friend Father Bannon put it, he lived in "Texas of the eighteenth century, with his Black Robes of Pimería Alta, . . . with the friars and soldiers of early California."[47] On January 30, 1953, Bolton died quietly.[48]

.   .   .

The Board of Regents was meeting in San Francisco when word reached them that Bolton was dead. They extolled the man who had served the university for so long, so well, and so faithfully. The *San Francisco Chronicle* called him "California's leading historian and beloved University of California professor."[49] The paper reported that Bolton "died while completing notes on a study of Father Garces, early Arizona and California missionary," as if the old professor had been hard at work when impertinent Death tapped him on the shoulder. Everyone knew the true stories about Bolton's rigorous work habits. "A late light burning in the Bancroft . . . meant that the eminent scholar was at work on his research."[50] The light burned no more.

There was a small funeral in the Berkeley Hills Chapel in which Fred Stripp, Baptist minister and colleague in the speech department, presided. Family and friends visited the funeral home. Mrs. Sproul attended for the president. Sydney Ehrman was there. John Hicks and Bolton's students who taught in the history department paid their respects.[51] Bolton was cremated and his remains were buried near his daughter Laura at Sunset View Cemetery on a hillside with a view of the Golden Gate. About a year later Gertrude died and was buried next to Bolton.

Two weeks after Bolton's death a memorial service was held for him in Newman Hall across the street from the Berkeley campus. Father Francis G. Quinan presided over a Catholic mass for Bolton's soul. "Here in our beloved country we differ about religion," Father Quinan observed afterward. "But the American way, thank God, is to respect those differences. And that was the way of this great man we honor this morning." Quinan thought that it was appropriate that people of all religious faiths had come together to honor Bolton. "In this age of ours . . . we need . . . to come closer together." Bolton was not a Catholic, but he appreciated the mass, Father Quinan said, because "it brought him back in spirit to the days of the old Padres—to a Serra . . . a Crespi, Padre Kino and other zealous friars." Bolton had shared these thoughts with Father Quinan, yet "his spiritual life he kept to himself." Still the priest assured his listeners that Bolton's faith was "healthy, unobtrusive, a living part of him." Then he read to the assembly Bolton's favorite piece of scripture, Chapter 13 of St. Paul's First Epistle to the Corinthians:

When I was a child I spoke as a child. Now that I have become a man I have put away the things of a child. We see now through a mirror in an obscure manner, but then face to face. Now I know in part, but then I shall know even as I have been known.[52]

Afterword

The Debatable Legacy

In 1994 I gave a lecture at the Huntington Library about Bolton as a cultural mediator. Afterward, Wilbur Jacobs and I sat on the patio outside the snack bar. A prominent Turner and Parkman scholar, Wilbur was also one of the key academic figures in the establishment in the 1970s of the field of Native American history. Not incidentally, he had chaired my doctoral committee at the University of California, Santa Barbara. He regarded Bolton as an apologist for the Catholic missions, which had caused terrible damage to Indians. I tried to explain that Bolton's racial and ethnic views were complex and in some ways progressive. "He's just like Turner," he replied. "Every time you think you have him on the side of the angels, he pops up somewhere else saying all the wrong things."

I learned something important from Wilbur during that exchange. Bolton did not have late-twentieth-century sensibilities, and it was a mistake to try to demonstrate that he did. He was, of course, a man of his own time. Historians may strive for objectivity, but as Bolton's life demonstrates, they cannot completely escape from their own historical moment, their culture, or their own past. Even so, Bolton was more than a man of his own time. His life shows that a historian can challenge the world to broaden its outlook and take new meanings from history.

Bolton found a seam in American history where he could work among the religious and ethnic fissures of his time. He believed and taught that Spaniards contributed to human progress by extending Christianity and European civilization. Working in a time when eugenicists and the Ku Klux Klan preached racism and nativism, Bolton championed the merging of civilizations and cultures. He straddled the U.S. border with Mexico and adopted a transnational outlook that defied the common prejudices of his age.

Bolton's idea that cultures met and melded in the borderlands was important, but he only sketched the concept. What did it mean that cultures met and somehow fused? What did that say about American history in general? Surely it meant that Turner's moving frontier concept had to be modified somehow. On these matters Bolton was silent or maddeningly vague. He hinted that the Hispanic and Anglo experiences should be compared, but he did not do it. A rigorous comparison of North American frontiers would have required a reconsideration of some of Turner's ideas: the relationship of free land, individualism, democracy, and American exceptionalism, for example. In one sense Bolton's failure to provide such an analysis is not surprising. He preferred narrative drama to critical analysis. Nevertheless, Bolton's disinterest in making direct comparisons of the Spanish Borderlands and Turner's Anglo-American frontier remains perplexing because the need for comparisons seemed so obvious. Why did he not do it? Perhaps it is best to take him at his word: Bolton wrote that he was Turner's devoted disciple. He believed that somehow he was proving that the Master was correct. Perhaps it is just as well that Bolton left comparisons to others. His attempts at comparative history in "Greater America" dwelled on dubious similarities rather than telling differences among American nations. Bolton thought that the history of the Americas lit the way to a cooperative future. Troubling inconsistencies did not matter in his grand panorama of the Americas or the borderlands.

Turner's coincident reluctance to incorporate Bolton's borderlands in his version of American history was likewise disappointing. One can only conclude that Turner simply did not think that the borderlands were in the mainstream of American history. In Turner's view Hispanic Americans were among the people swept aside by a stronger and more vigorous Anglo-American population.

Bolton's inclusive American history had virtues, but it also had flaws. His romantic perspective led him to make generalizations that did not bear scrutiny. For example, he thought that all adventurers were much alike. Not long after Charles Lindbergh made his transatlantic flight, Bolton wrote, "Not alone Lancelot, and Galahad, and Arthur and the Maid, rode beside Lindbergh.... With him were Narváez, De Soto, and Coronado, too, and many another 'who dared his own wild dreams to try' in these Spanish Borderlands."[1] The mythical Lancelot, the historical Coronado, and Lindbergh were out for high adventure, and differences did not matter to Bolton. A hero was a hero. Bolton silently included himself in the crowd of he-men whom he mentioned. Was he not an explorer too? Did he not traverse deserts, mountains, and canyons in search of adventure and fame? Like Parkman, Bolton assumed the role of heroic historian, one who blazed his own trails in pursuit of some past hero's story.

Bolton's style is no longer in vogue, but in his own time he had many admirers. Samuel Eliot Morison in his 1950 AHA presidential address proclaimed that "a historical career can be a great adventure, and not in ideas alone; witness the lives of Bolton and Trevelyan, men who write history that sings to the heart while it informs the understanding."[2] Bolton thanked Morison for the "bouquet" and hoped that Trevelyan would not be offended at the comparison.[3] Morison also admired Bolton's trail research and recommended that historians get out of the library to see the places where history had occurred.[4] Morison, who sailed with the U.S. Navy during World War II and retraced the routes of maritime explorers in his own sailboat, was especially well attuned to Bolton's method and perspective. The bouquet was thrown from one historian-explorer to another.

Bolton's instinct was to be open-minded and inclusive, although he did not find a formula that could include everyone on an equal footing. He believed that human progress meant that American Indians should adopt European values and institutions. This unexamined assumption led him to celebrate the extension of European polities and religions without giving due attention to the damage done to Native Americans. During Bolton's lifetime few readers would have disagreed with him. Modern readers may reject Bolton's positive assessment of Spanish conquest and colonization but should be grateful that Bolton published the Spanish documents that are bedrock resources for ethnohistory and the new borderlands history.

Just as Bolton's publications have continuing influence, so do his contributions to the University of California. As director of the Bancroft Bolton facilitated the collection of books and documents about the Americas from all over the world. When Turner was asked to estimate the scholarly worth of the Bancroft in 1904, he supposed that the presence of too much Spanish and Indian stuff devalued the library, because he thought the "American" period was far more important. What if Turner had joined the Berkeley faculty and influenced the collection of new material for the library? Surely he would not have thrown the Spanish and Indian records out the library window. But just as certainly he would have encouraged the collection of Anglo-American materials from the pioneer era. Accordingly the emphasis and strengths of the Bancroft would be different today—not necessarily worse, not wrong, but different.

Bolton's placement at Berkeley made a difference not only in his career but in the development of the University of California. If Bolton had not been hired in 1911, who could have attracted the hundreds of graduate students who studied with him? Who would have created a distinctive California school of history, known around the world? Could Frederick Teggart have done that? Herbert Priestley? Bolton was the perfect person for the job before 1940. The postwar years—or perhaps they should be called the post-Bolton years—were another matter. Bolton's ideas were new and invigorating in 1911. In 1941 it was time for something else. After three decades, Bolton's time as the principal architect of the University of California's formidable reputation in history had passed, but the institutional importance of his work remained. John Hicks and the other historians who built the postwar history department did not start from scratch; they already enjoyed the institutional prestige that Bolton had established during his generation of stewardship.

Bolton was of that generation of professors who were loyal servants of the institutions that employed them, a relationship that seems rarer, if not downright archaic, today. Perhaps Bolton and his peers, who engaged the emerging system of higher education and professional scholarship when it was new, appreciated its novelty and significance in ways that their successors do not. Bolton, Jameson, Turner, and other historians in the first half of the twentieth century created something of lasting value that was just as important as their ideas and their books. They built institutions—universities, archives, libraries, graduate programs, funding mechanisms—that still serve us as the essential foundations of scholarship.

Despite Bolton's single-minded devotion to scholarship, he was not a cloistered academic. He thought that history mattered, and he worked hard to inform the public about it. His contributions to the National Park Service, the California Historical Survey Commission, the Historic American Buildings Survey, and the State Department bespeak a man deeply involved with his own society. But public engagement came with risks, even for a professor as well-regarded and professionally entrenched as Bolton. His gentle criticism of an establishment hero like Thomas Starr King, mistaken identification of colonial ruins in Georgia, and erroneous authentication of the fake Drake plate caused public debate that could have damaged his career and the reputation of the university. Deft management of Bolton's few blunders—and good luck in the case of the plate—saved him from embarrassment, but those close shaves should remind us that no historian lives in an ivory tower. The public intellectual who does not choose his public words carefully soon becomes a subject for discussion and possible discipline from powers that govern the university.

Bolton thought hemispherically, but he lived locally. Bolton regarded groups like the Native Sons of the Golden West and the California Historical Society (as well as E Clampus Vitus, for that matter) as local constituencies vital to the university and to his discipline. Bolton cultivated local patriots so that they would support academic studies, but he also tried to broaden their concept of history by including the Hispanic past. If it seems that Bolton trod too gingerly among the sacred monuments of local patriots, he was not alone. In his presidential address, Morison urged historians to "deal gently with your people's traditions," lest they turn away from written history that deflates their heroes.[5]

Morison's admonition raised questions that should be asked about Bolton. How far should a historian go in praising heroes, local or otherwise? At what point does a historian become the architect of a false idol? Bolton went too far in exaggerating the qualities and accomplishments of his heroes. An admirable desire to include Spanish Catholic characters in American history motivated Bolton, but his uncritical adulation of Spanish colonizers pleased some and offended others, then and now. Bolton's assertion of heroic universality notwithstanding, in a diverse society a hero to one group may be a villain to another. Bolton wanted his heroes to speak to everyone for all time, but the world is too complicated for that. Ironically, Bolton helped to make American history more complicated by making it more inclusive.

Today Bolton's heroes are out of fashion, but his basic ideas about borderlands and the Americas, modified to suit the times, enjoy a resurgence in popularity. The academic world has its fashions, its momentary responses to new conditions and societal demands; so tomorrow's historians will no doubt move on to other topics and interpretive perspectives. Every generation writes history anew, and the relevance of Bolton's ideas will fade again. Yet he should be remembered for extending the borders of the American past, for making it more tolerant and diverse and less ethnocentric. Bolton opened the way to new interpretive possibilities in history. We have not reached their limit.

ABBREVIATIONS USED
IN THE NOTES

AHA   American Historical Association.

AHR   *American Historical Review.*

AHA-LC   Papers of the American Historical Association, Library of Congress, Washington, D.C. [box no., file name, as appropriate].

BFP   Bolton Family Papers. BL, C-B 841 [box number, subject as appropriate].

BiP   Ray A. Billington Papers, HEH [box number, folder title].

BL   Bancroft Library, University of California, Berkeley.

BP   Herbert E. Bolton Papers. BL, C-B 840. [Part I, II, or III, as appropriate][Out or In, as appropriate]: [box number, subject as appropriate].

CLSP   Constance Lindsay Skinner Papers, New York Public Library, New York.

FA   Max Farrand Collection, HEH.

HEH   Henry E. Huntington Library, San Marino, California.

HMSP   Henry Morse Stephens Papers. BL.

IA	Institutional Archives (HEH).
JP	J. Franklin Jameson Papers, Library of Congress, Washington, D.C. [box no., file name].
NSGW	Native Sons of the Golden West.
TU	Frederick Jackson Turner Collection, HEH. [box no.].
MLRP BP	Mary Leticia Ross Papers, 4–8. Papers of Herbert Eugene Bolton. Georgia Department of Archives and History, Morrow, Georgia.
MSS 5064	Frank Lockwood, "Correspondence Concerning Herbert E. Bolton," MSS 5064, Bancroft Library.
MVHA	Mississippi Valley Historical Association.
PBP-LMU	Papers of the Pacific Coast Branch of the American Historical Association. Charles Van der Ahe Library. Loyola Marymount University, Los Angeles.

NOTES

INTRODUCTION

1. Hurtado, "Parkmanizing the Spanish Borderlands," 149–167; Weber, "The Idea of the Spanish Borderlands," 3–20; Truett, "Epics of Greater America," 213–217.

2. Truett, "Epics of Greater America," 233–241; Hanke, *Do the Americas Have a Common History?* esp. 3–10; Magnaghi, *Herbert E. Bolton and the Historiography of the Americas,* 117–154; Delpar, *Looking South,* 1–40. For recent examples of transnational history, see J. H. Elliott, *Empires of the Atlantic World;* and Weber, *Bárbaros.*

3. Sandos, "Junípero Serra's Canonization"; Sandos, "Junipero Serra, Canonization, and the California Indian Controversy"; Hurtado, "Bolton, Racism and American History"; Hurtado, "More Shadows on the Brass"; Weber, "Turner, the Boltonians, and the Borderlands"; Weber, "Blood of Martyrs, Blood of Indians."

4. For example, see Brooks, *Captives and Cousins;* Blackhawk, *Violence over the Land;* Hackel, *Children of Coyote, Missionaries of Saint Francis;* Hurtado, *Intimate Frontiers;* Gutiérrez, *When Jesus Came, the Corn Mothers Went Away.*

5. Bannon, *Bolton;* and Caughey, "Herbert Eugene Bolton," 40–67.

CHAPTER 1

1. Bolton, "On Wisdom's Trail," 3.

2. Ibid., 4.

3. Frederick Bolton to Eugenie Bolton Johnson, 10/29/1953, BFP:3, miscellaneous.

4. Ibid.

5. Ibid.

6. BP:134.

7. Cozzens, "The Lost Trail," quotes in February 11, 1875, p. 43; April 22, 1875, p. 125.

8. Edwin Latham Bolton to Commissioner of Pensions, 9/24/1881, BP In: Rosalind Cady Bolton.

9. Edwin Latham Bolton to Commissioner of Pensions, 9/24/1881, BP In: Rosalind Cady Bolton; Frederick Bolton to Eugenie Bolton Johnson, 10/29/1953, BFP:3, miscellaneous.

10. HEB to Frederick, 12/13/1885, BFP.

11. HEB to Frederick, 1/15/1886, BFP.

12. HEB to Frederick, 2/8/1886, BFP.

13. HEB to Frederick, 4/17/1887, BFP.

14. HEB to Frederick, 10/31/1888, BFP.

15. HEB to Frederick, 5/22/1887, 7/19/1888, 4/10/1889, BFP.

16. HEB to Frederick, 10/3/1888, BFP.

17. HEB to Frederick, 10/16/1889, BFP.

18. Frederick Bolton to Eugenie Bolton Johnson, 10/29/1953, BFP:3.

19. HEB to Frederick, 2/25/1889, BFP.

20. HEB to Frederick, 10/22/1888, BFP.

21. Sulloway, *Born to Rebel*, 83–118 passim.

22. HEB to Frederick, 7/2/1887, BFP.

23. HEB to Frederick, 7/17/1887, BFP (emphasis in original).

24. HEB to Frederick, 9/9/1888, 10/3/1888, 10/31/1888, BFP.

25. HEB to Frederick, 11/4/1888, 5/5/1889, BFP.

26. HEB to Frederick, 5/1/1889, BFP.

27. "Constitution," in *Papers of the American Historical Association*, vol. 1, no. 1, *Report of the Organization and Proceedings, Saratoga, September 9–10, 1884* (New York: G. P. Putnam's Sons, 1885), 1, 11.

28. Novick, *That Noble Dream*, 22–24.

29. *Proceedings of the AHA, 1886*, 6.

30. Ibid., 63–64.

31. HEB to Frederick, 7/7/1889, BFP.

32. HEB to Frederick, 9/11/1889, BFP.

33. HEB to Frederick, 10/22/1889, BFP.

34. HEB to Frederick, 10/22/1889, 11/14/1889, BFP.

35. HEB to Frederick, 2/4/1890, BFP.

36. HEB to Frederick, 2/1/1890, BFP.

37. HEB to Frederick, 3/1/1890, BFP.

38. Conzen, *Immigrant Milwaukee*, 1–9 passim; Simon, *The City-Building Process*, 13–50.

39. Fraser, *Preparing America's Teachers*, 74–85.

40. HEB to Frederick, 3/7/1891, BFP.

41. HEB to Frederick, 9/6/1890, BFP.

42. HEB to Frederick, 9/13/1890, 4/17/1890, 10/11/1890, BFP.

43. HEB to Frederick, 9/27/1890, BFP.

44. HEB to Frederick, 4/3/1891, BFP.

45. HEB to Frederick, 7/9/1891, BFP.

46. HEB to Frederick, 11/9/1890, BFP.

47. HEB to Frederick, 6/20/1891, BFP.

48. HEB to Frederick, 3/20/1891, BFP.

49. HEB to Frederick, 7/9/1891, BFP.

50. HEB to Frederick, 6/13/1891, BFP.

51. HEB to Frederick, 7/25/1891, BFP.

52. HEB to Frederick, 7/15/1891, BFP.

53. HEB to Frederick, 8/33/1891 *[sic]*, BFP.

54. HEB to Frederick, 10/18/1891, 1/10/1892, BFP.

55. HEB to Frederick, 12/8/1891, BFP.

56. Curti and Carstensen, *University of Wisconsin*, 1:508.

57. HEB to Frederick, 10/18/1891, BFP.

58. HEB to Frederick, 3/12/1892, 11/22/1892, BFP.

59. HEB to Frederick, 10/31/1891, BFP.

60. HEB to Frederick, 9/25/1892, BFP.

61. HEB to Frederick, 10/23/1892, BFP.

62. HEB to Frederick, 11/22/1892, BFP.

63. HEB to Frederick, 12/4/1892, BFP.

64. HEB to Frederick, 12/16/1892, BFP.

65. HEB to Frederick, 9/25/1892, BFP.

66. HEB to Frederick, 2/4/1893, BFP.

CHAPTER 2

1. Curti and Carstensen, *University of Wisconsin*, 1:120–123, 501.

2. Brown, *Beyond the Frontier*, 16–18.

3. Haskins to Jameson, 2/27/1894, JP:92, Haskins.

4. Billington, *Turner*, 58–82, 108–159, 472–497; Bogue, *Turner*, 39–57, 91–144, 451–464.

5. Powicke, "Haskins," 649–656.

6. Becker quoted in Brown, *Beyond the Frontier*, 31.

7. Jacobs, "Frederick Jackson Turner—Master Teacher," 49–58.

8. Haskins to Jameson, 2/15/1891, JP:92, Haskins.

9. On Eliot and the "Wisconsin idea," see Hawkins, *Between Harvard and America*, 164, 166; James quoted at 78.

10. Franklin, *Life of Gilman*, 110–181; Hawkins, *Pioneer*, 19–20.

11. Franklin, *Life of Gilman*, 125.

12. Haskins to Jameson, 7/11/1891, JP:92, Haskins.

13. Bogue, *Turner*, 67–71.

14. HEB to Frederick, 9/16/1893, BFP.

15. HEB to Frederick, 9/30/1893, BFP.

16. HEB to Frederick, 9/16/1893, BFP.

17. HEB to Frederick, 1/28/1894, BFP.

18. HEB to Frederick, 10/21/1893, BFP.

19. HEB to Frederick, 1/28/1894, BFP.

20. HEB to Frederick, 12/10/1893, BFP.

21. HEB to Frederick, 1/5/1894, BFP.

22. Theta Delta Chi now advertises that it does not discriminate on the basis of race or religion, www.tdx.org; Horowitz, *Campus Life*, 77, 82–83, 145–148.

23. Steinberg, *Academic Melting Pot*, 9–11.

24. HEB, "How I Got That Way" [1944], BP Out: 155.

25. Becker, "Everyman His Own Historian," 246–55. See also, Wilkins, *Carl Becker*, 204–209.

26. Vincent, "Guy Stanton Ford," 16–23; Ford, "Trends and Problems of the Social Sciences," in *On and Off Campus*, 371–372.

27. Frederick Bolton to Eugenie Bolton Johnson, 10/29/1953, BFP:3, miscellaneous.

28. HEB to Frederick, 9/16/1894, BFP.

29. HEB to Frederick, 4/18/1894, 6/14/1894, BFP.

30. HEB to Frederick, 7/26/1894, BFP.

31. Wells quoted in Billington, *Turner*, 147.

32. Curti and Carstensen, *University of Wisconsin*, 1:525.

33. Harper quoted in Hofstadter and Metzger, *The Development of Academic Freedom in the United States*, 427–428.

34. HEB to Frederick, 9/28/1894, BFP.

35. HEB to Frederick, 3/8/1895, BFP.

36. HEB to Frederick, 3/26/1895, BFP.

37. *Tomah Journal*, quoted in Bannon, *Bolton*, 15; HEB to Frederick, 8/26/1895, BFP.

38. HEB to Frederick, 8/26/1895, BFP.

39. Jacobs, "'Turner, as I Remember Him,' by Herbert Eugene Bolton," 56.

40. HEB to Frederick, 12/2/1895, BFP.

41. HEB to Frederick, 1/13/1895 [1896], 1/19/1895 [1896], BFP.

42. HEB to Frederick, 7/25/1896, BFP.

43. HEB to Frederick, 8/17/1896, BFP.

44. HEB to Frederick, 10/18/1896, BFP.

45. Libby, "Geographical Distribution of the Vote of the Thirteen States," 1–116.

46. Jacobs, "Frederick Jackson Turner—Master Teacher," 49–58; Jacobs, "'Turner, as I Remember Him,' by Herbert Eugene Bolton," 54–61.

47. HEB to Frederick, 10/18/1896, BFP.

48. Clipping encl. in HEB to Frederick, 12/10/1896, BFP.

49. HEB to Frederick, 1/3/1897, BFP.

50. Ibid.

51. HEB to Frederick, 10/18/1896, BFP.

52. HEB to Frederick, 2/13/1897, BFP.

53. HEB to Frederick, 4/4/1897, BFP.

54. Carl Becker followed such a path to a Wisconsin PhD. Wilkins, *Carl Becker*, 46–49.

55. HEB to Frederick, 5/18/1897, BFP.

56. Turner to Becker, 7/3/1896, TU:2.

57. HEB to Frederick, 5/18/1897, BFP.

58. HEB to Frederick, 6/8/1897, BFP.

59. HEB to Frederick, 6/19/1897, BFP.

60. McMaster to Turner, 4/12/1897, TU:2; Goldman, *John Bach McMaster*, 67, n. 28.

61. Cf. Wood, *Early History of the University of Pennsylvania*, esp. 5; Cheyney, *History of the University of Pennsylvania*, 49–50.

62. Cheyney, *History of the University of Pennsylvania*, 287–288.

63. Goldman, *John Bach McMaster*, 4–30.

64. Ibid., 51.

65. McMaster quoted in ibid., 53.

66. Cheyney, *History of the University of Pennsylvania*, 290.

67. HEB to Frederick, 10/10/1897, BFP.

68. The thesis accepted in 1897 was filed at Clark in 1898 and published as *Hydro-Psychoses*.

69. HEB to Frederick, 10/27/1897, BFP.

70. HEB to Frederick, 7/25/1896, BFP.

71. HEB to Frederick, 11/14/1897, BFP.

72. HEB to Frederick, 12/22/1897, BFP.

73. HEB to Frederick, 1/5/1897 [1898], BFP.

74. HEB to Frederick, 1/27/1898, BFP.

75. Morgan, *America's Road to Empire*, 47–48; "University Day Programme," 2/22/1898, mailed 2/24/1898, BFP.

76. HEB to Frederick, 4/8/1898, BFP.

77. HEB to Frederick, 5/5/1898, BFP.

78. Goldman, *John Bach McMaster*, 74–78; quotation at 75.

79. Lodge quoted in ibid., 78.

80. HEB to Frederick, 8/21/1898, BFP.

81. HEB to Frederick, 9/11/1898; Gertrude Bolton to Olive Bolton, 9/21/1898, BFP.

82. Gertrude Bolton to Olive Bolton, 12/2/1898, BFP.

83. HEB to Frederick, 11/15/1898, 12/2/1898, BFP.

84. HEB to Frederick, 1/22/1899, 1/28/1899, BFP.

85. Doctor Wenner quoted in HEB to Frederick, 1/30/1899, BFP.

86. HEB to Frederick, 1/31/1899, 1/30/1899, BFP.

87. HEB to Frederick, 1/31/1899, 2/2/1899, BFP.

88. HEB to Frederick, 2/10/1899, BFP.

89. HEB to Frederick, 4/22/1899, BFP.

90. HEB to Frederick, 3/23/1899, BFP.

91. HEB to Frederick, 5/24/1899, BFP.

92. HEB to Frederick, 3/23/1899, BFP.

93. HEB to Frederick, 4/22/1899, BFP.

94. HEB to Frederick, 5/5/1899, 5/8/1899, BFP.

95. HEB to Frederick, 5/13/1899, 5/16/1899, BFP.

96. HEB to Frederick, 5/24/1899, BFP.

97. HEB to Frederick, 6/29/1899, 6/30/1899, 7/14/1899, BFP.

98. HEB to Frederick, 7/18/1899, BFP.

99. HEB to Frederick, 8/25/1899, BFP.

100. F. E. Bolton, "Random Memories," 72.

101. Ibid.

CHAPTER 3

1. HEB to Frederick, 9/29/1900, BFP.

2. Many letters could be cited, but this one is typical: HEB to Frederick, 10/30/1900, BFP.

3. HEB to Frederick, 1/14/1900, BFP.

4. Bolton to Sanford B. Dole, 4/7/1900, HEH Manuscript 27057, reprinted in Rolle, "A Note on the Younger Bolton."

5. "The Free Negro in the South Before the Civil War," typescript, BP Part III.

6. "The Acquisition of Florida Inevitable," attached to HEB to Frederick, 8/12/1900, BFP.

7. HEB to Frederick, 9/24/1900, BFP.

8. HEB to Frederick, 11/20/1900, BFP.

9. Carlton and Adams, "'A Work Peculiarly Our Own,'" 204; Barker, "Lester Gladstone Bugbee"; Bugbee, "Archives of Bexar."

10. Friend, "A Dedication to the Memory of George Pierce Garrison," 308.

11. Garrison to Jameson, 1/22/1898, JP:85, Garrison. Garrison, "The First Stage of the Movement for the Annexation of Texas," 72–96.

12. Barker quoted in Pool, *Eugene C. Barker*, 35.

13. Garrison to Jameson, 7/29/1901, 7/30/1901, JP:85, Garrison.

14. Excerpts from Haskins's letter were published in an Austin newspaper clipping that Bolton sent his brother in HEB to Frederick, 10/16/1901, BFP.

15. HEB to Frederick 1/16/1901, 3/21/1901, 4/12/1901, 4/27/1901, 5/18/1901, 5/29/1901, BFP.

16. HEB to Frederick, 6/3/1901, BFP.

17. HEB to Frederick, 9/1/1901, BFP.

18. HEB to Frederick, 9/13/1901, BFP.

19. Ibid.

20. HEB to Frederick, 9/22/1901, 10/1/1901, BFP.

21. Garrison to Jameson, 7/29/1901, JP:85, Garrison.

22. HEB to Frederick, 10/6/1901, BFP.

23. Barker quoted in Pool, *Eugene C. Barker*, 36–37.

24. HEB to Frederick, 10/16/1901, BFP.

25. Ibid.

26. HEB to Frederick, 10/26/1901, BFP.

27. Ibid.

28. Griffin, "To Establish a University of the First Class"; Prindle, "Oil and the Permanent University Fund"; Benedict, *A Source Book*, 397.

29. *A Critical Study of Nullification in South Carolina* (1896).

30. Benedict, *A Source Book*, 406–408.

31. Lane, *History of Education in Texas*, 151.

32. J. Cutler, *Lynch-Law*, 179, 183, 188; Littlefield, *Seminole Burning*, 5–6.

33. Lane, *History of Education in Texas*, 151–153.

34. Garrison to Jameson, 7/29/1901, JP:85, Garrison.

35. HEB to Frederick, 10/26/1901, BFP; Pool, *Eugene C. Barker*, 37.

36. Garrison described the holdings he had seen in "The Archivo General de Mexico," 430–431.

37. Garrison, "Southwestern History in the Southwest," quotation at 238.

38. The Bancroft Library, amassed by historian and bibliophile Hubert Howe Bancroft, had been for sale since the 1880s, but in 1902 there were no buyers. News clipping, inside cover of Thwaites, *The Bancroft Library*.

39. HEB to Frederick, 1/24/1902, BFP.

40. Boston: Houghton, Mifflin and Co., 1903.

41. HEB to Frederick, 1/5/1902, BFP.

42. HEB to Frederick, 12/6/1901, BFP.

43. HEB to Frederick, 2/1/1902, BFP.

44. HEB to Frederick, 6/17/1902, BFP.

45. Benedict, *A Source Book,* 823.

46. HEB to Frederick, 7/8/1902, BFP.

47. HEB to Frederick, 8/?/1902, BFP (postcard with date obliterated).

48. HEB to Frederick, 8/17/1902, BFP.

49. Bolton, "Some Materials for Southwestern History," 109.

50. Bolton, "Tienda de Cuervo's Ynspeccion."

51. HEB to Frederick, 9/10/1902, BFP; Blair and Robertson, *Philippine Islands.*

52. HEB to Frederick, 7/4/1903, BFP.

53. Garrison to McLaughlin, 7/10/1903, JP:85, Garrison.

54. Garrison to McLaughlin, 7/23/1903, JP:85, Garrison.

55. HEB to Frederick, 9/7/1903, BFP. Bolton erroneously states that he arrived in Mexico on August 27, but he meant July 27.

56. HEB to Mother, 8/21/1903, BFP, Miscellaneous.

57. HEB to Frederick, 9/7/1903, BFP.

58. HEB to Frederick, 12/25/1903, BFP.

59. Blair and Robertson, *Philippine Islands,* 18:29.

60. Dunn, "My Most Unforgettable Character" [1953], BP In.

61. Friends of the Bancroft Library, 1949, BP Out. Bolton mistakenly recalled that he met Jordan in Austin at the time of the earthquake, but Jordan was at home in Stanford then.

62. Jordan, *The Days of Man,* 2:151–153; quotation at 153.

63. "The Spanish Abandonment and Re-occupation of East Texas."

64. *With the Makers of Texas,* v–vii.

65. HEB to Frederick, 5/27/1904, BFP.

66. HEB to Frederick, 6/16/1905, BFP.

67. Garrison to Jameson, JP:85, Garrison; Bolton to Jameson, 2/27/1905, JP:61, Bolton.

68. Rothberg and Goggin, *John Franklin Jameson,* 3:5.

69. Jameson to HEB, 2/27/1905, JP:61, Bolton.

70. HEB to Turner, 6/10/1905, JP:61, Bolton.

71. Turner to Jameson, 6/30/1905, JP:132. This brief, hand-scrawled note was separated from Bolton's letter cited in the previous note.

72. HEB to Jameson, 9/2/1905, JP:61, Bolton.

73. Garrison to Jameson, 9/2/1905, JP:85, Garrison.

74. I have not found Jameson's September 1905 proffer in his papers or in Bolton's.

75. Garrison to Jameson, 9/21/1905, JP:85, Garrison.

76. HEB to Jameson, 11/15/1905, JP:61, Bolton.

77. "Material for Southwestern History in the Central Archives of Mexico."

78. Jameson to HEB, 1/4/1906, JP:61, Bolton.

79. "Will Investigate Mexican Archives," news clipping, encl. in HEB to Frederick, 1/14/1906, BFP.

80. HEB to Frederick, 1/14/1906, BFP.

81. HEB to Frederick, 4/18/1906, 10/9/1906, BFP.

82. HEB to Jameson, 1/18/1906, JP:61, Bolton.

83. Jameson to HEB, 1/22/1906, JP:61, Bolton.

84. Hodge, *Handbook of American Indians.*

85. HEB to Holmes, 4/18/1906, BP Out; HEB to Frederick, 10/9/1906, BFP.

86. HEB to Jameson, 9/3/1906; Jameson to HEB, 9/15/1906, JP:61, Bolton.

87. Jameson to HEB, 12/12/1906, JP:88, Guide to the Mexican Archives.

88. Garrison to Jameson, 12/13/1906, JP:85, Garrison.

89. Jameson to Garrison, 12/22/1906, JP:85, Garrison (emphasis in original).

90. Garrison to Jameson, 1/21/1907, JP:85, Garrison; Poole, *Eugene C. Barker,* 42.

91. Jameson to Garrison, 1/28/1907, JP:85, Garrison.

92. HEB to Jameson, 3/15/1907, JP:88, Guide to the Mexican Archives.

93. HEB to Frederick, 6/15/1907, BFP.

94. The mine was also known as the San Saba. HEB to Frederick, 6/7/1907, BFP; HEB, "The Discovery of the San Saba Mine," 1950, BP Out.

95. HEB to Frederick, 6/7/1907, BFP.

96. HEB to Frederick, 6/7/1907, BFP; HEB to J. Farley, 4/30/1910, BP Out; Pierre L. Russell to HEB, 12/29/1932, BP In.

CHAPTER 4

1. Turner to Henry Morse Stephens, 7/7/1902, TU:3.

2. Gale, "Farrand, Max."

3. For example, see Turner to Charles Van Hise, 8/3/1906, TU:7; Farrand to Turner, 8/23/1907, TU:9A; Jacobs, *Frederick Jackson Turner's Legacy,* 28.

4. In December, rumors about Stanford University and Turner began to appear in California newspapers. Farrand to Turner, 12/17/1904, TU:4.

5. Mirrielees, *Stanford,* 13–81.

6. While Bancroft wrote sections of the history, he relied on a staff of researchers and writers to compile much of his work. Caughey, *Bancroft,* 99–117.

7. Ibid., 349–365; "Bancroft Library May Go to the University," newspaper clipping, in Thwaites, *The Bancroft Library,* inside front cover.

8. Dillon, "Sutro"; Dillon, "Sutro Library," Burr quoted at 342.

9. Turner to Farrand, 10/4/1904, TU:4.

10. Farrand to Turner, 10/10/1904, 12/24/1904, TU:4.

11. Nagel, *Iron Will*, 203–204.

12. Stanford quoted in ibid., 204–208.

13. Cutler, *The Mysterious Death of Jane Stanford*, 9–25 passim. Cf. Nagel, *Iron Will*, 210–211; Ogle, "The Mysterious Death of Mrs. Leland Stanford."

14. Elliott, *Stanford University*, 128–129.

15. Turner to Farrand, 1/23/1905, TU:5.

16. Farrand to Turner, 12/17/1904, TU:4.

17. Stephens to Turner, 12/13/1904; Turner to Stephens, 12/17/1904, TU:4.

18. Caughey, *Bancroft*, 358–360.

19. Newspaper quoted in ibid., 364.

20. Thwaites, *The Bancroft Library*, 4, 19.

21. Ibid., 19, 20.

22. Thwaites quoted in Dangberg, *Teggart*, 39.

23. Wheeler to Turner, 1/20/1906, 2/21/1906, TU:6.

24. Memo, Board of Trustees, March 27, 1906, Stanford, TU:6A.

25. Notice form the Board of Regents, April 20, 1906, TU:7.

26. Jordan, *The Days of Man*, 2:168.

27. Fradkin, *The Great Earthquake*, 190.

28. Jordan to Turner, 4/18/1906, TU:6A.

29. Jordan to Farrand, 4/19/906, HM 16697, HEH.

30. Jordan to Turner, 4/20/1906, TU:6A.

31. Turner to Farrand, 4/26/1906, TU:6A.

32. Wheeler, *The Abundant Life*, 134. Quotation in HEB, "Friends of the Bancroft Library," 1949, BP Out.

33. Stephens to Turner, 5/2/1906, TU:6A.

34. Dillon, "Sutro Library," 344.

35. Stephens to Turner, 5/2/1906, TU:6A.

36. Caughey, *Bancroft*, 393; Dangberg, *Teggart*, 42.

37. Turner to Van Hise, 8/3/1906, TU:7.

38. Bohemian Club, *A Chronicle of Our Years*, 9–17.

39. Turner to Van Hise, 8/3/1906, TU:7.

40. Frances Bolton Appleton to Eugenie Bolton, 8/11/1953, transcript in author's possession. Quotations in HEB to Frederick, 8/18/1907, BFP.

41. Hodge, *Handbook of American Indians*. Bolton's book *The Hasinais* was published after his death.

42. HEB to Frederick, 8/18/1907, BFP.

43. HEB, "Rambles in Mexico," MLRP BP.

44. Engelhardt to HEB, 4/30/1907, 5/28/1907, 10/16/1907, 10/29/1907, and Engelhardt to Rev. P. Presidente, 10/16/1907, BP In, Engelhardt.

45. Engelhardt to HEB, 11/26/1907, BP In, Engelhardt.

46. Jameson to HEB, 10/10/1907, JP:88, Guide to the Mexican Archives.

47. HEB to Jameson, 10/14/1907, 10/16/1907, JP:88, Guide to the Mexican Archives.

48. "Papers of Zebulon M. Pike," 798–827.

49. Dana Carleton Munro to Frederick Jackson Turner, n.d. [1907], TU:9A.

50. Eugene C. Barker to HEB, 3/28/1908, BP In.

51. HEB to Gammon, Worsham, and Pope, 3/4/1908, 3/14/1908, BP Out.

52. For example, see BP In, Texas, Attorney General.

53. This and the following three paragraphs draw upon HEB, "Rambles in Mexico," MLRP BP.

54. Bolton spelled Corral's name with one *r*, but I have corrected the spelling when quoting him. On Corral's reputation, see Knight, *The Mexican Revolution*, 1:54, 73, 75–76, 202.

55. HEB, "Rambles in Mexico," MLRP BP.

56. Ibid.

57. HEB to Turner, 1/25/1908, TU:10.

58. Turner to HEB, 2/25/1908, BP In; HEB to Turner, 3/14/1908, TU:12.

59. 6th ed. (London: Rivingtons, 1902).

60. HEB, "On Wisdom's Trail," 54–55.

61. Barker to HEB, 3/28/1908, BP In.

62. Jordan to Turner, 6/9/1908; Adams to Turner, 6/30/1908, TU:11.

63. Adams to Turner, 7/25/1908, TU:11.

64. Adams to HEB, 8/31/1908, BP In.

65. Turner to Adams, 7/12/1908, TU:11.

66. Adams to Turner, 9/7/1908; Turner to Adams, 10/12/1908, TU:11.

67. HEB to Adams, 9/28/1908, BP Out.

68. Adams to Turner, 10/19/1908, 11/2/1908, TU:11.

69. Adams to Bolton, 11/2/1908, 11/24/1908, BP In.

70. HEB to Adams, 11/16/1908, BP Out.

71. Adams to Bolton, 11/24/1908, BP In.

72. HEB to Adams, 12/3/1908, BP Out.

73. Adams to Bolton, 12/19/1908, BP In; HEB to Adams, 12/26/1908, BP In [Bolton's copy kept in the Adams file].

74. HEB to S. E. Mezes, 6/4/1909, BP Out.

75. Turner to HEB, 3/25/1909, BP In.

76. Anonymous, "Visiting Faculty."

77. Stephens to HEB, 8/13/1910, BP In.

78. Stephens to Turner, 7/25/1909, TU:12.

79. Ibid.

80. Bogue, *Turner,* 251.

81. Stephens to Turner, 8/15/1909, TU:12.

82. "Academy of Pacific Coast History," AHA-LC, Box 460, Committee Misc.

83. E.g., Rudolph Taussig to Stephens, 9/20/1910 and 4/27/1915, HMSP, Box 8, In.

84. Stephens to Turner, 8/15/1909, TU:12.

85. Wheeler to Turner, 8/17/1909, TU:12.

86. Adams to Turner, 9/6/1909, TU:12.

87. Turner to Van Hise, 9/16/1909, TU:12. This letter is a mere fragment, but the meaning seems clear enough.

88. Telegram quoted in Haskins to Turner, 9/16/1909, TU:12.

89. Turner to HEB, 12/2/1909, BP In.

90. Turner quoted in Bogue, *Turner,* 253.

91. Teggart to Stephens, 5/10/1910, HMSP, Box 8, In.

92. Pool, *Barker,* 44.

93. HEB to Mezes, 7/30/1910, BP Out.

94. Ibid.

95. Ibid.; Stephens to HEB, 8/13/1910, BP In.

96. Bannon, *Bolton,* 74.

97. Stephens to HEB, 8/13/1910, BP In.

98. Stephens to HEB, 8/19/1910, BP In.

99. Stephens to HEB, 8/19/1910, BP In. Bolton's words, extracted from his letter of 8/24/1910, were typed onto Stephens's letter. Bolton's August 24 letter to Stephens does not exist.

100. Barker to HEB, 8/4/1910, 10/27/1910, BP In.

101. HEB to Stephens, 9/21/1910, BP Out.

102. Stephens to Bolton, 9/26/1910, BP In.

103. Pool, *Barker,* 44.

104. HEB to Frederick, 1/27/1910, BFP.

105. Billington, *Turner,* 298.

106. HEB to Frederick, 9/10/1909, BFP.

107. HEB to Jameson, 9/24/1910, JP:61, Bolton.

108. HEB to Jameson, 11/30/1910, JP:61.

109. HEB to Turner, 12/27/1910, BP Out.

110. Regents quoted in Dangberg, *Teggart,* 4.

111. Stephens to HEB, 4/13/1911, BP In.

112. HEB to Frederick, 7/17/[1911], BFP (Jameson quoted in this letter).

CHAPTER 5

1. Monroe Deutsch, "Introduction," in Wheeler, *The Abundant Life*, 3–19.

2. Wheeler, *The Abundant Life*, 39.

3. Ibid., 374–378.

4. Ryder quoted in Brucker, May, and Hollinger, *History at Berkeley*, 3.

5. Stephens to Turner, 9/16/1909, TU:12. Unfortunately, Stephens's handwriting is so crabbed and small that I cannot make out his word, but I think "possibilities" captures the sense of it.

6. For a recent assessment of Stephens, see Brucker, May, and Hollinger, *History at Berkeley*, 3.

7. Quotes in "Historical News," *AHR* 24 (July 1919), 747–748; Jameson, "The American Historical Review," 1–7.

8. Gale Randall, interview with author, 8/11/2010 (notes in author's possession).

9. The descriptions of faculty that follow are drawn from *Blue and Gold*, the University of California yearbook, for 1911, pp. 47–61, and for 1913, pp. 59, 63.

10. *White Servitude in Maryland; Colonial Opposition to Imperial Authority; James K. Polk.*

11. "The Viceroy of New Spain in the Eighteenth Century."

12. Dangberg, *Teggart*, 43–45; Teggart and Smith, *Diary of Gaspar de Portola*.

13. Kagan, *Spain in America*, 11, 25, 39–43, 258–59.

14. HEB to L. L. Bernard, 12/14/1928, BP Out.

15. HEB to Barrows, 5/4/1911, BP Out; Ferrier, *University of California*, 515–516; Barrows, "The Revolution in Mexico," 438–453.

16. Kroeber to HEB, 8/12/1912, 3/18/1918, BP In.

17. T. Kroeber, *Ishi in Two Worlds*, 117–120, 162–163. See also K. Kroeber and C. Kroeber, *Ishi in Three Centuries*, 3–9.

18. Quoted in Ferrier, *University of California*, 475.

19. Gebhard et al., *Guide to Architecture*, 259.

20. *Blue and Gold*, 1911, p. 140.

21. Paltridge, *History of the Faculty Club*, 15.

22. Ferrier, *University of California*, 453.

23. Sibley, *The Golden Book of California*, 75, 115.

24. *Blue and Gold*, 1913, p. 384.

25. This assessment is based on the Class of 1911, photographed as juniors for the *Blue and Gold* of 1911, n.p.

26. HEB to Frederick, 7/9/1911, BFP.

27. Hackett to HEB, 11/28/1909, 3/2/1910, BP In.

28. Bannon, *Bolton*, 283–290, gives the names, degrees, and dates of Bolton's graduate students. "A Bibliography of the Historical Writings of the Students of Her-

bert Eugene Bolton," in Ogden, Sluiter, and Crampton, *Greater America*, 549–672, provides the titles and dates of theses, dissertations, and other writings.

29. HEB, "Charles Edward Chapman," BP In, Chapman.

30. Chapman, *Catalogue of Materials in the Archivo General de Indias*.

31. Chapman to Frank Lockwood, 2/29/1932, MSS 5064. Chapman's description of events makes Teggart the only likely suspect.

32. "In Memoriam, Herbert Ingram Priestley, 1875–1944," BP In, Priestley.

33. Priestley to HEB, 9/21/1911, BP In. Bannon, in *Bolton*, 284, incorrectly gives Priestley's PhD as 1916.

34. Woodrow Wilson Borah, interview with author, 8/13/1992 (notes in author's possession).

35. Rippy, "This I Recall," BP In, Rippy. A revised version of this recollection was published as "Herbert Eugene Bolton: A Recollection," 166–171. The unpublished version is in some respects franker and has some information that does not appear in the article.

36. Borah, interview, 8/13/1992.

37. HEB Jr., "My Most Unforgettable Character."

38. 1911, BP Out, published in *Bolton and the Spanish Borderlands*, 23–31.

39. Ibid., 23.

40. Jameson to HEB, 9/26/1911, JP:88, Guide to the Mexican Archives.

41. HEB to Frederick, 1/14/1913, BP Out.

42. Jameson to HEB, 2/25/1913, JP:88, Guide to the Mexican Archives.

43. Jameson to HEB, 2/25/1913, 3/17/1913, JP:88, Guide to the Mexican Archives.

44. Bolton, *Guide*, iv.

45. Jameson, to HEB, 8/30/1913, JP:88, Guide to the Mexican Archives.

46. Bolton, *Guide*, viii.

47. Cleveland: Arthur H. Clark Company, 1914.

48. Bolton, *Athanase de Mézières*, 1:29.

49. Magnaghi, "Editor's Introduction," in Bolton, *Hasinais*, 3–21.

50. Bolton, *Texas*, v.

51. Ibid., vi.

52. HEB, "The Location of La Salle's Colony," 165–182.

53. Turner to HEB, 5/26/1914, BP In.

54. HEB to Turner, 6/4/1914, BP Out.

55. Turner to HEB, 10/13/1914, BP In.

56. Turner to HEB, 1/20/1916, BP In. This letter is excerpted in Jacobs, *The Historical World of Frederick Jackson Turner*, 215–216.

57. HEB to Turner, 1/27/1916, TU:30.

58. Stephens to Turner, 9/16/1909, TU:12.

59. Conmy, *The Origins and Purposes of the Native Sons*, 9–10.

60. Bates, *History of the Bench and Bar,* 286.

61. Davis to HEB, 1/27/1914, 2/4/1914, 2/6/1914, 4/9/1914, 5/18/1914, BP In.

62. Stephens to Jameson, 3/8/1919, JP:129, H. M. Stephens.

63. Davis, "University Fellowships," 7–8. See also Davis, "Our Early Law," 11–12; and Davis, "The Preservation of Our State History," 7–8.

64. Davis, "University Fellowships," 8.

65. HEB to Davis, 5/5/1913, BP Out.

66. Wheeler to HEB, 1/27/1913, BP In.

67. Davis, *Dark Side of Fortune,* 1–79 passim.

68. HEB to Doheny, 4/4/1914; HEB to Dunn, 5/2/1914, BP Out.

69. HEB to Doheny, 5/5/1914, BP Out.

70. Doheny to HEB, 5/7/1914, BP In.

71. HEB Jr., "My Most Unforgettable Character."

CHAPTER 6

1. HEB to Frederick, 10/18/1913, BFP. Herbert was born six weeks before Bolton sent the letter.

2. For example, HEB to Frederick, 1/27/1910, BFP.

3. HEB Jr., "My Most Unforgettable Character."

4. Ibid.

5. Ibid.

6. Ibid. Bolton wrote to his wife and family when he was away on research trips. Several dozen letters from Gertrude to Bolton are found under her name in BP In.

7. HEB Jr., "My Most Unforgettable Character."

8. Davis to HEB, 6/8/1915, 6/9/1915, BP In.

9. HEB to Hiram Johnson, 6/10/1915, BP Out.

10. California Historical Survey Commission, *Preliminary Report,* 9–18.

11. For example, see Coy, *Guide to the County Archives of California;* Coy, *The Genesis of California Counties;* Coy, *California County Boundaries.*

12. Davis to HEB, 5/18/1920, BP In.

13. (New York: The Macmillan Company, 1917), 3–8.

14. HEB to Stephens, 12/9/1915, BP Out.

15. HEB to Leuschner, 12/15/1915, HEB Out.

16. HEB to Frederick, 6/2/1914, BFP.

17. HEB to Allen Johnson, 10/16/1916, BP Out.

18. HEB to Frederick, 10/23/1892, BFP; Colin Calloway, "Introduction," in Parkman, *Pioneers of France,* vii–viii.

19. Parkman, *Pioneers of France,* 20.

20. Bannon, *Bolton,* 117.

21. *Dictionary of American Biography*, s.v. "Johnson, Allen"; "Personal," *AHR* 36 (April 1931): 660–661.

22. Johnson's principal works are *Stephen A. Douglas; Readings in American Constitutional History; Jefferson and His Colleagues; The Historian and Historical Evidence;* and Johnson and Robinson, *Readings in Recent American Constitutional History.*

23. "Mission as a Frontier Institution," reprinted in Bannon, *Bolton and the Spanish Borderlands,* 187–211.

24. HEB to Jameson, 4/13/1917, JP:288, *AHR.*

25. "American Acta Sanctorum," 302.

26. Jameson to HEB, 1/25/1916, JP:288, *AHR.*

27. Jameson to HEB, 6/7/1917; HEB to Jameson, 6/18/1917, JP:288, *AHR.*

28. Jameson to HEB, 6/7/1917, JP:288, *AHR.* These words appear in the published version with only slight modification. See Bolton, "Mission as a Frontier Institution," 188–189.

29. HEB to Jameson, 6/18/1917, JP:288, *AHR.*

30. Bolton, "Mission as a Frontier Institution," 211.

31. Weber, "Turner, the Boltonians, and the Borderlands," 66–81; Weber, *The Spanish Frontier in North America,* 1–13, 335–360.

32. Jameson to HEB, 9/24/1917, JP:288, *AHR.*

33. HEB to Jameson, n.d., JP:288, *AHR.*

34. Bolton, "Mission as a Frontier Institution," 187.

35. Hanna to HEB, 9/15/1917, [November] 1918, [December] 1918, 11/19/1919, BP In.

36. McLaughlin to HEB, 7/23/1918, BP In; HEB to McLaughlin, 7/28/1918, BP Out.

37. HEB to McLaughlin, 9/16/1918, BP Out.

38. HEB to McLaughlin, 4/30/1919, BP Out; McLaughlin to HEB, 5/7/1919, 1/26/1920, 3/3/1920, BP In.

39. Charles H. Cunningham to H. Morse Stephens, 12/18/1916, BP In.

40. HEB to Albright, 2/31/1917, BP Out; HEB to Albright, 5/28/1917, BP Out.

41. Swain, *Wilderness Defender,* 16–24, 35, 65, 56–60.

42. Rothman, *Preserving Different Pasts.*

43. Albright to HEB, 6/4/1917, BP In.

44. Bolton, *Kino's Historical Memoir.*

45. HEB to Albright, 6/18/1917, BP Out.

46. Mather to HEB, 6/23/1924, BP In, U.S. National Park Service.

47. Bolton to Edward Hyatt, 2/27/1915, BP Out.

48. Nisbet, *Teachers and Scholars,* 152.

49. Ibid., 151.

50. Bannon, *Bolton,* 106.

51. Wheeler to HEB, 5/17/1919, BP In, California, University, President.

52. Stephens to Jameson, 12/15/1918; Jameson to Stephens, 1/7/1919, JP:129, H. M. Stephens.

53. Nisbet, *Teachers and Scholars*, 153.

54. HEB to Barrows, 4/2/1917, BP Out; Bogue, *Turner*, 326.

55. HEB to Waldo G. Leland, 2/23/1918, BP Out; HEB to Isaiah Bowman, 7/12/1918, BP Out; HEB to Bailey Willis, 8/17/1918, BP Out.

56. "Suggested Plans of the War History Committee of the University of California," 1918; HEB to Roy Bolton, 2/6/1919, BP Out.

57. E. A. Dickson to HEB, 9/17/1917, BP In.

58. "Finding Aid for the Edward A. Dickson Papers, 1900–1954," UCLA, Special Collections, www.oac.cdlib.org/findaid/ask:/13030/tf9xonb6dk.

59. HEB to Dickson [1920], BP Out.

60. Dickson to HEB, 8/12/1919, BP In.

61. HEB to Dickson, 2/16/1920, BP Out; Dickson to HEB, 3/15/1920, BP In; Dickson to HEB, n.d., BP In. Bancroft staff marked this "1920," but it may have been written in 1919.

62. Bolton coedited the *Southwestern Historical Quarterly* and was advisory editor for the *Hispanic American Historical Review*, which Chapman edited. HEB to Davis, 8/7/1919, BP Out.

63. Doheny to HEB, 9/20/1917, BP In. This was addressed "Dear Sir" and was evidently sent to several other scholars.

64. "Memorandum of Agreement Between the University of California and the Doheny Research Foundation," BP In, Doheny Foundation.

65. Davis, in *Dark Side of Fortune*, 118, states that the foundation was "launched" in November 1918, but it must have begun in 1917. The Bolton Papers show that the foundation was in full swing by early 1918. "Executive Committee Meeting," 8/20/1918, BP In, Doheny Foundation.

66. Priestley to HEB, 2/6/1918, 3/27/1918, BP In.

67. HEB to Wheeler, 3/13/1918, BP Out.

68. HEB to Doheny, 10/16/1920, BP Out.

69. The description of Stephens's death and memorial service come from an anonymous letter to Jameson. The author was probably Bolton but may have been Teggart. JP:129, H. M. Stephens.

70. Thorpe, *Henry Edwards Huntington*, 387–394.

71. HEB to Margaret Sartori, 9/16/1919, 10/10/1919, BP Out.

72. HEB to John F. Davis, 8/17/1921, BP Out; HEB to Edward Eberstadt, 8/17/1921, BP Out; HEB to David Prescott Barrows, 8/31/1922, BP Out. The collection is now known as the Fort Sacramento Papers.

CHAPTER 7

1. HEB to Turner, 5/14/1919, TU:31A.
2. HEB to Frederick Bolton, 6/15/1919, BFP (emphasis in original).
3. "Southwestern History at the University of California," n.d., BP Out.
4. HEB to Frederick Bolton, 6/15/1919, BFP.
5. Magnaghi, *Bolton and the Historiography of the Americas*, 53–81, gives a detailed account of the establishment of the course and publication of Bolton's extensive published syllabus, *History of the Americas*.
6. Teggart, quoted in Dangberg, *Teggart*, 10.
7. HEB to Leuschner, n.d. [1923], BP Out.
8. "The list shows . . ." [1924], BP Out.
9. HEB to Professor McElroy, 2/20/1916, BP Out.
10. Hackett to HEB, [9/26?]/1918, BP In.
11. Hackett to HEB, 10/4/1918, BP In.
12. Vinson to HEB, 10/11/1917, BP In, Texas, University, President.
13. Gould, "The University Becomes Politicized," 255–276. Harper to HEB, 7/19/1924, BP In, Texas, University.
14. Barker to HEB, 5/12/1919, 7/15/1919, BP In.
15. *Southwestern Historical Quarterly* 20 (July 1916), 96–100. The tenor of Dunn's article compelled Barker to apologize to Bolton for not sending it to him for approval. Barker to HEB, 1/15/1917, BP In.
16. Hackett to HEB, n.d. [1919], BP In.
17. Hackett to HEB, n.d. [1919], BP In. This is a different letter than the one cited in the previous note.
18. Barker to HEB, 7/15/1919, BP In.
19. Barker to HEB, 1/15/1920, 1/21/1920, BP In.
20. Dunn to HEB, 12/28/1915, BP In.
21. HEB to Dunn [1916], BP Out.
22. Dunn to HEB, 10/8/1916, 11/24/1916, 1/17/1917, BP In.
23. New York: Macmillan, 1920.
24. Marshall to HEB, 3/14/1921, BP In.
25. Paxson to HEB, 12/16/1920, BP In.
26. Etulain, "After Turner," 159. These are inferences gleaned from Paxson's published writings: *The Last American Frontier; History of the American Frontier; When the West Is Gone.*
27. Bolton, *Kino's Historical Memoir;* Bolton and Marshall, *The Colonization of North America;* Bolton and Adams, *California's Story;* Bolton, "The Mission as a Frontier Institution," 42–61. In addition, Bolton published articles and chapters in the *San Diego Union; The Pacific Ocean in History*, ed. Bolton and Stephens (1917); the *Oakland*

Tribune; The Islander; the *Hispanic American Historical Review;* the *Catholic Historical Review;* and the *Daily Oklahoman.*

28. For an account of the Bolton-Clark controversy, see Bannon, *Bolton,* 121–29.

29. *Rim of Christendom,* xxi.

30. Turner to Charles Van Hise, 6/15/1906, TU:7.

31. Parkman, *Parkman Reader,* 3.

32. Jacobs, *Francis Parkman, Historian as Hero,* x.

33. Ibid., 90–94. Jacobs was not the only biographer to cast Parkman as a hero. See Wade, *Francis Parkman: Heroic Historian.*

34. Johnson to HEB, 10/18/1917, BP In.

35. Johnson to HEB, 1/20/1918, BP In.

36. Johnson to HEB, 2/6/1918, BP In.

37. HEB to Allen Johnson, 4/2/1919, BP Out.

38. Johnson to HEB, 4/23/1919, BP In, includes a long quotation from a letter from Glasgow to Bolton.

39. Ibid. Bannon published a lengthy quotation from this letter, but omitted the sections that appear above. Bannon, *Bolton,* 131–132.

40. HEB to Allen Johnson, 4/28/1919, BP Out; Johnson to HEB, May 11, 1919, BP In.

41. Ibid.

42. Barman, *Constance Lindsay Skinner,* 13–83.

43. Adams, "Biographical Sketch," 21; Skinner to Owen Small, 12/3/1930, in Eastman, *Constance Lindsay Skinner,* 8.

44. Johnson to Skinner, 1/3/1921, CLSP. Skinner, "Notes," 92, quotes Johnson as writing, "You can feel more than flattered by this interest on the part of America's greatest living historian," which was evidently a paraphrase of Johnson's letter.

45. Johnson to Skinner, 9/25/1919, CLSP.

46. Johnson to Skinner, 10/19/1919, CLSP.

47. Johnson to HEB, 1/5/1920, BP In.

48. Johnson to HEB, 3/7/1920, BP In.

49. Ibid.

50. HEB to Johnson, 3/18/1920, BP Out.

51. HEB to Johnson, 4/2/1920, BP Out.

52. HEB to Glasgow, 5/19/1920, BP Out.

53. Johnson to Skinner, 6/3/1920, CLSP.

54. *The Spanish Borderlands,* x.

55. Ibid., vii.

56. George Parmly Day to Bolton, 1/6/1922, BP In.

57. Bolton, *History of the Americas,* xx.

58. For an appraisal Bolton's racial views, see Hurtado, "Bolton, Racism, and

American History," 127–142. For an example of how Bolton's promotion of missionary heroes could lead him astray, see Sandos, "Junípero Serra's Canonization."

59. Turner to HEB, 8/12/1925, BP In.

60. Turner to HEB, 8/12/1925, BP In; Bolton, *Arredondo's Proof.*

61. Turner to HEB, 8/31/1925, BP In. The word "truly" is crossed out, but there is no way to know if Bolton or Turner made the change. Other marks on the letter indicate that Bolton was selecting quotes for blurbs, so it is likely that he struck the objectionable word "truly" for that purpose.

Turner referred to Bolton's *Arredondo's Proof.* I have not found a direct reference to *The Spanish Borderlands* in the Turner correspondence at the Bancroft or Huntington libraries.

62. Turner, *The Significance of Sections in American History.*

63. Steiner, "Frederick Jackson Turner and Western Regionalism," 103–135.

64. Turner, "The Development of American Society," 180–183.

65. Turner, *The Significance of Sections and American History,* 252, 315–316.

66. New York: Henry Holt, 1935.

67. Turner, *The United States,* 352, 354.

68. HEB to Turner, 9/15/1926, TU: 38. The "imitative disciple" term is in HEB to Turner, 12/27/1910, BP Out, and TU: 20. Bolton was commenting on Turner's "Geographic Sectionalism in America," reprinted in *The Significance of Sections in American History,* 193–206.

69. *The Significance of Sections in American History,* 193, 206.

70. Turner to HEB, 8/21/1930, BP In.

CHAPTER 8

1. AHA, *Annual Report,* 1920, 18.

2. Thomas Maitland Marshall to HEB, 8/22/1921, BP In.

3. Meany, "New York," www.nysm.nysed.gov/services/meanydoc.html.

4. HEB to Hodder, 10/8/1921, BP Out.

5. Hodder to Louis Paetow, 10/17/1921, BP In, Hodder. Professor Paetow evidently passed the letter to Bolton, who kept it in his file of letters from Hodder. AHA, *Annual Report,* 1921, 82. Bannon, in *Bolton,* 182n, reported that Bolton "had been considered" for the second vice presidency but deferred to Wilson. There is nothing in the official record of the nominating committee to indicate how seriously it was considering Bolton, but records for that year are sparse. AHA-LC, Box 451, Committee on Nominations.

6. HEB to Hodder, 12/2/1921, BP Out. Adams did not receive the nomination. Hodder to HEB 12/7/1921, BP In.

7. Teggart, "As to University Presidents," *Christian Science Monitor* (August 1, 1919), reprinted in Dangberg, *Teggart,* 245–247.

8. Dangberg, *Teggart,* 46–49.

9. Wheeler to HEB, 5/17/1919, BP In, California, University, President.

10. Nisbet, *Teachers and Scholars,* 154–155; Dangberg, *Teggart,* 48–52.

11. HEB to Barrows, 6/6/1921, BP Out.

12. Nisbet, *Teachers and Scholars,* 188–193; Ferrier, *University of California,* 511, 522; Kerr, *The Gold and the Blue,* 1:144.

13. Ferrier, *University of California,* 522–526.

14. HEB to Barrows, 4/6/1923, BP Out.

15. HEB to A. O. Leuschner, n.d. [1923?] [draft]; 10/31/1923, BP Out.

16. HEB to Frederick Bolton, 5/2/1920, BFP.

17. Woodrow Borah, interview with author, 8/13/1992 (transcript in author's possession).

18. Marshall to HEB, 8/22/1921, BP In.

19. Rippy to HEB, 10/14/1920, BP In.

20. Marshall to HEB, 5/24/1921, BP In; Mecham to HEB, 3/27/1922, BP In, Thomas Maitland Marshall.

21. Marshall to HEB, 5/24/1921, 6/2/1921, 6/28/1921, BP In.

22. This and the following quotations are from Bolton, "On Wisdom's Trail," 6–8, 54.

23. HEB to Frederick Bolton, 4/14/1912, BFP.

24. Jeanne Weir to HEB, 8/25/1914, BFP.

25. Frederick Bolton to HEB, 9/18/1923, BP In.

26. Hackett to HEB, 9/28/1923, BP In.

27. Ford to HEB, 9/28/1923; Hackett to HEB, 9/28/1923, BP In.

28. HEB quoted in Bannon, *Bolton,* 154.

29. Grace Mildred Bolton to HEB, 12/9/1923, BP In.

30. Pool, *Barker,* 124.

31. Barker to HEB, 3/15/1923, 11/14/1923, 5/18/1924, BP In.

32. Barker to HEB, 5/26/1923, BP In.

33. Barker to Goodwin, 6/18/1923, BP In, Eugene C. Barker; Bannon, *Bolton,* 156.

34. Hackett to HEB, 6/12/1923, BP In.

35. Hackett to HEB, 11/26/1923, BP In.

36. Hackett to HEB, 1/30/1924, BP In.

37. Barker to HEB, 11/14/1923, 2/26/1924, BP In.

38. Bolton had tried to hire Ford to replace Stephens. Ford to HEB, 7/12/1920, 4/26/1921, BP In.

39. Barker to Ford, 5/17/1924, BP In, Guy Stanton Ford.

40. Barker to HEB, 5/18/1924, BP In.

41. Barker to HEB, 5/31/1924; Hackett to HEB, 6/2/1924, BP In.

42. Barker [1924], BP In.

43. Great Register, Alameda County, California Room, State Library, Sacramento.

44. Frederick Bolton to HEB, 6/6/1924, BP In.

45. Engelhardt to HEB, 7/29/1924, BP In.

46. Barrows to HEB, 6/7/1924, BP In. Barrows's letter was written on campus. He was so anxious to get it to Bolton that he sent him the draft—perhaps hand-delivered it, though this is uncertain.

47. Resolution dated 6/7/1924, BP In, Native Sons of the Golden West.

48. Bannon, *Bolton*, 165.

49. "To the Alumni and Regents," June 1924, BP Out. Scribbled on fifteen telegram blanks, there appear to be three drafts, but it is impossible to know if Bolton combined parts of one draft with another. After making the notes to organize his thinking, he may have spoken off the cuff.

50. Hackett to HEB, 6/2/1924, BP In.

51. Bannon, *Bolton*, 167.

52. Hackett to HEB, 6/15/1924, BP In.

53. Hackett to HEB, 6/25/1924, BP In.

54. Hackett to HEB, 6/18/1924; Barker to HEB, 6/23/1924, BP In.

55. Moore to HEB, 6/15/1924, BP In, Texas, University.

56. Quoted in Pool, *Barker*, 129.

57. Barker sent his speech to Bolton (1925, BP In) and other professors around the country. Most of the address is in Pool, *Barker*, 131–133.

58. Pool, *Barker*, 134–135, 136.

59. Wallace Notestein et al., "To the Members of the American Historical Association," 7/1/1924, AHA-LC, Box 451, Nominating Committee Report, 1924; Notestein to Members of the Nominating Committee, 10/25/1924, 7/1/1924, AHA-LC, Box 451, Nominating Committee, 1923–1926; AHA, *Annual Report*, 1925, 28.

CHAPTER 9

1. Stern, *Eugenic Nation*, 21, 57–81, 123.

2. All quotations are from HEB, "Free Negro in the South" (BP, Part III, Articles and Essays, Carton 1), an unpublished synopsis of his dissertation.

3. Quotations in this paragraph are from Bolton, "On Wisdom's Trail," 15, 16, 19.

4. Bolton, "Mission as a Frontier Institution," in Bannon, *Bolton and the Borderlands*, 205–206.

5. Bolton to Ellison, 9/5/1916, BP Out.

6. *Anderson v. Mathews*, 174 Cal. 537, 163 Pac. 902. See also Castillo, "Twentieth-Century Secular Movements," 714–715; Forbes, *Native Americans of California and*

Nevada, 92–93; Fernandez, "Except a California Indian"; Goodrich, "The Legal Status of the California Indian," 163–166.

7. No correspondence directly connects Bolton with the Anderson case. However, Bolton wrote a two-thousand-word report on the question of Indian citizenship ("The Status of California Indians as Citizens," BP Out), and the "Brief of the Petitioner" (*Ethan Anderson v. Shafter Mathews*, Case Files, Records of the Supreme Court of California, Case no. 8035, WPA no. 22955, Bin no. 2236, State Archives, Sacramento, California [hereinafter cited as Case File]) closely follows Bolton's rationale. Most persuasively, approximately four hundred of Bolton's words are quoted *in extenso*, but without attribution, in Case File, 22–23.

8. "The Status of California Indians as Citizens," BP Out.

9. For a more detailed and sophisticated analysis of the problem of California Indian citizenship, see Akins, "Lines on the Land."

10. "Brief of the Petitioner," Case File; *Anderson v. Mathews*, 174 Cal. 537, 163 Pac. 902.

11. Nichols, "Civilization over Savage," 390 passim.

12. HEB to Gertrude, 6/6/1922, BP Out.

13. Calloway, "My Grandfather's Axe."

14. Prucha, *The Great Father*, 2:798–800.

15. HEB to Hewett, 12/4/1922, BP Out. Bolton learned of the Bursum Bill through an article in the *New Republic:* Henderson, "The Death of the Pueblos."

16. Ogden, Sluiter, and Crampton, *Greater America*, a festschrift, includes a complete list of HEB's graduate students and their theses, dissertations, and publications.

17. Davis to HEB, 1/27/1914, 2/4/1914, 2/6/1914, BP In.

18. Lummis, *Spanish Pioneers*, 2.

19. Davis to HEB, 5/18/1914, BP In.

20. Novick, *That Noble Dream*, 15, 172–174, 338–341, 365–366; Norwood, *Third Reich in the Ivory Tower*, 36–74 passim.

21. HEB to Frederick Bolton, 2/26/1904, BFP.

22. Banduragga, "One Hundred Years of History in Nevada," 3–14; Stensvaag, "'The Life of My Child,'" 3–20; HEB to Miss Weir, 6/20/1917, BP Out.

23. HEB to Marshall, 4/4/1922, BP Out; HEB to W. T. Root, 7/2/1926, BP Out.

24. Marshall to HEB, 7/15/1925, BP In; HEB to Marshall, 7/17/1925, BP Out.

25. HEB to W. T. Root, 7/2/1926, BP Out.

26. Whitaker to HEB, 7/3/1927, BP In; HEB to Whitaker, 7/14/1927, BP Out.

27. Leonard to HEB, 6/4/1927, BP In; HEB to E. L. Hardy, 6/8/1927, BP Out; HEB to DuFour, 7/11/1927; BP Out; HEB to E. L. Hardy, 11/29/1927, BP Out.

28. Synnott, "Anti-Semitism and American Universities," 233–234; Yeomans, *Abbott Lawrence Lowell*, 209–216.

29. Becker to HEB, 11/13/1935, BP In.

30. Published as Bolton, ed., *Historical Memoirs of New California*.

31. Transcript [1923], BP In, Native Sons of the Golden West.

32. See BP In, Ehrman; Bannon, *Bolton*, 171–174.

33. Transcript [1922], BP In, Native Sons of the Golden West.

34. Ibid.

35. Ibid.

36. Transcript [1923], BP In, Native Sons of the Golden West.

37. For positive assessments, see Royce, *California, from the Conquest*, 437–465; Bancroft, *History of California*, 6:745–754. Modern views of vigilantism are more negative: Brown, *Strain of Violence;* Caughey, *Their Majesties the Mob;* Senkewicz, *Vigilantes in Gold Rush San Francisco*.

38. Williams, *History of the San Francisco Committee of Vigilance of 1851*, 436–437.

39. John F. Davis to HEB, 9/22/1919, BP In.

40. HEB to Dean Lipman, 2/11/1927, BP Out.

41. Mitchell, "Joaquín Murieta"; Ogden, Sluiter, and Crampton, *Greater America*, 636.

42. Ogden, Sluiter, and Crampton, *Greater America*, 636.

43. HEB to Adams, 3/16/1920, BP Out.

44. This and following quotations are from Bolton and Adams, *California's Story*, 119, 135, 137, 190–210.

45. Campbell to HEB, 1/22/1926, BP In, California, University, President, W. W. Campbell.

46. Ibid.

47. Campbell to HEB, 11/10/1926, BP In, California, University, President, W. W. Campbell.

48. HEB to Campbell, 5/12/1927, BP Out.

49. HEB to William J. Hayes, 5/3/1927, BP Out.

50. HEB to Campbell, 5/12/1927, BP Out.

51. HEB to Young, 5/16/1927, BP Out.

52. HEB to Ellison, 5/5/1927, BP Out.

53. Ellison to HEB, 5/14/1927, BP In; HEB to Ellison, 5/16/1927, BP Out.

54. BP, Part III, Professional Activities, Cartons 2–5.

CHAPTER 10

1. Earl Pomeroy to author, 8/22/1990 (letter in author's possession). Pomeroy, who was a graduate student at Berkeley in the late 1930s, was quoting another graduate student. Pomeroy relished the story.

2. Bolton, *Anza's California Expeditions*.

3. HEB to Lockwood, 12/9/1927, BP Out.

4. Thompson, *El Maestro*, 45–53.

5. *With Padre Kino on the Trail; The Apache Indians.*

6. Lockwood quoted in Thompson, *El Maestro*, 1.

7. Ibid., 113–116.

8. HEB to Lockwood, 1/19/1928, BP Out.

9. 3:xv.

10. HEB Jr., "My Most Unforgettable Character."

11. "Map of Anza's Routes through Pimería Alta, 1774–1776," in Bolton, *Outpost of Empire*, facing p. 332.

12. HEB to Lipman, 2/4/1927, BP Out.

13. Bannon, *Bolton*, 283–286.

14. HEB to Lipman, 2/4/1927, BP Out.

15. HEB to Charles B. Lipman, 2/18/1928, BP Out.

16. Frank C. Lockwood, "Correspondence Concerning Herbert E. Bolton," MSS C-D 5064, Bancroft Library. Lockwood queried Bolton's students in order to write a biographical introduction to a festschrift, Hammond, *New Spain and the Anglo-American West.* Lockwood's essay was not included in the volume but was published as "Adventurous Scholarship."

17. Pomeroy to author, 9/10/1990 (letter in author's possession).

18. Leonard, interview with author, 8/8/1994 (notes in author's possession).

19. HEB to Rippy, 3/12/1929; HEB to Ellison, 3/9/1929, BP Out.

20. By "placement" I mean a full-time, permanent position in a college or university. A few of his students changed jobs. Thomas, for example, taught at Oklahoma and Alabama, so his career accounted for two "placements" of Bolton students. I compiled the placement record from "A Bibliography of the Historical Writings of the Students of Herbert Eugene Bolton," in Ogden, Sluiter, and Crampton, *Greater America*, 549–672, and from items I found in BP In and BP Out.

21. Pomeroy to author, 9/10/1990.

22. Ogden, Sluiter, and Crampton, *Greater America*, 549–672.

23. HEB, "Address of Professor H. E. Bolton before the Junior College Section of the California High School Teachers' Association, Berkeley, July 18, 1917," BP Out; HEB, "High School Class Visitations, May 20–24, 1918," BP Out.

24. I learned this from historian Iris Wilson Engstrand, who heard it from one of Bolton's women graduate students.

25. Angie Debo is perhaps the best-known example of gender discrimination in hiring between the wars. Leckie, *Angie Debo;* Wolff and Schrems, "Politics and Libel"; Lowitt, "'Dear Miss Debo,'" 372–405.

26. Paxson to HEB, 2/2/1923, BP In.

27. See, for example, Edward J. Lynch to HEB, 9/27/1934, BP In, NSGW.

28. Bannon, *Bolton*, 179n.

29. HEB to Ross, 7/22/1920, BP Out.

30. Ogden, Sluiter, and Crampton, *Greater America*, 653; Mendelson and Elling-son, *Mary Leticia Ross Papers*, 156.

31. Bolton, *Rim of Christendom*, xxi.

32. HEB to Ralph Kuykendall, 8/23/1932, BP Out; HEB to A. J. Cloud, 5/29/1935, BP Out.

33. HEB to H. A. Spindt, 3/20/1934 (with attachment), BP Out.

34. HEB to A. J. Cloud, 5/29/1935, BP Out; HEB to Guy Stanton Ford, 11/19/1935, BP Out.

35. Bolton, *History of the Americas*.

36. Turner to HEB, 2/4/1929, BP In.

37. HEB to Turner, 2/7/1929, BP Out.

38. HEB to Turner, 1/17/1928, TU:45.

39. Hackett to Bolton, 11/14/1928, BP In.

40. HEB to James F. Willard, 11/2/1928, BP Out.

41. Bogue, *Turner*, 429.

42. HEB to Willard, 12/11/1928, BP Out.

43. Willard to Turner, 6/22/1929, TU:42.

44. This and following quotations are from "Defensive Spanish Expansion and the Significance of the Borderlands," in Bannon, *Bolton and the Spanish Borderlands*, 59, 62, 64.

45. Willard to Turner, 6/22/1929, TU:42.

46. 4 vols. (Berkeley: University of California Press, 1926), 1:vii.

47. Bolton, "Introduction," in *Historical Memoirs*, 1:xxix, xc.

48. Bolton, *Fray Juan Crespi*, iii, iv.

49. Ibid., 50.

50. Bolton acknowledged Edward J. Hanna, archbishop of San Francisco, as a "constant source of inspiration." *Kino's Historical Memoir*, 1:26.

CHAPTER 11

1. Kerr, *The Gold and the Blue*, 1:17.

2. HEB to Ehrman, 4/2/1931, BP Out.

3. "Ehrman Replaces Foster as U.C. Regent," clipping, n.d.; Sidney M. Ehrman to HEB, 2/25/1930, BP In.

4. HEB to C. C. Young, 5/6/1930, BP Out.

5. Engelhardt to HEB, 11/20/1930, HEB In.

6. For example, Bolton, *A Pacific Coast Pioneer*, is a reprint of his introduction to *Fray Juan Crespi*, xiii–lxi. See also Bolton, *Arredondo's Historical Proof of Spain's Title*

to Georgia, 1–110, and Bolton, with Ross, *The Debatable Land*, which is a reprint of the introduction to *Arredondo*.

7. This and the following quotations are from Bolton, *Outpost of Empire*, viii, 15, 326–332.

8. Jacobs, *Historian as Hero*, 57–67.

9. Skinner, "The Lure of the Golden Gate," 3.

10. Bolton, *Outpost of Empire*, after p. 332.

11. HEB, *Outpost of Empire*, 333–334.

12. Adams to HEB, 5/10/1930, BP In; HEB, memo announcing Adams's death, 9/2/1930, BP Out.

13. HEB to Dexter Perkins, 1/19/1931, BP Out.

14. HEB to T. J. Wertenbaker, 2/10/1932, BP Out.

15. HEB to W. W. Campbell, 6/21/1930, BP Out.

16. "History" [January 1930]; HEB to Robert Gordon Sproul, 11/25/1933, BP Out.

17. Douglass, *The California Idea*, 140.

18. Bannon, *Bolton*, 189.

19. William J. Hayes to Robert Sproul, 5/9/1931, BP In, Native Sons of the Golden West; Bannon, *Bolton*, 178–179.

20. Bannon, *Bolton*, 179–180.

21. Bolton, *Rim of Christendom*, xx.

22. HEB to Sproul, 11/2/1931, BP Out.

23. Boston: Houghton Mifflin, 1924.

24. Paxson, *The Independence of the South American Republics*.

25. HEB to Paxson, 3/23/1932, BP Out. Bolton wrote Paxson three letters on the same day. The third is an undated draft but seems to follow the gist of the other letters.

26. HEB, "Our New Historians," 1932, BP Out.

27. Turner quoted in Billington, *Turner*, 415.

28. Ibid., 403–416; Bogue, *Turner*, 439.

29. Ford to Farrand, 5/8/1933, TU:50A.

30. His last letter to McMaster is 5/15/1927, BP Out, congratulating him for a new book.

31. McMaster quoted in Goldman, *John Bach McMaster*, 158.

32. Jacobs, "'Turner As I Remember Him,'" 54–61.

33. HEB to Rudolph L. Dalagher, 3/28/1932, BP Out; Jacobs, "'Turner As I Remember Him,'" 60.

34. HEB to Farrand, 11/21/1932, BP Out.

35. *The Significance of Sections in American History*.

36. HEB to Parish, 9/19/1931, BP Out.

37. Parish, "Comment and Historical News," 136.

38. HEB to Joseph Ellison, 1/24/1931, BP Out.

39. Boston: Little Brown, 1931.

40. Bannon, *Bolton*, 182–183.

41. HEB, "Our New Historians," 1932, BP Out.

42. HEB to Ford, 4/10/1931, BP Out.

43. Bolton, "Epic of Greater America," in Bannon, *Bolton and the Spanish Borderlands*, 302; first published in *American Historical Review* 38 (April 1933), 448–474.

44. This and following quotations are from Bolton, "Epic of Greater America," 324, 325, 328–329, 330, 331, 332, 332n8.

45. Bannon, *Bolton and the Spanish Borderlands*, 299–301.

46. Hanke, *Do the Americas Have a Common History?* 185–189; Magnaghi, *Bolton and the Historiography of the Americas*, 83–131, summarizes the critics.

47. Binkley quoted in Hackett to Lockwood, 11/25/1931, MSS C-D 5064, Bancroft Library.

48. HEB quoted in ibid.

49. Chapman to Lockwood, 2/29/1932, MSS C-D 5064, Bancroft Library.

50. HEB, Teggart, et al., to Chairman of the Institute for Social Sciences, 10/18/1932, BP Out.

51. Chapman to Lockwood, 2/29/1932, MSS C-D 5064, Bancroft Library.

52. Argus Press Clipping Director to HEB, 1/5/1933, BP In, "A."

53. Hackett to Lockwood, 12/19/1932, MSS C-D 5064, Bancroft Library.

54. Lockwood to Hackett, 1/4/1933, MSS C-D 5064, Bancroft Library.

55. Lockwood to Hackett, 10/4/1932, 1/13/1932, MSS C-D 5064, Bancroft Library.

56. Lockwood, "Adventurous Scholarship," 185–194.

57. HEB to Thomas C. Vint, 12/19/1933, BP Out.

58. For examples, see Irving F. Morrow to HEB, 12/12/1933, BP In, U.S. National Park Service; HEB to Conrad L. Wirth, 6/16/1934, BP Out.

59. For a typical letter recommending several students for National Park Service jobs, see HEB to Conrad L. Wirth, 4/17/1935, BP Out.

60. A guide to Brooks's papers may be found at www.trumanlibrary.org/hstpaper/brooksp.htm.

61. See *Information Science Pioneers*, s.v. "Vernon Dale Tate," accessed June 14, 2011, www.libsci.sc.edu/bob/isp/tatevd.htm.

62. Neasham's biography may be found in "Guide to the Aubrey Neasham Collection," Sacramento Archives and Collection Center, Online Archive of California, http://content.cdlib.org/view?docId=kt1h4nc623&doc.view=entire_text&brand=oac.

63. See *The Handbook of Texas Online*, s.v., "Dunn, William Edward," accessed June 14, 2011, www.tshaonline.org/handbook/online.

64. HEB to Philip C. Brooks, 5/25/1934, BP Out, gives some idea of Bolton's assiduous search for employment for his students.

65. HEB to Dunn, 2/10/1932, BP Out.

66. Gale Randall (HEB's granddaughter), interview with the author, 8/11/2010 (notes in author's possession).

67. Bannon, *Bolton*, 154–155.

68. Edward J. Lynch to HEB, 5/24/1933, 6/26/1934, 8/5/1937, 9/13/1938; John T. Regan to HEB, 6/10/1940, all in BP In, Native Sons of the Golden West.

69. Becker, *Modern History*.

70. Becker to HEB, 12/1/1935, BP In.

71. Bolton to Mrs. Henry Gratton Doyle, 12/6/1935; HEB to Becker, 12/6/1935, BP Out.

CHAPTER 12

1. *Arredondo's Historical Proof;* Bolton and Ross, *The Debatable Land.*

2. HEB to Ross, 7/22/1920, BP Out; Ross, "The Anglo-Spanish Conflict in the Caribbean Area."

3. HEB to Ross, 7/22/1920, BP Out.

4. HEB to Ehrman, 6/26/1925, BP Out.

5. *Arredondo's Proof,* facing p. xviii, facing p. 80.

6. "French Intrusions and Indian Uprisings"; "The French on the Savannah"; "The Spanish Settlement of Santa Elena"; "The Restoration of the Spanish Missions in Georgia"; "With Pardo and Boyano on the Fringes of the Georgia Land."

7. *New York Times,* 6/3/1934, quoted in Floyd, "Certain Tabby Ruins," 182.

8. Floyd, "Certain Tabby Ruins"; Thomas, "Saints and Soldiers"; Weber, *The Spanish Frontier,* 349–350.

9. Floyd, "Certain Tabby Ruins," 4.

10. Bolton, "On Wisdom's Trail," 19–29.

11. HEB to Conrad L. Wirth, 6/16/1934, BP Out. See also Dudley C. Bayliss to HEB, 11/26/1934, BP In, U.S. National Park Service.

12. HEB to James A. Hall, 6/18/1934; HEB to Conrad L. Wirth, 6/16/1934, BP Out.

13. Floyd, "Certain Tabby Ruins," 26–27, 37–40, 58–60, 174–177, 180–181.

14. Dudley C. Bayliss to HEB, 5/1/1935, BP In, U.S. National Park Service; Edmund Abrahams to HEB, 11/17/1939, BP In, U.S. National Park Service.

15. Pomeroy to author, 8/22/1990 (letter in author's possession).

16. The essential story of the plate is in Hanna, *Lost Harbor,* 242–262. See also Hurtado, "More Shadows on the Brass." On the Clampers' involvement in the fabrication of the plate, see Von der Porten, Spitze, et al., "Who Made Drake's Plate of

Brass?"; and Chandler, *ECV*. I have also benefited from an unpublished manuscript: Edward Von der Porten and James Spitze, with Raymond Aker and Robert W. Allen, "The Mystery of the Plate of Brass: California's Greatest Hoax and the Search for Its Perpetrators," which the authors generously shared with me.

17. Chandler, *ECV*, 3–5.

18. E Clampus Vitus, *Credo Quia Absurdum*, 9.

19. "The Knave," *Oakland Tribune*, quoted in Chandler, *ECV*, 15.

20. Camp and Mood, "George Ezra Dane," 91–93.

21. As will be seen, some interested parties claimed that the plate was discovered in 1933.

22. Von der Porten, Spitze, et al., "Who Made Drake's Plate of Brass?" 122; E Clampus Vitus, *Ye Preposterous Booke of Brasse*, 2.

23. Josephine Hyde to HEB, 8/6/1921, BP In, Drake Association.

24. E Clampus Vitus, *Ye Preposterous Booke of Brasse*, 55.

25. Shinn quoted in Hanna, *Lost Harbor*, 243.

26. Bolton, "Francis Drake's Plate of Brass," 1.

27. Ibid., 1–16; Watson, "Drake and California," 19–24.

28. Undated note; Bill of Sale, 3/3/1937, both BP In, Drake Correspondence.

29. Bolton, "Francis Drake's Plate of Brass," 2.

30. Chickering to Templeton Crocker, 2/23/1937, BP In, Drake Correspondence.

31. The next day, Chickering, the careful lawyer, typed his recollection of the day, A.L.C., "Memorandum," 3/1/1937, BP In, Drake Correspondence.

32. A.L.C., 3/3/1937, BP In, Drake Correspondence.

33. Ibid.

34. Thirteen of the nineteen donors had graduated from the university. Chickering to Sproul, 4/12/1937, BP In, Drake Correspondence.

35. HEB to Sproul, 3/5/1937, BP In, Drake Correspondence.

36. Announcement, California Historical Society Luncheon, 4/6/1937, BP In, Drake Correspondence.

37. "Drake's Plate of Brass," typescript [April 1937], BP In, Drake Correspondence. The published version is Bolton, "Francis Drake's Plate of Brass," also issued separately as "Drake's Plate of Brass," in *Drake's Plate of Brass*.

38. "Drake's Plate of Brass," typescript [April 1937], BP In, Drake Correspondence.

39. Caldeira's statement, taken by Chickering, is in "Personalia and Marginalia," *California Historical Society Quarterly* 16 (June 1937): 192.

40. Edwards "Ned" Metcalf, in conversation with author, 4/15/1993, Huntington Library, San Marino, California.

41. "Interview with William Caldeira," 4/9/1937, BP In, Drake Correspondence; "Drake Plate Theory Upset by Oaklander," *Oakland Tribune*, 4/16/1937, 1, 2.

42. Bolton, "Francis Drake's Plate of Brass."

43. Chickering to Sproul, 5/6/1937, BP In, Drake Correspondence.

44. "The Cross of Saint Thomas and the Plate of Brass, or Parson Fletcher Vindicated," BP In, Drake Correspondence.

45. Quoted from photograph in Von der Porten, Spitze, et al, "Who Made Drake's Plate of Brass?" 125. The authors do not believe that the maker of this plate forged the first one. However, he may have used the same tools and brass stock.

46. ECV, *Ye Preposterous Booke of Brasse*, 9–10.

47. Haselden, "Is the Drake Plate of Brass Genuine?" 271–274.

48. Sproul to HEB, 5/3/1937, BP In, Drake Correspondence.

49. HEB to Sproul, 5/6/1937; Sproul to HEB, 10/29/1937, BP In, Drake Correspondence.

50. This bit of lore is from Peter Blodgett, H. Russell Smith Foundation Curator, Western American Manuscripts, Huntington Library.

51. Haselden, *Scientific Aids*, 4, 61–67.

52. There are hundreds of Drake plate letters in HEH, IA 32.5.11.7.

53. Vincent Harlow to Haselden, 7/22/1937; Robin Flower to Haselden, 9/1/1937, HEH, IA 32.5.11.7. Flower, a British Museum expert, had already responded to an inquiry from Chickering. Flower included a copy of his letter to Chickering in his letter to Haselden.

54. HEB to Haselden, 7/28/1937, HEH-IA.

55. Haselden, "Is the Drake Plate of Brass Genuine?" 274.

56. Chickering, "Some Notes with Regard to Drake's Plate of Brass," 280.

57. Bocqueraz, "Finding of the Drake Plate."

58. Haselden to Caley, 9/16/1937, HEH-IA.

59. Haselden to Sproul, 9/30/1937, HEH-IA.

60. HEB, "Comments on Captain Haselden's Letter of October 16, 1937," BP In, Drake Correspondence.

61. Bolton, "Francis Drake's Plate of Brass," 11.

62. Chickering to Ralph L. Phelps, 4/30/1937, BP In, Drake Correspondence.

63. Sproul to HEB, 10/29/1937, BP In, Drake Correspondence.

64. Ibid.

65. Fink to Hildebrand [November 1937?], BP In, Drake Correspondence.

66. Allen L. Chickering to Hildebrand, 12/3/1937, BP In, Drake Correspondence.

67. Haselden to Caley, 9/25/1937, HEH-IA.

68. Fink to HEB, 3/21/1938; HEB to Fink, 3/26/1937, BP In, Drake Correspondence.

69. HEB to Chickering, 3/26/1938; Chickering to HEB, 3/16/1938, BP In, Drake Correspondence.

70. Chickering to HEB, 5/18/1939, BP In, Drake Correspondence.

71. This and following quotations are from Fink and Polushkin, *Drake's Plate of Brass Authenticated*, 11, 14, 18, 25.

72. Haselden to Sproul, 12/8/1938; Sproul to Haselden, 12/21/1938, HEH-IA.

73. Haselden to Douglas S. Watson, 12/10/1938, HEH-IA.

74. Caley to Haselden, 12/30/1938, HEH-IA.

75. Bolton, "Francis Drake's Plate of Brass," 7.

76. Eli R. Deming to HEB, 4/17/1937, BP In, Drake Correspondence.

77. William A. Hamilton to HEB, 2/7/1939, BP In, Drake Correspondence.

78. "Signed 'Francis Drake,'" BP In, Drake Correspondence.

79. HEB to R. G. Ellis, 6/8/1938, BP In, Drake Correspondence.

CHAPTER 13

1. Hicks et al., "Final Report of the Committee of Ten."

2. Edgar E. Robinson to Dexter Perkins, 12/16/1938, AHA-LC, Box 86, Secretary file, 1935–39.

3. "Financial Aid Given by the American Historical Association to the Pacific Coast Branch," Garver, "History," PCB-LMU.

4. Quoted in ibid. For membership figures, see "Pacific Coast Branch Report," AHA-LC, Box 102, Secretary file, PCB.

5. Thomson to Read, 3/12/1938, AHA-LC, Box 110, Secretary file, PCB.

6. Thompson to Read, 3/21/1938, AHA-LC, Box 86, Secretary file, 1935–39.

7. "Status of the Pacific Coast Branch of the American Historical Association," AHA-LC, Box 110, Secretary file, PCB.

8. Hicks et al., "Final Report of the Committee of Ten."

9. The students were Charles Hackett, Irving B. Leonard, J. Fred Rippy, and Arthur Scott Aiton. HEB to Hull, 9/19/1935, BP Out.

10. Johnson to "Dear Mother" [fall 1935], copy in author's possession.

11. HEB to Sproul, 9/19/1935; HEB to Hull, 10/14/1945, BP Out.

12. HEB to Hull, 9/14/1937, BP Out.

13. HEB to Leonard, 11/1/1938; HEB to Sproul, 11/28/1938, BP Out.

14. HEB to Sproul, 11/26/1938, BP Out.

15. HEB to [Gertrude Janes Bolton?], 12/5/1938, BP Out.

16. Ibid.

17. HEB to Cherrington, 3/14/1939, BP Out.

18. HEB to Leonard, 3/14/1939, BP Out; Dunn to HEB, 4/27/1939, BP In.

19. HEB to Leonard, 3/14/1939, BP Out.

20. HEB to Caughey, 4/7/1939, BP Out.

21. HEB to Cherrington, 4/22/1939; HEB to Willard E. Givens, 8/11/1939, BP Out.

22. HEB to Mood, 9/18/1939, BP Out.

23. DeConde, *A History of American Foreign Policy*, 538–543.

24. HEB to Amelio L. Guerra, 8/10/1939, BP Out.

25. HEB to George F. Gerling, 11/28/1939, BP Out.

26. "Bolton Boss Debunker," newspaper clipping, BP Out, Box 152.

27. Bolton, *Pageant in the Wilderness*.

28. Nussbaum to Preston T. Hutchins, 12/13/1939, BP In, Nussbaum.

29. Nussbaum to Hutchins, 12/13/1939, BP In, Nussbaum.

30. Paxson to HEB, 5/2/1939, BP In.

31. "Annual Salaries, 1931–1940," December 1939, BP Out. Bolton penciled in Kerner's new salary and wrote "2 additional" at the foot of the page.

32. Sproul to HEB, 10/12/1938, BP In, California, University, President.

33. Lerner, "Ernst H. Kantorowicz."

34. Schevill quoted in HEB to Sproul, 6/27/1939, BP Out.

35. Lerner, "Ernst H. Kantorowicz."

36. HEB to Kantorowicz, 7/24/1939, BP Out.

37. HEB to Miss Schieber, 5/8/1920, BP Out.

38. "Reply form," 1920, BP Out (emphasis in original).

39. HEB to Sproul, 4/15/1940, BP Out.

40. Kinnaird, "American Penetration of Spanish Louisiana."

41. HEB to Monroe Deutsch, 8/14/1939, BP Out.

42. HEB to Sproul, 1/9/1940, BP Out. Bolton's recommendation took the form of eight letters to Sproul, all dated 1/9/1940. For convenience I cite them here and below as one communication.

43. Ibid.

44. HEB to Sproul, 4/25/1940, BP Out.

45. Ibid.

46. Ibid.

47. Brucker, May, and Hollinger, *History at Berkeley*, 52; Puryear, Bingham, and Maslenikov, "Robert Joseph Kerner"; Riasanovsky, Feldman, Roseberg, and Segal, "Raymond James Sontag"; Barth, Brown, Hammond, and Strong, "Walton Elbert Bean"; Alden, "Engel Sluiter."

CHAPTER 14

1. HEB to Edward W. Mumford, 2/8/1940, BP Out.

2. Catholic University of America (1929), Saint Mary's College (1929), University of San Francisco (1930), Marquette University (1937). "List of Honorary Degrees," January–February 1950, BP Out. Bolton had also received honorary degrees from the

University of Toronto (1931) and the University of New Mexico (1937), but these were not included in the above-mentioned list. Bannon, *Bolton*, 236.

3. Peter T. Conmy to HEB, 3/19/1940, BP In, Conmy; HEB to Conmy, 4/29/1940, BP Out.

4. Paxson to Allen L. Chickering, 5/14/1940, BP In, Paxson.

5. HEB to Andres Pastoriza, 5/23/1940, BP Out.

6. HEB to Mrs. Boyle Workman, 7/18/1940, BP Out.

7. Bolton, *Coronado*, 427.

8. A detailed account of the trip may be found in Neasham, "Coronado's Trail," November 1941, BP In, Neasham.

9. HEB to Gertrude, 8/19/1940, 8/16/1940, BP Out.

10. HEB to Gertrude, 8/19/1940, BP Out.

11. Ibid.

12. Bolton, *Coronado*, 427; HEB to Neasham, 9/7/1940, BP Out.

13. HEB to Cherrington, 1/28/1941, BP Out.

14. HEB to Gertrude, 1/23/1941; HEB to Cherrington, 1/28/1941, BP Out.

15. HEB to Nettels, 3/5/1941, BP Out.

16. HEB to Gertrude, 3/7/1941, 3/10/1941, 3/14/1941, 3/18, 1941, 3/22/1941, BP Out.

17. HEB to Hillory Tolson, 4/4/1941, BP Out.

18. Dickson to Bolton, 5/14/1941, BP In.

19. [Dickson], "Centennial History of California" [1941?], BP Out. This document is in the front of the first 1941 folder. Though unsigned, it conforms with the ideas that Dickson expressed in other correspondence.

20. HEB to Sproul, 6/13/1941, BP Out.

21. 5/6/1941, BP Out.

22. HEB to Gregory Crampton, 7/15/1941, BP Out.

23. Bolton mistakenly wrote "hitch-hiking" to Rainbow Bridge, in ibid. Cf. "Boat Trip Down the San Juan and Colorado Rivers," BP, Part III, Carton 1, Notes, Santa Fe trip, 1939.

24. HEB to Gregory Crampton, 7/15/1941, BP Out.

25. HEB to Powell, 7/31/1941, BP Out.

26. HEB to Marten Ten Hoor, 4/2/1941, BP Out; Borah to HEB, 10/15/1941, BP In.

27. HEB to Claudius O. Johnson, 11/6/1941, 12/22/1941, BP Out.

28. [HEB], "Charles Edward Chapman," BP In, Chapman. This appears to be a eulogy that Bolton read to the Native Sons.

29. Bannon, in *Bolton*, 218, claims it was a stroke. Bolton, writing at the time, described Priestley's illness as "heart trouble." HEB to Claudius O. Johnson, 12/22/1941, BP Out.

30. HEB to Claudius O. Johnson, 12/22/1941, BP Out.

31. HEB to Mrs. Alvin Bolton, 2/7/1942, BP Out.

32. Lawrence Kinnaird, Frederic L. Paxson, and Lesley Byrd Simpson, "Herbert Ingram Priestley," *In Memoriam*, 1944, BP In, Priestley.

33. HEB to Sproul, 3/12/1942, BP Out.

34. Dickson to HEB, 12/13/1941, BP In.

35. Dickson to Sproul, 12/26/1941, BP In, Dickson.

36. HEB to Sproul [1942], BP Out. This draft may not have been sent to Sproul.

37. HEB to Rippy, 3/25/1942, BP Out. This is a "Rough draft much revised," as indicated in the margin.

38. HEB to Rippy, 9/4/1942, BP Out.

39. Rippy to HEB, 9/7/1942, BP In; HEB, "Rippy" [9/1942?], BP Out.

40. Dickson to HEB, 1/19/1942; Dickson to James Corley, 2/17/1942, BP In.

41. Dickson to HEB, 1/19/1942, BP In.

42. HEB to Sproul, 4/1/1942, BP Out.

43. HEB to Sproul, 2/18/1942, BP Out.

44. HEB to Dickson, 4/18/1942, BP Out.

45. Chappell to D. G. Maclise, 5/26/1942, BP Out.

46. HEB to Dickson, 7/31/1942, BP Out.

47. Dickson to HEB, 9/8/1942, BP In.

48. O'Brien to HEB, 5/16/1942, 12/23/1943, BP In, Serra Cause.

49. O'Brien to HEB, 3/27/1947, BP In, Serra Cause.

50. HEB to Dickson, 10/23/1942, BP Out.

51. "Confidential; A Meeting of the Committee on the Centennial History," 10/9/1942, BP In, Dickson.

52. HEB to Dickson, 10/23/1942; HEB to Sproul, 10/23/1942, BP Out.

53. Dickson to HEB, 10/26/1942, BP In.

54. HEB to Dickson, 11/10/1942, BP Out.

55. Dickson to HEB, 5/18/1943, BP In.

56. Dickson to HEB, 2/2/1945, BP In.

57. HEB to Sproul, 5/6/1943, BP Out.

58. HEB to Sproul, 6/28/1943, BP Out.

59. HEB to Sproul, 9/16/1943, BP Out.

60. Borah, Elberg, and Parsons, "James Ferguson King."

61. "Report of the of the Executive Secretary on the Activities of the American Historical Association," AHA-LC, Box 132, Executive Committee Reports.

62. Edgar B. Wesley to Ford, 4/15/1943; Ford to Wesley, 5/1/1943; Edgar E. Robinson to Ford, 5/5/1943; Ford to Robinson, 5/10/1943; Arthur M. Schlesinger to Ford, 5/7/1943; Ford to Schlesinger, 5/10/1943, all in AHA-LC, Box 141, Committee on History Teaching.

63. There is no direct evidence that Jones and Bolton knew each other, but they were undergraduates at Wisconsin at the same time.

64. Jones to Ford, 7/9/1943, AHA-LC, Box 141, Committee on History Teaching.

65. Bessie Louise Pierce, "Adjustment of the College Curriculum to Wartime Conditions and Needs," enclosure, Fred J. Kelly, memo, "Reports on Adjustment of the College Curriculum to Wartime Conditions and Needs," n.d., AHA-LC, Box 141, Committee on History Teaching.

66. Ibid.

67. Robinson, "Statement of the Problem," in "Stanford Conference of California College and University Teachers of American History," 8/27–28/1943, AHA-LC, Box 141, Committee on History Teaching.

68. "Stanford Conference of California College and University Teachers of American History," 8/27–28/1943, AHA-LC, Box 141, Committee on History Teaching.

69. Truett, "Epics of Greater America," 234. The course analysis was compiled by Stanford's Thomas A. Bailey.

70. "Stanford Conference of Junior College Teachers of American History," 8/27–28/1943, AHA-LC, Box 141, Committee on History Teaching.

71. Paxson to Professor Guttridge et al., 7/7/1944, BP In, Paxson.

72. Ibid.

73. Hicks, *My Life with History*, 280.

74. Magnaghi, *Bolton and the Historiography of the Americas*, 124–126.

CHAPTER 15

1. Bannon, *Bolton*, 222.

2. "We don't teach much by preachment. We teach best by infection. We have to have the bug ourselves. When the bug gets sick our ability to teach declines. When the bug dies the teacher is dead, even though he may still occupy the platform and draw his pay. To teach we have to have a live healthy bug. Even discipline for its own sake usually shoots under the mark." "Dicho" [1944], BP Out.

3. Mrs. Donald Cutter, interview with author, August 3, 2002, Tucson.

4. HEB to P. B. Fay, 8/1/1944, BP Out.

5. HEB to Mrs. Herbert Hamlin, 12/1/1944; HEB to Lewis Wetzlar, 12/1/1944, BP Out.

6. HEB to Sproul, 4/18/1944, BP Out.

7. HEB to Aubrey Drury, 1/27/1944, BP Out; HEB to Hackett, 5/15/1944, BP Out; M. R. Tillotson to HEB, 6/6/1944, BP In, U.S. National Park Service.

8. HEB to Geiger, 1/27/1944, BP Out.

9. HEB to William L. Schurz, 6/8/1944; HEB to Herschel Brickell, 10/17/1944, BP Out.

10. HEB to Hammond, 2/2/1945, BP Out; Hammond to HEB, 3/7/1945, BP In.

11. Hammond to HEB, 9/22/1945, BP In.

12. HEB to E. B. Fred, 4/16/1945, 6/2/1945, BP Out.

13. Berkeley: University of California Press, 1945.

14. Ogden, Sluiter, and Crampton, *Greater America*, iv; Bannon, *Bolton*, 249.

15. "Dr. Bolton Is Honored at Banquet," *San Francisco Chronicle*, 12/31/1945, "Metropolis" section, p. 9, clipping, BP Out.

16. Borah to HEB, 3/29/1946, BP In.

17. HEB to A. R. Davis, 8/3/1948, BP Out. See also HEB to W. O. Aydelotte, 7/26/1948, BP Out.

18. Borah to HEB, 8/24/1948, BP In; Brucker, May, and Hollinger, *History at Berkeley*, 53.

19. HEB to Florence Escott, 5/2/1946, BP Out.

20. Pan-Americanism, n.d., 1947, BP Out.

21. Caughey to Robert J. Kerner, 8/30/1946, BP In, Caughey.

22. HEB to Caughey, 6/17/1947, BP Out.

23. Chronicles of California [1947]; HEB to Samuel T. Farquhar, 6/17/1947, BP Out.

24. MA thesis, University of California, Berkeley, 1947.

25. Wiley, "Jedediah Smith and the West"; Aurora Hunt, "U.S. Sentries on the Western Frontier."

26. Caughey to HEB, 6/21/1947, BP In, Caughey.

27. HEB to Farquhar, 6/21/1947, BP Out.

28. HEB to Farquhar, 6/17/1947, BP Out.

29. HEB to Farquhar, 6/21/1947, BP Out.

30. HEB to Farquhar, 7/21/1947, BP Out.

31. HEB to Caughey, 7/22/1947, 8/6/1946, BP Out.

32. Caughey to HEB, 10/10/1948, BP In, Caughey.

33. HEB to Paul Brooks, 6/24/1946; HEB to Edward C. Aswell, 6/25/1946, BP Out.

34. Bannon, *Bolton*, 231; HEB to William E. Larned, 8/8/1947, BP Out; newspaper clipping, 11/13/1948, BP Out.

35. HEB to Anderson, 2/10/1940, BP Out.

36. HEB to Harvey, 11/10/1947, BP Out.

37. HEB to Larned, 9/16/1947, BP Out.

38. HEB to Anderson, 5/14/1948; HEB to Larned, 5/14/1948; HEB to Harvey, 7/8/1948, BP Out.

39. Estimated Income, 1950, BP Out.

40. "New World," *Time*, 12/5/1949, 108–109.

41. HEB to Eisenhower, 8/30/1950, BP Out.

42. Bolton, *Coronado,* vii. The small maps are at p. 412.

43. Ibid., x, 139.

44. Ibid., 413–422, quotation at 414.

45. HEB to Howard J. Savage, 1/12/1948, BP Out; Bannon, *Bolton,* 242.

46. HEB to Howard J. Savage, 1/12/1948, BP Out.

47. Application for Travel Expenses, 3/14/1947, BP Out; Bannon, *Bolton,* 232.

48. HEB to John J. Van Nostrand, 11/13/1951, BP Out.

49. Estimated Income, 1950, BP Out.

50. Geiger, "Beatification of Fray Junípero Serra."

51. Sandos, "Junípero Serra's Canonization."

52. O'Brien to HEB, 12/7/1948, BP, Part III, Serra Cause, Bibliography.

53. O'Brien to HEB, 1/20/1949, 3/27/1950, BP In, Serra Cause.

54. O'Brien to HEB, 2/21/1949, BP In, Serra Cause.

55. Draft, "The Confessions of a Wayward Professor," 1949, BP Out, published in *Americas* 6 (January 1950), 359–362.

56. Questions 1 and 2, 1948, BP Out.

57. Sandos, "Junípero Serra's Canonization," 1260; Costo and Costo, eds., *The Missions of California.*

58. Collected and republished as Cook, *The Conflict between the California Indian and White Civilization.*

59. Hurtado, "California Indian Demography, Sherburne F. Cook, and the Revision of American History"; Jacobs, "Sherburne Friend Cook: Rebel-Revisionist."

60. McWilliams, *Southern California Country,* 29, 30.

61. Borah to HEB, 2/4/1939, 6/28/1939, BP In.

62. Bolton and Marshall, *The Colonization of North America,* 22.

63. Cook's estimate of the population of California Indians in 1769 increased over time from 135,000 to 310,000. See Cook, *The Population of the California Indians.* The debate about Indian population decline continues. See, for example, Denevan, *The Native Population of the Americas in 1492;* Thornton, *American Indian Holocaust and Survival;* Thomas, *Columbian Consequences,* vol. 1.

64. Sandos, "Junípero Serra's Canonization."

CHAPTER 16

1. Unless otherwise noted, the discussion of the loyalty oath controversy is drawn from Gardner, *The California Oath Controversy,* 1–47.

2. Kerr, 9/29/1969, quoted in "The Loyalty Oath Controversy," Regional Oral History Office, BL, http://bancroft.berkeley.edu/ROHO.

3. Dickson quoted in Gardner, *The California Oath Controversy,* 260.

4. The statement is cited in full in ibid., 34–36.

5. Dickson to Ehrman, 4/14/1950, John Francis Neylan Papers, Banc Mss C-B 881, Box 177: 1950 #2, BL (available online in the California Loyalty Oath Digital Collection).

6. Kerr, 9/29/1969, quoted in "The Loyalty Oath Controversy," Regional Oral History Office, BL, http://bancroft.berkeley.edu/ROHO.

7. G. Stewart, *The Year of the Oath*, 9.

8. In the 1970s Powell served on my doctoral committee at Santa Barbara, where graduate students characterized him as pro-Franco, a fascist, and a phalangist among other things. They perhaps overstated the case, but he was certainly situated on the right wing of the political spectrum, according to his niece, Mary Alice Pisani.

9. Powell to Billington, 2/12/1951, MVHA, 1948–1960, BiP.

10. Caughey to Billington, 1/7/1951, MVHA, 1948–1960, BiP. Caughey's *Indians of Southern California in 1852* was the result of his fellowship at the Huntington Library.

11. Caughey to Billington, 2/20/1951; Caughey to Ralph Bieber, 3/27/1951; "Resolution proposed to the MVHA," all in MVHA, 1948–1960, BiP.

12. Hicks, *My Life with History*, 282–287.

13. Halberstam, *The Coldest Winter*, 175, 191–192, 384–386.

14. Quoted in Gardner, *The California Oath Controversy*, 158.

15. Conmy to HEB, 9/21/1950, BP In, Conmy.

16. Ibid.

17. Conmy's record is reconstructed from Conmy to HEB, 8/25/1929, 3/2/1939, and 9/21/1950, BP In, Conmy.

18. HEB to Hammond, 1/14/1949; "To Whom It May Concern," 11/4/1950, BP Out.

19. Notes [1949?], BP Out.

20. HEB to Albright, 3/?/1949, BP Out. See also HEB to Birge, 3/11/1949; HEB to Waldo Leland, 3/21/1949, both in BP Out.

21. HEB to Waldo Leland, 3/21/1949; HEB to "Dear Guy" [Ford], [1949], BP Out.

22. Howard M. Houseal, 11/14/1950, BP In, Contra Costa Junior College.

23. HEB to Ehrman, 2/23/1950, BP Out.

24. HEB to Joel B. Ricks, 5/8/1950, BP Out.

25. HEB to A. R. Mortensen, 10/17/1950, BP Out.

26. "In Memoriam: Charles Wilson Hackett," www.utexas.edu/faculty/council/2000–2001/memorials/SCANNED/hackett.pdf; Bannon, *Bolton*, 250.

27. HEB, "Charles Wilson Hackett," n.d., 1951, BP In, Hackett.

28. *San Francisco Chronicle*, 3/16/1951, p. 1, col. 6; "Local Matron Leaps from Gate Bridge," *Berkeley Daily Gazette*, 3/15/1951, p. 1, col. 7.

29. Bolton, *Pageant*, 1; quotation at 3.

30. Ibid., 2.

31. Ibid., 124.

32. Blackhawk, *Violence over the Land;* Brooks, *Captives and Cousins.*

33. Bolton, *Pageant,* 3.

34. Thomas Johnson, email to author, 5/12/2011.

35. HEB to Lewis F. Haines, 7/12/1951, 8/15/1951, BP Out.

36. Jacobs, "'Turner as I Remember Him.'"

37. Ibid., 58–59.

38. Jacobs, personal conversation with author, 1998.

39. Jacobs, "'Turner as I Remember Him,'" 54.

40. HEB to Robert J. Drake, 8/31/1951, BP Out.

41. HEB to James W. Gallagher, 11/13/1951, BP Out.

42. HEB to Chickering, 1/8/1952, BP Out.

43. Bannon, *Bolton,* 250; HEB to Frederick, 9/13/1901, BFP.

44. Quinan, "In Memoriam," 2/12/1953, BP Out.

45. Albright to HEB, 8/31/1952, BP In.

46. Thickens to Bannon, 8/26/1952, BP Out.

47. Bannon, *Bolton,* 250.

48. "Prof. Bolton, U.C. Historian, Taken by Death," *Oakland Tribune,* 1/30/1953, p. 1, col. 10.

49. "Private Funeral Monday for Dr. Herbert Bolton," *San Francisco Chronicle,* 1/31/1953, p. 4, col. 1.

50. "Prof. Bolton, U.C. Historian, Taken by Death," *San Francisco Chronicle,* 1/30/1953, p. 1, p. 10, col. 4.

51. "Friends Who Called," n.d., 1953, BP Out.

52. Quinan, "In Memoriam," 2/12/1953, BP Out.

AFTERWORD

1. Bolton, "Defensive Spanish Expansion," in Bannon, *Bolton and the Borderlands,* 42.

2. Morison, "Faith of a Historian," 274.

3. HEB to Morison, 2/15/1951, BP Out.

4. Morison, "Faith of a Historian," 273.

5. Ibid., 270–271; quote at 271. Morison was also warning historians away from dialectical materialism and communism.

BIBLIOGRAPHY

A NOTE ON THE BOLTON PAPERS

The Herbert E. Bolton Papers (C-B 840) is a large three-part collection at the Bancroft Library. Part I consists of historical documents that Bolton collected in Mexico and elsewhere. Bolton's voluminous correspondence constitutes Part II. Part III consists of materials related to Bolton's myriad professional activities—syllabi, lecture notes, book and article drafts, news clippings, photographs, and miscellany. Excellent finding aids for all three parts are available on the Bancroft website. Unless otherwise noted, in the present work BP In and BP Out refer to Part II. BP Out is arranged chronologically by year. In cases where the year is known but the month and day are not, such items are placed at the beginning of the year. BP In is arranged alphabetically by the correspondent's last name and chronologically within that file. There are files for institutions, such as the Native Sons of the Golden West and National Park Service. In some cases (e.g., the Serra Cause) there are materials in Parts II and III.

The Bolton Family Papers (C-B 841), also at the Bancroft, is another important collection of letters, from Herbert to his brother Frederick. It is the best source of information about Bolton before he joined the Berkeley faculty. Because the brothers were both academics, their letters reveal some of the details of their professional lives as well as personal matters.

UNPUBLISHED SOURCES

Bancroft Library, University of California, Berkeley

Hubert Howe Bancroft Collection.

Herbert Eugene Bolton Papers, C-B 840.

Herbert Eugene Bolton Jr. "My Most Unforgettable Character," MSS C-2 190.

Bolton Family Papers, C-B 841.

Leon Bocqueraz. "Finding of the Drake Plate," MSS C-D 4008A.

Alfred Louis Kroeber Correspondence and Papers.

Irene D. Paden. "Dr. Bolton as I Knew Him," MSS C-D 5035:5.

Frank C. Lockwood. "Correspondence Concerning Herbert E. Bolton," MSS 5064.

H. Morse Stephens Papers, C-B 926.

Academy of Pacific Coast History (Hubert Howe Bancroft Collection).

California Room, State Library, Sacramento, California

Great Register.

California State Archives, Sacramento

Records of the Supreme Court of California.

Department of Archives and History, Atlanta, Georgia

"On Wisdom's Trail." Papers of Herbert Eugene Bolton. Mary Leticia Ross Papers.

Henry E. Huntington Library, San Marino, California

Ray A. Billington Papers.

Max Farrand Collection.

Frederick Jackson Turner Collection.

Institutional Archives, 32.5.11.7 (Drake Plate Correspondence).

Manuscript 27057 (HEB to Sanford B. Dole, 4/7/1900).

Library of Congress, Washington, D.C.

Papers of the American Historical Association.

J. Franklin Jameson Papers.

Charles Van der Ahe Library, Loyola Marymount University, Los Angeles

Papers of the Pacific Coast Branch of the American Historical Association.

Pan American University–Pan American Archives, Edinburg, Texas

Alfred B. Thomas Papers.

University of Oklahoma, Norman

Evans Hall, Administration.

Personnel Files, Alfred B. Thomas.

WORKS BY BOLTON

1900

"Our Nation's First Boundaries." *The Western Teacher* 9 (October 1900): 64–67.

1902

"De Los Mapas." *Texas State Historical Association Quarterly* 6 (July 1902): 69–70.

"Some Materials for Southwestern History in the Archivo General de México." *Texas State Historical Association Quarterly* 6 (October 1902): 103–112; 7 (January 1904): 196–213.

1903

"Tienda de Cuervo's Ynspección of Laredo, 1757." *Texas State Historical Association Quarterly* 7 (January 1903): 187–203.

Trans. "'Affairs in the Philipinas Islands, by Fray Domingo de Salazar." In *The Philippine Islands, 1493–1803*, edited by Emma Helen Blair and James Alexander Robertson, vol. 5, 210–255. 55 vols. Cleveland: Arthur H. Clark Company, 1903–1909.

Trans. "Two Letters to Felipe II." In *The Philippine Islands, 1493–1803*, edited by Emma Helen Blair and James Alexander Robertson, vol. 6, 76–80. 55 vols. Cleveland: Arthur H. Clark Company, 1903–1909.

1904

With Eugene C. Barker. *With the Makers of Texas: A Source Reader in Texas History.* New York: American Book Company, 1904.

Trans. "Trade between Nueva España and the Far East. In *The Philippine Islands, 1493–1803*, edited by Emma Helen Blair and James Alexander Robertson, vol. 18, 57–64. 55 vols. Cleveland: Arthur H. Clark Company, 1903–1909.

Trans. "Events in the Filipinas Islands, from the Month of June 1617, until the Present Date in 1618." In *The Philippine Islands, 1493–1803*, edited by Emma Helen Blair and James Alexander Robertson, vol. 18, 65–92. 55 vols. Cleveland: Arthur H. Clark Company, 1903–1909.

Trans. "Description of the Philippinas Islands." In *The Philippine Islands, 1493–1803*, edited by Emma Helen Blair and James Alexander Robertson, vol. 18, 93–106. 55 vols. Cleveland: Arthur H. Clark Company, 1903–1909.

Trans. "Relation of the Events in the Filipinas Islands and in the Neighboring Provinces and Realms, from July, 1618, to the Present Date in 1619." In *The Philippine Islands, 1493–1803*, edited by Emma Helen Blair and James Alexander Robertson, vol. 18, 204–234. 55 vols. Cleveland: Arthur H. Clark Company, 1903–1909.

Trans. "Letter from Francisco de Otaço, S.J., to Father Alonso de Escovar." In *The Philippine Islands, 1493–1803*, edited by Emma Helen Blair and James Alexander Robertson, vol. 19, 35–39. 55 vols. Cleveland: Arthur H. Clark Company, 1903–1909.

Trans. Relation of Events in the Philippinas Islands and Neighboring Provinces and Kingdoms, from July, 1619, to July, 1620." In *The Philippine Islands, 1493–1803*, edited by Emma Helen Blair and James Alexander Robertson, vol. 19, 42–70. 55 vols. Cleveland: Arthur H. Clark Company, 1903–1909.

1905

"Practical Suggestions Concerning the Organization of Historical Materials in High School Work." *Texas School Journal* (March 1905): 1–7.

"The Spanish Abandonment and Re-occupation of East Texas, 1773–1779." *Texas State Historical Association Quarterly* 9 (October 1905): 67–137.

1906

"The Founding of Mission Rosario: A Chapter in the History of the Gulf Coast." *Texas State Historical Association Quarterly* 10 (October 1906): 113–139.

"Massanet or Manzanet." *Texas State Historical Association Quarterly* 10 (July 1906): 101.

"The Old Stone Fort at Nacogdoches." *Texas State Historical Association Quarterly* 10 (April 1906): 283–285.

1907

"Spanish Mission Records at San Antonio." *Texas State Historical Association Quarterly* 10 (April 1907): 297–307.

1908

"Material for Southwestern History in the Central Archives of Mexico." *AHR* 13 (April 1908): 510–527.

"The Native Tribes from the East Texas Mission." *Texas State Historical Association Quarterly* 11 (April 1908): 249–276.

"Notes on Clark's 'The Beginnings of Texas.'" *Texas State Historical Association Quarterly* 12 (October 1908): 148–158.

Ed. "Papers of Zebulon M. Pike, 1806–1807." *AHR* 13 (July 1908): 798–827.

1909

"Portola's Letters Found." *San Francisco Call*, October 17, 1909.

1910

"Records of the Mission Nuestra Señora del Refugio." *Texas State Historical Association Quarterly* 14 (October 1910): 164–166.

More than 100 articles on Indian tribes in Texas and Louisiana. *Handbook of Indians North of Mexico*, edited by Frederick Webb Hodge. 2 Pts. Smithsonian Institution, Bureau of American Ethnology, Bulletin 30. Washington, D.C.: Government Printing Office, 1907–1910.

1911

Trans. and ed. "Expedition to San Francisco Bay in 1770: Diary of Pedro Fages." Academy of Pacific Coast History, *Publications* 2 (July 1911): 141–159.

"Father Kino's Lost History, Its Discovery and Its Value." Bibliographical Society of America, *Papers* 6 (1911): 9–34.

"The Jumano Indians in Texas, 1650–1771." *Texas State Historical Association Quarterly* 15 (July 1911): 66–84.

1912

"The Obligation of Nevada toward the Writing of Her Own History." Nevada Historical Society, *Third Biennial Report . . . 1911–1912* (1913): 62–79.

"The Spanish Occupation of Texas, 1519–1690." *Texas State Historical Association Quarterly* 16 (July 1912): 1–26.

1913

Guide to the Materials for the History of the United States in the Principal Archives of Mexico. Washington, D.C.: Carnegie Institution of Washington, 1913.

"The Admission of California." *University of California Chronicle* 15 (October 1913): 554–566.

"Spanish Activities on the Lower Trinity River, 1746–1771." *Texas State Historical Association Quarterly* 16 (April 1913): 339–377.

"New Light on Manuel Lisa and the Spanish Fur Trade." *Texas State Historical Association Quarterly* 17 (July 1913): 61–66.

1914

Athanase de Mézières and the Louisiana-Texas Frontier, 1768–1780. 2 vols. Cleveland: Arthur H. Clark Company, 1914.

"The Founding of the Missions on the San Gabriel River." *Texas State Historical Association Quarterly* 17 (April 1914): 323–378.

"Mexico, Diplomatic Relations with." In *Cyclopedia of American Government*, edited by Andrew Cunningham McLaughlin and Albert Bushnell Hart, vol. 2, 422–425. 3 vols. New York: Appleton, 1914.

1915

Texas in the Middle Eighteenth Century: Studies in Spanish Colonial History and Administration. Berkeley: University of California Press, 1915.

"The Location of La Salle's Colony on the Gulf of Mexico." *Mississippi Valley Historical Review* 2 (September 1915): 165–182. Also in *Texas State Historical Association Quarterly* 27 (January 1924): 171–189.

1916

Ed. *Spanish Exploration in the Southwest*. New York: Scribner's, 1916.

"The Beginnings of Mission Nuestra Señora de Refugio." *Texas State Historical Association Quarterly* 19 (April 1916): 400–404.

"The Writing of California History." *Grizzly Bear* 19 (May 1916): 4.

1917

Trans. and ed. "Explorers' Visits to San Diego Bay Told of in Diaries." *San Diego Union*, January 1, 1917.

"The Explorations of Father Garcés on the Pacific Slope." In *The Pacific Ocean in History*, edited by Henry Morse Stephens and Herbert E. Bolton, 317–330. New York: Macmillan, 1917.

"French Intrusions in New Mexico, 1749–1752." In *The Pacific Ocean in History*, edited by Henry Morse Stephens and Herbert E. Bolton, 389–407. New York: Macmillan, 1917.

"The Mission as a Frontier Institution in the Spanish-American Colonies." *AHR* 23 (October 1917): 42–61.

"The Spanish Mission in California: Their Relation to the General Colonial Policy." *Oakland Tribune*, April 22, 1917.

1918

"Cabrillo and Vizcaíno Visit Catalina Island, 1542–1602." *The Islander* (Avalon, Santa Catalina Island, California), July 16, 1918.

Ed. "General James Wilkinson as Advisor to Emperor Iturbide." *Hispanic American Historical Review* 1 (May 1918): 163–180.

1919

Ed. *Kino's Historical Memoir of Pimería Alta: A Contemporary Account of the Beginnings of California, Sonora, and Arizona by Father Eusebio Francisco Kino, S.J., Pioneer Missionary, Explorer, Cartographer, and Ranchman, 1683–1711.* 2 vols. Cleveland: Arthur H. Clark Company, 1919.

Trans. and ed. "Father Escobar's Relation of the Oñate Expedition to California." *Catholic Historical Review* 5 (April 1919): 19–41.

Ed. "The Iturbide Revolution in the Californias." *Hispanic American Historical Review* 2 (May 1919): 188–242.

1920

With Thomas Maitland Marshall. *The Colonization of North America, 1492–1783.* New York: Macmillan, 1920.

"The Old Spanish Fort on Red River." *Daily Oklahoman* (Oklahoma City), April 11, 1920.

1921

The Spanish Borderlands: A Chronicle of Old Florida and the Southwest. The Chronicles of America Series, vol. 23. New Haven: Yale University Press, 1921.

1922

With Ephraim Douglass Adams. *California's Story.* Boston: Allyn and Bacon, 1922.

1924

"An Introductory Course in American History." *Historical Outlook* 15 (January 1924): 17–20.

1925

Arredondo's Historical Proof of Spain's Title to Georgia: A Contribution to the History of One of the Spanish Borderlands. Berkeley: University of California Press, 1925.

With Mary Ross. *The Debatable Land: A Sketch of the Anglo-Spanish Contest for the Georgia Country.* Berkeley: University of California Press, 1925.

"The Mormons in the Opening of the West." *Deseret News* (Salt Lake City), October 24, 31, November 14, 25, 1925. Also in *Utah Genealogical and Historical Magazine* 16 (January 1926): 40–72.

"Spanish Resistance to the Carolina Traders in Western Georgia, 1680–1704." *Georgia Historical Quarterly* 9 (June 1925): 115–130.

1926

Ed. *Historical Memoirs of New California, by Fray Francisco Palóu, O.F.M.* 4 vols. Berkeley: University of California Press, 1926.

Palóu and His Writings. Berkeley: University of California Press, 1926.

"José Francisco Ortega." *Grizzly Bear* 38 (January 1926): 1.

1927

Ed. *Fray Juan Crespi, Missionary Explorer on the Pacific Coast, 1769–1774.* Berkeley: University of California Press, 1927.

A Pacific Coast Pioneer. Berkeley: University of California Press, 1927.

"Juan Crespi, a California Xenophon." *Touring Topics* 19 (July 1927): 23, 48.

1928

History of the Americas: A Syllabus with Maps. Boston: Ginn, 1928. New edition, 1935.

"Escalante in Dixie and the Arizona Strip." *New Mexico Historical Review* 3 (January 1928): 41–72.

"Cabrillo, Juan Rodríguez," "López de Cardenas, García," "Coronado, Francisco Vázquez," "Crespi, Juan," "Kino, Eusebio Francisco," "de Mézières y Clugny," and "Palóu, Francisco." In *Dictionary of American Biography.* 20 vols. New York: Scribner's, 1928–1936.

1930

Ed. *Anza's California Expeditions.* 5 vols. Berkeley: University of California Press, 1930.

"Defensive Spanish Expansion and the Significance of the Borderlands." In *The Trans-Mississippi West: Papers Read at a Conference Held at the University of Colorado, June 18–June 21, 1929,* edited by James Field Willard and Colin Brummitt Goodykoontz, 1–42. Boulder: University of Colorado, 1930.

1931

Ed. *Font's Complete Diary: A Chronicle of the Founding of San Francisco.* Berkeley: University of California Press, 1931.

Outpost of Empire: The Story of the Founding of San Francisco. New York: Alfred A. Knopf, 1931.

"Anza Crosses the Sand Dunes." *Touring Topics* 23 (May 1931): 7.

"The Capitulation at Cahuenga." *Touring Topics* 23 (November 1931): 7.

"Coming of the Cattle." *Touring Topics* 23 (March 1931): 7.

"Coronado Discovers Zuñi." *Touring Topics* 23 (January 1931): 8.

"The Founding of San Diego Mission." *Touring Topics* 23 (April 1931): 7.

"Fremont Crosses the Sierra." *Touring Topics* 23 (October 1931): 7.

"Gold Discovered at Sutter's Mill." *Touring Topics* 23 (December 1931): 9.

"Jedediah Smith Reaches San Gabriel." *Touring Topics* 23 (June 1931): 7.

"Oñate in New Mexico." *Touring Topics* 23 (February 1931): 8.

"Trapper Days in Taos." *Touring Topics* 23 (July 1931): 7.

"In the South San Joaquin Ahead of Garcés." *California Historical Society Quarterly* 10 (September 1931): 211–219.

1932

The Padre on Horseback: A Sketch of Eusebio Francisco Kino, S.J., Apostle to the Pimas. San Francisco: Sonora Press, 1932.

1933

"The Epic of Greater America." *AHR* 38 (April 1933): 448–474.

1934

"Pack Train and Carreta." *California Monthly* 33 (November 1934): 4, 6.

1935

"The Black Robes of New Spain." *Catholic Historical Review* 21 (October 1935): 257–282.

1936

Cross, Sword and Gold Pan. Los Angeles: Primavera Press, 1935.

Rim of Christendom: A Biography of Eusebio Francisco Kino, Pacific Coast Pioneer. New York: Macmillan, 1936.

"Archives and Trails." *California Monthly* 37 (October 1936): 19, 40–42.

"The Jesuits in America: An Opportunity for Historians." *Mid-America* 18 (October 1936): 223–233.

1937

"Francis Drake's Plate of Brass." In *Drake's Plate of Brass: Evidence of His Visit to California in 1579*, 1–42. Special Publication No. 13. San Francisco: California Historical Society, 1937. Reprinted in *California Historical Society Quarterly* 16 (March 1937): 1–16.

1939

Wider Horizons of American History. New York: Appleton-Century, 1939.

"Escalante Way—An Opportunity for the National Park Service." In *American Planning and Civic Annual,* edited by Harlean James, 266–273. Washington, D.C.: American Planning and Civic Association, 1939.

1940

"Cultural Coöperation with Latin America." *National Education Association Journal* 29 (January 1940): 1–4.

"Alta California," "California, Russians in," "California, Spanish Exploration of," "California Missions," "California under Mexico," and "California under Spain." In *Dictionary of American History.* 6 vols. New York: Scribner's, 1940.

1949

Coronado, Knight of Pueblos and Plains. New York: Whittlesey House, 1949.

Coronado on the Turquoise Trail, Knight of Pueblos and Plains. Coronado Cuatro Centennial Publications, edited by George P. Hammond, vol. 1. Albuquerque: University of New Mexico Press, 1940.

1950

"The Confessions of a Wayward Professor." *The Americas* 6 (January 1950): 359–362.

Pageant in the Wilderness: The Story of the Escalante Expedition to the Interior Basin, Including the Diary and Itinerary of Father Escalante. Salt Lake City: Utah State Historical Society, 1950.

1964

Bolton and the Spanish Borderlands, edited by John Francis Bannon. Norman: University of Oklahoma Press, 1964.

1987

The Hasinais: Southern Caddoans As Seen by the Earliest Europeans, edited by Russell Magnaghi. Norman: University of Oklahoma Press, 1987.

WORKS ABOUT BOLTON AND HIS WORK

Almaráz, Félix. "The Making of a Boltonian: Carlos E. Castaneda of Texas—The Early Years." *Red River Valley Historical Review* 1 (Winter 1974): 329–350.

Bannon, John Francis. "Herbert Eugene Bolton: His *Guide* in the Making." *Southwestern Historical Quarterly* 73, no. 1 (1969): 35–55.

———. *Herbert Eugene Bolton: The Historian and the Man.* Tucson: University of Arizona Press, 1978.

Bolton, Frederick E. "Random Memories of an Admiring Brother." *Arizona and the West* 4, no. 1 (1962): 72.

Caughey, John W. "Herbert Eugene Bolton." In *Turner, Bolton, and Webb: Three Historians of the American Frontier,* edited by Wilbur R. Jacobs, John W. Caughey and Joe B. Frantz, 41–74. Seattle: University of Washington Press, 1965.

Cummins, Light T. "Getting beyond Bolton: *Columbian Consequences* and the Spanish Borderlands, a Review Essay." *New Mexico Historical Review* 70 (1995): 201–215.

Cummins, Victoria H., and Light T. Cummins. "Building on Bolton: *The Spanish Borderlands* Seventy-Five Years Later." *Latin American Research Review* 35 (2000): 230–243.

Delpar, Helen. *Looking South: The Evolution of Latin Americanist Scholarship in the United States, 1850–1975.* Tuscaloosa: University of Alabama Press, 2008.

Dunn, William Edward. Review of *Texas in the Middle Eighteenth Century,* by Herbert E. Bolton. *Southwestern Historical Quarterly* 20 (July 1916): 96–100.

Emery, Edwin. "Bolton of California." *California Monthly* (September 1941): 12–13, 39–43.

Escudero, Carlos R. "Historian in Action." *California Monthly* (September 1941): 14–16, 43–44.

Friend, Llerena B. "Herbert Eugene Bolton and the Texas State Library." *Texas Libraries* 35 (Summer 1973): 48–64.

Gilbert, Hope. "He Followed the Trails of the Desert Padres." *Desert Magazine* (July 1950): 27–31.

Gutiérrez, Ramón A., and Elliott Young. "Transnationalizing Borderlands History." *Western Historical Quarterly* 41 (Spring 2010): 27–53.

Haines, Francis. "Go Write a Book: Nez Perce, Horses, and History." *Western Historical Quarterly* 4 (April 1973): 124–131.

Hammond, George P., ed. *New Spain and the Anglo-American West: Historical Contributions Presented to Herbert Eugene Bolton.* 2 vols. Lancaster, Pa.: Lancaster Press, 1932.

————. "In Memoriam: Herbert Eugene Bolton, 1870–1953." *The Americas* 9 (April 1953): 391–398.

Hanke, Lewis, ed. *Do the Americas Have a Common History: A Critique of the Bolton Theory*. New York: Alfred A. Knopf, 1964.

Holmes, Jack D. L. "Interpretations and Trends in the Study of the Spanish Borderlands: The Old Southwest." *Southwestern Historical Quarterly* 74 (1971): 461–477.

Hurtado, Albert L. "Herbert E. Bolton, Racism, and American History." *Pacific Historical Review* 62 (May 1993): 127–142.

————. "Parkmanizing the Spanish Borderlands: Bolton, Turner, and the Historians' World." *Western Historical Quarterly* 26 (Summer 1995): 149–167.

————. "More Shadows on the Brass: Herbert E. Bolton and the Fake Drake Plate." In *Frontier and Region: Essays in Honor of Martin Ridge*, edited by Robert C. Ritchie and Paul Hutton, 215–230. Albuquerque: University of New Mexico Press, 1997.

————. "Romancing the West in the Twentieth Century: The Politics of History in a Contested Region." *Western Historical Quarterly* 32 (Winter 2001): 417–435.

————. "California's Fantasy Heritage and the Professional Empire of Herbert E. Bolton." In *Alta California: Peoples in Motion, Identities in Formation, 1769–1850*, edited by Steven W. Hackel, 197–214. Berkeley and San Marino: University of California Press in association with the Huntington Library and the University of Southern California, 2010.

————. "Professors and Tycoons: The Creation of Great Research Libraries in the American West," *Western Historical Quarterly* 41 (Summer 2010): 149–169.

————. "Herbert E. Bolton and the Bancroft Library." In *The Bancroft Library at 150: A Sesquicentennial Symposium*, edited by Charles B. Faulhaber, 97–108. Berkeley, Calif.: Bancroft Library, 2011

Jacobs, Wilbur R., ed. "'Turner, As I Remember Him,' by Herbert Eugene Bolton." *Mid-America* 36 (January 1954): 54–61.

Jacobs, Wilbur R., John W. Caughey, and Joe B. Frantz. *Turner, Bolton and Webb: Three Historians of the American Frontier*. Seattle: University of Washington Press, 1965.

Jacobsen, Jerome V. "Herbert E. Bolton." *Mid-America* 35 (April 1953): 75–80.

Karel, Anastasia. "A Tale of Two Collections: The Papers of Herbert Bolton and George Hammond." *Newsletter of the Friends of the Bancroft Library* (Spring 2009): 6–7.

Kessell, John L. "Bolton's *Coronado*." *Journal of the Southwest* 32 (Spring 1990): 83–96.

Langum, David J. "Herbert Eugene Bolton." In *Historians of the American Frontier: A Bio-bibliographical Sourcebook*. Edited by John R. Wunder. New York: Greenwood, 1988.

Lockwood, Frank. "Adventurous Scholarship: Dr. Herbert E. Bolton." *Catholic World*, 138 (November 1933): 185–194.

Magnaghi, Russell M. 1975. "Herbert E. Bolton and the Sources for American Indian Studies." *Western Historical Quarterly* 6 (January 1975): 33–46.

———. *Herbert E. Bolton and the Historiography of the Americas*. Westport, Conn.: Greenwood Press, 1998.

McCaughey, Robert A. "Four Academic Ambassadors: International Studies and the American University before the Second World War." *Perspectives in American History* 12 (1979): 561–607.

Nash, Gerald D. *Creating the West: Historical Interpretations, 1890–1990*. Albuquerque: University of New Mexico Press, 1991.

Ogden, Adele, Engel Sluiter, and Gregory Crampton, eds. *Greater America: Essays in Honor of Herbert Eugene Bolton*. Berkeley: University of California Press, 1945.

Onis, Jose de. "The Americas of Herbert E. Bolton." *The Americas* 12 (October 1955): 157–168.

Price, B. Byron. "Bolton, Coronado, and the Texas Panhandle." In *Coronado and the Myth of Quivira*, edited by D. Everett. Canyon, Texas: Panhandle-Plains Historical Society, 1985.

Rippy, James F. "Herbert Eugene Bolton: A Recollection." *Southwest Review* 39, no. 3 (1954): 166–171.

Rolle, Andrew F. "A Note on the Younger Bolton." *The Americas* 10, no.4 (1954): 421–424.

Ross, Mary, comp. *Writings and Cartography of Herbert Eugene Bolton*. Los Angeles: n.p., 1932.

Rundell, Walter, Jr. "Webb to Bolton." *Panhandle-Plains Historical Review* 50 (1977): 77–80.

Sandos, James A. "Junípero Serra's Canonization and the Historical Record." *American Historical Review* 93 (December 1988): 1253–1269.

———. "Junípero Serra, Canonization, and the California Indian Controversy." *Journal of Religious History* 15, no. 3 (1989): 311–329.

———. "Junípero Serra and California History." *The Californians* 7 (March-August 1989): 18–25.

Skinner, Constance Lindsey. "The Lure of the Golden Gate." *New York Herald Tribune Books*, August 2, 1931, p. 3.

Super, Richard R. "Teaching 'A History That Only God Could Write:' The History of the Americas." *History Teacher* 16 (May 1983): 339–354.

Truett, Samuel. "Epics of Greater America: Herbert Eugene Bolton's Quest for a

Transnational American History." In Schmidt-Nowara and Nieto-Phillips, *Interpreting Spanish Colonialism*, 213–247.

Voght, Martha. "Herbert Eugene Bolton as a Writer of Local History." *Southwestern Historical Quarterly* 72 (1969):313–323.

Weber, David J. "Turner, the Boltonians, and the Borderlands." *American Historical Review* 91 (February 1986): 66–81.

———. "Blood of Martyrs, Blood of Indians: Toward a More Balanced View of Spanish Missions in Seventeenth-Century North America." In Thomas, *Archaeological and Historical Perspectives on the Spanish Borderlands East*, 429–448.

———. "The Idea of the Spanish Borderlands." In *The Spanish Borderlands in Pan-American Perspective*, vol. 3 of *Columbian Consequences*, edited by David Hurst Thomas, 3–20. Washington, D.C.: Smithsonian Institution Press, 1991.

———. "A New Borderlands Historiography: Constructing and Negotiating the Boundaries of Identity." In Hackel, *Alta California*, 215–234.

Worcester, Donald E. "Herbert Eugene Bolton: The Making of a Western Historian." In *Writing Western History: Essays on Major Western Historians*, edited by Richard Etulain, 193–213. Albuquerque: University of New Mexico Press, 1991.

OTHER WORKS

Adams, Dorothy. "Biographical Sketch." In *Constance Lindsay Skinner, Author and Editor: Sketches of Her Life and Character, With a Checklist of Her Writings and the "Rivers of America" Series*, edited by Ann Heidbreder Eastman. N.p.: Women's National Book Association, 1980.

AHA. *Annual Report of the American Historical Association*. Washington, D.C.: Government Printing Office, various years.

———. *Papers of the American Historical Association*, vol. 1, no. 1, *Report of the Organization and Proceedings, Saratoga, September 9–10, 1884*. New York: G. P. Putnam's Sons, 1885.

Akins, Damon B. "Lines on the Land: The San Luis Rey River Reservations and the Origins of the Mission Indian Federation." Ph.D. diss., University of Oklahoma, Norman, 2009.

Albright, George Leslie. *Explorations for Pacific Railroads, 1853–1855*, edited by Herbert E. Bolton. Berkeley: University of California Press, 1921.

Alden, Dauril. "Engel Sluiter (1906–2001)." *Hispanic American Historical Review* 82 (May 2002): 329–331.

Almaráz, Félix D. 1981. Carlos E. Castañeda's Rendezvous with a Library: The Latin

American Collection, 1920–1927—The First Phase. *Journal of Library History* 16 (2): 315–328.

Bancroft, Hubert Howe. *History of California.* 7 vols. San Francisco: The History Company, 1886–1890.

Banduragga, Peter L. "One Hundred Years of History in Nevada: The Story of the Nevada Historical Society, 1904–2004." *Nevada Historical Society Quarterly* 47, no. 1 (2004): 3–14.

Barker, Eugene C. "Lester Gladstone Bugbee, Teacher and Historian." *Southwestern Historical Quarterly* 49 (July 1945): 1–35.

Barman, Jean. "Constance Lindsay Skinner and the Marketing of the Western Frontier." In *Canadian Papers in Rural History*, edited by D. H. Akenson. Gananoque, Ontario: Langdale Press, 1996.

————. *Constance Lindsay Skinner: Writing on the Frontier.* Toronto: University of Toronto Press, 2002.

Barrows, David P. "The Revolution in Mexico." *University of California Chronicle* 13 (October 1911): 438–453.

Barth, Gunther, Delmer M. Brown, George P. Hammond, and Edward W. Strong, "Walton Elbert Bean," *University of California in Memoriam*, September 1978. http://sunsite.berkeley.edu/uchistory/archives_exhibits/in_memoriam/index4.html.

Bates J. C., ed. *History of the Bench and Bar of California.* San Francisco: Bench and Bar Publishing Company, 1912.

Becker, Carl L. "Everyman His Own Historian." In *Everyman His Own Historian: Essays on History and Politics*, edited by Carl L. Becker, 246–255. New York: F. S. Crofts & Company, 1935.

————. *Modern History: The Rise of a Democratic, Scientific, and Industrialized Civilization.* New York: Silver, Burdett and Company, 1935.

Benedict, H. Y., ed. *A Source Book Relating to the History of the University of Texas: Legislative, Legal, Bibliographical, and Statistical.* University of Texas Bulletin No. 1757. Austin: University of Texas, 1917.

Billington, Ray Allen. *Frederick Jackson Turner: Historian, Scholar, Teacher.* New York: Oxford University Press, 1973.

Bingham, Alfred M. *Portrait of an Explorer: Hiram Bingham, Discoverer of Machu Picchu.* Ames, Iowa: Iowa State University Press, 1989.

Bingham, Hiram. *Inca Land: Explorations in the Highlands of Peru.* Boston: Houghton Mifflin, 1922.

Blackhawk, Ned. *Violence over the Land: Indians and Empires in the Early American West.* Cambridge, Mass.: Harvard University Press, 2006.

Blair, Emma Helen, and James Alexander Robertson, eds. *The Philippine Islands, 1493–1803.* 55 vols. Cleveland: Arthur H. Clark Company, 1903–1909.

Bogue, Allan G. *Frederick Jackson Turner: Strange Roads Going Down.* Norman: University of Oklahoma Press, 1998.

———. "'Not by Bread Alone': The Emergence of the Wisconsin Idea and the Departure of Frederick Jackson Turner." *Wisconsin Magazine of History* 86, no. 1 (2002): 10–23.

Bohemian Club. *A Chronicle of Our Years, Commemorating the Seventy-Fifth Anniversary of the Founding of the Bohemian Club of San Francisco.* San Francisco: Grabhorn Press, 1947.

Bolton, Frederick E. *Hydro-Psychoses.* Worcester, Mass.: J. H. Orpha, 1899.

Borah, Woodrow, Sanford Elberg, and James J. Parsons. "James Ferguson King." *University of California in Memoriam, 1985.* http://sunsite.berkeley.edu/uchistory/archives_exhibits/in_memoriam/index4.html.

Brewer, Thomas B. "The 'Old Department' of History at the University of Texas, 1910–1951." *Southwestern Historical Quarterly* 70, no. 2 (1966): 229–246.

Brooks, James F. *Captives and Cousins: Slavery, Kinship, and Community in the Southwest Borderlands.* Chapel Hill: University of North Carolina Press, 2002.

Brown, David S. *Richard Hofstadter: An Intellectual Biography.* Chicago: University of Chicago Press, 2006.

———. *Beyond the Frontier: The Midwestern Voice in American Historical Writing.* Chicago: University of Chicago Press, 2009.

Brown, Richard Maxwell. *Strain of Violence: Historical Studies of Violence and Vigilantism.* New York: Oxford University Press, 1975.

Brucker, George A., Henry F. May, and David A. Hollinger. *History at Berkeley: A Dialog in Three Parts.* Berkeley: University of California, Center for Studies in Higher Education and Institute of Governmental Studies, 1998.

Bugbee, Lester Gladstone. "The Archives of Bexar." *University Record* 1 (October 1899): 339–345.

Burns, Edward McNall. *David Starr Jordan: Prophet of Freedom.* Stanford, Calif.: Stanford University Press, 1953.

Bustamante, Adrian. "'The Matter Was Never Resolved': The *Casta* System in Colonial New Mexico, 1693–1823." *New Mexico Historical Review* 66 (April 1991): 143–164.

California Historical Survey Commission. *Preliminary Report of the California Historical Survey Commission.* Sacramento: State Printing Office, 1917.

Calloway, Colin G. "My Grandfather's Axe: Living with a Native American Past." In

Reflections on American Indian History: Honoring the Past, Building a Future, edited by Albert L. Hurtado, 3–31. Norman: University of Oklahoma Press, 2008.

Camp, Charles L. "Bancroft, Old and New." In *GPH: An Informal Record of George P. Hammond and His Era in the Bancroft Library*. Berkeley: Friends of the Bancroft Library, 1965.

Camp, Charles L., and Fulmer Mood. "George Ezra Dane." *California Folklore Quarterly* 1 (January 1942): 91–93.

Carlton, Don E., and Katherine J. Adams. "'A Work Peculiarly Our Own': Origins of the Barker Texas History Center, 1883–1950." *Southwestern Historical Quarterly* 86, no. 2 (1982): 197–230.

Carstensen, Vernon. "Wisconsin Regents: Academic Freedom and Innovation, 1900–1925." *Wisconsin Magazine of History* 48, no. 2 (1965): 101–110.

Castillo, Edward D. "Twentieth-Century Secular Movements." In *Handbook of North American Indians*, vol. 8, *California*, edited by Robert F. Heizer. Washington, D.C.: Smithsonian Institution, 1976.

Caughey, John Walton. *Hubert Howe Bancroft, Historian of the West*. Berkeley: University of California Press, 1946.

———, ed. *The Indians of Southern California in 1852: The B. D. Wilson Report and a Selection of Contemporary Comment*. San Marino, Calif.: Huntington Library Press, 1952.

———, ed. *Their Majesties the Mob*. Chicago: University of Chicago Press, 1960.

Chandler, Robert J. *ECV: 75 Years of Making History*. San Francisco: E Clampus Vitus, 2007.

Chapman, Charles E. *Catalogue of Materials in the Archivo General de Indias for the History of the Pacific Coast and the American Southwest*. Berkeley: University of California Press, 1919.

Chappell, Maxine. "Bodie and the Bad Man: Historical Roots of a Legend." MA thesis, University of California, Berkeley, 1947.

Cheyney, Edward Potts. *History of the University of Pennsylvania, 1740–1940*. Philadelphia: University of Pennsylvania Press, 1940.

Chickering, Allen L. "Some Notes with Regard to Drake's Plate of Brass." *California Historical Quarterly* 16 (September 1937): 275–281.

Conmy, Peter Thomas. *The Origins and Purposes of the Native Sons and Native Daughters of the Golden West*. San Francisco: Dolores Press, 1956.

Conzen, Kathleen Neils. *Immigrant Milwaukee, 1836–1860: Accommodation and Community in a Frontier City*. Cambridge, Mass.: Harvard University Press, 1976.

Cook, Sherburne F. *The Conflict between the California Indian and White Civilization.* Berkeley: University of California Press, 1976.

———. *The Population of the California Indians, 1769–1970.* Berkeley: University of California Press, 1976.

Cook, Sherburne F., and Woodrow Borah. *Essays in Population History.* 3 vols. Berkeley: University of California Press, 1971–1979.

Cooper, John Milton Jr., ed. "Frederick Jackson Turner and the Wisconsin Idea: A Recently Discovered Letter." *Wisconsin Magazine of History* 57, no. 4 (1974): 310–312.

Costo, Rupert, and Jeannette Henry Costo, eds. *The Missions of California: A Legacy of Genocide.* San Francisco: Indian Historian Press, 1987.

Coulter, E. Merton, ed. *Georgia's Disputed Ruins.* Chapel Hill: University of North Carolina Press, 1937.

Coy, Owen C. "The Settlement and Development of the Humboldt Bay Region, 1850–1875." PhD diss., University of California, Berkeley, 1918.

———. *Guide to the County Archives of California.* Sacramento: State Printing Office, 1919.

———. *The Genesis of California Counties.* Sacramento: State Printing Office, 1923.

———. *California County Boundaries: A Study of the Division of the State into Counties and the Subsequent Changes in Their Boundaries, with Maps.* Sacramento: State Printing Office, 1923.

———. *The Humboldt Bay Region, 1850–1875: A Study in American Colonization of California.* Los Angeles: California State Historical Association, 1929.

Cozzens, Samuel Woodworth. "The Lost Trail," *The Youth's Companion,* serialized in 48, nos. 6–17 (1875): 43, 51, 59, 67, 75, 83, 91, 99, 109, 117, 125, 133.

Curti, Merle, and Vernon Carstensen. *The University of Wisconsin, 1848–1925: A History.* 2 vols. Madison: University of Wisconsin Press, 1949.

Cutler, James Elbert. *Lynch-Law: An Investigation into the History of Lynching in the United States.* New York: Longmans, Green, and Company, 1905.

Cutler, Robert W. P. *The Mysterious Death of Jane Stanford.* Stanford, Calif.: Stanford University Press, 2003.

Dangberg, Grace. *A Guide to the Life and Works of Frederick J. Teggart.* Reno, Nev.: Grace Dangberg Foundation, 1983.

Davis, John F. "University Fellowships in Pacific Coast History." *California Outlook* 12 (April 19, 1913): 7–8.

———. "Our Early Law and the Admission of California." *California Outlook* 12 (April 26, 1913): 11–12.

————. "The Preservation of Our State's History." *California Outlook* 12 (May 3, 1913): 7–8.

Davis, Margaret Leslie. *Dark Side of Fortune: Triumph and Scandal in the Life of Oil Tycoon Edward L. Doheny.* Berkeley: University of California Press, 1998.

DeConde, Alexander. *A History of American Foreign Policy.* 2nd ed. New York: Charles Scribner's Sons, 1971.

Delpar, Helen. *Looking South: The Evolution of Latin Americanist Scholarship in the United States, 1850–1975.* Tuscaloosa: University of Alabama Press, 2008.

Denevan, William M., ed. *The Native Population of the Americas in 1492.* Madison: University of Wisconsin Press, 1976.

Dickinson, Donald C. *Henry E. Huntington's Library of Libraries.* San Marino, Calif.: Huntington Library Press, 1995.

Dillon, Richard H. "The Sutro Library." *News Notes of California Libraries* 51 (April 1956): 338–352.

————. "Sutro, Adolph Heinrich Joseph." *American National Biography Online.* www.anb.org.

Douglass, John Aubrey. "Creating a Fourth Branch of State Government: The University of California and the Constitutional Convention of 1879." *History of Higher Education Quarterly* 32, no. 1 (1992): 31–72.

————. *The California Idea and American Higher Education: 1850 to the 1960 Master Plan.* Stanford, Calif.: Stanford University Press, 2000.

Dugger, Ronnie. "The University of Texas: The Politics of Knowledge." *Change* 6, no. 1 (1974): 30–39, 60–61.

Dutschke, C. W. *Guide to the Medieval and Renaissance Manuscripts in the Huntington Library.* 2 vols. San Marino, Calif.: Huntington Library, 1989.

E Clampus Vitus. *Ye Preposterous Booke of Brasse Which Includes Divers Strange and Surprising Vituscan Voyages, Learned Discourses, Pious Anecdotes, Missionary Pilgramages, Merry Tales and Histories and a Fulle and Compleate Historie of Ye Plate of Brasse Set Up on Our Fair Shores by Ye Buccaneer Franke Drake.* N.p.: Press of Ye Greate Hi-OH [1937].

————. *Credo Quia Absurdum, Being a Compilation of Historic Documents and Trivia Pertinent to a Full Understanding of the Meaning and Purpose of the Ancient and Honorable Order of E Clampus Vitus.* Placerville, Calif.: n.p., 1949.

Eastman, Ann Heidbreder, ed. *Constance Lindsay Skinner, Author and Editor: Sketches of Her Life and Character, With a Checklist of Her Writings and the "Rivers of America" Series.* N.p.: Women's National Book Association, 1980.

Edwards, Harry Stillwell. *Eneas Africanus.* 1st ed., 1920. 2nd ed., New York: Grosset and Dunlap, 1940.

Elliott, J. H. *Empires of the Atlantic World: Britain and Spain in America, 1492–1830.* New Haven: Yale University Press, 2006.

Elliott, Orrin Leslie. *Stanford University: The First Twenty-Five Years.* Stanford, Calif.: Stanford University Press, 1937.

Ellison, Joseph. *California and the Nation, 1850–1869: A Study in the Relations of a Frontier Community with the Federal Government.* Berkeley: University of California Press, 1927.

Etulain, Richard W. "After Turner: The Western Historiography of Frederic Logan Paxson." In *Writing Western History: Essay on Major Western Historians,* edited by Richard W. Etulain, 137–165. Albuquerque: University of New Mexico Press, 1991.

Faulhaber, Charles. *The Bancroft Library, 1900–2000.* Berkeley: Center for Studies in Higher Education, University of California, 2000.

Fernandez, Ferdinand F. "Except a California Indian: A Study in Legal Discrimination." *Southern California Quarterly* 50 (June 1968): 169–170.

Ferrier, William Warren. *Origin and Development of the University of California.* Berkeley: Sather Gate Book Shop, 1930.

Fink, Colin, and E. P. Polushkin. *Drake's Plate of Brass Authenticated: The Report on the Plate of Brass.* San Francisco: California Historical Society, 1938.

Fitzgibbon, Mother Richard Marie. "The American Catholic Historical Association Secretaryship of Peter Guilday, 1919–1941." *Records of the American Catholic Historical Society of Philadelphia* 77, no. 4 (1966): 195–241.

Floyd, Marmaduke. "Certain Tabby Ruins on the Georgia Coast." In *Georgia's Disputed Ruins,* edited by E. Merton Coulter, 3–189. Chapel Hill: University of North Carolina Press, 1937.

Forbes, Jack D. *Native Americans of California and Nevada: A Handbook.* Healdsburg, Calif.: Naturegraph, 1969.

Ford, Guy Stanton, ed. *Dictatorship in the Modern World.* Minneapolis: University of Minnesota Press, 1935.

———. *On and Off Campus.* Minneapolis: University of Minnesota Press, 1938.

Fradkin, Philip L. *The Great Earthquake and Firestorms of 1906: How San Francisco Destroyed Itself.* Berkeley: University of California Press, 2005.

Franklin, Fabian. *The Life of Daniel Coit Gilman.* New York: Dodd, Mead and Company, 1910.

Frantz, Joe B. "Eugene C. Barker." *Great Plains Journal* 18 (1979): 65–71.

Fraser, James W. *Preparing America's Teachers: A History*. New York: Teachers College Press, 2007.

Friend, Llerena. "A Dedication to the Memory of George Pierce Garrison, 1853–1910." *Arizona and the West* 17, no. 4 (1975): 304–308.

Friends of the Bancroft Library. *GPH: An Informal Record of George P. Hammond and His Era in the Bancroft Library*. Berkeley: Friends of the Bancroft Library, 1965.

———. *Some Treasures of the Bancroft Library Celebrating the Dedication of the Enlarged and Remodeled Library, May 6th, 1973*. Berkeley: Friends of the Bancroft Library, 1973.

Frugé, August. *A Skeptic among Scholars: August Frugé on University Publishing*. Berkeley: University of California Press, 1993.

Gale, Robert L. "Farrand, Max." *American National Biography Online*. www.anb.org.

Gardner, David P. *The California Oath Controversy*. Berkeley: University of California Press, 1967.

Garrison, George P. "A Memorandum of M. Austin's Journey from the Lead Mines in the County of Wythe in the State of Virginia to the Lead Mines in the Province of Louisiana West of the Mississippi, 1796–1797." *American Historical Review* 5 (April 1900): 518–523.

———. "The Archivo General de Mexico." *The Nation* 72 (May 30, 1901): 430–431.

———. "Southwestern History in the Southwest." In AHA, *Annual Report of the American Historical Association, 1901*, 233–242.

———. *Texas, A Contest of Civilizations*. American Commonwealths. New York: Houghton, Mifflin and Company, 1903.

———. "The First Stage of the Movement for the Annexation of Texas." *American Historical Review* 10 (October 1904): 72–96.

———, ed. *Diplomatic Correspondence of the Republic of Texas*, 3 vols. In AHA, *Annual Report of the American Historical Association*, 1907, 1908.

———. "The First Twenty-Five Years of the University of Texas." *Southwestern Historical Quarterly* 60, no. 1 (1956–57): 106–117.

Gebhard, David, Roger Montgomery, Robert Winter, John Woodbridge, and Sally Woodbridge. *A Guide to Architecture in San Francisco and Northern California*. 2nd ed. Santa Barbara, Calif.: Peregrine Smith, 1976.

Geiger, Maynard F. "Beatification of Fray Junípero Serra." In *Some California Catholic Reminiscences for the United States Bicentennial*, edited by F. J. Weber, 127–137. New Haven: Knights of Columbus for the California Catholic Conference, 1976.

Goldman, Eric F. *John Bach McMaster: American Historian*. Philadelphia: University of Pennsylvania Press, 1943.

Goodrich, Chauncey Shafter. "The Legal Status of the California Indian." Parts 1 and 2. *California Law Review* 14 (January–March 1926): 83–100, 157–187.

Goodykoontz, James F., and Colin B. Willard, eds. *The Trans-Mississippi West: Papers Read at a Conference Held at the University of Colorado, June 18–June 21, 1929.* Boulder: University of Colorado, 1929.

Gould, Lewis L. "The University Becomes Politicized: The War with Jim Ferguson, 1915–1918." *Southwestern Historical Quarterly* 86, no. 2 (1982): 255–276.

Griffin, Roger A. "To Establish a University of the First Class." *Southwestern Historical Quarterly* 86, no. 2 (1982): 135–160.

Griswold, Robert L. *Fatherhood in America: A History.* New York: Basic Books, 1993.

Guilday, Peter. *John Gilmary Shea, Father of American Catholic History, 1824–1892.* New York: United States Catholic Historical Society, 1926.

Gutiérrez, Ramón. *When Jesus Came, the Corn Mothers Went Away: Marriage, Sexuality, and Power in New Mexico, 1500–1846.* Stanford, Calif.: Stanford University Press, 1991.

Habberton, John. *Helen's Babies; with Some Account of Their Ways, Innocent, Crafty, Angelic, Impish, Witching, and Repulsive.* Boston: Loring, 1876.

Hackel, Steven W. *Children of Coyote, Missionaries of Saint Francis: Indian-Spanish Relations in Colonial California, 1769–1850.* Chapel Hill: University of North Carolina Press, 2005.

———, ed. *Alta California: Peoples in Motion, Identities in Formation, 1769–1850.* Western Histories, edited by William J. Deverell. Berkeley and San Marino: University of California Press in association with the Huntington Library and the University of Southern California, 2010.

Halberstam, David. *The Coldest Winter: America and the Korean War.* New York: Hyperion, 2007.

Hanna, Warren L. *Lost Harbor: The Controversy over Drake's California Anchorage.* Berkeley: University of California Press, 1979.

Haselden, Reginald Berti. *Scientific Aids for the Study of Manuscripts.* Oxford: Oxford University Press, 1935.

———. "Is the Drake Plate of Brass Genuine?" *California Historical Society Quarterly* 17 (1937): 71–74.

Hawkins, Hugh. *Pioneer: A History of the Johns Hopkins University, 1874–1889.* Ithaca, N.Y.: Cornell University Press, 1960.

Hawkins, Hugh. *Between Harvard and America: The Educational Leadership of Charles W. Eliot.* New York: Oxford University Press, 1972.

Henderson, Alice Corbin. "The Death of the Pueblos." *New Republic*, November 29, 1922, pp. 11–13.

Hicks, John D. *My Life with History: An Autobiography*. Lincoln: University of Nebraska Press, 1968.

———et al. "Final Report of the Committee of Ten on Reorganization and Policy, December 29, 1939." www.historians.org/pubs/archives/CommitteeofTen.cfm.

Hodge, Frederick Webb, ed. *Handbook of American Indians North of Mexico*. 2. vols. Washington, D.C.: Government Printing Office, 1907–1910.

Hofstadter, Richard. *The Progressive Historians: Turner, Beard, Parrington*. New York: Alfred Knopf, 1968.

Hofstadter, Richard, and Walter P. Metzger. *The Development of Academic Freedom in the United States*. New York: Columbia University Press, 1955.

Horowitz, Helen Lefkowitz. *Campus Life: Undergraduate Cultures from the End of the Eighteenth Century to the Present*. Chicago: University of Chicago Press, 1987.

Hunt, Aurora. "U.S. Sentries on the Western Frontier from Letters Written by the California Column." Paper prepared for History 199, University of California, Berkeley [1939?]. Bancroft Library.

Hurtado, Albert L. "California Indian Demography, Sherburne F. Cook, and the Revision of American History." *Pacific Historical Review* 58 (August 1989): 323–343.

———. *Intimate Frontiers: Sex, Gender, and Culture in Old California*. Albuquerque: University of New Mexico Press, 1999.

Jackson, Kenneth T. *The Ku Klux Klan in the City, 1915–1930*. New York: Oxford University Press, 1967.

Jacobs, Wilbur R. "Frederick Jackson Turner—Master Teacher." *Pacific Historical Review* 23 (February 1954): 49–58.

———, ed. *Frederick Jackson Turner's Legacy: Unpublished Writings in American History*. San Marino, Calif.: Huntington Library, 1965.

———. *The Historical World of Frederick Jackson Turner, with Selections from His Correspondence*. New Haven: Yale University Press, 1968.

———. "Sherburne Friend Cook: Rebel-Revisionist (1896–1974)." *Pacific Historical Review*, 54 (1985): 191–199.

———. *Francis Parkman, Historian as Hero: The Formative Years*. Austin: University of Texas Press, 1991.

———. *On Turner's Trail: 100 Years of Writing Western History*. Lawrence: University Press of Kansas, 1994.

Jameson, J. Franklin. "American Acta Sanctorum." *AHR* 13 (January 1908): 286–302.

———. "The American Historical Review, 1895–1920." *AHR* 26 (October 1920): 1–7.

Johnson, Allen. *Stephen A. Douglas: A Study in American Politics*. New York, Macmillan, 1908.

———. *Readings in American Constitutional History, 1776–1876*. Boston: Houghton Mifflin Company, 1912.

———. *Jefferson and His Colleagues: A Chronicle of the Virginia Dynasty*. New Haven: Yale University Press, 1921.

———. *The Historian and Historical Evidence*. New York: Charles Scribner's Sons, 1926.

Johnson, Allen, and William A. Robertson, eds. *Readings in Recent American Constitutional History, 1876–1926*. New York: Charles Scribner's son, 1927.

Jordan, David Starr. *The Days of Man; Being Memories of a Naturalist, Teacher, and Minor Prophet of Democracy*. 2 vols. Yonkers-on-Hudson, N.Y.: World Book Company, 1922.

Kagan, Richard L. *Spain in America: The Origins of Hispanicism in the United States*. Urbana and Chicago: University of Illinois Press, 2002.

Kerr, Clark. *The Gold and the Blue: A Personal Memoir of the University of California, 1949–1967*. 2 vols. Berkeley: University of California Press, 2001, 2003.

Kinnaird, Lawrence. "American Penetration of Spanish Louisiana." PhD diss., University of California, 1928.

———. *Spain in the Mississippi Valley, 1765–1794*. 4 vols. Washington, D.C.: U.S. Government Printing Office, 1946–1949.

Knight, Alan. *The Mexican Revolution*. 2 vols. Cambridge: Cambridge University Press, 1986.

Kroeber, Karl, and Clifton Kroeber, eds. *Ishi in Three Centuries*. Lincoln: University of Nebraska Press, 2003.

Kroeber, Theodora. *Ishi in Two Worlds: A Biography of the Last Wild Indian in North America*. Berkeley: University of California Press, 1961.

Lane, J. J. *History of Education in Texas*. Contributions to American Educational History, ed. Herbert B. Adams, vol. 35. Washington, D.C.: Government Printing Office, 1903.

Lanham, Url. *The Bone Hunters*. New York: Columbia University Press, 1973.

Leckie, Shirley. *Angie Debo: Pioneering Historian*. Norman: University of Oklahoma Press, 2000.

Leebrick, Karl C. "The English Expedition to Manila in 1762, and the Government of the Philippine Islands by the East India Company." PhD diss., University of California, Berkeley, 1917.

Lerner, Robert E. "Ernst H. Kantorowicz." In *Medieval Scholarship: Biographical Stud-*

ies on the Formation of a Discipline, edited by Helen Damico and Joseph B. Zavadil, vol. 1, 263–276. 3 vols. New York: Garland, 1995.

Levy, David W. *The University of Oklahoma: A History*, vol. 1, *1890–1917*. Norman: University of Oklahoma Press, 2005.

Libby, Orin Grant. "The Geographical Distribution of the Vote of the Thirteen States on the Federal Constitution, 1787–8." *Bulletin of the University of Wisconsin, Economics, Political Science, and History Series* 1, no. 1 (1894): 1–116.

Littlefield, Daniel F. *Seminole Burning: A Story of Racial Vengeance*. Jackson: University of Mississippi Press, 1996.

Lockwood, Frank C. *The Apache Indians*. New York: Macmillan, 1938.

———. *With Padre Kino on the Trail*. Tucson: University of Arizona Press, 1934.

Lowitt, Richard. "'Dear Miss Debo': The Correspondence of E. E. Dale and Angie Debo." *Chronicles of Oklahoma* 77 (Winter 1999–2000): 372–405.

Lummis, Charles F. *The Spanish Pioneers*. 7th ed. Chicago: A. C. McClurg, 1918.

McCormac, Eugene I. *White Servitude in Maryland, 1634–1820*. Johns Hopkins University Studies in Historical and Political Science, ser. 22, no. 3–4. Baltimore: Johns Hopkins University Press, 1904.

———. *Colonial Opposition to Imperial Authority during the French and Indian War*. University of California Publications in History. Berkeley: University of California Press, 1911.

———. *James K. Polk: A Political Biography*. Berkeley: University of California Press, 1922.

McMaster, John Bach. *A History of the People of the United States*. 8 vols. New York and London: D. Appleton and Company, 1883–1906.

McWilliams, Carey. *Southern California Country: An Island on the Land*. New York: Duell, Sloan and Pearce, 1946.

Meany, Joseph F. "New York: The State of History." www.nysm.nysed.gov/services/meanydoc.html.

Mendelson, Johanna, comp., and Paul Ellingson, ed. *Mary Leticia Ross Papers: A Descriptive Inventory*. Atlanta: Georgia Department of Archives and History, 1979.

Mirrielees, Edith R. *Stanford: The Story of a University*. New York: G. P. Putnam's Sons, 1959.

Mitchell, Richard G. "Joaquin Murieta: A Study of Social Conditions in Early California." MA thesis, Berkeley, University of California, 1927.

Morgan, H. Wayne. *America's Road to Empire: The War with Spain and Overseas Expansion*. New York: John Wiley and Sons, 1965.

Morison, Samuel Eliot. "Faith of a Historian." *AHR* 56 (January 1951): 261–275.

Muto, Albert. *The University of California Press: The Early Years, 1893–1953*. Berkeley: University of California Press, 1993.

Nagel, Gunther W. *Iron Will: The Life and Letters of Jane Stanford*. Rev. ed. Stanford, Calif.: Stanford Alumni Association, 1985.

Nichols, David A. "Civilization over Savage: Frederick Jackson Turner and the Indian." *South Dakota History* 2 (Fall 1972): 383–405.

Nisbet, Robert. *Teachers and Scholars: A Memoir of Berkeley in Depression and War*. New Brunswick, N.J.: Transaction, 1992.

Norwood, Stephen H. *The Third Reich in the Ivory Tower: Complicity and Conflict on American Campuses*. New York: Cambridge University Press, 2009.

Novick, Peter. *That Noble Dream: The "Objectivity Question" and the American Historical Profession*. Cambridge: Cambridge University Press, 1988.

Nuttall, Zelia. *Codex Nuttall: Facsimile of an Ancient Mexican Codex Belonging to Lord Zouche of Harynworth, England*. Cambridge, Mass.: Peabody Museum of American Archaeology and Ethnology, Harvard University, 1902.

———. *The Book of the Life of the Ancient Mexicans, Containing an Account of Their Rites and Superstitions: An Anonymous Hispano-Mexican Manuscript Preserved at the Biblioteca Nazionale Centrale, Florence, Italy*. Berkeley: University of California, 1903.

———, trans. and ed. *New Light on Drake: A Collection of Documents Relating to His Voyage of Circumnavigation, 1577–1580*. London: Hakluyt Society, 1914.

Ogden, Adele, Engel Sluiter, and Gregory Crampton, eds. *Greater America: Essays in Honor of Herbert Eugene Bolton*. Berkeley: University of California Press, 1945.

Ogle, Gary. "The Mysterious Death of Mrs. Leland Stanford." *Pacific Historian* 25 (Spring 1981): 1–7.

Paltridge, James Gilbert. *A History of the Faculty Club at Berkeley*. Berkeley: Faculty Club of the University of California, 1990.

Parish, John C. "Comment and Historical News." *Pacific Historical Review* 1 (March 1932): 136.

Park, Hyong-Kyu. "Eugene C. Barker: A Historian from East Texas." *East Texas Historical Journal* 34, no. 1 (1996): 68–70.

Parkman, Francis. *Pioneers of France in the New World*. 1885. Reprint, Lincoln: University of Nebraska Press, 1996.

———. *The Parkman Reader*, edited by Samuel Eliot Morison. Boston: Little, Brown, 1955.

Paxson, Frederic Logan. *The Independence of the South American Republics: A Study in Recognition and Foreign Policy*. Philadelphia: Ferris and Leach, 1903.

————. *The Last American Frontier*. New York: Macmillan, 1910.

————. *History of the American Frontier*. Boston: Houghton Mifflin, 1924.

————. *When the West Is Gone*. New York: Henry Holt, 1930.

Pelfrey, Margaret Cheney, and Patricia A. *A Brief History of the University of California*. Berkeley: University of California, distributed by the University of California Press, 2004.

"Personalia and Marginalia." *California Historical Society Quarterly* 16 (June 1937): 192.

Pool, William C. *Eugene C. Barker, Historian*. Austin: Texas State Historical Association, 1971.

Powicke, F. M. "Charles Homer Haskins." *English Historical Review* 52 (October 1937): 649–656.

Prindle, David F. "Oil and the Permanent University Fund: The Early Years." *Southwestern Historical Quarterly* 86, no. 2 (1982): 277–298.

Prucha, Francis Paul. *The Great Father: The United States Government and the American Indians*. 2 vols. Lincoln: University of Nebraska Press, 1984.

Puryear, V. J., W. Bingham, and O. A. Maslenikov. "Robert Joseph Kerner, History: Berkeley." *University of California in Memoriam*, April 1958. http://sunsite.berkeley.edu/uchistory/archives_exhibits/in_memoriam/index4.html.

Riasanovsky, Nicholas, Gerald D. Feldman, Hans W. Roseberg, and Edward B. Segal. "Raymond James Sontag." *University of California in Memoriam*, July 1975. http://sunsite.berkeley.edu/uchistory/archives_exhibits/in_memoriam/index4.html.

Rorabaugh, W. J. *Berkeley at War: The 1960s*. New York: Oxford University Press, 1989.

Ross, Mary. "The Anglo-Spanish Conflict in the Caribbean Area and the North American Mainland, 16th and 17th Centuries." MA thesis, University of California, Berkeley, 1919.

————. "French Intrusions and Indian Uprisings in Georgia and South Carolina, 1577–1580." *Georgia Historical Quarterly* 7 (September 1923): 251–281.

————. "The French on the Savannah." *Georgia Historical Quarterly* 8 (September 1924): 167–194.

————. "The Spanish Settlement of Santa Elena (Port Royal) in 1578." *Georgia Historical Quarterly* 9 (December 1925): 352–379.

————. "The Restoration of the Spanish Missions in Georgia, 1598–1606." *Georgia Historical Quarterly* 10 (September 1926): 171–199.

————. "With Pardo and Boyano on the Fringes of the Georgia Land." *Georgia Historical Quarterly* 14 (December 1930): 267–285.

Rothberg, Morey, and Jacqueline Goggin, eds. *John Franklin Jameson and the Development of Humanistic Scholarship in America*. 3 vols. Athens: University of Georgia Press, 1993.

Rothman, Hal. *Preserving Different Pasts: The American National Monuments*. Urbana: University of Illinois Press, 1989.

Royce, Josiah. *California, from the Conquest in 1846 to the Second Vigilance Committee in San Francisco: A Study in American Character*. Boston: Houghton Mifflin and Company, 1886).

Schmidt-Nowara, Christopher, and John M. Nieto-Phillips, ed. *Interpreting Spanish Colonialism: Empires, Nations, and Legends*. Albuquerque: University of New Mexico Press, 2005.

Senkewicz, Robert M. *Vigilantes in Gold Rush San Francisco*. Stanford, Calif.: Stanford University Press, 1985.

Sibley, Robert, ed. *The Golden Book of California*. Berkeley: California Alumni Association, 1937.

Simon, Roger D. *The City-Building Process: Housing and Services in New Milwaukee Neighborhoods, 1880–1910*. Rev ed. Transactions of the American Philosophical Society, Vol. 86, pt. 6. Philadelphia: American Philosophical Society, 1996.

Skinner, Constance Lindsay. *Pioneers of the Old Southwest: A Chronicle of the Dark and Bloody Ground*. Chronicles of America, vol. 18. New Haven: Yale University Press, 1919.

———. *Adventures of Oregon: A Chronicle of the Fur Trade*. Chronicles of America, vol. 22. New Haven: Yale University Press, 1920.

———. "Notes Concerning My Correspondence with Frederick Jackson Turner." *Wisconsin Magazine of History* 19 (September 1935): 91–103.

Smith, Donald E. "The Viceroy of New Spain in the Eighteenth Century." AHA, *Annual Report of the American Historical Association*, 1908 (1909), 169–181.

Spurgeon, Selena A. *Henry Edwards Huntington, His Life and Collections: A Docent Guide*. San Marino, Calif.: Huntington Library, 2002.

Stadtman, Verne A. *The University of California, 1868–1968*. New York: McGraw-Hill, 1970.

Steinberg, Stephen. *The Academic Melting Pot: Catholics and Jews in American Higher Education*. New York: McGraw-Hill, 1974.

Steiner, Michael C. "Frederick Jackson Turner and Western Regionalism." In *Writing Western History: Essays on Major Western Historians*, edited by Richard W. Etulain, 103–135. Albuquerque: University of New Mexico Press, 1991.

Stensvaag, James T. "'The Life of My Child': Jeanne Elizabeth Wier, the Nevada

Historical Society, and the Great Quarters Struggle of the 1920s." *Nevada Historical Society Quarterly* 23, no. 1 (1980): 3–20.

Stephens, Henry Morse. *Revolutionary Europe*. 6th ed. London: Rivingtons, 1902.

———. "Valuable Work on Behalf of California History." *Grizzly Bear* 16 (April 1915): 1–2.

Stern, Alexandra Minna. *Eugenic Nation: Faults and Frontiers of Better Breeding in Modern America*. Berkeley: University of California Press, 2005.

Stewart, George R. *The Year of the Oath: The Fight for Academic Freedom at the University of California*. Garden City, N.Y.: Doubleday, 1950.

Stewart, Robert Ernest, and Mary Frances Stewart. *Adolph Sutro: A Biography*. Berkeley: Howell-North, 1962.

Stone, Irving, ed. *There Was Light: Autobiography of a University, Berkeley, 1868–1968*. Garden City, N.Y.: Doubleday and Company, 1970.

Sulloway, Frank J. *Born to Rebel: Birth Order, Family Dynamics, and Creative Lives*. New York: Vintage Books, 1996.

Swain, Donald C. *Wilderness Defender: Horace M. Albright and Conservation*. Chicago: University of Chicago Press, 1970.

Synnott, Marcia Graham. "Anti-Semitism and American Universities: Did Quotas Follow the Jews?" In *Anti-Semitism in American History*, edited by David A. Gerber, 233–271. Urbana: University of Illinois Press, 1986.

Teggart, Frederick, and Donald E. Smith, eds. *Diary of Gaspar de Portola during the California Expedition of 1769–1770*. Publications of the Academy of Pacific Coast History, vol. 1, no. 3. Berkeley: University of California, 1909.

Thomas, David Hurst. "Saints and Soldiers at Santa Catalina: Hispanic Designs for Colonial America." In *The Recovery of Meaning: Historical Archaeology in the Eastern United States*, edited by Mark P. Leone and Parker B. Potter, Jr., 73–140. Washington, D.C.: Smithsonian Institution Press, 1988.

———, ed. *Archaeological and Historical Perspectives on the Spanish Borderlands West*. Vol. 1 of *Columbian Consequences*. Washington, D.C.: Smithsonian Institution Press, 1989.

Thompson, William M. *El Maestro on Horseback: Francis Cummins Lockwood, 1864–1948*. Tucson: Westernlore Press, 1990.

Thornton, Russell. *American Indian Holocaust and Survival: A Population History since 1492*. Norman: University of Oklahoma Press, 1987.

Thorpe, James. *Henry Edwards Huntington: A Biography*. Berkeley: University of California Press, 1994.

Thwaites, Reuben G. *The Bancroft Library: A Report Submitted to the President and Regents of the University of California.* Berkeley: n.p., 1905.

Turner, Frederick Jackson. "Editor's Note." *Bulletin of the University of Wisconsin, Economics, Political Science, and History Series.* Vol. 1, no. 1 (1894): iii–vii.

———. *The Frontier in American History.* New York: Henry Holt, 1920.

———. "Geographic Sectionalism in America." *Annals of the Association of American Geographers* 16 (June 1926): 85–93.

———. *The Significance of Sections in American History.* New York: Henry Holt, 1932.

———. *The United States, 1830–1850: The Nation and Its Sections.* New York: Holt, Rinehart and Winston, 1935.

———. *Rereading Frederick Jackson Turner: "The Significance of the Frontier in American History" and Other Essays.* Commentary by John Mack Faragher. New York: Henry Holt, 1994.

———. "The Development of American Society." In *Frederick Jackson Turner's Legacy: Unpublished Writings in American History,* edited by Wilbur R. Jacobs. San Marino, Calif.: Huntington Library, 1965.

"Visiting Faculty." In *Blue and Gold.* Berkeley: University of California, 1908.

Von der Porten, Edward, and James M. Spitze, with Raymond Aker, Robert W. Allen. "Who Made Drake's Plate of Brass? Hint: It Wasn't Francis Drake." *California History* 81 (September 2002): 116–133, 168–171.

Vigness, David M. "A Dedication to the Memory of Charles Wilson Hackett, 1888–1951." *Arizona and the West* 7, no. 1 (1965): 1–4.

Vincent, George E. "Guy Stanton Ford: An Appreciation." In *On and Off Campus,* edited by Guy Stanton Ford, 16–23. Minneapolis: University of Minnesota Press, 1938.

Wade, Mason. *Francis Parkman: Heroic Historian.* New York: Viking, 1942.

Wallace, Anthony F. C. *Rockdale: The Growth of an American Village in the Early Industrial Revolution.* New York: Alfred A. Knopf, 1978.

Watson, Douglas S. "Drake and California: The Finding of Evidence of His Visit and Its Implications." *California Historical Society Quarterly* 16, no. 1, part 2 (March 1937): 19–24.

Weber, David J. *The Spanish Frontier in North America.* New Haven: Yale University Press, 1992.

———. *Bárbaros: Spaniards and Their Savages in the Age of the Enlightenment.* New Haven: Yale University Press, 2005.

Wheeler, Benjamin Ide. *The Abundant Life: Benjamin Ide Wheeler.* Berkeley: University of California Press, 1926.

Wiley, Francis. "Jedediah Smith and the West." PhD diss., University of California, Berkeley, 1941.

Wilkins, Burleigh Taylor. *Carl Becker: A Biographical Study in American Intellectual History.* Cambridge, Mass.: MIT Press and Harvard University Press, 1961.

Williams, Mary Floyd. *History of the San Francisco Committee of Vigilance of 1851: A Study of Social Control on the California Frontier in the Days of the Gold Rush.* Berkeley: University of California Press, 1921.

Wissler, Clark, Constance Lindsay Skinner, and William Wood. *Adventures in the Wilderness.* The Pageant of America, vol. 1. New Haven: Yale University Press, 1925.

Wolff, Suzanne H., and Cynthia J. Schrems. "Politics and Libel: Angie Debo and the Publication of *And Still the Waters Run.*" *Western Historical Quarterly* 22 (May 1991): 185–203.

Wood, George B. *Early History of the University of Pennsylvania from Its Origin to the Year 1827.* 3rd ed. Philadelphia: J. B. Lippincott Company, 1896.

Writers' Program, Work Projects Administration. *Berkeley: The First Seventy-Five Years.* Berkeley: Gillick Press, 1941.

Wrobel, David. *The End of American Exceptionalism: Frontier Anxiety from the Old West to the New Deal.* Lawrence: University Press of Kansas, 1993.

———. *Promised Lands: Promotion, Memory, and the Creation of the American West.* Lawrence: University Press of Kansas, 2002.

Wrobel, David, and Michael C. Steiner, eds. *Many Wests: Place, Culture, and Regional Identity.* Lawrence: University Press of Kansas, 1997.

Yeomans, Henry Aaron. *Abbott Lawrence Lowell, 1856–1943.* Cambridge, Mass.: Harvard University Press, 1948.

INDEX

Note: The abbreviation HEB has been used throughout. Figures are denoted by Fig. and the figure number; these refer to the photograph gallery the follows page 158.

academic freedom: Adams's promise of, 70–71; Barker's speech on, 142; loyalty oath in context of, 253–56; Wells-Ely controversy and, 27–28

Academic Senate (UC), 254

Academy of American Franciscan History, 257–58

Academy of Pacific Coast History, 72

Acheson, Dean, 256

Adams, Ephraim D.: on academic freedom, 70–71; as AHA president, 171; death of, 178, 210; work: *California's Story* (with HEB), 154–55

Adams, Herbert Baxter, 21–22

Adams, James Truslow, 180, 183, 186

African Americans: beliefs about, 44, 48, 145–46; equality struggles of, 250. *See also* slaves and slavery

AHA. *See* American Historical Association (AHA)

Aiton, Arthur, 133, 222

Albion College (Mich.), 38

Albright, Horace, 104–5, 259, 263

Albright, Leslie, 104

Allen, William F., 21

Ambrose, Genevieve, 108

America: use of term, xv, 183, 186. *See also* Americas

American Association of University Professors, 106, 130

American Commonwealth series, 47

American Council of Learned Societies, 259

American Historical Association (AHA): cross-country travel to conference, 5–6; expeditions of HEB praised at, 267; founding and goals of, 12; generational and regional changes in, 178–79, 210–14; HEB as president-elect and president of, 178–79, 181, 210; HEB's presidential address for, 183–87; HEB's "Two Types of Courses

American Historical Association (AHA)
(*continued*)
   in American History" presented to,
   133–34; loyalty oath controversy and,
   255–56; meetings mentioned, 54, 69,
   178; nominations for office (1921, 1924,
   1928), 129–30, 143, 171; Panama-
   Pacific Historical Congress of, 98–99;
   Pike papers discovery announced at,
   66, 67; presidents after HEB, 210–11;
   presidents before HEB, 23, 26, 98–99,
   101, 129, 134, 171, 210; reorganization
   proposed, 212–13; Southwest historical studies report for, 47; structure of
   leadership (1929), 211; Turner's frontier thesis presented to, 22; U.S. history teaching initiative of, 235–36.
   See also Pacific Coast Branch (AHA)
American Historical Review: editor of, 41,
   53, 82; HEB's articles: introduction
   and Pike's papers, 66; on Mexican
   archives, 54; "The Mission as a Frontier Institution in the Spanish American Colonies," 101–4, 128, 148
American Indians: assimilation of, 147,
   267; childhood reading about, 8, 19;
   graduate student research on, 148;
   HEB's articles in handbook on, 55, 65,
   84; in HEB's *Coronado*, 247; in HEB's
   Escalante book, 261; legal issues of,
   146–48, 250; number in California,
   310n63; as objects of missionary attention, 90–91, 102, 173–74, 177; population decline in colonial period, 249–50
Americanism: use of term, 237
American Philosophical Society, 247
American Revolution, 8, 19, 151–52, 217
Americans: use of term, xv
American West: AHA representation
   and meetings in context of, 178–79;
   AHA resolution on, 12; childhood
   reading about, 19; McMaster's interest
   in, 33; Wheeler's view of, 80–81. *See*

also Southwest; Spanish America;
   Spanish Borderlands; *and specific states*
Americas: conflicts and differences among
   nations of, 185, 186–87; curriculum ter-
   minology and, 238–39; FDR's use of
   term, 216; Good Neighbor Policy and,
   214–15, 216, 225, 227. *See also* history
   of the Americas (hemispheric history)
Anasazi ruins, *Fig. 13*
Anderson, Clinton P., 245–46
Anderson, Ethan, 146–47
Andrews, Charles McLean, 134
Anglo-American history: assumptions
   about Spanish in, 122–24, 125–26;
   Drake plate as venerable relic of, 208;
   ethnocentric view of, 81; HEB's discussions of, 151–53, 268; as HEB's
   heritage, 6, 209; indigenous population decline in, 250; key repository
   of materials on, 62; missions' role in,
   101–4, 128; Turner's privileging of,
   126–28; vigilantism in, 153, 154, 155.
   See also anti-Catholic attitudes; frontier thesis (Turner, 1893)
Anglos: Mexican attitudes toward, 65;
   organizations of, 93; use of term, xv
anthropology department (Calif.), 84
anti-Catholic attitudes: in California mi-
   lieu, 3, 93, 257, 258; historical research
   as counter to, 148; in narrative of Spanish America, 40, 123–24, 125–26; in
   Parkman's writing, 100; rejection of,
   144. *See also* Anglo-American history
anti-Semitism: allegations about HEB's,
   219–20; common experiences of,
   148–50; of fraternity, 26; pragmatic
   approach to, 150–51, 229, 242
Anza, Juan Bautista de: exploring trails
   of, 159, 160, 161–62; publications on,
   176–78
Anza's California Expeditions (HEB),
   161–62, 176–78
archives: Catholic history documents in,

258; funds for foreign research in, 93–94; guides to Mexican materials of, 52–55, 56, 65, 77, 78, 89; researcher's death in foreign location, 104; Texas Bexar Archives, 40, 47, 51; Zacatecas, 66, 68. *See also* Archivo Nacional (Mexico); Bancroft Library; historical documents; Huntington Library; Museo Nacional (Mexico City); National Archives

Archivo Nacional (Mexico): Garrison's role in exploiting, 57; guide to materials of, 52–55, 56, 65, 77, 78, 89; HEB's first travel to and publication from, 48–50; schedule of, 51, 65

Arizona: Anza's trail, 161–62; Coronado's trail, 225–27; Escalante's trail, 218; Kino's trail, 105, 119. *See also* Spanish colonizers and missions

Arizona Coronado Commission, 225

Arredondo's Historical Proof of Spain's Title to Georgia (HEB), 167, 192–94

assimilation, 146–47, 267

Athanase de Mézières and the Louisiana-Texas Frontier, 1768–1780 (HEB), 89–91, 112

Austin (Texas): HEB's first impression of, 44; political figures' challenge to direction of university courses, 45–46; university faculty circle and activities in, 48. *See also* Texas; University of Texas

Bancroft, George, 30

Bancroft, Hubert Howe, 59, 61–62, 154, 279n38

Bancroft Library (University of California, Berkeley): appraisal of original collection, 62; building on campus for, 62, 64; directors after HEB, 221–23, 241; Doheny's failure to fund, 109–10; Drake plate acquired by, 197–98, 207; focus of, 111; HEB's collection in, 258; HEB's control of, 112–13, 267;

HEB's interest in, 69, 71, 77; HEB's Mexican manuscripts in, 105–6; HEB's retirement from, 218–19; HEB's return in WWII, 229–30, 240; HEB-Teggart relationship and, 77–78, 105–6; HEB working in, *Fig. 23;* highlighted in international exposition, 98–99; historical demography drawn from, 249–50; keys to, 88; leadership needed for, 74, 75; negotiations for acquiring, 61–62, 82; origins of, 59; Priestley's role at, 87, 106; reputation assured, 110; for sale since 1880s, 279n38; saved from earthquake and fire (1906), 64; special strengths of, 59; Turner's evaluation of, 60, 71; university's relationship to, 79–80; Venegas manuscript of, 259

Bancroft Prize, 246

Bank of America, xv, 257

Bannon, John Francis, 89, 187, 240, 263

Barat College of the Sacred Heart (Lake Forest), 165–66

Barker, Eugene C.: angry at HEB's hiring, 44; considered for Byrne professorship, 180; Garrison's attitude toward, 41; HEB's friendship with, 50, 69; HEB's students hired by, 115–16; HEB's university absence and, 55, 56; role in history department of Texas, 76; teaching of, 45; on Texas presidency, 135, 136, 137, 139, 141–42; work: *With the Makers of Texas* (with HEB), 50, 52, 154

Barron, George Haviland, 195–96

Barrows, David Prescott, 83–84, 131–32, 138–39

Bean, Walter, 223

Beard, Charles, 35

Bear Flag Revolt (1846), 152, 195

Becker, Carl L.: as AHA president, 179, 210; fellowship process and, 31; fraternity of, 26; HEB's defense of, 190–91;

Becker, Carl L. *(continued)*
　　historical views of, 26–27; on Rosen-
　　berg as Jew, 150; on Turner's voice, 23
beliefs (HEB): about Spain in America,
　　40; ethnocentric, pro-missionary per-
　　spective, 3, 90–91, 123–26, 144–47;
　　exclusions of, 26, 86; general discus-
　　sions of, 144–47; inclusive sense of
　　history in, 151–55, 267; on race, 44,
　　48, 145–46, 266; southern white
　　influences on, 44, 48; Texas cultural
　　assumptions about, 45–47; youthful
　　prejudices abandoned, 27. *See also*
　　politics; religious beliefs
Bemis, Edward W., 28
Bénard, Emile Henri, 84–85
Berkeley. *See* University of California,
　　Berkeley
Bernard Moses Memorial Lecture, 228
Billington, Ray Allen, 256
Binkley, William, 188
Boaz, Franz, 84
Bocqueraz, Leo, 200, 203
Bohemian Club, *Fig. 6*, 64, 81, 93
Bolton, Alvin (brother), 229
Bolton, Edwin Latham (father), 6–8, 209
Bolton, Eugenie (daughter), 52, 189,
　　214, 263
Bolton, Frances (daughter), 31, 36, 189
Bolton, Frederick (brother): anti-
　　communism and, 253; on church
　　going, 48; as dean of school of edu-
　　cation at Washington, 134; departure
　　for and return from Germany, 30,
　　31; education of, 11, 13, 14–15, 16, 18,
　　29, 33–34; financial assistance from,
　　26; on Gertrude Janes, 10; on hard
　　work, 7; as high school principal, 15,
　　16; marriage of, 19, 25; teaching at
　　college, 35; teaching at high school,
　　8–9, 11; on Texas presidency, 138
Bolton, Gertrude ("Tootie," daughter),
　　65, 170, 189

Bolton, Gertrude Janes (wife): courtship
　　and marriage of, 16, 17, 19–20, 25, 29;
　　death of, 264; expedition role of, 161–
　　62; health concerns of, 34, 96, 189;
　　HEB driven by, 249, 261; HEB's cor-
　　respondence with, 97, 226, 227, 246,
　　287n6; on HEB's honors, 214; high
　　school years, 10; home destroyed in
　　wildfire (1923), 135; household econ-
　　omy of, 29, 39, 96–97; intelligence
　　and academic excellence of, 14, 19;
　　Philadelphia stay of, 36; teaching of,
　　15–16, 27; Texas move and, 43, 48;
　　Texas presidency offer and, 138; at
　　University of Wisconsin, 25. *See also*
　　family life and children
Bolton, Grace (sister), 135
Bolton, Helen (daughter; later Schneider),
　　39, 42–43, 189, 262–63
Bolton, Herbert, Jr. (son), 88, 96–97, 98,
　　162, 189
Bolton, Herbert Eugene (HEB): birth, 6;
　　courtship and marriage, 16, 17, 19–20,
　　25, 29; death, 263–64; photographs,
　　Figs. 1–3, 9–18, 23. *See also* Bolton,
　　Gertrude Janes (wife); family life and
　　children; wages and income (HEB)
—beliefs. *See* beliefs (HEB)
—characteristics: affability, 9–10, 16;
　　ambition to be somebody, 10; appear-
　　ance, 5; behavior toward subordinates
　　vs. superintendents, 17–18; cigarette
　　smoking, 52, 88, 218, 240–41, 262;
　　contradictions in, 1–3; ego and arro-
　　gance, 101, 142–43; failure to observe
　　poverty, 146; gentleness and encour-
　　agement, 97, 163–64; hard work and
　　discipline, 7–8, 17–18, 64–65; health
　　concerns, 218, 240–41; lack of exec-
　　utive decisiveness, 142; learning
　　and maintaining social skills, 25–26;
　　misogyny as young man, 19; nocturnal
　　studies, 88–89, 97; optimism, 217; per-

Corral, Ramon, 68–69, 89
Cortés, Hernán, 49, 136
Coy, Owen C., 98, 107, 108
Cozzens, Samuel Woodworth, 8
Craven, Avery, 221, 222
Crespi, Juan, 151, 173
Cuba: HEB's views on (1898), 34–35
Culleton, James H., 232
Cunningham, Charles, 115–16

Dane, George Ezra, 194, 195, 196, 199
Dartmouth College, 42
Davis, John F.: Catholicism of, 148;
    death of, 175–76; graduate fellowships
    supported by, 93–94; HEB's request
    for opinion of, 153; HEB's work sup-
    ported by, 106, 152; hemispheric
    approach to California history and,
    114; as historical survey chair, 98;
    War History Committee and, 107, 108
Debatable Land, The (HEB and Ross), 167
Debo, Angie, 297n25
democracy: in California history, 151–52;
    vigilantes and, 153, 154, 155
DeVoto, Bernard, 235
Dewey, John, 106
Díaz, Porfirio, 69, 89, 185–86
Dickson, Edward A.: attitude toward
    HEB and history, 107–8; California
    centennial projects of, 227–28, 230–
    34; HEB's treatment of Caughey
    compared with, 243–44; loyalty
    oath supported by, 234, 253–55
Dictionary of American Biography, 100
Diocesan Historical Commission, 232
doctoral programs: comparison of, 162;
    dual problems in development of, 24–
    25; fellowship policies and, 31–32;
    historical research collections and,
    47; mentor–graduate student rela-
    tionships in, 117; placement of Cal
    graduates from, 133. See also histori-
    cal profession; students, graduate;

University of California, Berkeley,
    history department
Dodd, William E., 104
Doe, Charles Franklin, 84
Doe Library (University of California,
    Berkeley), Fig. 8, 62, 84, 85. See also
    Bancroft Library
Doheny, Edward I., 94, 108–10
Doheny Foundation, 109–10
Dominican Republic: HEB honored by,
    224–25
Drake, Francis, 196, 201, 208–9, 262
Drake plate: attacks on authenticity of,
    201–3; belief in authenticity, 197–98,
    199–201, 204, 207–9; condition of,
    205–6; ECV's perfidy in concealing
    truth, 209; fabrication and inscrip-
    tion of, 195–96; HEB's reflections on,
    262; inspiration for, 194–95; negotia-
    tions for, 197, 198, 199, 204; Shinn's
    discovery of, 196–97, 200; testing of,
    204–7
Drake University, 228
Dressler, Albert, 195
DuFour, Clarence, 149
Duke University, 165, 166
Dumke, Glenn S., 234
Duncalf, Frederic, 142
Dunn, William E. ("Eddie"): as HEB's
    student, 51, 164–65; later positions of,
    189, 215; position of, 115–16; proposi-
    tion for HEB, 116–17; Spain research
    of, 94
Dunne, Peter Matsen, 238

E Clampus Vitus (ECV, fraternal orga-
    nization): Drake plate hoax and, 195–
    96, 199–201, 209; HEB's talks on
    Drake for, 196, 201; HEB's view of,
    268; revival of, 194–95
Ehrman, Sidney Hellman, endowed pro-
    fessorship, 175, 180–81, 219–20, 221,
    223

Ehrman, Sidney M.: California centennial project and, 232; Drake plate funds from, 199; festschrift involvement of, 242; HEB's *Coronado* and, 259; HEB's funeral and, 264; HEB's work supported by, 150–51, 152, 192; loyalty oath and, 254

Eisenhower, Dwight D., 246

Eliot, Charles W., 23–24

Ellison, Joseph, 157

Ellison, William Henry, 160, 165

Ely, Richard T., 24–25, 27–28

Emerson, Ralph Waldo, 6

Engelhardt, Zephyrin, *Fig. 10*, 66, 138, 176, 232

Epic of America, The (Adams), 183, 186

"Epic of Greater America, The" (HEB), 183–87, 217, 266

Equestrian Order of Saint Sylvester, 258

Escalante, Francisco Silvestre Vélez de: exploring trails of, 159, 217–18, 228; HEB's book on, 247–48, 259–61; planned book about, 225

eugenics: assimilation vs., 146; Jews as viewed in, 148–49; widespread belief in, 144–45, 265–66

European countries: broad commonalities among, 185; HEB's travel and research in, 179–80

Ewing, Russell, 225

expansionism: McMaster's support for, 35; new course on, 47–48; racial issues in, 145, 146

expeditions. *See* travels and expeditions (HEB)

Faculty Club (and Glade), *Figs. 7, 18,* 85, 110

Faddis, Miss (instructor), 16

Fairchild (Wis.) High School, 15, 16, 17–20

family life and children: Big Papa and Big Mama in, 97, 261; family photo-graph, *Fig. 9;* financial needs of, 31, 36, 77, 107, 225, 226; Gertrude's management of, 29, 39, 96–97; home destroyed in wildfire (1923), 135; losses in, 260, 262–63; Mexico City stay of, 65; new home for (1930s), *Figs. 21, 22,* 189–90; outings and visits, 83, 97, 151, 162; support for HEB's work, 97–98

Farquhar, Samuel, 243–44

Farrand, Max: as AHA president, 210; background of, 58–59; Jordan's correspondence with, 63; Turner's friendship with, 58, 60, 171, 181; Turner's posthumous books overseen by, 182; Yale position for, 69

federal government: HEB's connections to, 104–5, 189; Indian policy of, 147–48; Latin American policy of, 214–15, 216–17. *See also* Historic American Buildings Survey (HABS); National Park Service; U.S. Department of State; *and other agencies*

Federation of Graduate Clubs, 30–31, 34

Ferguson, James, 115–16

Fessenden, Ellen, 167

Fessenden, Josephine, 167

Fink, Colin, 205–7, 209

Fish, Carl, 236

Fiske, John, 19, 30

Fletcher, Parson, 201, 204, 206, 208

Florida: in Spanish Borderlands, 103, 123; U.S. acquisition of, 40

Flower, Robin, 303n53

Floyd, Marmaduke, 193

Ford, Guy Stanton: AHA role of, 210, 211, 212; assistance after wildfire, 135; fraternity of, 26; HEB'S appeal to, 259; historical views of, 27, 184; Texas presidency rejected by, 136, 137; on Turner's death, 181; U.S. history teaching initiative of, 235–36

Fort Caroline, 123

Franciscan order research assistance, 66

Fray Juan Crespi (HEB), 151, 173

Friedenwald, Herbert M., 33

Friend, Llerena, 41

frontier thesis (Turner, 1893): approach and summary of, 22; HEB on modification of, 186, 187; HEB's borderlands concept and implications for, 126–28, 170–73, 177–78, 182, 266; HEB's loyalty to, 120, 127, 170, 266; HEB's reflections on, 262; HEB's Spanish missions juxtaposed to, 101–3; historical standpoint of, 99; history teaching adjustments for, 118. *See also* Anglo-American history

Fuchs, Klaus, 252

Fuller, William, 196, 201

Garcés, Francisco, 261, 263

Garrison, George Pierce: Carnegie proposals of, 50, 52–53, 55–56; death of, 57, 75; HEB recruited by, 43; HEB's first impression of, 44; HEB's hopes to please, 48; HEB's Mexican research supported by, 50–51; HEB's outmaneuvering of, 52–55, 56, 57, 66; hopes for University of Texas, 40–42; politics and controversies of university and, 45, 46, 47; works: introduction, *With the Makers of Texas* (HEB and Barker), 50, 52; *Texas, A Contest of Civilizations*, 47

Gayley, Charles Mills, 130

Geiger, Maynard, 232, 241

gender, graduate degrees by, *168–69*. *See also* women

Georgia: mistaken identification of mission ruins in, 192–94; Spain's title to, 167–68; in Spanish Borderlands, 1

Georgia Historical Quarterly, 193

Georgia's Disputed Ruins (report), 193–94

Georgia Society of the Colonial Dames of America, 193

Germany: academic model of, 12, 220; Jewish immigrant from, 219–20

Giannini, Amadeo Peter, 257

Giannini, L. Mario, 257

Gillan (professor), 16, 17

Gilman, Daniel Coit, 24

Glasgow, Robert, 100, 121, 124

gold rush, 155, 227–28, 246

Good Neighbor Policy: HEB's lectures on, 227; hemispheric history linked to, 214–15, 216, 225

Goodwin, Cardinal, 238

Grand Canyon: Castañeda's description of, 247; HEB's expeditions to, *Fig. 14*, 218, 228

Granite (Wis.): lumber company job in, 13

Great Britain: removed from center of American history, 118. *See also* Anglo-American history

Greater America (festschrift, 1945), 242

Great Hall (University of California, Berkeley), 85

Guerra de Tejas. *See* Mexican-American War

Guide to the Materials . . . in the Principal Archives of Mexico (HEB), 52–55, 56, 65, 77, 78, 89

Guinn, James M., 98

HABS (Historic American Buildings Survey), 189, 193–94, 268

Hackett, Charles W. ("Hackie"): on AHA Nominating Committee, 171; assistance after wildfire, 135; death of, 260; on HEB biographical sketch, 187, 188; as HEB's student, 86, 164–65; position of, 115–16; on Texas presidency, 136, 137, 139, 140–42

Hakluyt, Richard, 204

Hale, George Ellery, 111

Hammond, George P.: as Bancroft Library director, 241; festschrift involvement of, 187; HEB's Coro-

historical documents *(continued)*
Turner's preferences for collecting, 60; Venegas manuscript, 259; women's translation of, 50–51, 167. *See also* cartographic materials

Historical Memoirs of New California (Palóu, ed. by HEB), 173

historical profession: age divisions in, 134, 164–65; AHA presidency as pinnacle, 129; anti-communism's effects on, 234, 252–58; checks on race and religion of candidates, 148–50; circles of connections in, 41–42, 43, 53, 57, 64, 73, 134; doctorates required in, 106; emergence of, 12; financial reward issue in, 246; generational and regional changes in, 178–79, 210–14; inside game in, 76–77; institutional relationships of, 268; local political influences on, 45–46; objectivity and historical context of, 265–66; as role models for graduate students, 117; Stephens's role in, 82–83; trans-Mississippi West conference of, 171–72. *See also* academic freedom; American Historical Association (AHA); doctoral programs; historian; universities and colleges; *and specific institutions*

Historic American Buildings Survey (HABS), 189, 193–94, 268

historic sites and trails: HABS work and, 189, 193–94, 268; mistaken identification of Spanish mission ruins (Ga.), 192–94; official status in research on, 105. *See also* travels and expeditions (HEB)

history: context of writing, 265–66; decision to study, 27, 29; early interest in, 19; of hemisphere vs. nations, 114; inclusive, broadened perspective on, 151–55, 267; of oaths, 254; philosophical spectrum in, 67. *See also* Anglo-American history; California history; frontier thesis (Turner, 1893); history of the Americas (hemispheric history); Latin American studies and history; national histories; Native American history; Spanish Borderlands; Spanish colonizers and missions; transnational history

history courses: curriculum reorganized at Cal, 113–15; demand for U.S. history in, 235–39; European expansionism, 47–48; European history, 44–45; hemispheric emphasis in, 2; map for, *Fig. 12; Spanish Borderlands* used in, 125; Teggart's interference in, 132. *See also* history of the Americas (hemispheric history)

History of Education in Texas (Lane), 46

History of the American Frontier (Paxson), 180

History of the American People (McMaster), 33

history of the Americas (hemispheric history): AHA presidential address on, 183–87, 217; California textbook incorporating, 155; conceptualization of, 2, 133–34; course on, 104, 112, 113–14, 126, 170–71, 216; easterners' rejection of, 217; foreign policy context of, 214–17; map for, *Fig. 12*; others' reservations about approach, 118; Pacific Coast and Basin defined in, 182–83; resurgence of concept, 269; social and political context of, 265–66; standpoint of, 99; text organized on, 117–19; Turner's ideas juxtaposed to, 126–28; virtues and flaws of, 266–67; WWII backlash against, 235–39. *See also* Spanish Borderlands

Hodder, Frank C., 130

Holmes, William A., 55

Holocaust, 250

Hoover, Herbert, 154

Houghton Mifflin (publisher), 244

Philippine Commission, 83

Philippine Islands: educational work in, 83, 87; historical documents collection on, 49, 50, 51

Pike, Zebulon Montgomery, 66–67

Pioneers of the Old Southwest (Skinner), 122

Pius XII (pope), 258

Plan of Iguala (Mexico, 1821), 147

political science department (Calif.), 83

politics: avoidance of controversy, 141, 142–43, 211; declined to discuss, 137–38; questions about, 10; universities as separate from, 139–40. *See also* communism

Polushkin, E. P., 206–7

Pomeroy, Earl, 164, 194, 296n1

Pontiac (Parkman), 19

Portolá, Gaspar de, 259

Powell, Philip, 229, 256–57, 311n8

Powicke, F. M., 22

Prather, W. L., 43, 45, 46–47, 55

Prescott, William Hickling, 19

Priestley, Herbert Ingram: as Bancroft Library director, 222, 224; courses taught by, 114, 132, 239; death of, 229, 230, 306n29; dismay at HEB's use of budget, 133; Doheny Foundation work of, 109; HEB's replacement and, 221; as HEB's student, 87; position of, 162, 166; student of, 229

primary sources. *See* cartographic materials; historical documents

Princeton Institute for Advanced Studies, 256

Princeton University, 166, 203–4, 229

professionalization, 12, 14–15. *See also* historical profession

Professors' Faculty Club (Philadelphia), 37

Prolegomena to History (Teggart), 106, 107

Protestantism: Drake plate as venerable relic of, 208; narrative about triumph of, 123–24, 125–26. *See also* Anglo-American history; anti-Catholic attitudes; frontier thesis (Turner, 1893)

publications (HEB): as chronicle vs. critical analysis, 92–93; *Coronado* as culmination of, 246–47; detailed vs. pleasing to read, 117–19, 121; Ehrman's funds for, 150–51, 152, 192; first article, 40; foreword to book, 262; ideas underlying, 91–92; introductions to edited documents, 176–77; listed by year, 315–22; maps and photographs in, 162; multiple ongoing projects, 119, 121; plans for, 88–89, 93; writing lessons for, 125, 167, 176. *See also* cartographic materials

publications, specific (HEB): *Anza's California Expeditions*, 161–62, 176–78; *Arredondo's Historical Proof of Spain's Title to Georgia*, 167, 192–94; *Athanase de Mézières and the Louisiana-Texas Frontier, 1768–1780*, 89–91, 112; *California's Story* (with Adams), 154–55; *The Colonization of North America, 1492–1783* (with Marshall), 117–19; *Coronado* (joint publication), 241, 244–47, 259; *The Debatable Land* (with Ross), 167; "Drake's Plate of Brass," 199–200; "The Epic of Greater America," 183–87, 217, 266; *Fray Juan Crespi*, 151, 173; *Guide to the Materials . . . in the Principal Archives of Mexico*, 52–55, 56, 65, 77, 78, 89; *The Hasinais*, 65, 90–91, 282n41; *Kino's Historical Memoir of Pimería Alta*, 105, 119–21, 170; *With the Makers of Texas* (with Barker), 50, 52, 154; "The Mission as a Frontier Institution in the Spanish American Colonies," 101–4, 128, 148; "The Need for the Publication of a Comprehensive Body of Documents Relating to the History of Spanish

context underlying, 117; approach to, 3; demand for equal recognition in works, 101–2, 113; HEB on Berkeley move and, 77; HEB's congratulations for Turner's Harvard move, 73–74; HEB's hopes to engage Turner in discourse, 133–34, 170–73, 266; key differences in, 60, 64, 67, 119–21, 126–28; Turner's assistance with position for HEB, 37, 38

Tuskegee Institute, 146

"Two Types of Courses in American History" (HEB), 133–34

United States, 1830–1850, The (Turner), 127, 182

universities and colleges: anti-communism's effects on, 234, 252–58; demand for U.S. history in, 235–39; discrimination against Jews in, 26, 148–50; doctoral training issues for, 24–25; enrollment decline in WWI, 107; funds from public land sales for, 21; growing importance of midwestern and western, 210–14; president's role in, 138–39, 142–43, 155; set theory analogy of, 79–80. *See also* academic freedom; doctoral programs; historical profession; students; *and specific institutions*

University of Arizona, 225

University of California, Berkeley: Academic Senate's role at, 131–32; anthropology department of, 84; Bernard Moses Memorial Lecture, 228; building boom of, *Fig. 8*, 84–85; Coronado quadricentennial and, 225; depression years at, 175, 179, 180–81, 190; Doheny Foundation at, 109–10; Drake plate conveyed to, 199; faculty recruitment agreement with Stanford, 71, 75, 76; foundation of, 24; HEB's History 8 popularity at, 113–14; HEB's

interest in, 69; HEB's legacy for, 267–68; HEB's students hired by, 166; interlocking network of, 79–80; loyalty oath controversy at, 234, 252–58; mandatory retirement age at, 180; political science department of, 83; presidential crisis of, 130–33; publishing arm of, 72 (*see also* University of California Press); religious matters at, 93; research board of, 112; student life and sports at, 85–86; Sutro's library rejected by, 60; Turner recruited by, 58, 61, 64, 72–73; Turner's summer teaching at, 62; War History Committee of, 107–8; wartime curriculum report of, 237–39. *See also* Bancroft Library; Doe Library

University of California, Berkeley, history department: anti-communist political climate of, 234, 252–58; Bancroft Library's relationship to, 79–80; cost-cutting measures of, 219; endowed professorships established in, 175, 180–81, 183, 219, 222–23; focus of, 75, 77, 83, 87, 98–99, 113–14; graduate education development of, 162–63; graduate funding and fellowships of, 93–94, 104, 164, 167, 190, 257–58; HEB as chair of, 80, 112–13, 163; HEB recruited by, 75–78; HEB's consolidation of power in, 133–34, 188, 190–91, 267–68; HEB's replacement in, 219–23; HEB's retirement from, 218–19; HEB's return in WWII, 229–32, 234–35, 240; HEB's vision for, 77–78; Huntington's cooperation with, 111; ranking of, 115; reputation of, 81–82, 98, 106, 110, 183; revisionist, broadened direction of, 151–55; Sather Professor of History of, 82, 179, 221–23; Teggart's interference in, 74–75, 132; U.S. history required, 238–39. *See also* history courses; students

Text:	10.25/14 Fournier
Display:	Fournier
Compositor:	BookMatters, Berkeley
Indexer:	Margie Towery
Printer and binder:	Sheridan Books, Inc.